Africa in World Politics

Third Edition

Africa in World Politics

*The African State System
in Flux*

edited by

John W. Harbeson
City University of New York

Donald Rothchild
University of California, Davis

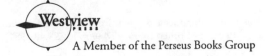

A Member of the Perseus Books Group

Copyright © 2000 by Westview Press, A Member of the Perseus Books Group

Published in 2000 in the United States of America by Westview Press, 5500 Central Avenue, Boulder, Colorado 80301-2877, and in the United Kingdom by Westview Press, 12 Hid's Copse Road, Cumnor Hill, Oxford OX2 9JJ

Find us on the World Wide Web at www.westviewpress.com

Library of Congress Cataloging-in-Publication Data
Africa in world politics / edited by John W. Harbeson, Donald Rothchild.—3rd ed.
    p.   cm.
  Includes bibliographical references and index.
  ISBN 0-8133-3613-9 (pb.)
  I. Harbeson, John W. (John Wills), 1938– . II. Rothchild, Donald S.
DT30.5 .A3543 1999
960.3'2—dc21

                                                    99-048912

10   9   8   7   6   5   4   3

Contents

Tables and Illustrations

Acronyms

AAF	Angolan Armed Forces
ACP	African, Caribbean, and Pacific
ACRI	African Crisis Response Initiative
ADF	Alliance of Democratic Forces
ADFL	Alliance of Democratic Forces for the Liberation of the Congo
AEF	Afrique Equatoriale Française
AFRC	Armed Forces Revolutionary Council
ANC	African National Congress
AOF	Afrique Occidentale Française
CAR	Central African Republic
CDR	Coalition for the Defense of the Republic
CEAO	West African Economic Community
CEEAC	Economic Union of the States of Central Africa
CFA	Communauté Financière Africaine (African Finance Community)
CLM	Congo Liberation Movement
CNDD	Conseil National pour la Défense de la Démocratie
CNK	Comité National du Kivu
CNONG	Conseil National des Organisations Non-Gouvernementales
COMESA	Common Market for East and Southern Africa
CRD	Congolese Rally for Democracy
CSSDCA	Conference on Security, Stability, Development and Cooperation in Africa
DAC	Development Assistance Committee
DROC	Democratic Republic of the Congo
EAC	East African Cooperation
ECA	Economic Commission for Africa
ECOMOG	Economic Community Monitoring Group
ECOWAS	Economic Community of West African States
EDF	European Development Fund
EEC	European Economic Community
EIB	European Investment Bank
EO	Executive Outcomes

EPLF	Eritrean Peoples' Liberation Front
EPRDF	Ethiopian People's Revolutionary Democratic Front
EU	European Union
Eurodad	European Network on Debt and Development
FAR	Forces Armées Rwandaises
FDD	Forces pour la Défense de la Démocratie
FDI	foreign direct investment
FLEC	Frente de Liberação do Enclave do Cabinda (Cabindan Enclave Liberation Front)
FNLA	National Front for the Liberation of Angola
FOF	Forces of the Future
FRELIMO	Mozambique Liberation Front
FTAs	Free Trade Agreements
FY	fiscal year
GATT	General Agreement on Tariffs and Trade
GDP	gross domestic product
GHAI	Greater Horn of Africa Initiative
GPRA	Provisional Government of the Algerian Republic
GSP	Generalized System of Preferences
GUNT	Transitional Government of National Unity
HIPCs	Heavily Indebted Poor Countries
IFIs	international financial institutions
IGAD	Intergovernmental Authority on Development
IGADD	Inter-Governmental Agency on Drought and Development
IMF	International Monetary Fund
IPA	International Peace Academy
ISI	import-substitution industrialization
JCET	Joint/Combined Exchange Training
LPC	Liberian Peace Council
MAGIC	Modern Africa Growth and Investment Company
MIGA	Multilateral Investment Guarantee Organization
MPLA	Popular Movement for the Liberation of Angola
NALU	National Army of Liberation of Uganda
NAOF	New Africa Opportunity Fund
NGO	nongovernmental organization
NMG	Neutral Monitoring Group
NPFL	National Patriotic Front of Liberia
NPRC	National Provisional Ruling Council
NRM	National Resistance Movement
OAU	Organization of African Unity
ODA	overseas development assistance
OECD	Organization for Economic Cooperation and Development
OIC	Organization of the Islamic Conference

OPIC	Overseas Private Investment Corporation
PDD	Presidential Decision Directive
PTA	Preferential Tariff Area
PVOs	private voluntary organizations
RDC	Rally for a Democratic Congo
RECAMP	Reinforcement of African Capabilities for Peacekeeping
RENAMO	Mozambique National Resistance
REPAs	Regional Economic Partnerships
RFF	Republican Federalist Forces
RPA	Rwanda Patriotic Army
RPF	Rwanda Patriotic Front
RSA	Republic of South Africa
RUF	Revolutionary Unity Front
SACU	Southern African Customs Union
SADC	Southern African Development Community
SADR	Sahrawi Arab Democratic Republic
SFA	Special Facility for Africa
SLA	Sierra Leone Army
SMC	Standing Mediation Committee
SNA	Somali National Alliance
SPA	Program of Assistance to Africa
SPLA	Sudan People's Liberation Army
SPLM	Sudan People's Liberation Movement
SRSG	Special Representative of the Secretaries-General
SSA	sub-Saharan Africa
SSLM	Southern Sudanese Liberation Movement
Stabex	Stabilization of Export Earnings
SWAPO	South–West African People's Organization
Sysmin	Stabilization of Minerals
TEU	Treaty on European Union
UDEAC	Customs Union of the Central African States
UDEAC-CEMAC	Economic and Monetary Union of Central African States
UDSP	Union for Democracy and Social Progress
UEAC	Economic Union of Central Africa
UEMOA	Economic and Monetary Union of West African States
ULIMO	United Liberation Movement for Democracy
UMA	Maghrib Arab Union
UNCTAD	United Nations Conference on Trade and Development
UNDP	United Nations Development Program
UNESCO	United Nations Educational, Scientific, and Cultural Organization
UNITA	National Union for the Total Independence of Angola

UNITAF   United Nations Task Force
UNOSOM II United Nations Operation in Somalia
USAID   U.S. Agency for International Development
USITA   U.S. International Trade Commission
WTO   World Trade Organization
ZCTU   Zimbabwean Confederation of Trade Unions
ZDI   Zimbabwe Defense Industries

PART ONE
Introduction

1

The African State and State System in Flux

DONALD ROTHCHILD
JOHN W. HARBESON

The sub-Saharan African state, and its state system, are in flux, and the manifestations of this new reality are as numerous, diverse, and complex as its implications are important. Within the literature of international relations, the future of the state as its preeminent and bedrock institution has been a subject of some speculation, at least since John Herz's arresting 1951 essay.[1] In sub-Saharan Africa today, the speculations of Herz and others are being put to the test. The process has sometimes been dramatically violent, the costs in human terms have proved extensive, the implications are uncertain, and the likely outcomes remain matters for debate. This theme is present, stated explicitly or implicitly, in all the chapters of this volume. In the current introductory chapter, we survey the evidence of these processes of potentially tectonic change, draw out some of the contributions to this theme in the chapters that follow, and explore the issues that these processes present in both existential and theoretical terms.

Manifestations of
a State System in Crisis

There is nothing subtle about much of the evidence showing the African state and its state system to be in flux. Somalia remains the quintessential example of a failed state following the combination of the collapse of the Siad Barre regime, a major outbreak of drought-induced famine, and a disastrous U.S.-led intervention, as discussed by Donald Rothchild and Jeffrey Herbst in Chapters 7 and 13 of this volume. Today, there is no Somali state, as the term is normally understood. Equally remarkable, but less noticed, has been the lack of evidence that any Somali faction currently has the capability or resolve to restore the status quo ante. The long-term consequences of Ethiopia's effort to transform itself from an empire to a confederation of ethnically defined regions remain uncertain. The brutal ongoing border war between Ethiopia and Eritrea reflects deeper unresolved issues created by the simultaneous processes of Ethiopia's transformation and Eritrea's winning of independence from Ethiopia as the postcolonial era's first new African state. Thus, any semblance of a functioning regional Horn of Africa state system has been shattered. Only the non-Horn members of the Intergovernmental Authority on Development (IGAD), Uganda and Kenya, have any capacity to bring that organization's external influence to bear on events in these countries.[2]

State weakness and state system frailty have been mutually reinforcing in Africa during post–Cold War times. In central Africa, the embattled regime of President Laurent-Désiré Kabila struggles to prevent a complete collapse, even a de facto partition, of the Democratic Republic of the Congo (formerly Zaire), long predicted by observers of former President Mobutu Sese Seko's *ancien régime*. Major interventions by troops from eight other states or insurgencies in support of, or in opposition to, Kabila have undermined any semblance of a regional state system in the middle of Africa; moreover, domestic state weakness, which afflicts most of these intervening regimes, has had negative effects on their economies and, in the case of Zimbabwe, fueled opposition to the long-running government of President Robert Mugabe.[3] Zimbabwe's and Angola's interventions, an extension of their economic and political interests, have helped to sustain the Kabila regime; however, with the financial costs of the war increasing, and given the Angola government's need to use its strength to contain the expanding civil war with Union for the Total Independence of Angola's (UNITA) re-armed guerrilla force, Kabila may find himself more exposed to rebel probes than before.[4] Uganda, Rwanda, and Burundi have all intervened to prevent ethnically based cross-border extensions of their domestic state crises, but there is little indication to date that their contribution to the shattering of interstate norms has done more than perpetuate, enlarge, and deepen their respective sources of domestic state difficulties at home. In Chapter 14, René Lemarchand details the escalation of the Great Lakes crisis from the time the Rwanda incursion was launched to the present. Despite the continent-wide ramifications of this confrontation, diplomatic efforts by the Southern African Development Community and the Organization of African Unity (OAU), as well as mediation efforts by South Africa and Zambia, have not proved effective thus far.

The southern and West African experiments exemplify a regional extension of the globally centered theory of hegemonic stability, whereby regional hegemons underwrite the stability of neighboring states. That the results have been inconclusive in both experiments has been evident to participants and observers alike, as Robert Mortimer and Jeffery Herbst make clear in Chapters 8 and 13, respectively. Whether the underlying cause is a misapplication of theory or a theoretical flaw in its regional extension is open to debate.

On the one hand, South Africa, by virtue of its size and power, naturally dominates the southern African region, although Zimbabwe's pretensions to similar status have underlain the personal animosity that surfaces from time to time between President Mugabe and President Nelson Mandela of South Africa. South Africa's own record in the region is not beyond reproach. Its intervention to arrest potential instability in tiny Lesotho, resulting from a disputed national election, left neighboring states wondering about South Africa's motives. Was South Africa acting in pursuit of interests shared by all its neighbors and itself, as the theory postulates? Or was it a narrower and perhaps false conception of its national interest alone that threatened rather than reassured the states of the region?

On the other hand, Nigeria, as the executive arm of the Economic Community of West African States (ECOWAS), has had mixed results in its efforts to restore and stabilize democratic rule in Liberia and Sierra Leone. Such an initiative extends still further the reach of hegemonic stability theory, which has generally *assumed* a system of stable, functioning states and addressed itself to the political and economic *behavior* of those states within the international arena. But no theory—including hegemonic stability theory—has been fashioned to address the domestic *reconstruction* of member-states that the disintegration of both Liberia and Sierra Leone made necessary. As Mortimer recounts in Chapter 8, tensions and conflicts among *regimes* have obstructed the deeper task of restoring or reconstructing the stability of the *state itself*. Yet the self-interests of the regime of General Sani Abacha in Nigeria in terms of economic and political aggrandizement clearly undermined its concentration on the larger objective of stabilization in the West African region. In addition, the footprints of warlords and mercenaries acting without reference to the goals of state reconstruction, about which William Reno writes in Chapter 12 and elsewhere, have been found in the Liberian and Sierra Leonean sagas as well.[5] It remains to be seen whether a new democratically elected Olusegun Obasanjo administration in Nigeria, coming to power as this book goes to press, will be able to reshape or rehabilitate Nigeria's putative role as a West African regional hegemon.

The dramatic examples of state and regional state systems in disarray or verging upon collapse have appeared to buttress the position of those who argue that post–Cold War glimmerings of an African political and economic renaissance are in grave danger of being extinguished. These signs of decline have produced appearances of political chaos, vast dislocations, and human immiseration, all of which principally profit people such as warlords and mercenaries who harbor no loyalty to the African state or state system. Such turmoil suggests not an emergent post–Cold War *transformation* of the inherited colonial state and African state system but, rather, their decay and dissolution—a situation that foreshadows descent into a Hobbesian state in which (as Hobbes himself hypothesized) pervasive individual rational self-interest might *not* allow for a possible escape into a secure political order.

The dramatic demonstrations of states and state systems in flux, however, may or may not portend what the Afro-pessimists have been predicting for the long run. Given the profound restructuring of the former colonial states and the state system under way in Africa, any attempt to discern the outcomes of such a transformation would be premature—especially in light of important ramifications of the post–Cold War restructuring of the *global* political order that is still developing. Therefore, it also seems much too early to foreclose the possibility that the creative, stable, and legitimate reordering of received state and state system structures will emerge. In sum, *flux* may or may not ultimately prove to be a synonym for *decay*.

The definitive meaning of this chapter's title—"The African State and State System in Flux"—may be determined as much by the less spectacular and more incremental indicators of change in the more stable reaches of the continent as by dramatic cases of state collapse, civil war, or revolution. In those African states that have managed to preserve some degree of stability and coherence, which factors have influenced the direction of political change? And which factors have engendered the profound decay experienced elsewhere, strengthened and reinforced the received former colonial state structures, or induced significant evolutionary modification of these structures toward something more stable and more genuinely African? We find that these factors fall broadly into two categories: (1) those shaping the contours of states both individually and collectively, and (2) those determining the design of the African state *system*, including influences that emanate both from within and from outside the continent.

Before we proceed to these interrelated themes, however, a measure of definitional clarity is required. Some scholars have suggested that it is nearly impossible to specify the state as a separate variable or constellation of variables, because of the difficulty involved in distinguishing it from governments or regimes.[6] Indeed, it has been commonplace in both the academic and policymaking literatures to refer to the *state* as though there *were* no significant, operational distinctions among state, government, or regime. Moreover, dictatorial regimes have been complicit in this analytical confusion. Such regimes act as though they *perceive* their interests to be indistinguishable from those of the states they rule—a syndrome pervasive within, but by no means exclusive to, sub-Saharan Africa. Yet it is both possible and necessary to fashion a distinction among states, governments, and regimes. This must be done carefully because of the evidence, noted above, that governments of the day not only have harmed themselves by their misrule but also have undermined or even shattered the continued acquiescence of their peoples to be governed together as one community. Conversely, regimes that act in concert with others to restore, rebuild, or strengthen the foundations of the polity have the capacity to promote legitimate and self-sustaining governance. The same logic regarding responsible and responsive governance applies to state systems as well.[7]

African States in Flux

Max Weber's conception of the state has remained a benchmark for most contemporary analysis. For Weber, the defining properties of the state include (1) its unchallenged control of the territory within the defined boundaries under its control, (2) its monopolization of the legitimate use of force within its borders, and (3) its reliance upon impersonal rules in the governance of its citizens and subjects. There has, however, been a tendency to broaden this defining list of state properties over the years. Charles Tilly appears to include membership in a *system* of states as part of the definition of the state itself, a position reinforced by such writers as Reno, Christopher Clapham, and Robert H. Jackson.[8] Moreover, Tilly implicitly builds into his analysis a state's capacity to extract resources for its own support. Crawford Young, in his definitive study of the African colonial state, develops the notion that stateness is about *rational* rulemaking;[9] he further increases the complexity of the concept of the state by observing that "today, the concept of the nation is universally absorbed into state doctrine."[10] In doing so, he raises the further intriguing problem, particularly in African contexts, of what the viable basis or bases must be for the existence of truly *multinational* states.

What factors have been most influential in stabilizing and transforming states, so defined, in post–Cold War Africa? To what extent and in what ways have these variables engendered a further weakening of already fragile states or, alternatively, strengthened and possibly transformed them? Among the factors generally regarded as critical in terms of increasing prospects for an African political renaissance, scholars have stressed the following: favorable patterns of ethnic relations, the reduction of corruption, the strengthening of civil society, the reform and liberalization of economic policies, an emphasis on the doctrine of state responsiveness to legitimate public demands, respect for civil rights, reliance upon the emergence of more capable "new leaders," and expanded democratization.

With respect to a further strengthening of the responsive state, these elements of a possible African renaissance fall into two general categories: (1) those factors related to the assumption that democratization is a means to increase the capacity and durability of the state, and (2) those related to the assumption that the prior existence of a stable state is necessary for the realization of democratic ends. On the one hand, if the concept of "nation" is intrinsic to the concept of the state, how can frameworks of stable interethnic relations be forged from immensely complex ethnic mosaics using democratic procedures? Although elements of transparency, noncorruptibility, and accountability can in principle be nurtured in nondemocratic political regimes, they can more plausibly survive over time in a democracy because these elements are normally regarded as part of its definition. The surfacing of a disparate array of new African heads of state—emblematic of a new generation, reputedly more realistic and pragmatic than the more visionary rulers of independence times, many of whom have come to power at the head of revolutionary armies—has captured the imagination of many policymakers and academics.[11] These heads of state have included Yoweri Museveni of Uganda, Meles Zenawi of Ethiopia, Issayas Afewerki of Eritrea, Paul Kagame of Rwanda, and, in some listings, Kabila of the Democratic Republic of the Congo. Apart from an implicit assumption that their more practical outlooks would incline them toward a greater openness to World Bank and International Monetary Fund guidelines on structural adjustment, precisely *how* they and their revolutionary movements have proposed to regenerate their frail states has not become explicit. Meanwhile, each has been at war—with one or more of the others. In Chapter 13 Herbst suggests that the aim of these new leaders has gone beyond capturing the state to include capturing the state system as well.

On the other hand, the emergence and rapid spread of democratic initiatives have been hailed as principal harbingers of a political renaissance in the Third World in the post–Cold War era. In little more than half a generation, most of Latin America and the Caribbean have succeeded in throwing off authoritarian rule and in installing fairly stable forms of democratic governance in its place.[12] Could sub-Saharan Africa now replicate this achievement, and, if so, could it do so in ways comparable to models established by democratic transitions in the Americas or southern Europe?[13] In almost all cases in these latter contexts, a democratic regime supplanted an *ancien régime* where the existence of the state itself was not at issue. In these cases, national political identity has been relatively secure and the possibility of ethnic communities attempting to secede or plunging a country into civil war has been relatively remote. Not surprisingly, therefore, the literature on democratic transitions, still largely grounded in the experiences of the Americas and southern Europe, also tends tacitly to *assume* a state whose existence is not at issue. Although the classical and contemporary literatures both postulate civil society as the temporal and logical foundation of a democratic state, the current reality in much of sub-Saharan Africa is one in which the process of *democratizing* the state takes for granted the prior existence of a tolerant, stable state *per se*. Although the interface between processes of economic and political liberalization remains a subject of debate, the dependence of these upon a stable state has been implicit in most of the literature.

Thus, the launching of democratization initiatives in sub-Saharan Africa poses a critical and relatively unexamined question: To what extent and under what circumstances may democratic initiatives not just represent ends in themselves but display *instrumental* importance in either furthering or undermining the strengthening of states? The preliminary evidence offers some basis for cautious optimism, much of it from southern Africa. In Mozambique, a newly democratic country has begun to stitch together the wounds of decades of civil war.[14] Both the Mozambique Liberation Front (FRELIMO), which won a very close election in 1994, and the Mozambique National Resistance (RENAMO), its erstwhile military adversary, have appeared to collaborate as government and loyal opposition, overseeing the first steps toward long-suppressed economic development. In South Africa and Namibia, apartheid regimes have yielded to majority-based ones, sustaining both as viable states while effectively ending their long civil wars. In these cases, a key element in these state-restoring transitions appears to have been the formation of comprehensive and detailed political pacts between the warring adversaries *prior* to the holding of the initial nonracial, multiparty elections.[15] Furthermore, in Benin and Ghana, democratically elected regimes appear to have lent political stability to these states, improving the prospects for renewed economic growth and development.

Processes of pact formation may sometimes link the pursuit of democratization and state reconstruction. Several countries in eastern and central Africa have appeared to lend support to this contention, by negative example. Meles Zenawi's Tigrean-led regime in Ethiopia has staked the possibility of a postimperial state in his country upon a confederal structure that allows the nationalities considerable scope for self-determination, even to the point of secession under certain circumstances. Meles has in effect gambled that the regions will not seek to follow Eritrea into independence if the right to exercise that option is guaranteed to them in advance. However, the failure of a 1991 Transition Conference to reach consensus, on such issues as the formation of a neutral security force, demobilization of armies, and the confederal structure itself, impinged negatively on both state reconstruction and democratization. (The conference was attended by nearly all the parties that had united to overthrow Mengistu Haile Mariam's military dictatorship.)[16] Moreover, the failure of Ethiopia and Eritrea at the outset to fully define and address issues attending the birth of Eritrea as a new state, resulting in the bitter war that has erupted between them, has not only harmed state formation and democratization in both countries but further undermined the Horn of Africa as a regional state system.[17]

Elsewhere, it remains to be seen whether the Museveni government's effort to restore the Ugandan state in a hostile regional environment has been hindered or advanced by his insistence on retaining the National Resistance Movement (NRM) as a kind of Platonic guardian institution rather than permitting the resumption of democratic multiparty politics. Finally, the government of Frederick Chiluba has restricted eligibility to run for president to third-generation Zambians under the provisions of its new constitution. The transparent purpose of this ploy—to disqualify former President Kenneth Kaunda from advancing his candidacy again— has both sapped Zambian democracy of real content and represented an assault on the multicultural melting-pot foundations of the Zambian state.[18]

Much of the literature on democratization emphasizes both the critical potential influence of an *ancien régime* in determining the fate of a democratic transition and the implicit assumption that a change of regime is a *sine qua non* of any such transition. Michael Bratton and Nicolas van de Walle, in their important study of the early stages of democratic transitions in sub-Saharan Africa, broadly follow this literature and anticipate the staying power of neopatrimonial governing practices, even *after* a new regime ostensibly committed to democracy has been elected.[19] They are somewhat more sanguine about the prospects for democratic transitions from military or single-party regimes. On the whole, however, this literature does not deal with the question of whether, how, or in what circumstances the processes of democratization might prove instrumental in strengthening the fabric of the state upon which it ultimately depends for its existence. Although the shadow of neopatrimonialism has indeed darkened the prospects for democracy in Africa, the case of Kenya suggests the limits of this generalization. The regime of Daniel arap Moi in Kenya, a classic example of neopatrimonialism at work, has not been able to prevent violent ethnic challenges to the fabric of the state following its two multiparty elections. Violent clashes in Nairobi and elsewhere prior to the 1997 elections appear to have forced Moi to reverse course and to entertain the possibility of further democratization. Although the matter remains undecided at this juncture, the Kenya case suggests the possibility that neopatrimonial regimes may be susceptible to corrosion in the face of civil society pressure, even as civil society remains susceptible to co-optation by residual neopatrimonialism.

Finally, in Chapter 15, Francis Deng argues that a changing state system may have begun to internationalize an altered definition of the contemporary state itself.[20] He contends that the pervasiveness and imperatives of humanitarian disasters, caused by retrograde governments and magnified by weak or inept ones, have prompted a new African emphasis upon the limits of state sovereignty in contemporary times. Representing an extension of the thesis advanced by Robert H. Jackson and Carl Rosberg that recognition and membership in the United Nations system have served as a powerful de jure legitimator of de facto weak states, the contemporary theory has evolved that governments are answerable internationally *within their borders* for their citizens' enjoyment of internationally defined human rights regimes.[21] In essence, major states and international organizations are in the process of becoming active *partners* of governments in making basic human rights part of the working foundations of contemporary states.

The evolving principle of responsible state sovereignty signifies an amendment not only of the Weberian conception of the state but also of the core tenets upon which the United Nations system was established. Moreover, rules for implementing this doctrine are yet to be codified. Thus, it remains to be seen whether responsible state sovereignty can be made equally enforceable in cases where militarily powerful governments preside over states whose foundations they may be undermining as well as in cases where the regime and the state have both disintegrated.

A State System in Flux

The weakness currently experienced by many African states is inevitably reflected in the wider state system in which they are embedded. With the end of the Cold War, African states, largely left to fend for themselves, have frequently found themselves hard-pressed to fulfill the primary tasks they have set for themselves—namely, securing their borders, achieving economic growth and development, and providing good governance. Whereas some states have demonstrated a capacity to achieve their main goals in a difficult international environment, others have displayed weak capabilities, being unable to regulate their societies effectively or implement their public policies throughout the territory nominally under their control. The problem of weak regulatory capacity is accentuated in some African states by the existence of a low level of political legitimacy. In cases involving a lack of public consensus over the valid exercise of public authority, the dominant ruling elite may turn to repressive tactics to compensate for its lack of legitimate authority. In this situation, the people become alienated from their state, and, with the state acting in an arbitrary and autocratic manner, its political elite can become a source of insecurity, ineffectiveness, and oppression.[22]

Two indicators of the declining inability of some state leaders to provide their citizens with the basic essentials of an internationally secure environment are the increasing porousness of state borders and the growing frequency of external military interventions. Where central government institutions are unable to control private interests (i.e., warlords, corporations, mercenary enterprises) within their border, it is not surprising that these actors serve their special purposes through activities that run counter to those of their state or neighboring states. As Reno shows in Chapter 12, relatively autonomous warlords (sometimes with the protection of private security firms) carry on their predatory economic activities in the territory of a neighboring state unsupervised and unaccountable to legitimate authorities. Ineffective state control has a number of possible deleterious effects, including smuggling, currency transfers and abuses, illegal arms deliveries, attacks on co-ethnics across the border, hostile radio and television broadcasts, support for military coups, terrorist campaigns, oil and water cutoffs, and environmental degradation. The inability of state leaders and institutions to oversee activities and extract revenues from these private actors leaves the state gravely weakened in terms of fulfilling its economic, political, and security tasks.

In addition, the weak state may be exposed to interventions by neighboring states that are affected by the intrusions of predatory interests into their political space. Insecurity at international borders and unscrupulous private behavior do not occur in isolation and therefore can set the stage for a decline in African state norms, as set out under the Charter of the Organization of African Unity. Military and political interventions, indicated by the growing international war in the Democratic Republic of the Congo (as Lemarchand effectively discusses in Chapter 14), threaten the African normative order with a terrifying destruction. The journal *Africa Confidential* no doubt overstates the finality of the collapse of norms, but its grim conclusion on the fragility of interstate norms is an appropriate warning regarding current trends rapidly unfolding on the continent: "Africa's hallowed doctrine of non-interference in the affairs of sovereign states has been abandoned. Borders are no longer sacrosanct. Even that institutional pillar of non-interference, the Organization of African Unity . . . has been deafeningly silent in the face of new regional alliances."[23] In a change from old realist attitudes about the presence of weak states on a border, African leaders in the well-functioning states now view this proximity as potentially menacing to their well-being.

As agreed by the Heads of African States and Governments at Addis Ababa in 1963, the Charter of the Organization of African Unity sought to establish a normative order that would permit the continent's sovereign states to live alongside one another in peace and amity. Declaring as one of its purposes the defense of their sovereignty, territorial integrity, and independence, the Charter went on to declare their members' adherence to the principles of respect for the sovereignty and territorial integrity of all member-states, noninterference in the internal affairs of states, and unreserved condemnation of political assassination and subversive activities on the part of a neighboring state or any other states. These principles, pushed by the more moderate Monrovia bloc at the Addis Ababa negotiations, represent a victory for interstate order and moderation over more radical challenges to the status quo.

As African economies weakened in the face of both heavy international constraints and poor policy decisions (see the discussions by Thomas Callaghy and Nicolas van de Walle in Chapters 3 and 11, respectively), and as political elites have become isolated from their citizens and increasingly prone to adopt authoritarian measures, state frailty contributed to the weakness of the African state system. The OAU itself, unable to collect its dues and gripped with immobilism regarding intrastate violations of human rights generally and minority ethnic and religious freedoms in particular, proved unable to offer the effective leadership on interstate matters envisaged in the Charter. Ethnic cleansing, mass violence, and civil wars emerged and took a terrible toll on human life and property. As they spilled across international borders, there was often no effective international agency willing to halt the conflagration and prepared to attempt to restore the peaceful order envisioned by the Charter. In 1991, in a turn toward the doctrine of responsible governance, Ambassador A. Haggag, the assistant secretary general of the OAU, told conferees from all over Africa who were assembled at the Kampala Forum that "the principle of non-interference in the internal affairs of States is increasingly coming under scrutiny, given the obvious fact that wars and conflicts have inflicted heavy damage on many of the African States concerned, with the resultant destruction of the economic, social and cultural fabric of our people."[24] Only three years later, as genocidal fury swept Rwanda and some 800,000 people were brutally massacred, it became increasingly evident that the institutions of interstate amity and cooperation were inadequate to cope with impending state and interstate dangers.

It must be emphasized that many states in Africa continue to accept and work within the OAU's prescribed normative order. They display stable states and borders, and they practice cooperative economic, political, and military relations with neighboring countries. Being relatively poor and lacking effective military forces for the most part, they are not inclined to assume the costs and risks of major cross-border interventions. As a consequence, the norms set out in the OAU Charter survive, partly because weak states have a continued interest in maintaining principles of nonintervention and sovereignty and partly because they are conscious of their inability to project force. Moreover, already possessing sufficient territory to meet their population needs, they have little incentive to expand their domains through conquest.

What is becoming apparent at the same time is an increasing tendency on the part of other states to disregard OAU norms on nonintervention and to take unilateral military actions against their neighbors. For example, Sudan, in a mutually damaging relationship, has been charged with giving military support to the Lord's Resistance Army in Uganda, whereas Uganda, Eritrea, and Ethiopia are reportedly aiding the Sudan People's Liberation Army insurgency across their borders. Such actions undercut the very norms of interstate relations that provide a measure of stability in an environment increasingly in need of a firm normative foundation. Countries interceding in a neighboring country in violation of OAU norms suffer a loss of reputation, causing elites in other states to distrust their willingness to bargain in good faith or to keep to the agreements they sign.[25] How, then, can one explain the preparedness of leaders to take advantage of weak states in their neighborhood to act unilaterally and to extend their military influence outward, thus rendering the continent's interstate rules and institutions more and more ineffective? To see how structural weakness in a neighboring state creates incentives to intercede in the domestic affairs of another country, we will look briefly at recent military interventions in Sierra Leone, Congo-Brazzaville, Lesotho, and the Democratic Republic of the Congo. What emerges is a variety of overlapping interests that impel rulers to take substantial risks for perceived political, material, or security benefits.

With the decline of the state's administrative control of its borderland areas in Liberia and Sierra Leone, warlords such as Charles Taylor in Liberia engaged in a thriving trade in timber and diamonds—essentially free of revenue obligations to central authorities. Formal bureaucratic influences were gravely weakened by the existence of such autonomous economic institutions in both countries, for central authorities were denied the capacity to develop the countryside economically and were obstructed in their ability to halt the internal wars emerging between various political and ethno-military factions along the frontier. In this situation of lawlessness, Taylor's decision in 1991 to back Foday Sankoh's Revolutionary Unity Front (RUF) insurgent forces across the border in Sierra Leone extended and internationalized his private commercial undertakings at great cost to the stability and well-being of the Sierra Leone government. According to Reno, "Liberian fighters appeared, with Charles Taylor's backing, to incorporate diamond-producing areas of Sierra Leone for their own enrichment in Taylor's aggressive Shadow State—what Taylor calls 'Greater Liberia.'"[26] In 1999, Taylor, by now the elected president of Liberia, has continued to assist the rebel forces in Sierra Leone. The destabilizing effects of this continuing support for the RUF insurgents have become a source of international concern, leading U.S. assistant secretary of state for African Affairs Susan Rice to warn of possible sanctions in conjunction with its allies if Taylor persisted with this tactic.[27]

In Congo-Brazzaville, where in October 1997 the elected president, Pascal Lissouba, was locked in a bitter struggle with the former military ruler, General Denis Sassou-Nguesso, a four-month-long impasse was broken when Angolan troops formed an alliance with Sassou-Nguesso and broke down Lissouba's defenses. The Angolans brought heavy equipment, including artillery and jet aircraft, to bear against government forces. In intervening in the internal Congo-Brazzaville conflict, the Angolans had important strategic interests at stake. For one thing, they suspected Lissouba of commercial dealing with UNITA and believed their border to be more secure with their ally, Sassou-Nguesso, in control of the state. For another, they suspected Lissouba of being supportive of the Cabindan Enclave Liberation Front (FLEC), an independence movement in Angola's rich oil-producing enclave of Cabinda. For the Angolans, then, intervention was worth the risks in terms of enhanced security for the Popular Movement for the Liberation of Angola (MPLA) regime that would follow from a Sassou-Nguesso victory.[28]

South Africa's intervention in Lesotho in September 1998, supported by troops from Botswana, was initiated by Acting President Mangosuthu Buthelezi to prevent a possible military coup and to protect the Katse Dam and surrounding reservoir that supplies vitally needed water supplies to South Africa. In an effort to stabilize a small neighbor and guard against possible spillover effects from this enclave to adjacent areas in South Africa, an initial force of 800 troops was sent to the capital, Maseru, where they were surprised by heavy resistance from the Lesotho armed forces and opposition elements. South African forces were embarrassed by the poor performance of their forces under fire, creating doubts about South Africa's role as a third-party peacekeeper in other major disputes on the continent. The dam and water supplies were protected, but looters and arsonists did major damage to central Maseru before the crisis was brought to an end.

Finally, the ongoing Congo crisis of the late 1990s underlines the decline of OAU norms on interstate relations and the mixed incentives that political actors display when engaging in interventions across Africa's international borders. As former Zairian dictator Mobutu Sese Seko's legitimacy disappeared, and as his ability to extract resources and exercise effective administrative control over the lands and people nominally under his control declined, his weak state became increasingly vulnerable to internal and external attack. By 1996, his most formidable opponent, former Katangese politician Laurent Kabila, was able to forge a coalition of political and ethnic-based forces that could hold on to its eastern province heartland and then launch a well-executed offensive that ultimately seized Kinshasa, the capital city. A critical element spearheading Kabila's coalition, formally known as the Alliance of Democratic Forces for the Liberation of the Congo (ADFL), were the Banyamulenge people. These Zairians of Tutsi origin had deep grievances over the government's threat both to deny them Zairian citizenship and to expel them from the country. In neighboring Rwanda and Burundi, Tutsi-led administrations expressed concern over the fate of their co-ethnics across the border. Moreover, these governments (as well as that of Uganda), troubled by the Mobutu government's failure to halt cross-border raids by armed Hutu militias, claimed legitimate security concerns in eastern Zaire. Such internal and external security interests led them to back Kabila's ADFL insurgents in their successful assault on the Zairian heartland, which culminated with Mobutu's overthrow.

As Lemarchand discusses in Chapter 14, Kabila, fearing a devastating loss in popular support in Kinshasa and its environs if he remained loyal to his Banyamulenge vanguard forces, shifted his alliance partners in the Congo and the wider region and began to act aggressively toward Tutsi influences in the army as well as the population residing in the eastern Congo.[29] Angry Tutsi warriors, feeling betrayed and vulnerable to victimization, reacted by bolstering the growing forces of rebellion in their heartland area. In this they were actively backed by Rwanda and Uganda, whose leaders argued that, after years of cross-border attacks by armed militia, they had legitimate security concerns in eastern Congo.[30]

In response to the growing rebel threat, the governments of Angola, Zimbabwe, Namibia, and Chad and the insurgent movement UNITA rallied to sustain the beleaguered Laurent Kabila. The backing of Angola and Zimbabwe was critically important to Kabila's forces, for their heavily armed troops limited the rebel advances during the early battles. However, as the Angolan army faced a renewed opposition from a re-armed UNITA (now engaged in the Congo to reopen smuggling routes for diamonds and military equipment), it reduced its costly commitment to Kabila. Similarly, Zimbabwe's government, under heavy criticism at home for a costly venture in the Congo that allegedly involved the financial interests of the president's family, reduced its commitments there in 1999. Thus, a mix of security and economic motives provided an incentive to intervene, but as the costs and risks rose (particularly for Angola and Zimbabwe), the interveners opted for prudence and cut down on their involvement.[31]

These acts of military intervention have weakened the structure of the African state system, undercutting basic system norms on state sovereignty and nonintervention. In an effort to shore up the state system, and to broaden the OAU's normative principles to include those regarding basic human rights, state actors, alone or in coalition with others, have intervened to restore order and a return to respect for the rights of peoples to life and fundamental freedoms. For example, South Africa has attempted to mediate the escalating conflict in Central Africa, the OAU has sought to resolve the long-simmering conflict in the Western Sahara, ECOWAS has pushed a peace process in both Liberia and Sierra Leone, and, under the leadership of former President Julius Nyerere of Tanzania, seven regional governments in the Great Lakes region imposed sanctions on the government of Pierre Buyoya following his seizure of power in Burundi in 1996. But the efforts of Africa's third parties to build support for a stable peace process, and thus to reinforce the normative order, have had limited success at best. Generally lacking financial and military capabilities, these powers do not find themselves in a position to enforce agreements or to sustain a commitment to the peace process over an extended period of time. Moreover, they lack the ability to influence the preferences of local actors through the use of packages of pressures and incentives. As a consequence, the "supports" of the African state system as conceived in Addis Ababa frequently appear to lack the collective capacity to protect the normative order against those prepared to take the law into their own hands.

Conclusion

In this chapter, we have discussed the linkage between African state weakness and state system frailty. State weakness displays a spillover effect, threatening the normative order upon which African interstate relations rest. The inability of some states to protect their borders, or to prevent insurgents, smugglers, currency manipulators, or terrorists from using their territory to engage in malevolent activities in neighboring countries, invites retaliation. Also, stronger African countries, intent on quick economic gains or insecure over the possibility of attacks from across borders, may seize the opportunity of weakness in an adjoining state to assist a beleaguered head of state or a friendly insurgent movement. There is neither an outside enforcer present following the disengagement of the former colonial or Cold War powers, nor a local hegemon on the scene willing and able to enforce OAU norms on sovereignty and nonintervention, leaving Africa's relatively weak states exposed and unable to protect the security of their citizens. Paradoxically, as the contagion of disorder spreads, even the well-functioning African states are entrapped by the continent's growing insecurity.

In the chapters that follow, the various authors probe both the sources of fluidity and weakness and the efforts to arrest their spiraling effects. They also examine the responses of the industrialized countries, mesmerized as they are by the new challenges of technologies and largely disengaged from Africa's struggle for security and development. To be sure, when famine or genocide strikes, external actors may display a momentary concern with Africa's pain, but soon afterward they retreat to the sidelines. Clearly, only a new commitment, in Africa and abroad, can begin to break this cycle of marginality and despair.

Notes

1. John Herz, "The Rise and Demise of the Territorial State" (1951), reprinted in John H. Herz, *The Nation-State and the Crisis of World Politics* (New York: McKay, 1976), pp. 99–124. See also John Herz, "The Territorial Nation-State Revisited: Reflections on the Future of the Nation-State," in ibid., pp. 226–253.

2. The other IGAD members are Eritrea and Ethiopia.

3. Major external interveners have included the governments of Uganda, Burundi, Rwanda, Chad, Zimbabwe, Angola, and Namibia, as well as the insurgent movement known as the National Union for the Total Independence of Angola (UNITA). For a fuller picture of these various intervening forces, see Chapter 14 in this volume and René Lemarchand, "Congo-Kinshasa: The Wages of War," *Africa Confidential* 39, no. 23 (November 20, 1998), pp. 1–3.

4. On the roots of the civil war in Angola, see Donald Rothchild, *Managing Ethnic Conflict in Africa: Pressures and Incentives for Cooperation* (Washington, D.C.: Brookings Institution, 1997), pp. 111–145.

5. William Reno, *Corruption and State Politics in Sierra Leone* (Cambridge, Eng.: Cambridge University Press, 1995); and William Reno, *Warlord Politics and African States* (Boulder: Lynne Rienner Publishers, 1998).

6. Leonardo Villalon and Philip Huxtable (eds.), *The African State at the Critical Juncture: Disintegration and Reintegration* (Boulder: Lynne Rienner Publishers, 1998).

7. Charles Tilly, *Coercion, Capital and European States 1990–1992* (Boulder: Lynne Rienner Publishers, 1992).

8. Ibid. See also William Reno, *Warlord Politics and African States* (Boulder: Lynne Rienner Publishers, 1998); Christopher Clapham, *Africa and the International System* (London: Cambridge University Press, 1996); and Robert H. Jackson, *Quasi-States: Sovereignty, International Relations, and the Third World* (Cambridge, Eng.: Cambridge University Press, 1990).

9. Crawford Young, *The African Colonial State in Comparative Perspective* (New Haven: Yale University Press, 1994), p. 20.

10. Ibid., p. 32.

11. Marina Ottaway, *Africa's New Leaders* (Washington, D.C.: Carnegie Endowment, 1999).

12. Samuel Huntington, *The Third Wave: Democratization in the Late Twentieth Century* (Norman: University of Oklahoma Press, 1991); Robert Putnam, *Making Democracy Work: Civic Traditions in Modern Italy* (Princeton: Princeton University Press, 1993); Guillermo O'Donnell and Philippe Schmitter, *Transitions from Authoritarian Rule: Tentative Conclusions About Uncertain Democracies* (Baltimore: Johns Hopkins University Press, 1986); and Juan Linz and Alfred Stepan, *Problems of Democratic Transitions and Consolidation* (Baltimore: Johns Hopkins University Press, 1996).

13. Michael Bratton and Nicolas van de Walle, *Democratic Experiments in Africa: Regime Transitions in Comparative Perspective* (Cambridge, Eng.: Cambridge University Press, 1997).

14. Cameron Hume, *Ending Mozambique's War: The Role of Mediators and Good Offices* (Washington, D.C.: United States Institute of Peace Press, 1994).

15. John W. Harbeson, "Rethinking Democratic Transitions: Lessons from Eastern and Southern Africa," in Richard Joseph (ed.), *State Conflict and Democracy in Africa* (Boulder: Lynne Rienner Publishers, 1999), pp. 39–57. See also Caroline Hartzell and Donald Rothchild, "Political Pacts as Negotiated Agreements: Comparing Ethnic and Non-Ethnic Cases," *International Negotiation* 2, no. 1 (1997), pp. 147–171.

16. John W. Harbeson, "Elections and Democratization in Post-Mengistu Ethiopia," in Krishna Kumar (ed.), *Post-Conflict Elections, Democratization and International Assistance* (Boulder: Lynne Rienner Publishers, 1998), pp. 111–131.

17. John W. Harbeson, *Peace, Democracy and National State in the Horn of Africa: The Cases of Eritrea and Ethiopia* (Washington, D.C.: United States Institute of Peace, 1999), forthcoming.

18. Michael Bratton and Nicolas van de Walle, "A First at Second Elections in Africa with Illustrations from Zambia," in Joseph (ed.), *State Conflict and Democracy in Africa*, pp. 377–409.

19. Ibid.

20. See also Francis M. Deng, Sadikiel Kimaro, Terrence Lyons, Donald Rothchild, and I. William Zartman, *Sovereignty as Responsibility: Conflict Management in Africa* (Washington, D.C.: Brookings Institution, 1996).

21. Robert H. Jackson and Carl G. Rosberg, "Why Africa's Weak States Persist: The Empirical and the Juridical in Statehood," *World Politics* 35, no. 1 (1982), pp. 1–24.

22. Mohammed Ayoob, *The Third World Security Predicament: State Making, Regional Conflict, and the International System* (Boulder: Lynne Rienner Publishers, 1995); Kalevi J. Holsti, *The State, War, and the State of War* (Cambridge, Eng.: Cambridge University Press, 1996); Christopher Clapham, *Africa and the International System* (Cambridge, Eng.: Cambridge University Press, 1996); and Stephen John Stedman, "Conflict and Conciliation in Sub-Saharan Africa," in Michael E. Brown (ed.), *The International Dimensions of Internal Conflict* (Cambridge, Mass.: MIT Press, 1996).

23. "Africa: Big Men, Big Countries, Big Hopes," *Africa Confidential* 39, no. 1 (January 19, 1998), p. 1.

24. Ambassador A. Haggag, "Statement," in Olusegun Obasanjo and Felix G. N. Mosha (eds.), *Africa: Rise to Challenge* (New York: Africa Leadership Forum, 1992), p. 304.

25. David A. Lake, "Regional Security Complexes: A Systems Approach," in David A. Lake and Patrick M. Morgan (eds.), *Regional Orders: Building Security in a New World* (University Park: Pennsylvania State University Press, 1997), p. 51.

26. Reno, *Corruption and State Politics in Sierra Leone*, p. 169.

27. Paula Wolfson, "Congress—Sierra Leone," *Voice of America* (March 23, 1999), pp. 1–2.

28. "Congo: Former Dictator's Victory," *Africa Research Bulletin* 34 (Political, Social, and Cultural Series), no. 10 (October 1–31, 1997), pp. 12862–12864.

29. Mark Turner, "Congo Leader Turns on His Former Supporters," *Financial Times* (August 8–9, 1998), p. 4.

30. Scott Stearns, "Congo Rebels," *Voice of America* (August 31, 1998), p. 1. (A useful website in this connection is Gopher://gopher.voa.gov/00/newswire/mon/CONGO_REBELS.) Some months afterward, the European Union released a statement recognizing Uganda's "legitimate security concerns" in the Congo. See Ian Fisher, "Uganda's Helping Hand to Congo Rebels Raises Questions About Motives," *New York Times*, December 21, 1998, p. A8.

31. "Congo-Kinshasa: The Wages of War," *Africa Confidential* 39, no. 23 (November 20, 1998), pp. 1–3; and "Angola quits the Congo . . . leaving Kabila exposed," *Daily Mail and Guardian*, February 19, 1999. A website with related information is located at http://www.mg.co.za/mg/news/99feb2/19feb-congo.html.

PART TWO

Historical Parameters

2

The Heritage
of Colonialism

CRAWFORD YOUNG

Africa, in the rhetorical metaphor of imperial jingoism, was a ripe melon awaiting carving in the late nineteenth century. Those who scrambled fastest won the largest slices and the right to consume at their leisure the sweet, succulent flesh. Stragglers snatched only small servings or tasteless portions; Italians, for example, found only desserts on their plate. In this mad moment of imperial atavism—in Schumpeterian terms, the objectless disposition toward limitless frontier expansion—no one imagined that a system of states was being created. Colonial rule, assumed by its initiators to be perpetual, later proved to be a mere interlude in the broader sweep of African history; however, the steel grid of territorial partition that colonialism imposed long appeared permanent. Although possibly threatened by the patterns of disorder and state collapse that emerged in the 1990s, the stubborn resilience of the largely artificial boundaries bequeathed by the colonial partition is surprising.

Colonial heritage is the necessary point of departure for analysis of African international relations. The state system—which, transnational vectors notwithstanding, is the fundamental structural basis of the international realm—inherits the colonial partition. A few African states have a meaningful precolonial identity (Morocco, Tunisia, Egypt, Ethiopia, Burundi, Rwanda, Madagascar, Swaziland, Lesotho, and Botswana), but most are products of the competitive subordination of Africa—mostly between 1875 and 1900—by seven European powers (Great Britain, France, Germany, Belgium, Portugal, Italy, and Spain).

African Colonial Heritage Compared

The colonial system totally transformed the historical political geography of Africa in a few years' time, and the depth and intensity of alien penetration of subordinated societies continues to cast its shadow.[1] The comprehensive linkages with the metropolitan economies in many instances were difficult to disentangle. In the majority of cases in which decolonization was negotiated, the colonizer retained some capacity to shape the choice of postcolonial successors and often—especially in the French case—enjoyed extensive networks of access and influence after independence was attained. The cultural and linguistic impact was pervasive, especially in sub-Saharan Africa. Embedded in the institutions of the new states was the deep imprint of the mentalities and routines of their colonial predecessors. Overall, colonial legacy cast its shadow over the emergent African state system to a degree unique among the major world regions.

In Latin America, although colonial administrative subdivisions shaped the state system, Spain and Portugal swiftly ceased to be major regional players after Creole elites won independence in the nineteenth century. Great Britain and, later, the United States were the major external forces impinging upon the region. In Asia, the first target and long the crown jewel of the colonial enterprise, imperial conquest tended to follow the contours of an older state system; not all Asian states have a historical pedigree (as is true of the Philippines, Pakistan, Papua New Guinea), but a majority do. The circumstances surrounding Asian independence, the discontinuities imposed by the Japanese wartime occupation of Southeast Asia, and the larger scale of most Asian states and the greater autonomy of their economies all meant that the demise of the colonial order there was far more sharp and definitive than was the case in Africa.

Perhaps the closest parallel to Africa in terms of durable and troubled colonial impact on regional international relations is found in the Middle East. The partition of the Ottoman domains in the Levant between Great Britain and France and the imperial calculus employed in territorial definitions and structures of domination left in their wake a series of cancerous conflicts. Thrones had to be found for Great Britain's Hashemite allies; the duplicity of incompatible wartime promises to Arabs and Zionists bore the seeds of inextricable conflict over whether the Palestine mandate awarded to Great Britain by the League of Nations would develop as a Jewish homeland or an Arab state; Great Britain invented Jordan as a territory for its wartime ally Prince Abdullah; Lebanese borders were drawn so as to maximize the zone of dominance for Maronite Christians; Sunni Arab nationalism in Syria was countered by heavy recruitment of minority Alawites for the colonial militia; and Kurdish state demands were denied so that oil-rich zones could be attached to the

British-Iraqi mandate.[2] The unending turbulence in this region provides daily confirmation of the colonial roots of many intractable contemporary conflicts. But even here, colonial penetration of Middle Eastern Arab societies and economies was much less than was the case in Africa, and the erstwhile colonial connections weigh less heavily.

In the African instance, the shadow of the colonial past falls upon the contemporary state system in several critical respects. The sheer number of sovereign units and the weakness and vulnerability of many due to their small scale are the most obvious. The continuing importance of former economic and political colonial linkages, most of all for the twenty states formerly under French rule, significantly shapes regional politics— both as an active channel of influence and as a negative point of reference. Most of the festering regional crises that torment the continent—Western Sahara, the Horn, the Great Lakes region, Angola—are rooted in one way or another in ill-considered decolonization strategies driven by metropolitan interests. In this chapter, I will consider these components of the colonial heritage in turn.

Fragmentation of Africa

The African continent in 1993 (and its offshore islands) contained no fewer than fifty-three sovereign units (using UN membership as the criterion)—nearly one-third of the world total.[3] Although this large number is advantageous in terms of guaranteeing a voice in international forums where the doctrine of sovereign equality ensures equal voting rights for states large and small, this is little compensation for the disabilities of being tiny. Sheer economic weakness is one disadvantage. Most African states had a GNP less than the Harvard University endowment or the profits of a major multinational corporation. The limits of choice imposed by a narrow national market and circumscribed agricultural and mineral resource bases rendered most states highly vulnerable to the vagaries of commodity markets and the workings of the global economic system. Although some minuscule mercantile states elsewhere have achieved prosperity—Singapore is an obvious example—and tiny sovereignties perched on vast oil pools may accumulate enormous wealth—Bahrain, Qatar, and United Arab Emirates are cases in point—the rapid Iraqi military seizure of Kuwait in 1990 (which was rolled back only by a vast U.S.-led military intervention) amply demonstrated the vulnerability of the small state, however rich. Of the microstates among Africa's fifty-three polities, only Mauritius has prospered.

The full scope of the fragmentation of independent Africa was not apparent until the virtual eve of independence. Most of the vast sub-Saharan domains under French domination were joined in two large administrative federations, Afrique Occidentale Française (AOF) and Afrique Equatoriale Française (AEF). Political life, however, germinated first at the territorial level; the crucial 1956 *Loi-cadre* (framework law) located the vital institutions of African political autonomy at this echelon. Although some nationalist leaders dreamed of achieving independence within the broader unit, especially in the AOF, the wealthier territories (Ivory Coast, Gabon) were opposed to this. In the final compressed surge toward independence, the interaction of divisions among nationalist leaders and movements, combined with French interests, resulted in twelve states of modest size rather than two large ones.[4] In the 1950s, Great Britain did promote federations of its colonial possessions as a formula for self-government in the West Indies, the United Arab Emirates, and Malaysia, as well as in east and central Africa, but with indifferent success. In east and central Africa, the fatal flaw was linking the project of broader political units to the entrenchment of special privilege for the European settler communities. Thus contaminated, the federation idea was bound to fail.[5] In instances in which large territories had been governed as single entities—Nigeria, Sudan, Congo-Kinshasa—independence as one polity was possible, although all three countries have, at times, been beset by separatist pressures.

Once sovereignty gave life to colonial territories as independent nations, the African state system has proven to be singularly refractory to broader movements of unification. The 1964 unification of Tanganyika and Zanzibar to form Tanzania and the 1960 unification of British Somaliland and Italian-administered Somalia at the moment of independence remain the sole cases of political amalgamation. At the turn of the century, the Tanzania union with Zanzibar is being questioned; and in the wake of the collapse of a Somali state in 1991, Somaliland reemerged as a separate unit, although unrecognized by the international community.

Dream of African Unity

The dream of a broader African unity persists, first nurtured by intellectuals of the diaspora and expressed through a series of pan-African conferences beginning in 1900, then embraced by the radical wing of African nationalism in the 1950s, above all by Kwame Nkrumah of Ghana. The Organization of African Unity (OAU) was created in 1963 to embody this dream, but even its charter demonstrated its contradictions. The OAU was structured as a cartel of states whose territorial integrity was a foundational principle. Rather than transcending the state system, the OAU consolidated it.

The urgency of regional and ultimately continental unification is repeatedly endorsed in solemn documents, including the 1980 Lagos Plan of Action and the 1989 African alternative framework to structural adjust-ment programs of the Economic Commission for Africa.[6] Innumerable re-gional integration schemes have been launched, of which the most impor-tant are the Union du Maghreb Arabe, the Economic Community of West African States, the Southern African Development Coordination Council, and the various customs and monetary unions of the francophonic West African states.[7] But the goal of effective integration remains elusive; the impact of the colonial partition remains an enduring obstacle.

The colonial origins of most African states weighed heavily upon the consciousness of postindependence rulers. Initially, the fundamental ille-gitimacy of the boundaries was a central tenet of pan-African national-ism; the 1945 Manchester Pan-African Congress excoriated "the artificial divisions and territorial boundaries created by the Imperialist Powers." As late as 1958, the Accra All-African Peoples' Conference denounced "artificial frontiers drawn by the imperialist Powers to divide the peoples of Africa" and called for "the abolition or adjustment of such frontiers at an early date."[8] But once African normative doctrine was enunciated by the states rather than by nationalist movements, the tone changed, and the sanctity of colonial partition frontiers was asserted. The consensus of the first assembly of African independent states—also in Accra in 1958—was expressed by Nkrumah, the leading apostle of African unification: "Our conference came to the conclusion that in the interests of that Peace which is so essential, we should respect the independence, sovereignty and territorial integrity of one another."[9]

The OAU Charter makes reference to territorial integrity no fewer than three times; at the Cairo OAU summit in 1964, the assembled heads of state made the commitment even more emphatic through a solemn pledge to actively uphold existing borders, a level of responsibility that goes significantly further than the mere passive recognition of the inviola-bility of frontiers.[10] Although a certain number of boundary disputes have arisen in independent Africa, the principle of the sanctity of colonial partition boundaries—the juridical concept of *uti possidetis*—remains a cornerstone of a solidifying African regional international law.[11] Most of the disputes have been resolved by negotiation, applying the colonial treaties as the point of juridical reference.[12] The enduring fear of the fragility of the African state system paradoxically endows the artificial colonially imposed boundaries with astonishing durability. The one ap-parent exception—the independence of Eritrea from Ethiopia in 1993—can be said to prove the point. Eritrean nationalists grounded their claim to self-determination in the argument that Eritrea, as a former Italian colonial territory, should have had the opportunity for independence like all other former colonies, rather than being forcibly joined (in the Eritrean view) to Ethiopia by the international community.

The colonial system profoundly reordered economic as well as political space. During their seventy-five years of uncurbed sovereignty, colonial powers viewed their African domains as veritable *chasses gardées* (private preserves). Metropolitan capital enjoyed privileged access; to varying degrees, other capital was viewed with reserve or even hostility (especially by the Portuguese until the final colonial years). The security logic of the colonial state joined the metropolitan conviction that the occupant was entitled to exclusive economic benefits in return for the "sacrifice" of supplying governance services to foster trade and investment linkages, which tied African territories to metropolitan economies as subordinated appendages. Territorial infrastructures, particularly the communications systems, were shaped by the vision of imperial integration; road nets ran from the centers of production to the ports and colonial capitals. Although over time a shrinkage of the once-exclusive economic ties with the erstwhile colonizers has occurred, these bonds were so pervasive that they have been difficult to disentangle. It is no accident that regional economic integration schemes joining states once under different colonial jurisdictions have had only limited success; the most resilient mechanism of regional economic cooperation has been the CFA franc zone, a product of the economic space defined by the former French empire in sub-Saharan Africa.

Influence of Former Colonizers

The colonial occupation of Africa, which occurred relatively late in the global history of imperial expansion, was comparatively dense and thorough. The multiplex apparatus of domination—which was constructed to ensure the "effective occupation" stipulated by the 1884–1885 Berlin Conference as a condition for the security of the proprietary title and to extract from the impoverished subjects the labor service and fiscal tribute to make alien hegemony self-financing, as metropolitan finance ministries required—was unlikely to dissolve instantly once the occupying country's flag was lowered on independence day. Over time, the many linkages binding the decolonized state to the former metropole—linkages both manifest and submerged—have slowly eroded. They were a central dimension in the international relations of new states, especially in the early years of independence. Even four decades later, especially in the case of France, colonial connections still play a role.

Several factors influence the importance of ties with former colonizers. In those cases where independence was won through armed liberation struggles rather than bargaining, the power transfer brought initial rupture (Algeria, Guinea-Bissau, Mozambique, Angola). In some other cases (Guinea, Congo-Kinshasa), the circumstances of independence brought immediate crisis and discontinuity in relationships; even though relations were ultimately restored, the degree of intimacy between the two countries could never be the same. Generally, the smaller erstwhile colonial powers played a less visible role than did the two major imperial occupants, Great Britain and France.

Italy was largely eliminated as a result of its having been on the losing side in World War II. Although it regained a ten-year trust territory mission in Somalia in 1950, Rome was never permitted to return to Libya and Eritrea and quickly ceased to be a factor in either territory. Spain was the last country to enter the colonial scramble, and it had only a superficial hold on its territories in northwest Africa (former Spanish Morocco, Ifni, Western Sahara, Equatorial Guinea). Its minor interests were swallowed up in postcolonial turmoil in its erstwhile domains (the Moroccan annexation of Western Sahara, Macias Nguema's capricious tyranny in Equatorial Guinea from its independence in 1968 until 1979). Emblematic of Spain's elimination from Africa was the affiliation of Equatorial Guinea with the French-tied Communauté Financière Africaine (CFA) franc zone after Macias Nguema was overthrown in 1979.[13]

Belgium retained an important and uninterrupted role in its small former colonies of Rwanda and Burundi, but its economic interests in these states were not large. In Zaire, where the financial stake was considerable, relationships were punctuated with repeated crises.[14] The sudden and aborted power transfer left inextricably contentious disputes over the succession to the extensive colonial state holdings in a wide array of colonial corporations. These disputes were seemingly resolved several times, only to reemerge in new forms of contention.[15]

In the Portuguese case, an imperial mythology of the global Lusotropical multiracial community was a keystone of the corporatist authoritarianism of the Salazar-Caetano *Estado Novo*. However, the utter discrediting of this regime by its ruinous and unending colonial wars in Africa from 1961 to 1974 brought it repudiation. More broadly, in the postcolonial era, a common element for the minor participants in the African partition was an abandonment of earlier notions that overseas proprietary domains validated national claims to standing and respect in the international arena.

Particularly intriguing has been the relative effacement over time of Great Britain on the African scene. Great Britain has long seen itself as a great power, although the resources to support such a claim silently ebbed away as a result of imperial overreach, according to one influential analysis.[16] In the 1950s, as the era of decolonization opened for Africa, conventional wisdom held that Great Britain was the most likely of the colonizers to maintain a permanent role in its vast colonial estates because of the flexible framework for evolution supplied by the British Commonwealth. This illusion proved to be based upon false inferences deduced from the older constellation of self-governing dominions, which had remained closely bound in imperial security relationships with London. Many thought the Commonwealth could preserve a British-ordered global ensemble beyond the formal grant of sovereignty in Asia and Africa. The illusion of permanence in which British imperialism so long basked dissipated slowly.[17] The doctrine enunciated at the 1926 Imperial Conference still dominated official thinking as the African hour of self-government approached. This document perceived the future as incorporating "autonomous communities within the British Empire, equal in status, in no way subordinate one to another in any aspect of their domestic or external affairs, though united by a common allegiance to the Crown and freely associated as members of the British Commonwealth of Nations."[18] As one of its commentators then wrote, "The British Empire is a strange complex. It is a heterogeneous collection of separate entities, and yet it is a political unit. It is wholly unprecedented; it has no written constitution; it is of quite recent growth; and its development has been amazingly rapid."[19]

Slow erosion overtook these lyrical notions of a global commonwealth's operating in a loose way as a political unit in world affairs so that Great Britain's claim to major power status might survive the decolonization of the empire. India's independence in 1947 was a crucial turning point; the true jewel in the imperial crown, it metamorphosed from the pivot of empire security to a self-assertive "neutralist" Asian power—an outcome that should have ended the illusion that an enlarged commonwealth could remain in any sense a "political unit." Yet when African members of the Commonwealth began joining Ghanaian independence in 1957, some of the older mystique persisted.

For most former British territories, joining the Commonwealth formed part of the *rite de passage* of independence; only Egypt and Sudan declined to enter its ranks.[20] Paradoxically, as the Commonwealth became numerically dominated by Asian, African, and Caribbean member states, it ceased to serve as a loose-knit, worldwide, British-inspired combine, and its meetings became occasions for heated attacks on British policy in Rhodesia and South Africa. Instead of an ingenious instrument for the subtle nurture of British global influence imagined by its designers, the Commonwealth thus seemed a funnel for unwelcome pressures upon British diplomacy. Even imperial nostalgia could not stave off recognition of these facts; waning British interest removed the Commonwealth's energizing center. In the words of a recent study, "The Commonwealth has survived only in [a] very attenuated form. . . . [It is] still a useful argumentative forum for its governments, offering a place for small states to be heard, extending benefits (albeit on a modest scale) to its members, and providing opportunities for discussion of problems of common interest."[21] This adjustment in the British images of the Commonwealth goes hand in hand with the gradual reduction of London's self-perception— from global hegemon to middle-sized European power.

The diminishing mystique of the Commonwealth as the vessel for a global British role helps to explain the relative effacement of Great Britain on the African scene. In the first years of African independence, British disposition for intervention was still visible. In the army mutinies that swept Uganda, Kenya, and Tanganyika in 1964, British troops intervened to check the mutineers, at the request of the embattled regimes. In Nigeria, Great Britain initially had a defense agreement; however, this was annulled in 1962 due to Nigerian nationalist pressure. In a number of cases, national armies remained under British command for a few years after independence; in 1964, the British commander of the Nigerian army refused the solicitation of some Nigerian leaders to intervene after scandal-ridden national elections brought the country to the brink of disintegration. Security assistance and economic aid in modest quantities continue, and in a few cases—most notably Kenya—influence remains significant. But since 1970, the relatively subdued role of Britain, if set against the expectations of 1960, is what stands out.

The French Connection

The case of France, which has played a pervasive role in the seventeen sub-Saharan states formerly under its rule, is completely different from that of Great Britain. The political, cultural, economic, and military connection that Paris has maintained with the erstwhile *bloc africain de l'empire* has been frequently tutelary, often intrusive, and sometimes overtly interventionist. The intimacy and durability of this linkage are as surprising as the eclipse of the United Kingdom. When African independence loomed on the horizon, France still suffered from its World War II humiliation and bitter internal divisions. The country was weakened by the chronic instability of the Fourth Republic, with one-third of its electorate aligned with the antiregime Stalinist French Communist party and its army locked in unending and unwinnable colonial wars—first in Indochina, then in Algeria. *France Against Itself* was the title of the most influential portrait of this epoch;[22] few anticipated the recapture of its European status and sub-Saharan role as regional hegemon under the Fifth Republic.

In grasping the pervasive African role of the resurrected postcolonial France, one needs first to draw a sharp distinction between the Maghreb and sub-Saharan Africa—a distinction that is sometimes overlooked amid the fascination with the French connection. In reality, French influence was shattered in what had been the most important parts of the former empire—North Africa and Indochina. In terms of the size of the economic stake, the AOF and especially the AEF were far behind the core regions of the imperial era. Psychologically, the heart of overseas France was Algeria, whose northern portions were considered to be full French departments. The savagery of the eight-year war for Algerian independence, especially the self-destructive fury of its final phases, compelled the exodus of most of the 1 million French settlers and the abandonment of much of their stranglehold on the Algerian economy.[23] The independent Algerian state pursued a consistently radical anti-imperial foreign policy, rendered financially possible by its relatively ample oil and natural gas revenues. Although Tunisia and Morocco were less assertive in international politics and leaned toward Western positions in their nonalignment, neither accepted the degree of French tutelage that was common in sub-Saharan Africa.

Several factors explain the comprehensive nature of the French relationship with sub-Saharan states formerly under its domination.[24] The terminal colonial effort in this zone to construct an elusive "federalism" as permanent institutional bonding, although it failed in its manifest goal of defining political status short of independence, had important consequences. The representation accorded emergent African leaders in the Fourth and (briefly) the Fifth Republics in French institutions drew much of the sub-Saharan independence generation into the heart of French political processes. In the Algerian instance, Paris representation was dominated by settler interests and a small number of collaborating Algerians; Tunisia and Morocco, which had a different international legal status, were not given parliamentary seats.

Although electoral manipulation occurred in sub-Saharan Africa as well, those Africans chosen were nonetheless far more representative of emergent political forces than the few Algerians who served in the French Parliament. As early as the 1946 constitutional deliberations, Leopold Senghor of Senegal played an influential role. By the late Fourth Republic, African leaders held ministerial positions (Felix Houphouet-Boigny of the Ivory Coast, Modibo Keita of Mali). Until literally the eve of independence, the "federal" formula that the Fifth Republic Constitution sought to institutionalize had the assent of most of the current political class, with the exception of the more radical intelligentsia—especially the students. The referendum approving the Fifth Republic Constitution in 1958 drew large, usually overwhelming majorities in all sub-Saharan territories except Guinea, reflecting the strong wishes of the African leadership for its approval. Jarring as his words now sound, Houphouet-Boigny spoke for a political generation in his often-quoted 1956 statement: "To the mystique of independence we oppose the reality of fraternity." The degree of incorporation of the sub-Saharan African political elite into the

French political world has no parallel, and it left a lasting imprint on the texture of postcolonial relationships. Successive French presidents from Charles de Gaulle to Jacques Chirac brought to office long-standing intimate ties with many sub-Saharan political leaders.

The original Fifth Republic concept of sub-Saharan territorial autonomy—with an array of core sovereign functions (e.g., defense, money, and justice) vested in the France-centered French community—swiftly vanished.[25] In its place emerged an array of devices giving institutional expression to intimacy. Some form of defense accords was negotiated with fourteen sub-Saharan ex-colonies;[26] French troops were permanently garrisoned in Djibouti, the Central African Republic, Gabon, the Ivory Coast, and Senegal; and a reserve intervention force earmarked for swift African deployment was held in readiness in France. Except for Guinea, Mali, Mauritania, and Madagascar, all these ex-colonies remained within a French currency zone (and Guinea and Mali eventually sought reentry).

By the 1970s, Franco-African summit conferences became a regular and lavish part of the diplomatic landscape; often these attracted more heads of state than did the OAU summits. *Francophonie* as a cultural instrument finds expression in the French educational systems and linguistic policies; the nurture of the French language enjoys a priority in French diplomacy that is unique among former colonizers. In the Maghreb, *francophonie* competes with the active policies of affirmation of the Arab language and culture; in sub-Saharan Africa (excepting Madagascar and Mauritania), retention of French as the primary state vehicle has been internalized as a political value by most of the state class.[27] Even a populist leader such as Alphonse Massemba-Debat of Congo-Brazzaville exclaimed in the late 1960s that the Congolese and the French were "Siamese twins," separable only by surgery.[28] Senghor, who was the most intellectually brilliant member of the independence political generation, summed up the pervasive relationship as *francité* (Frenchness, Francehood).[29] His induction into the *Académie Française* was, in his own eyes, a crowning achievement in a splendid career. A neologism such as *francité* has plausible resonance in the Franco-African case, but its analogues would be preposterous in characterizing any other postcolonial ties.

A singular form of tutelary, or dependent, linkages results from this broad-front set of connections, not all of which are well captured in the visible aspect of politics or in the asymmetrical core-periphery economic flows to which "dependency theory" draws attention. The francophonic African community counts upon the senior French partner to defend its interests within the European Community and among the international financial institutions, both public and private. Priority access to French aid is assumed, including periodic budgetary bailouts for the more impoverished states.[30] French willingness to occasionally intervene militarily to protect clients is of crucial importance; Guy Martin tallies twenty instances of such intervention between 1963 and 1983.[31] As then-President Valéry Giscard d'Estaing stated, "We have intervened in Africa whenever an unacceptable situation had to be remedied."[32] Perhaps even more critical to the nurture of tutelary standing are French security services of a more clandestine nature. French intelligence services furnish invaluable protection to rulers through their capacity to monitor and penetrate opposition groups and to foil potential conspiracies by providing early warning to incumbents. These security operations have always enjoyed high-level attention in Paris through such presidential advisers as the late éminence grise Jacques Foccart; François Mitterrand, as president, had entrusted these functions to his son, Jean-Christophe Mitterrand.

As of this writing, there are some signs that the silken threads binding francophonic Africa to France are fraying. France had made no move to prevent the overthrow of Hissene Habré by armed insurgents enjoying Libyan support in Chad at the end of 1990, although French troops in Chad could easily have prevented the takeover. Nor did France lift a finger to avert the collapse of the Moussa Traore regime in Mali in April 1991.[33] Supporting the CFA franc zone is more expensive and less profitable than it once was. Pessimism has spread concerning Africa's infirm economic and political condition. Protection of friendly incumbents appears to have lost some of its attractions, inasmuch as France, in early 1990, moved away from its long-held view that single-party rule, with its corollary of life presidency, was the most "realistic" political formula for Africa.[34] But the closely woven fabric of the French connection is too sturdy to quickly unravel, and France was more ambivalent toward democratization than the other former colonial powers.

Struggle to Eliminate Colonial Influence

The importance of the colonial past in shaping contemporary African international relations is thus beyond dispute. At the same time, the colonial system serves—paradoxically—as a negative point of reference for the African concert of nations. The legitimacy of the first generation of African regimes was rooted in the regimes' achievement—by conquest or negotiation—of independence. The transcendent unifying principle of the pan-African movement from its inception has been opposition to both colonialism and racism, evils that were joined on the African continent. The independent states that assembled to create the OAU in 1963 were divided on many questions of ideology and interpretation of nonalignment; all could rally behind the combat to complete the liberation of Africa from colonial occupation and regimes of white racial domination. The elemental notion of African solidarity arose out of the shared experience of racial oppression, a point made explicit by W.E.B. Du Bois many years ago:

> There is slowly arising not only a curiously strong brotherhood of Negro blood throughout the world, but the common cause of the darker races against the intolerable assumption and insults of Europeans has already found expression. Most men in this world are coloured. A belief in humanity means a belief in coloured men. The future world will in all reasonable possibility be what coloured men make of it.[35]

Nearly five decades later, Julius Nyerere translated these thoughts into African nationalist language: "Africans all over the continent, without a word being spoken, either from one individual to another, or from one African country to another, looked at the European, looked at one another, and knew that in relation to the European they were one."[36]

Indeed, at the moment of the OAU's creation, many of the most arduous independence struggles still lay ahead, including those in the Portuguese territories, Zimbabwe, and Namibia, as well as the mortal combat with apartheid in South Africa. The OAU has a mediocre record in coping with conflicts within Africa (e.g., in Somalia, Liberia, Eritrea, and Western Sahara; the Nigerian civil war; the Zaire rebellions; and the conflict between Chad and Libya). However, its anticolonial role has been important in providing a continental focus for African liberation diplomacy.

Within their own territorial domain, independent states faced a compulsion to demarcate themselves from their colonial past, to render visible the new status. The superficial symbolic accoutrements of independence—flags and postage stamps—might serve for a time. Africanization of the state apparatus might help as well, although, over time, the perception could arise that the real benefits of this change accrued above all to state personnel.

The imperative of demarcation eventually spread to the economic realm. In the 1970s, a wave of seizures of foreign assets with potent colonial connotations swept through Africa: Idi Amin's "economic war" against the Asian community in 1972, Mobutu Sese Seko's "Zairianization" and "radicalization" campaigns of 1973 and 1974, Tanzania's socialization measures after the 1967 Arusha Declaration, the 1972 and 1976 Nigerian "indigenization decrees," the copper mine nationalizations in Zambia and Zaire, and parallel measures in many other countries. Measures of expropriation of foreign assets almost exclusively affected holdings associated with the colonial past. This circumstance partly reflected a distinction often drawn between postindependence investments, which involved contractual commitments (presumably) freely made by the African state, and those investments made under alien sovereignty, which lacked moral standing (and doubtless had been well amortized). More important, steps to indigenize the economy reflected pressures to move beyond purely political independence, which would be denatured if all the structures of economic subordination remained intact. By the 1980s, this surge of economic demarcation had run its course; the deepening economic crisis and heightened vulnerability to external pressures made such measures infeasible. In addition, the measures were frequently discredited by the chaotic improvisation of their implementation and consequent dislocations (Zaire, Uganda) or by the perception that only narrow mercantile classes had benefited (Nigeria).[37]

The compulsion for demarcation from the colonial past was driven by psychological as well as political and economic factors. Particularly in sub-Saharan Africa, the colonial era brought a broad-front assault upon African culture that was far more comprehensive than similar experiences in the Middle East and Asia. The "colonial situation," to borrow Georges Balandier's evocative concept,[38] was saturated with racism. African culture was, for the most part, regarded as having little value, and its religious aspect—outside the zones in which Islam was well implanted—was subject to uprooting through intensive Christian evangelical efforts, which were often state supported. European languages supplanted indigenous ones for most state purposes; for the colonial subject, social mobility required mastering the idiom of the colonizer. In innumerable ways, colonial subjugation in Africa brought not only political oppression and economic exploitation but also profound psychological humiliation. In the nationalist response to colonialism, psychological themes are prevalent to a degree unique in Third World anti-imperialist thought. Frantz Fanon, the Martinique psychiatrist who supplied so powerful a voice to the Algerian revolution, was only the most eloquent such spokesman.[39]

Such doctrines as *négritude* and "African personality" were central components in nationalist thought, asserting the authenticity and value of African culture. This dimension of African nationalism gave a special emotional edge to the postcolonial quest for demarcation, as well as to the fervor of African state reaction to racism and colonialism.

Colonial heritage as a negative point of reference also influenced the contours of Cold War intrusion into Africa. Both the United States and the Soviet Union represented themselves as alternatives to the African nations' exclusive reliance upon the erstwhile colonizers for succor and support. Particularly in the early phases of independence, visible Soviet linkages served as a badge of demarcation. The extravagant fears of all colonizers—and of the West generally—regarding "Communist penetration" of Africa enhanced the value of Soviet relations, even if Soviet economic assistance was minimal. For those states that wanted (or felt compelled to undertake) a more comprehensive break with the Western colonial system, for a brief moment in the early 1960s and again in the late 1970s, the Soviet bloc appeared to offer an alternative—a hope that quickly proved illusory.

Colonial Roots of Regional Crises

A final legacy of the colonial system is the series of regional crises it has left in its wake, particularly in southern Africa and the Horn. In southern Africa, the roots of conflict can ultimately be traced to the catastrophic British mistake of transferring power to an exclusively white regime in South Africa in 1910. Imperial security calculus at the time focused exclusively upon the relationships between the English and Afrikaner communities. Virtually the only concession to African interests was the retention of colonial sovereignty over the Basutoland, Bechuanaland, and Swaziland protectorates. The terms of the Act of Union ultimately led to apartheid in South Africa. The year before the doctrine of "paramountcy of native interests" was proclaimed for Kenya in 1924, Great Britain granted full internal self-government to the white settlers in Southern Rhodesia (now Zimbabwe), an error that resulted in a costly liberation war before independence based upon equal rights for all Zimbabweans was won in 1980. When the hour of decolonization sounded elsewhere in Africa, South Africa, Rhodesia, and the Portuguese were in a position to construct a solid redoubt of white domination, which left the oppressed no other choices than passive acceptance of permanent exploitation or armed uprising. The ensuing militarization of society on all sides had far-reaching consequences: Some of these were positive, such as the 1974 army coup that ended corporatist autocracy in Portugal; others were much more negative, such as the entrenchment of competing insurgent movements in Angola. When independence came to Angola and Mozambique after the 1974 Portuguese coup, the white redoubt shrank, but it escalated its efforts to new and more destructive levels by arming, supplying, and guiding insurgent forces—the União Nacional para a Independência Total de Angola and the Resistência Nacional Mozambiquano. The ultimate cost is incalculable: literal destruction of civil society in Mozambique and endless civil war with heavy external involvement in Angola entailing a colossal wastage of its precious oil revenues, which are entirely absorbed in military operations.[40] The dismantling of apartheid in the 1990s—deracialization of the South African polity to undo the false decolonization of 1910—helped bring this infernal cycle of violence to an end in Mozambique, but the war in Angola continues to ravage the country.

In the case of the Horn, the spiral of decomposition affecting both Ethiopia and Sudan reflects choices made at the moment of decolonization when external strategic interests overrode regional considerations.

The decision by the UN General Assembly in 1952 to turn Eritrea over to Ethiopia was powerfully influenced by the United States' desire to enjoy an air and communications base at Asmara and to nurture a developing military cooperation with Ethiopia. Eritrean preferences were divided at the time, and significant sentiment in favor of union existed among the highland populations. However, there was overwhelming insistence on distinctive autonomous institutions for Eritrea (elected assembly as well as its own government, language rights, and flag); the reluctant and apprehensive acquiescence of coastal Muslims to the federation, as a fait accompli imposed from without, was absolutely conditioned upon this autonomy. Once the veil of sovereignty enveloped Eritrea, Ethiopia progressively dismantled the autonomous institutions, finally moving to full annexation in 1962 with no protest from the United Nations or the United States. (The latter was the chief sponsor of the settlement.) The result was a thirty-year war for independence, finally achieved in 1993— but not before the war had inflicted untold devastation on Eritrea and bankrupted Ethiopia.[41]

In the case of Sudan, as Sudanese nationalism—Arab centered and concentrated in the north—forced the pace of change in the 1950s, British state interests were, above all, anti-Egyptian, particularly after the Free Officers seized power in Cairo in 1952. The prime British objective in the decolonization negotiations was to ensure that Sudan became independent, separate from its "condominium" partner Egypt. The ransom of this goal was deference to the desire of the northern Sudanese for a unitary state under their control. The deepening fears of the southern Sudanese regarding their subordination to a state that defined itself as Arab and Muslim (identities they did not share), as well as their marginalization by the northern elite, were ignored. As in Eritrea, the reaction was swift; by 1960, a hydra-headed revolt was in evidence in a number of southern zones. Southern insurrection was brought to a momentary halt in 1972 by a creative political settlement; however, by 1983, its terms had been flagrantly violated, and guerrilla war had broken out again—this time at a higher level of violence and associated with widespread famine-induced starvation, which took 250,000 lives in 1988. Beyond the guerrilla forces and the national army, diverse groups of armed bands have proliferated, and the banalization of violence permeates daily existence. The indictment of decolonization policy and of earlier colonial policies that encouraged regional division in Sudan cannot cover all of the miscalculations, insensitivities, and repression that have followed 1956 independence in Sudan. Colonial legacy is nonetheless an inseparable element in any pattern of explanation.[42]

The Western Sahara is yet another festering sore in which an aborted decolonization opened the wound. In this instance, although Spain belatedly abandoned its short-lived (1958–1973) experiment to fully incorporate the colony as an "overseas province," the brief effort begun in 1973 to encourage institutions of autonomy was soon caught between the independence demands of the Frente Popular para la Liberación de Saguia el Hamra y Rio de Oro and Moroccan annexation claims. With Franco on his deathbed and amid grave fears about the instability that might lie ahead, Spain simply abandoned the territory when faced with the threat of the October 1975 Moroccan *marche verte*.[43]

Thus, in various ways, the colonial heritage intrudes into postindependence African international relations. Perhaps four decades after the great surge to independence in 1960, the colonial shadow will begin to fade. Important new trends that may tug colonial legacy further into the background will have a critical impact in the new millennium. The end of the Cold War will certainly have a profound influence. The depth of the economic crisis, along with a widening consensus that regional integration that bridges the old colonial divisions is indispensable to overcoming them, may lead to innovations in the state system that will begin to transcend the colonial partition. For the first forty years of African independence, however, colonial heritage has powerfully shaped the African international system.

Notes

1. For a more extended argument on the pathology of the African colonial state, see Crawford Young, *The African Colonial State in Comparative Perspective* (New Haven: Yale University Press, 1994).

2. Great Britain was awarded a mandate over the former Ottoman provinces by the League of Nations; these provinces became Iraq, which in turn achieved nominal independence in 1930 but remained within a British sphere of influence until the late 1950s. In the extensive literature on these themes, I have found especially useful Charles Issawi, *An Economic History of the Middle East and North Africa* (New York: Columbia University Press, 1972); Peter Sluglett, *Britain in Iraq 1914–1932* (London: Ithaca Press, 1976); William Roger Louis, *The British Empire in the Middle East 1945–1951: Arab Nationalism, the United States, and Postwar Imperialism* (Oxford: Clarendon Press, 1984); George Antonius, *The Arab Awakening* (New York: Capricorn Books, 1965); and Mary C. Wilson, *King Abdulla, Britain and the Making of Jordan* (Cambridge, Eng.: Cambridge University Press, 1987).

3. This total does not include Western Sahara, which is recognized as a member state by the Organization of African Unity but not by the United Nations. Eritrea and South Africa were added in the 1990s.

4. The most careful political history of this process of fragmentation is Joseph-Roger de Benoist, *La Balkanisation de l'Afrique Occidentale Française* (Dakar: Nouvelles Editions Africaines, 1979). His study clearly demonstrates that the balkanization was less a product of Machiavellian French design than the outcome of a

complicated interplay of African political competition and French improvised response. Resentment of the distant bureaucratic despotism of the AOF's French administrative headquarters was common in the outlying territories. Those nationalist leaders who, at various times, fought to preserve the unit—Leopold Senghor, Sekou Toure, Modibo Keita—were constrained both by their own rivalries and by the absence of a strong popular attachment to the AOF as a geographical entity.

5. Among the works on this subject, see Arthur Hazlewood (ed.), *African Integration and Disintegration* (London: Oxford University Press, 1967); Joseph S. Nye, *Pan-Africanism and East African Integration* (Cambridge, Eng.: Cambridge University Press, 1965); Patrick Keatley, *The Politics of Partnership* (Harmondsworth, Ind.: Penguin Books, 1964); Philip Mason, *Year of Decision: Rhodesia and Nyasaland in 1960* (London: Oxford University Press, 1960); and Donald Rothchild, *Toward Unity in Africa: A Study of Federalism in British Africa* (Washington, D.C.: Public Affairs Press, 1960).

6. Robert S. Brown and Robert J. Cummings, *The Lagos Plan of Action vs. the Berg Report* (Lawrenceville, Va.: Brunswick Publishing, 1984); and United Nations Economic Commission for Africa, *African Alternative Framework to Structural Adjustment Programmes for Socio-Economic Recovery and Transformation* (AAF-SAP), E/ECA/CM, 15/6/rev. 3, 1989.

7. See, among others, Ahmed Aghrout and Keith Sutton, "Regional Economic Union in the Maghreb, *Journal of Modern African Studies* 28, no. 1 (1990), pp. 115–139; and Elaine A. Friedland, "S.A.D.C.C. and the West: Cooperation or Conflict?" *Journal of Modern African Studies* 23, no. 2 (1985), pp. 287–314.

8. Saadia Touval, *The Boundary Politics of Independent Africa* (Cambridge, Mass.: Harvard University Press, 1972), pp. 22–23, 56–57.

9. Quoted in ibid., p. 54.

10. Onyeonoro S. Kamanu, "Secession and the Right of Self-Determination: An O.A.U. Dilemma," *Journal of Modern African Studies* 12, no. 3 (1974), pp. 371–373.

11. *Uti possidetis* is derived from a Roman private law concept, which holds that, pending litigation, the existing state of possession of immovable property is retained. Translated into international law, the phrase means that irrespective of the legitimacy of the original acquisition of territory, the existing disposition of the territory remains in effect until altered by a freely negotiated treaty. For a passionate attack on this doctrine by a Moroccan jurist, see "L'uti possidetis' ou le non-sens du 'principle de base' d l'OUA pour le réglement des differends territoriaux," *Mois en Afrique* 217–218 (February-March 1984), pp. 3–30.

12. For major studies on African boundary issues, see Touval, *The Boundary Politics of Independent Africa*, as well as Carl Gosta Widstrand (ed.), *African Boundary Problems* (Uppsala: Scandinavian Institute of African Studies, 1969); A. I. Asiwaju, *Partitioned Africans: Ethnic Relations Across Africa's International Boundaries 1884–1984* (London: C. Hurst, 1984); Yves Person, "L'Afrique Noire et ses frontières," *Revue Française d'Etudes Politiques Africaines* 80 (August 1972), pp. 18–42; and Ian Brownlie, *African Boundaries: A Legal and Diplomatic Encyclopedia* (Berkeley: University of California Press, 1979).

13. On the limited nature of Spanish rule, see Ibrahim Sundiata, *Equatorial Guinea* (Boulder: Westview Press, 1989); and Tony Hodges, *Western Sahara: The Roots of a Desert War* (Westport, Conn.: Lawrence Hill, 1983).

14. For thorough details, see Gauthier de Villers, "Belgique-Zaire: Le grand affrontement," *Cahiers du CEDAF* 1–2 (1990).

15. For details on the *contentieux*, see Crawford Young and Thomas Turner, *The Rise and Decline of the Zairian State* (Madison: University of Wisconsin Press, 1985), pp. 276–325.

16. Paul Kennedy, *The Rise and Fall of the Great Powers: Economic Change and Military Conflict from 1500 to 2000* (New York: Vintage Books, 1987).

17. This phrase is drawn from the intriguing study by Francis G. Hutchins, *The Illusion of Permanence: British Imperialism in India* (Princeton: Princeton University Press, 1967).

18. Quoted in Cecil J. B. Hurst et al., *Great Britain and the Dominions* (Chicago: University of Chicago Press, 1928), p. 9.

19. Ibid., p. 3.

20. South Africa, which had been a member since its accession to "dominion" status in 1910, quit in 1961 in the face of increasing attacks from the swelling ranks of African members.

21. Dennis Austin, *The Commonwealth and Britain* (London: Routledge and Kegan Paul, 1988), pp. 62, 64.

22. Herbert Luthy, *France Against Itself* (New York: Meridian Books, 1959).

23. For a graphic account of the holocaust during the final year of the Algerian war, with a mutinous army and a murderous settler force—the Organization de l'Armée Secrète—see Paul Henissart, *Wolves in the City: The Death of French Algeria* (New York: Simon and Schuster, 1970).

24. Useful studies on this topic include Edward Corbett, *The French Presence in Black Africa* (Washington, D.C.: Black Orpheus Press, 1972); Guy Martin, "Bases of France's African Policy," *Journal of Modern African Studies* 23, no. 2 (1985), pp. 189–208; George Chaffard, *Les carnets secrets de la décolonisation* (Paris: Calmass-Levy, 1965); Pierre Pean, *Affaires africaines* (Paris: Fayard, 1983); and Charles-Robert Ageron, *Les chemins de la decolonisation de l'empire français 1936–1956* (Paris: Editions du CNRS, 1986).

25. For a painstaking account by a highly informed French observer, see Joseph-Roger de Benoist, *Afrique Occidentale Française de 1944 à 1960* (Dakar: Nouvelles Editions Africaines, 1982).

26. Martin, "Bases of France's African Policy," p. 204.

27. One encounters some exceptions among the intelligentsia; one example was the late Cheikh Anta Diop of Senegal, a cultural nationalist of great influence who strongly urged promotion of the most widely spoken Senegalese language, Wolof. But overall, the commitment to French as the cultural medium is far more entrenched in the former French sub-Saharan territories than anywhere else in Africa.

28. Quoted in Corbett, *The French Presence*, p. 66.

29. Leopold Sedar Senghor, *Ce que je crois: Négritude, francité et civilisation de l'universel* (Paris: B. Crasset, 1988).

30. In theory, financial injections to meet budgetary crises—most commonly, payments to civil servants—have long ceased; in practice, they continue to occur. For fascinating details on the process and its political importance, see Raymond Webb, "State Politics in the Central African Republic," Ph.D. dissertation, University of Wisconsin–Madison, 1990.

31. Martin, "Bases of France's African Policy," p. 194.

32. Quoted in ibid.

33. See "France and Africa: The End of an Era" in the special issue of *Africa Report* 36, no. 1 (December-January 1991).

34. For details, see *Africa Confidential* 31, no. 5 (March 9, 1990).

35. Quoted in Victor Bakpetu Thompson, *Africa and Unity: The Evolution of Pan-Africanism* (London: Longman, 1969), p. 36.

36. Lecture by Julius Nyerere at Wellesley College, Wellesley, Massachusetts, April 1961; from my notes.

37. For details, see Crawford Young, *Ideology and Development in Africa* (New Haven: Yale University Press, 1982).

38. Georges Balandier, "The Colonial Situation," in Pierre van den Berghe (ed.), *Africa: Social Problems of Change and Conflict* (San Francisco: Chandler Publishing, 1965), pp. 36–57.

39. See, for example, Frantz Fanon, *Black Skin, White Masks* (New York: Grove Press, 1967). On this theme, see also O. Mannoni, *Prospero and Caliban: The Psychology of Colonization* (London: Methuen, 1956); and A. Memmi, *Portrait du colonisé, précédé du portrait du colonisateur* (Paris: Buchet-Chastel, 1957).

40. For some calculations on the magnitude of the damage done by South African destabilization in the region, see Joseph Hanlon, *Beggar Your Neighbors: Apartheid Power in Southern Africa* (Bloomington: Indiana University Press, 1986).

41. On the Eritrean case, see Bereket Habte Selassie, *Conflict and Intervention in the Horn of Africa* (New York: Monthly Review Press, 1980); I. M. Lewis (ed.), *Nationalism and Self-Determination in the Horn of Africa* (London: Ithaca Press, 1983); Richard Sherman, *Eritrea: The Unfinished Revolution* (New York: Praeger, 1980); John Markakis, "The Nationalist Revolution in Eritrea," *Journal of Modern African Studies* 26, no. 4 (1987), pp. 643–668; and Mesfin Araya, "The Eritrean Question: An Alternative Explanation," *Journal of Modern African Studies* 28, no. 1 (1990), pp. 79–100.

42. For two excellent scholarly monographs reflecting southern and northern Sudanese perspectives, see Dunstan M. Wai, *The Africa-Arab Conflict in the Sudan* (New York: African Publishing House, 1978); and Mohammed Omar Beshir, *The Southern Sudan: Background to Conflict* (London: William Blackwood and Sons, 1968).

43. Half a million Moroccans signed on to participate in this proposed citizen invasion and annexation of Western Sahara; 145,000 actually began the move to the frontier. For details, see Hodges, *Western Sahara*.

3

Africa and the World Political Economy: More Caught Between a Rock and a Hard Place

THOMAS M. CALLAGHY

At the dawn of the twenty-first century, Africa must quickly select the path it wishes to follow. On the one hand, it could allow the forces of implosion and ethnic warfare to become the masters of its fate, to the advantage of a few potentates lacking vision or warlords with transient alliances. Thus history would repeat itself, with all the suffering that this entails, and this old continent would be at the mercy of all types of corruption. Africa would be stripped of the wealth of its soil and the promise of its youth and left marginalized, adrift in the wake of history.

> Since the early 1990s, many countries in sub-Saharan Africa ... have been implementing sound macroeconomic policies and structural reforms. ... But despite these reforms, poverty remains widespread, private investment is subdued, and many African countries continue to depend heavily on external assistance.
>
> —*Alassane D. Ouattara*[1]

Marginalization and Dependence

In the middle of the nineteenth century, Africa underwent a wrenching adjustment from one set of terrible realities to another. With the end of the slave trade, African societies had to find other ways to interact with the world economy and with powerful foreign states, all in the context of seriously disrupted economies and considerable political flux. In the period just before the imposition of direct colonial domination, Africa found itself both marginalized from the world economy and highly dependent on it. Referring to this era, a leading historian of Africa has pointed to "the paradox of Africa's simultaneous involvement and marginalization in the world economy; . . . Africa was becoming less significant to the world economy at the same time [that] it involved itself more closely in international commercial relationships." This paradox operated in the opposite direction as well: The world's "increasing involvement in the African economy . . . [was] at odds with the decreasing economic importance of Africa" for the world economy.[2] At the dawn of the twenty-first century, this paradox still holds true; in fact, it is more applicable now than it was at the middle of the last century. As we shall see, this paradox and the dilemmas that arise from it are well captured by Dr. Ouattara's words.

Increased Marginalization: "Post-Neocolonialism"

The increased marginalization of Africa is twofold—economic and politico-strategic—and both aspects are tightly linked in their consequences. The first, primarily economic aspect is that Africa is no longer very important to the major actors in the world economy (equity investors, multinational corporations, international banks, and the economies of the major Western countries) and in its changing international division of labor. The second aspect of its marginalization is that, with the end of the Cold War, African countries have little politico-strategic importance for the major world powers.

Africa generates a declining share of world output. The main commodities it produces are either becoming less and less important or being more effectively produced by other developing countries. Trade is declining; few want to lend; and an even smaller number want to invest, except in narrowly defined mineral enclave sectors.

Africa's per capita income levels and growth rates have declined since the first oil crisis in 1973, whereas its percentage of worldwide official development assistance rose from 17 percent in 1970 to about 38 percent in 1991. After 1970, nominal gross domestic product (GDP) rose more slowly than that of other developing countries, whereas real GDP growth rates dropped dramatically.[3]

Other developing countries performed better despite the poor world economic climate, especially in the 1980s. Cross-regional comparisons are quite revealing. For the period 1982–1992, average GDP growth for Africa was 2.0 percent; for South Asia, the most comparable region, it was 5.2

percent; and for East Asia, it was 8.0 percent. The rate for all developing countries was 2.7 percent. The GDP per capita rates are even more revealing: Africa –1.1 percent, South Asia 2.9 percent, and East Asia 6.4 percent. At these rates of per capita GDP growth, it would be forty years before Africa returned to mid-1970s levels. The World Bank's baseline projections for Africa in the 1990s were more optimistic, but, as we shall see, its projections for the 1990s met with very mixed results.

In addition, African export levels stayed relatively flat or actually declined after 1970, whereas those of other developing countries rose significantly. For example, the continent's share of developing-country agricultural primary product and food exports declined from 17 percent to 8 percent between 1970 and 1990, with South and East Asian exports growing rapidly. If the 1970 share had been maintained, export earnings in the early 1990s would have been significantly higher. Average annual growth rates for all exports fared poorly.

Africa's marginalization becomes even more obvious when its performance is compared with that of other low-income countries. This is particularly true in regard to South Asia, with which Africa has the most in common. South Asia is composed of Bangladesh, Bhutan, Burma, India, Maldives, Nepal, Pakistan, and Sri Lanka. The difference in per capita GDP growth between the two regions is striking: Africa's declined dramatically whereas that of South Asia rose slowly but steadily. Moreover, Africa's population growth rate continued to climb whereas that of South Asia began to decline.

The most startling differences between the two regions relate to the level and quality of investment. Africa's investment as a percentage of GDP declined in the 1980s whereas that of South Asia continued to increase despite the difficult economic conditions of the decade. South Asia followed better economic policies and, above all, provided a much more propitious socioeconomic and politico-administrative context for investment. This disparity is most vividly manifested in the comparative rates of return on investment: Africa's fell from 30.7 percent in the 1960s to just 2.5 percent in the 1980s whereas South Asia's increased slowly but steadily, if only marginally, from 21.3 percent to 22.4 percent in the same period.

A similar picture emerges from the comparative figures for the growth of production for both agriculture and industry. In 1965 manufacturing accounted for 9 percent of economic activity in Africa, and by the late 1980s it had risen to only 11 percent; in addition, much of it was extremely inefficient by world standards, and the results of privatization had been very mixed. As a result, by 1990 there was little interest on the part of major actors in the world economy in lending or investing in Africa.

Given this dismal economic performance, both substantively and comparatively, it is not surprising that world business leaders took an increasingly jaundiced view of Africa. As one business executive put it, "Who cares about Africa; it is not important to us; leave it to the IMF and the World Bank."[4] Some observers have referred to this phenomenon as *post-neocolonialism*. For the most dynamic actors in a rapidly changing world economy, even a neocolonial Africa was not of much interest, especially after the amazing changes wrought in Asia, Latin America, and Eastern Europe in the early and mid-1990s. According to this viewpoint, the African crisis really should be left to the international financial institutions as a salvage operation, and if that effort works, fine; if not, so be it; the world economy will hardly notice.

Thus, whatever one thinks about the role of foreign investment and finance capital, it is important to remember that Africa increasingly imposes enormous difficulties for these actors, such as political arbitrariness, spreading civil war and other forms of strife, and administrative, infrastructural, and economic inefficiency. Foreign capital has a considerable ability to select the type of state with which it cooperates; thus it is doubtful that Africa will play any significant role in current shifts in the patterns of production in the international division of labor, especially after the international economic crisis that began in Asia in 1997 and spread to Russia and parts of Latin America. For most external businesspeople, Africa had become a voracious sinkhole that swallowed their money with little or no longer-run return. Two arresting facts further underscore Africa's marginalization by the early 1990s: (1) The amount of external financing done in 1991 through bonds for East Asia was $2.4 billion, and, for South Asia $1.9 billion, whereas it was zero for Africa; and (2) flight capital at the end of 1990 as a percentage of GDP was 14.9 for South Asia, 18.9 for East Asia, and 27.8 for developing Europe and Central Asia, whereas it was 80.3 for Africa.

Some observers had hoped that a postapartheid South Africa would help lead the region to sustained growth. Such a hope now appears quite unrealistic. South Africa faces enormous difficulties, although foreign investment is more likely to go there than elsewhere in Africa.

From this perspective, the lament of international organizations and development economists about the intractable underdevelopment of Africa is not just a conspiratorial attempt to conceal the pillage of Africa but, rather, a reflection of the fact (although they would not put it this way) that Africa, from the standpoint of major private economic actors, is an underexploited continent with weak states and weak markets.

Indeed, disinvestment emerged as a new trend. During the 1980s, for example, 43 of 139 British firms with industrial investments in Africa withdrew their holdings (mostly from Zimbabwe, Nigeria, and Kenya)—

despite ongoing economic reforms. Ironically, the retrenchment was due in part to the economic reforms themselves, as they removed overvalued exchange rates and import tariff protection. The British firms were unwilling to inject new capital to make their investments efficient by world standards of competitiveness. As noted, the second aspect of Africa's marginalization is politico-strategic, but it entails negative economic consequences as well. Africa has become of much less interest to the major world powers after the end of the Cold War. As one senior African diplomat described the situation, "We are an old tattered lady. People are tired of Africa. So many countries, so many wars."[5] The rise of warlords in regional and civil wars similar to those in nineteenth-century Africa has challenged the very notion of the nation-state borrowed at the time of independence in the 1960s. By the late 1990s Africa's first major interstate war was raging in Central Africa in the aftermath of the overthrow of the Mobutu regime in Zaire. When linked to ongoing or renewed wars in Angola and the Sudan, as well as new ones in Sierra Leone and between Eritrea and Ethiopia, the impact on attempted economic reform is likely to be great.

Debates about Africa used to pit internationalists concerned about big power rivalry against regionalists concerned with African issues. Ironically, the internationalists largely ceded the field to the regionalists after the unsuccessful intervention in Somalia. The regionalists used to call for the major powers not to turn Africa into an international battlefield but, rather, to let Africans solve their own problems—in short, to leave Africa alone. After the internationalists declared the game over, the regionalists desperately searched for a rationale to keep external interest, and resources, focused on Africa. Malign neglect became the more common reaction, especially as the major powers became concerned with security crises in Europe.

At the same time, however, the dramatic changes of 1989, Africa's politico-strategic marginalization, and the search for a new foreign policy rationale by Western industrial democracies in the early 1990s meant that economic conditionality was joined by forms of political conditionality, under the assumption that economic and political liberalization must go hand in hand. Hence, despite these forms of marginalization, Africa was becoming more dependent on often quite intrusive external actors.

Increased Involvement: The New Neocolonialism

In the 1980s Africa became more tightly linked to the world economy in two major respects: (1) by an extreme dependence on external public actors, particularly the IMF and the World Bank, in the determination of African economic policy; and (2) by the liberal or neoclassical thrust of this economic policy conditionality, which tried to push the continent toward more intense reliance on and integration with the world economy. Both of these aspects were linked directly to Africa's debt crisis.

In 1974 total African debt was about $14.8 billion; by 1992 it was over $150 billion, or more than 100 percent of Africa's total GNP. South Asia's percentage was only 36.3; and East Asia's, 27.9. Much of the rise came from international financial institutions (IFIs), especially the IMF and the World Bank, and it resulted largely from the borrowing associated with externally sponsored economic reform programs, usually referred to as structural adjustment. In 1980 IFI debt equaled 19 percent of the total; by 1992 it accounted for 28 percent, and by 1998 it had reached 32 percent. As we shall see, until 1996 this debt could not be formally rescheduled or diminished, and significant arrears accumulated, with the result that some countries were cut off from IMF and World Bank assistance. Much of the rest of Africa's debt was bilateral or government-guaranteed, private medium- and long-term debt and thus was rescheduled by Western governments through the Paris Club—not by the private banks, as in Latin America and Asia. A key norm of the debt regime was that countries could obtain Paris Club rescheduling relief without being in the good graces of the IMF and the World Bank.

This difficult external debt burden and the resulting desperate need for foreign exchange made African countries very dependent on a variety of external actors, all of whom used their leverage to "encourage" economic liberalization. This process, which some referred to as the *new neocolonialism*, meant intense dependence on the IMF, the World Bank, and major Western countries for the design of economic reform packages and the resources needed to implement them. This leverage, in turn, was converted into economic policy conditionality—specific economic policy changes in return for borrowed resources. The main thrust of these economic reform efforts was to integrate African economies more fully into the world economy by resurrecting the primary-product export economies that existed at the time of independence and making them work right this time by creating a more "liberal" political economy.

One good indicator of this increased international involvement was the number of African countries with ongoing relationships with the IMF and the World Bank. Between 1970 and 1978, African countries accounted for 3 percent of total assistance from IMF-approved economic reform programs. Their share of the total number of IMF programs for this period was 17 percent; by the end of 1979 it had risen to 55 percent. In 1978 only two African countries had agreements with the IMF; in March 1990, twenty-eight countries had such agreements (60 percent of the total agreements). Despite the large number of new members from Eastern Europe and the former Soviet Union, African countries still accounted for 38 percent of the agreements in September 1993. By February 1999, 41 percent of the agreements were with African countries, despite an increased number of programs due to the Asia crisis. Most of these countries also had simultaneous agreements with the World Bank. Finally, African countries had the highest number of repeat programs of any region of the world.

In sum, Africa's dismal situation was not caused primarily by its relationship to the world economy or to dominant countries or actors in the international state system; rather, it is the *combined* result of the effects of world market forces, the international state system and its international financial institutions, African socioeconomic structures, and the nature and performance of African state structures. Africa has always been relatively marginal to the world economy. It was now becoming even more so, and at an accelerating rate. In many respects, Africa was lost between state and market. It wandered between an ineffective, sometimes collapsing state and weak markets, both domestic and international, and the latter were increasingly indifferent. Many African officials failed to realize just how unimportant Africa was becoming to the world economy; they feared it and sought to run from it. Many of them are still looking for a shortcut, a quick fix, even though world events since 1980 demonstrate that one does not exist. If African countries are to survive, changes must be made in their economic priorities. If not, changes in the world political economy will continue to pass Africa by, with very serious long-term consequences for the people of the continent.[6]

The Political Economy of Attempted Economic Reform in the 1980s and 1990s

By the early 1980s the key question was not whether Africa had a serious economic crisis but, rather, what needed to be done about it. Avoidance of the problem and policy drift were common reactions, despite external warnings and pressure. Much of the African response was to rail against the prescriptions of external actors. For those governments that did decide to attack the problem (whether out of conviction or a desperate need for foreign exchange and debt rescheduling), the dilemmas were enormous, the risks great, and the uncertainties pervasive. Throughout the 1980s and early 1990s economic reform did take place in Africa in large and small ways. Many countries went through the motions or at least appeared to do so, resulting in a series of small reforms. Few cases of multisector, sustained reform appeared, however. Ghana and Uganda, in fact, were the only clear-cut examples, and they illustrated the enormous difficulties involved. Dr. Kwesi Botchwey, Ghana's longtime finance minister, portrayed these difficulties vividly:

> We were faced with two options, which we debated very fiercely before we
> finally chose this path. I know because I participated very actively in these
> debates. Two choices: We had to maneuver our way around the naiveties of
> leftism, which has a sort of disdain for any talk of financial discipline, which
> seeks refuge in some vague concept of structuralism in which everything
> doable is possible. . . . Moreover, [we had to find a way between] this naiveté
> and the crudities and rigidities and dogma of monetarism, which behaves as
> if once you set the monetary incentives everybody will do the right thing
> and the market will be perfect.[7]

As the Rawlings regime in Ghana and the Museveni regime in Uganda
discovered, neither position is fully correct: Not everything is possible,
and policy incentives do not ensure that markets will work well. In addition, a revenue imperative exists whatever path is chosen. Resources have
to come from somewhere. A quite rare conjuncture of factors allowed the
economic reform efforts in Ghana and Uganda to be sustained, and their
success at large reform—itself still fragile—is rare on the continent.

Economic Reform and the Implicit Bargain

Africans and external actors alike have asked how serious attempts at
economic reform could be prevented from collapsing, as several did in
quite dramatic fashion—in Zambia and Nigeria, for example. How could
the many other efforts that were limping along become more effective
and sustainable? How could the enormous burdens of such efforts be
softened or ameliorated? In a very real sense, these were classic issues of
statecraft, at both the national and international levels.

Africans have long maintained that substantial resource flows and debt
relief are required for sustained reform. One of the lessons of Ghana and
Uganda is that they are certainly necessary but not sufficient conditions.
By the early 1990s, external actors began to realize that increased resource
flows and debt relief were going to be required for Africa. This realization
began to sink in as the enormous obstacles to reform and the possibility
of widespread failure became increasingly apparent. Whether the resource flows and debt relief will actually come is another matter. The special new lending facilities of the IMF and the World Bank, such as the
Fund's Enhanced Structural Adjustment Facility, were steps in that direction, but substantial support for them from the major powers remained
precarious.

At the same time, a larger problem existed—one that was directly
linked to Africa's increasing marginalization from the world economy. An
implicit bargain was struck between the IFIs and the major Western countries on the one hand and the Africans on the other. The provisions of the
bargain were that if African countries successfully reformed their

economies in a neoorthodox direction with the help and direction of the IMF and the World Bank, then new international private bank and bond lending and equity plus direct foreign investment would be available to underpin and sustain the reform efforts.

By the early 1990s this implicit bargain was still very far from being upheld. It was not the fault of the IMF and the World Bank (both of which had worked to increase voluntary lending and direct foreign investment) or of reforming African governments. Rather, it was a legacy of Africa's thirty-year history of dismal economic performance (a track record that banks and investors do not forget easily) and of structural shifts in the world economy and state system that made other areas of the world more attractive to investors. Proponents of neoorthodox reform in Africa argued that this track record could be overcome if Africa provided relatively predictable environments for investment. Even if the African end of the bargain were to be fulfilled (which is not likely), the bargain would hold only if other areas of the world did not provide better opportunities. The "flight to safety" that followed the onset of the Asia crisis in 1997 demonstrated that, under conditions of uncertainty and shattered expectations, capital would return to the heartland of the world economy and not to marginalized areas such as Africa.

During a speech in March 1990, Michel Camdessus, the managing director of the IMF, provided a good description of this implicit bargain—what he called "the unwritten contract"—and, seemingly without intending to do so, also characterized the precarious nature of it. The speech is worth quoting at length:

> In other words, we must all strive to come back to what I would call the core idea of the unwritten contract of international cooperation: that countries adopt good policies, and that these [are] supported by adequate internal and external financing. . . . Every country has responsibility for its own destiny, and the main source of its future prosperity lies in its own efforts. Foreign investment and other assistance can only supplement the actions of the country itself. . . .
>
> In view of the rapid growth in Africa's debt-servicing burden, strenuous efforts to reduce the debt overhang must continue. For the future, African countries will need to be prudent about their borrowing, both as regards its scale and terms, and be careful to use new resources wisely and efficiently, so that they contribute to growth and external viability.
>
> The availability of the traditional types of finance will be limited. But I am sure that the Fund itself will be able to continue to play successfully its role as a catalyst of international financing, if African countries come forward with economic programs that are strong enough, and credible enough, to convince Africans themselves to invest in Africa. If this occurs—and it is possible—then the banks can be expected to overcome their hesitations, to sup-

port their long-term customers, and to direct their new lending to those countries that are creating growth and good business opportunities. They will lend on a very selective basis, and within limits, although these limits may expand for countries that succeed in their adjustment efforts.

Other forms of private lending can become more important. For example, there may be wider scope for direct and portfolio investment in many African countries. But this will happen only for those countries that consistently show a good economic performance, and that attract and welcome financing from abroad. This includes, not least, their own flight capital. By persevering with sound policies, any African country can gradually increase the confidence of its own population and of foreign investors in its long-term potential. . . .

You all know that the Fund also has heavy ongoing responsibilities in the global debt strategy, and new challenges in helping Eastern European countries to reform. Despite these demands on our resources, we shall be able to continue to support all African countries that are prepared to persevere with far-reaching reforms and that back up these reforms with firm financial discipline.[8]

Note the extent to which this description of the terms of the "unwritten contract" was hedged by repeated and careful qualifications. These reflected the degree of Africa's marginalization, larger changes in the international division of labor and state system, and the enormity of the economic and political obstacles to restructuring African political economies after thirty years of decline. The message was that the international system is indeed geared toward self-help and that resources would flow only to those who helped themselves. In the 1980s Africa's share of global foreign investment was 4.5 percent; by 1990 it was only 0.7 percent. In the early mid-1990s, net foreign investment for the whole region rose, but three-quarters of it was in the mineral sectors and much of it in South Africa and Nigeria.

Economic conditionality is not only an international fact of life, as the Asian crisis reminded us, but also a key element of the implicit bargain. The exceptions make this point. Between 1985 and early 1987, for example, the Kaunda government in Zambia half-heartedly implemented a very unpopular IMF–World Bank economic reform package. After deadly riots, strikes, and protests, Kaunda terminated the program in May 1987, announcing that Zambia would formulate and implement its own reform package without external resources and the conditionality that came with them. If Zambia after 1987 was an example of what African economic reform would look like without conditionality, Africa was in serious trouble. The tough decisions were simply not made, the economy continued to decline, and external actors essentially cut off resource flows. By the early 1990s, however, conditionality went wild in Africa; overly minute and cross-cutting conditionality stimulated game playing by both African and external officials—game playing that tended to undermine the efficacy of reform and the scarce resources that existed to support it.

In addition, the capacity of African states to absorb new resources effectively can be easily overloaded. Although more resources are definitely needed to increase the chances of sustained economic reform, only so much can be absorbed, both technically and politically. Inefficient programs and renewed rent-seeking are real possibilities, as the post-Kaunda democratic government of Frederick Chiluba in Zambia demonstrated. One way of coping with this problem was to use expatriates. A striking new expatriatization quietly took place in many African countries, as will also occur in Nigeria at present. In mid-1990, the head of the World Bank noted "the extraordinary fact that there are more expatriate advisors in Africa today than at the end of the colonial period."[9] Although this expatriatization increased the technical capacity of some African governments, it can also become a sensitive political issue.

Learning: The Fear of Failure

By the mid-1980s, some international officials had began to realize that many efforts at economic reform in Africa would fail unless changes were made in how the programs were designed and implemented. This often quite palpable fear of failure became an impetus to international learning. One senior World Bank official addressed the problem bluntly and honestly in 1987:

> The alternative—a series of failed programs in Africa—is not worth thinking about, and not only because of the human suffering. . . . The basic idea of moving to a market economy, shifting policies out of grandiosity to step-by-step solid progress, will be discredited. If they fail in a series of countries . . . then it is a failure of our approach to the economy, a failure of our institutions, a failure of our political will, and there's no way that we'll be able to say that it is just the failure of Africa! So we have a very, very big stake in this.[10]

This realization prompted a reassessment of the economic reform process, and by the end of the decade some learning was taking place—slowly and unevenly—among both external actors and certain African officials.

External officials began to realize that stop-go cycles of reform were a fact of life and that they needed to learn to adjust to them. Both sides became more attuned to the need for the politics of fine-tuning—the more careful calibration of policy measures, instruments, pace, timing, and sequencing, especially regarding the sensitive issues of food, health, fuel, and wages—in order to modulate the socioeconomic and political impacts of adjustment measures and thereby increase the chances of sustained reform. External officials believe, for example, that Zambia's 1985–1987 reform effort might not have failed if these lessons had been learned earlier.

Structural adjustment is an enormously difficult and politically sensitive task in Africa, especially as the benefits are often uncertain and come quite far down the road. Reform is often complicated by other factors, such as drought, famine, civil and regional wars, destabilization, and AIDS. The hardest thing to accept is that even successful neoorthodox reform will not eliminate Africa's marginality to the world economy in the short and medium runs. It might, however, begin to lessen and prevent the continent—or parts of it, at least—from becoming totally unimportant to the world economy. Livable societies are hard to build without productive connections to the world economy. If a sizable number of African countries do not make such connections, state failure will become a more widespread phenomenon on the continent.

Although some policy lessons have been learned, Africa's problems are larger still. Even if proper policy lessons are implemented and resources are found to support them, it is not clear that they would result in a high number of sustained large reform efforts. A link clearly exists between debt and structural adjustment in Africa, but it is not predominantly a causal one. The need for structural adjustment long predated the debt crisis, despite the views of many Africans; the debt crisis merely brought the structural adjustment crisis to a head. Even if the debt crisis were somehow miraculously solved tomorrow—through a total writeoff, for example—the structural adjustment crisis would remain. The case of Nigeria has shown that massive amounts of new resources can intensify rather than ameliorate economic decline.

For Africa, the task of confronting this decline is enormous—much larger than for any other region of the world, with the possible exception of Central Asia. External actors have learned that Africa is a special case; it has not responded as neoclassical theory predicted it should. As the World Bank has noted:

> The supply response to adjustment lending in low-income countries, especially in SSA [sub-Saharan Africa] has been slow because of the legacy of deep-seated structural problems. Inadequate infrastructure, poorly developed markets, rudimentary industrial sectors, and severe institutional and managerial weaknesses in the public and the private sectors have proved unexpectedly serious as constraints to better performance—especially in the poorer countries of SSA. Greater recognition thus needs to be given to the time and attention needed for structural changes, especially institutional reforms and their effects.[11]

Note the revealing use of the word *unexpectedly:* It indicates a changed perception—that Africa is a particularly difficult case. It is a case not of re-ordering policies but, rather, one of constructing a whole new context—what the World Bank has called an "enabling environment."

In a sense, for Africa *both* the structuralist and neoliberal sides are correct: As the structuralists maintain, there are enormous economic and social structure obstacles to development; and as the adherents of neoliberalism maintain, the state is also an impediment. *And* both sets of obstacles inhibit both import substitution industrialization and export-oriented economic activity, public and private. The structuralists are correct in maintaining that socioeconomic obstacles prevent neoclassical monoeconomics—the presumption that economic processes work the same everywhere—from being fully operative in Africa, as the World Bank has "unexpectedly" dis-covered; and the neoliberals are correct in maintaining that the nature of the state in Africa makes import substitution industrialization ineffective and wasteful, as many African structuralists still have not admitted.

The structuralists do have a theory of reform; but it is a weak one, be-cause its instrument of reform—the state—is itself terribly ineffective in Africa. Yet in the course of attempted reform, the external proponents of neoclassical change have confronted an orthodox paradox: In order to im-plement such reform, they, too, have to use what they perceive to be the major obstacle to reform—the African state—as the primary instrument of reform. Many people know what kind of state is needed, but nobody knows how to obtain it. Other than getting the state out of the economy, the neoclassical strategists did not have a theory of state reform, and they have found that getting the state out of the economy is much more diffi-cult than expected—politically, administratively, and technically. In addi-tion, the adherents of neoorthodoxy are learning that their own pro-claimed instrument of reform—the market—is also terribly weak in Africa. Over time it becomes increasingly clear that nobody understands the functioning of African economies; even the basic data for the formal economy are extremely limited and unreliable, and systematic data on the informal economy are still very weak.

After nearly forty years of independence, most of Africa is neither ef-fectively socialist nor capitalist; it is not even competently statist. Socialist and statist efforts have yielded few results, and modern capitalism hardly exists. Current liberalization efforts may not have a major impact in many places, and the rest of the world increasingly passes the continent by. In many respects, then, African countries are still lost between state and market, and, although successful large reform is not impossible (as Ghana and Uganda have demonstrated), it takes an extraordinary confluence of forces to bring it about and to sustain it.

Debates and False Hopes in the 1990s

Despite the learning that had occurred by the end of the 1980s—with obstacles to reform apparent on all sides—the key question remained: What should Africa do to cope with its devastating economic crisis? The answer put forth by the external actors, led by the IMF and the World Bank, was to persevere with the neoliberal thrust of reforms, with modifications to make them work more effectively. Many Africans remained unconvinced. This fundamental disagreement simmered quietly throughout the 1980s behind what appeared to many as an increasing consensus around a modified neoorthodox position.

This disagreement burst forth with surprising vigor in what could be called the "bloody spring of 1989." A major battle ensued between the World Bank and the UN Economic Commission for Africa (ECA), as the former tried to defend structural adjustment and the latter tried to attack it and present its own alternative strategy.[12]

What was taken as consensus by powerful external actors had actually been a quiet waiting game generated by the desperate need of African countries for external resources and the hope of a major bailout through substantial debt relief, higher export prices, greatly increased bilateral and multilateral aid, commercial bank lending, or direct foreign investment. When these things failed to materialize, a sense of betrayal set in for many Africans. For their part, the World Bank and other external actors helped to generate this crisis by being unduly optimistic about the expected results of the reform efforts in order to sell them. In an attempt to sustain positive expectations, the Bank fell victim to what I call the "fault of analytic hurry"—wanting to see things as real before they are. A backlash from failed expectations should not have been a surprise. The time frame was too narrow, the data were unreliable, reform measures were not fully or consistently implemented, and designating strong versus weak reformers was often arbitrary, misleading, and fleeting. In addition, expectations about positive outcomes were out of line with what could really be expected. Even if all reform measures were fully implemented in a sustained manner, the results would not be spectacular; they would be modest at best. And although even modest results would be a major accomplishment, they would unfortunately not be perceived that way by most Africans or many private actors in the world economy.

In 1993 the debate flared up again. This time, IMF and the World Bank had to defend themselves on a wider variety of fronts, most urgently at the annual Fund-Bank meetings. Africa was a major topic of discussion because, compared to other regions, it was not doing well in the area of economic reform. The IMF and the World Bank now conceded that reform had been modest and that it was taking longer than they expected.

They admitted that in 1980–1990 half of the IMF programs broke down, as did two-thirds of World Bank structural adjustment loans. By their own reckoning, in 1990–1991 only one of twenty-six countries with reform efforts did well, whereas in fourteen others results were only fair and in eleven they were poor to very poor.

Earlier in 1993, Oxfam had issued a stinging attack on structural adjustment entitled *Africa Make or Break: Action for Recovery*,[13] complemented by criticisms from the Environmental Defense Fund, Development Gap, Christian Aid, and others. Oxfam declared bluntly that IMF reform in Africa had failed and that if the Fund did not undergo major reform it should withdraw from Africa. At the same time, some Western legislators complained of the marginal reform results in Africa funded by the taxes of their citizens, while academics and Asian governments insisted that there were statist lessons to be learned from East Asian experience. Japan held a major conference on Africa in October in which it pushed these views while making no new pledges of assistance. The Japanese were quite dissatisfied with a recently released World Bank report entitled *The East Asian Miracle: Economic Growth and Public Policy*,[14] which was meant to reassess neoclassical economic views in light of the Asian experience; they believed that the report greatly underplayed the importance of statist policies that they thought could be copied by other countries, including African ones. It was clear that African views had not changed much either. Structural adjustment was still largely seen as an externally imposed evil, and many Africans believed that the world should accept an African alternative *and* pay for it.

But what was this alternative? Had it evolved and become more coherent, more viable? The answer was no. A viable African alternative to IMF and World Bank reform did not exist, especially given the weak state capabilities. An East Asian statist option was also clearly not possible. Desires for transformation do not an alternative make. The Fund-Bank strategy *was* a second-best one, but a modified version of it was probably the most viable option: As Ghana's Kwesi Botchwey was fond of saying, "Structural adjustment is very painful, but structural maladjustment is much worse."[15] This is a reflection of how hemmed in Africa really is.

The Rise of Political Conditionality: Governance and Democracy

Part of the modified version of structural adjustment, based on the poor track record of the 1980s, was the new notion of "good governance." The World Bank's emphasis on governance emerged from its learning about the primary importance of creating a more facilitative sociopolitical context for structural adjustment in Africa. Due to the dramatic changes in the world in 1989–1990 and the search for a new foreign policy thrust to replace containment (what the Clinton administration called "enlargement" of the world's free community of market democracies), governance was quickly transformed by the major Western industrial democracies into political conditionality focusing on the promotion of democracy and civil society. The convergence of these two policy thrusts—one largely technocratic from the World Bank, the other distinctly political from the major powers—posed a real dilemma for African leaders.

But was political conditionality a good idea, especially regarding the prospects for major economic change? The presumption of the mutually reinforcing character of political and economic reform in Africa relies on an extension of neoclassical economic logic: Economic liberalization creates sustained growth, growth produces winners as well as losers, and winners will organize to defend their newfound welfare and create sociopolitical coalitions to support continued economic reform. This logic, however, may not hold for much of Africa.

Successful economic reform in Africa has been rare, requiring a special conjuncture of factors, such as those that have existed in Ghana since 1983 and in Uganda since 1987. Central to the aforementioned logic is the argument that successful reform comes from insulating the policy process from the rent-seeking and distributional pressures that so dominated the first thirty years of independence in Africa. Ghana under Rawlings and Uganda under Museveni demonstrate that successful and sustained economic reform is possible without the presence of an *existing* societal support coalition. The former did major reform, then engaged in careful political liberalization; the latter started major reform and created a political structure that was far from fully democratic. In both cases, external actors acquiesced on the political side because major economic reform was under way.

The winners of economic reform in Africa are few, appear only slowly over time, and are difficult to organize politically. The neoclassical political logic of reform is too mechanistic for the African context; there are real transaction costs to organizing winners, not just infrastructural ones. Cocoa farmers, for example, have other cross-cutting interests, political loyalties, and histories of organization that make direct political organization in support of a given set of economic policies difficult. Other organizational bases of political solidarity exist—ethnic, regional, religious, linguistic, and patron-client—that make mobilization around policy-specific economic interests difficult. Even where such organizations might be possible, they would not likely be strong enough to support the full range of economic measures, thereby threatening the viability of reform. Economic learning by political leaders and societal groups is possible, but it is usually a fragile creature, requiring special circumstances to survive—and it can easily be upset.

The progress of democratization in Africa has been very uneven, especially in its relationship to economic reform. At one end of the spectrum,

Jerry Rawlings in Ghana kept his options open by resisting pressure to liberalize politically until he was ready; then he launched a rapid and controlled liberalization process. Catching the opposition off guard, he won a presidential election, and the opposition boycotted subsequent parliamentary elections. Rawlings later won a second round of elections. The result was a slowly expanding democracy that allowed Rawlings to continue the impressive economic reform effort. At the other end of the spectrum, the military government of General Ibrahim Babangida in Nigeria botched a long, complex, and manipulated liberalization process by abrogating presidential elections in June 1993. The resulting crisis led to General Babangida's resignation and a devastating downward spiral into brutal repression and massive corruption. After eight years of effort, Nigeria had neither democracy nor effective economic reform. Only in early 1999 did Nigeria emerge from this nightmare. Whether President Olusegun Obasanjo can make democracy work in Nigeria and engage in serious economic reform remains very open to question. The track record of the previous civilian government was very far from such an outcome, being one of the most venal and unproductive regimes in Nigeria's history.

External actors used political conditionality in Kenya only to find it undermined by the maneuvering of the Moi government *and* the inability of the opposition to come up with a single presidential candidate and slate of legislators. They reopened resource flows anyway. In Zambia, where a full transition did take place in late 1992, the new government of Frederick Chiluba had problems with political factionalism, resurgent corruption, ethnic and regional tension, and renewed authoritarian tendencies—largely of its own making—and it produced very uneven economic performance despite early good intentions and lots of external help.

Is this version of the "thesis of the perverse effect"[16]—that political liberalization might have no positive impact on the chances for sustained economic reform—likely to hold across the board for Africa? No, but it is important to assess particular cases carefully. A probabilistic rather than deterministic perverse effect is likely to operate. If not handled properly, political conditionality linked to democratization might impede rather than facilitate the productive relinking of Africa to the world economy. The widespread emergence of what Richard L. Sklar has called "developmental democracies" is not likely in Africa anytime soon.[17]

Undue Expectations Yet Again: Africa's "Renaissance" in the Mid-1990s

Nonetheless, by early 1998 a new African renaissance was being widely proclaimed—one based on relatively narrow data, however. Key external actors rushed to proclaim that Africa had turned the corner after three years of improved growth. What is more, they projected that this growth would continue.

The first signs that an African renaissance was being proclaimed came in early 1997, just six months before the full onset of the Asia crisis. In January, for example, a *Financial Times* headline trumpeted that "Fast Growth Forecast Targets Asia and Africa." By the time President Clinton made his historic trip to Africa in March 1998, the trumpets were getting louder. *Time* magazine had a cover story entitled "Africa Rising: After Decades of Famine and War, Life Is Finally Looking Up for Many Africans." By mid-1998, when the depth of the Asia crisis was finally being realized, the trumpets of external actors were reaching full blast. The IMF's Ouattara gave a speech in mid-June at an "Africa-U.S. Economic Conference" in Arlington, Virginia, on "The IMF's Role in the Unfolding African Renaissance." And shortly thereafter, Michel Camdessus, the Fund's managing director, told a summit of OAU heads of state in Ouagadougou that Africa is a "Continent on the Move."[18]

What was this latest burst of optimism based on? The answer is a narrow bed of sand, and, as we shall see, a shifting one at that. It was based on a three-year "surge" of growth. In mid-1998 the IMF noted that real GDP growth for 1990–1994 was 1.6 percent; and for 1995–1997, 4.3 percent. The per capita growth figures for the respective periods were –2.0 percent and 1.4 percent. The IMF pointed out that, in 1996, twenty-one African countries had growth rates of over 5 percent; and eleven, over 7 percent. Whereas in 1990 fifteen countries had negative growth rates, in 1996 only four did. In October (by which time the Asia crisis had spread to Russia and was heading for Brazil), the IMF actually revised its 1995–1997 average growth figure up to 5.2 percent. By April 1999, however, the figure for the same three years was down to 4.5 percent. According to the IMF, this 1995–1997 "renaissance" was based on much better policies and implementation, good commodity prices, and relatively decent weather. By early October 1998, the *Financial Times* was already quietly and politely noting that the "Renaissance Train Has Been Delayed."[19] Much of the 1995–1997 growth took the form of rising capacity utilization from the very low base reached by the end of the 1980s. Although investment in Africa rose from 1990 to 1996, it did so mostly in the minerals sectors. This investment increase still left Africa with a smaller percentage of foreign direct investment than it had enjoyed a decade earlier; public investment was still a third of rates for the rest of the developing world, whereas average savings rates were a very low 18 percent of GDP. In addition, 25 percent of foreign exchange earnings were going to actual debt service. If debt service due was being paid, the figure would have been far, far higher.

The IMF's figures were consistently higher than those of the World Bank. The Bank's April 1999 figure for 1995–1997 was only 3.8 percent—

this was the big boom. The Bank's figure for 1994–1998 was by then only 3.1 percent, and it was predicting 1999 growth at 2.5 percent, whereas the Fund's figure was 2.9 percent. An equally revealing comparison is the one for 1996–1998. In December 1998 the Bank's figure for this period was 3.4 percent; by April 1999 it had decreased to 3.2 percent. On the other hand, the Fund's October 1998 figure for the same period was 5.1 percent, and by April 1999 it had been lowered to 4.1 percent. A more sobering perspective came from the Bank when it pointed out that sustained growth of the 1995–1997 variety for a decade would still result in a per capita income that was 5 percent less in 2006 than in 1974. An equally revealing figure surfaced in the Bank's April 1999 *World Development Indicators*, which put the 1965–1997 average growth rate at only 2.6 percent. For real progress, it is necessary to have average growth rates at least in the 6–7 percent range consistently over time. Indeed, what brought major structural change to Asia was a growth rate higher than this for more than twenty years. Undue bursts of cheerleading optimism that quickly becomes hollow do not do anybody any good—a lesson that appears very hard for powerful external actors to learn.

These actors had also learned another lesson, however—one linked to declining levels of aid, which fell from $13.9 billion in 1990 to $10.7 billion in 1996. The mantra of the major donors was becoming "less aid, more trade and investment"—a belated, meager, and cheaper effort to help fulfill the implicit bargain. This new trend, and its limits, can be seen in the saga of the Clinton administration's "Growth and Opportunity Act." Meant to lower trade barriers to African goods and stimulate investment, this act had still not come out of Congress in any form by May 1999.

The Impact of the Asia Crisis and Contagion on Africa

Owing to Africa's marginalization, its countries were relatively insulated from the devastating blows of the Asia crisis, except for South Africa. As one IMF analyst put it, "Given the rudimentary state of financial markets in most sub-Saharan African countries and the rather limited amounts of private capital flowing into them, the financial contagion from the Asia crisis was effectively limited to South Africa."[20] The major impact came from terms of trade changes; but it is important, here, to differentiate among oil exporters, oil importers, and the CFA countries. In April 1999 the IMF estimated the 1998 and 1999 real income effects[21] for Africa as a whole to be –2.4 percent and –0.6 percent, respectively. For oil exporters the figures were –13.3 percent and –3.5 percent, for oil importers –0.2 percent and 0.0 percent, and for the CFA zone –1.6 percent and –0.6 percent. South Africa, the only African economy really integrated into the world economy, was hit by a steep devaluation of the rand, high interest rates, and declining trade and investment from Asia and elsewhere. Growth dropped to zero in 1998 and was expected to rise to only 0.6 percent in 1999. Foreign direct investment fell from $1.7 billion in 1997 to about $1 billion in 1998, whereas portfolio equity flows fell from $1.5 billion to $336 million. Business confidence was at a twelve-year low. Nigeria was very badly hit by the drop in oil prices just as the dramatic return to democracy was taking place. Its "growth" rate was expected to be –1.5 percent in 1999. All of Africa was going to be affected by slower growth in Europe and even stronger competition from Asian countries, due to their steep currency devaluations and urgent need to export themselves out of trouble.

Many Africans bitterly resented the enormous Asian rescue packages and the preemptory one for Brazil from the IFIs and Western countries that had been saying they did not have more resources for Africa. Despite the comparatively modest impact of the Asia crisis on Africa due to its marginalization, there was an even more sobering lesson learned from the Asia crisis: the imperative to have solid and internationally capable banking sectors. Even if large private resource flows were to come to Africa, structural impediments such as extremely weak banking sectors would inhibit the effective use of them.

On top of this, one must factor in the serious impact of growing civil conflict in Sierra Leone, Sudan, Eritrea, and Ethiopia—and, above all, in central Africa, where the continent's first major interstate war rages on with more than seven countries involved. This war is preventing reform from beginning in such places as what is left of Laurent Kabila's Congo. Even more sobering is the prospect of diverting the progress made by one of Africa's few star reformers—Museveni's Uganda. An arc of devastating armed conflict now exists from Eritrea to Angola. As the World Bank bluntly put it in April 1999, these conflicts pose "the biggest threat to Sub-Saharan Africa's near-term prospects, derailing . . . still fragile recovery and threatening the stability of the entire central African region." In many of the same regions, HIV infection rates are having a devastating effect. And emerging in areas of conflict and weakening state structures are regional economies that fuse control of coercion with control of trade, with the rise of what Janet Roitman calls garrison-entrepôts (in the greater Chad basin, for example). This scenario is accompanied by the criminalization of much economic activity. Will Reno has shown how warlords and weak sovereigns create their own linkages to private actors in the world economy using the shabby remains of external sovereignty, resulting in "a new internal configuration of power in place of formal state bureaucracies." Such rulers have realized that they "can manipulate transnational commercial transactions and outsiders' willingness to recognize them as mediators between local and world economies to accumulate wealth and control associates." These new configurations of power and ties to the world economy reflect Africa's ongoing marginalization rather than its lessening. Even in places such as Mozambique, where real rebuilding progress has been made, the extremely low base from which it is moving means that a long time will pass before the country is able to link itself productively to the world economy, as South Africa has begun to do. Finally, the hopes once held that South Africa would be a major engine of growth for the region are seriously in doubt for now.[22]

Africa and New Global Economic Governance

The Asia crisis and its spread were seen by many, including mainstream economists, as a major challenge to the legitimacy of the IMF and the World Bank, also evidenced by quite vigorous public differences between the two. Much like the Latin American debt crisis in 1982, the Asia crisis set off a major and quite varied flurry of proposals for a "new international financial architecture."[23] Because of its marginality, Africa had, in fact, been quietly leading the way in the 1990s toward new financial architecture and broader forms of global economic governance.

One of the primary results of structural adjustment in Africa has been rising levels of external debt. In 1998 Africa's long-term debt was $176 billion. Unlike most other regions of the world, this debt was mostly "official" debt owed to major Western countries, the International Monetary Fund, and the World Bank. Africa owed an incredible 76 percent of it to bilateral and multilateral creditors (44 percent and 32 percent, respectively)—itself a major indicator of marginalization. Since the late 1950s the bilateral debt has been rescheduled by creditor countries organized into a mechanism that came to be known as the Paris Club, whereas the multilateral debt could not be rescheduled. The Paris Club became the core of the international debt regime for official debt—by which I mean the actors, norms, processes, and mechanisms focused around countries unable to service their public and publicly guaranteed debt. As will be shown below, the practices of this international debt regime evolved in important ways over the 1980s as it became increasingly clear that poor countries, for whom structural adjustment worked least well, were usually unable to cope with their mounting debt loads. The rising debt burden of poor countries, most of which were African, thus became an increasing concern of key actors in the international arena—some creditor countries, agencies of the UN system such as the United Nations Conference on Trade and Development (UNCTAD), a wide-ranging group of nongovernmental organizations (NGOs), and, of course, debtor countries themselves. By 1996 this situation had led to the innovative "Heavily Indebted Poor Country (HIPC) Debt Initiative," discussed here. As part of the so-called North-South Dialogue of the New International Economic Order efforts of the 1970s and early 1980s, African and other Third World countries failed in their efforts to negotiate more generous and generalized norms for the debt regime; yet innovation in the 1990s was possible. Why?

The sources of change in the debt regime lay elsewhere—in the complex and uneven relations between some of the actors in the international debt regime (see Figure 3.1); in the activities of NGOs focused on debt, constituting what have been called principled-issue networks with their largely normative discourses and evolving capacities; and in fragments of an epistemic community of economists and other scholars who work on development issues, some of whom have played key roles as consultants and advisers to actors on both sides of the battles over debt. These three sets of actors have constituted a triple helix of relationships, of connections, that have led to important but still limited innovations in the way that the international debt regime functions

The three "genetic" strands of the triple helix—the international debt regime, the NGO debt networks, the epistemic community—are wrapped around a central structural dilemma of the international political economy to which actors in the three strands have reacted in varying ways. The structural dilemma is the emergence of an international underclass of weak states and economies that have not been able to benefit as easily or quickly from economic reform and democratization as those elsewhere in the world. This dilemma poses major difficulties for the functioning and evolution of the international political economy, as well as for international peace well into the next century. The driving force for change in the transnational governance of official debt has been the synergy among various forms of power, knowledge, and discourse as they interacted with this underlying structural dilemma. Each of the strands has used its power, knowledge, and discourses to shape the overall pattern of governance of official debt.

The actors of the international debt regime reacted haltingly and un- evenly as they slowly came to the realization that something had to be done about the structural dilemma despite its nonclassic geostrategic character. This realization was fostered—forced to the fore—by networks of NGOs working on debt and development that deployed an increasingly coherent moral discourse about social purpose aiming to gain representation and accountability for debtors. In turn, this NGO discourse was backed by a growing social movement and progressively more sophisticated knowledge about the technicalities and functioning of the international regime for official debt. The NGOs were assisted by sympathetic fragments of the epistemic community of economists, mostly but not exclusively by those outside the institutions of the international debt regime. Some of those inside the organizations of the international debt

FIGURE 3.1   The International Debt Regime for Public Debt

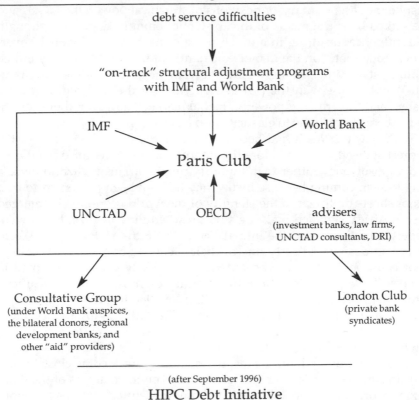

debt service difficulties

"on-track" structural adjustment programs
with IMF and World Bank

IMF   World Bank

Paris Club

UNCTAD   OECD   advisers
(investment banks, law firms,
UNCTAD consultants, DRI)

Consultative Group   London Club
(under World Bank auspices,   (private bank
the bilateral donors, regional   syndicates)
development banks, and
other "aid" providers)

(after September 1996)
HIPC Debt Initiative

regime accepted or were influenced by the content of the moral discourse. These insiders and outsiders—mostly academic economists—used their technical knowledge of economic theory, debt, rescheduling, and the operations of the international financial institutions to propose alternative norms, mechanisms, and practices to tackle the underlying structural dilemma of official debt. In the process, both groups of economists contributed to and were influenced by the moral discourses on debt and development of the NGOs. Loose, mostly informal networked connections have been made between the three strands of the triple helix, which pushed the evolution of the governance structures as they interacted with the underlying structural dilemma. The triple helix of transnational governance of official debt helped both to reproduce existing national and international structures and to alter them and the way they work.

A key implication of this argument is that the structure of transnational debt governance was shifted haltingly and unevenly beyond the largely state- and IFI-centric strand of the international debt regime. Over time, despite the absence of major positions of structural power, the NGOs and the sympathetic fragments of the epistemic community grew in strength and influence, resulting in a much more complex web of global governance—one rooted in the democratic nature of the world's highly industrialized states and strikingly different from the pattern of the early Bretton Woods era. Given the power structures of the international state system and the growing power of global markets, however, there continued to be distinct limits to elasticity and change.

By the early 1990s it had become increasingly clear that many of the poorest states that came before the international regime for official debt had an insolvency rather than liquidity problem. This realization was a long time in coming because insolvency had not been perceived to be a major short-run threat to the stability of the world economy. It emerged first in Africa, signaled by Zaire's first rescheduling in 1976, but it went largely unnoticed until the mid-1980s. By 1996 the IMF and the World Bank had designated forty-one of their members as "heavily indebted poor countries" (HIPCs) whose debt was unlikely ever to be repaid in full (see Table 3.1). The debt of these countries, mostly public or official rather than private, rose from $55 billion in 1980 to $183 billion only a decade later and to $215 billion by 1995. (This latter figure totaled more than twice their export earnings.) Of these forty-one countries, thirty-three are in sub-Saharan Africa. Most of the HIPCs have high levels of poverty and limited domestic resources and, in effect, come close to constituting an international underclass of states on the margins of the globalizing world economy. All but six fall into the United Nations Development Program's lowest human development category. According to the NGOs, these countries are in a vicious circle of economic and social decline.

The Paris Club is a complex and powerful, yet rarely recognized, hybrid international organization—one that reveals a lot about the evolution of the international political economy and the nature of transnational governance processes. One of the most powerful international organizations in operation over the last several decades, it has directly affected the lives of millions of people, although technically it does not exist. It is not a formal organization with a charter, legislated set of rules, fixed membership, large bureaucracy, or fancy building; rather, it is usually described as an ad hoc "forum" of creditor countries that reschedules the public and publicly guaranteed debt of "developing" states. It is far more, however, and has evolved significantly from its beginnings with Argentina in 1956 to Russia becoming its largest debtor, then creditor member in the mid-1990s. A small secretariat is housed in the French Treasury, and numerous officials are assigned to its operations in the creditor countries and the

TABLE 3.1 HIPCs: Characteristics of Existing External Debt

| | Total External Debt (End-1996)[1] | | Eligible for Paris Club Stock-of-Debt Operations on Naples Terms[2] | Debt by Principal Non–Paris Club Creditor Group[3] | | Multilateral Institutions | | |
	Total (In billions of U.S. dollars)	Of Which: Multilateral (In percent)		Debt to Russia	Commercial Banks	IMF	World Bank	Other
Angola	9.3	2.4		✓				
Benin	1.6	60.8	✓[4]					✓
Bolivia	4.8	61.6	✓[4]				✓	✓
Burkina Faso	1.2	95.8	✓[4]					
Burundi	1.2	85.6				✓		
Cameroon	8.1	22.8	✓		✓		✓	
Central African Republic	0.9	75.9	✓				✓	
Chad	1.0	83.4	✓					✓
Congo, Democratic Republic of the	9.9	27.7						✓
Congo, Republic of	4.8	15.0						✓
Côte d'Ivoire	12.4	35.8	✓		✓		✓	
Equatorial Guinea	0.3	49.4	✓		✓			
Ethiopia	5.1	52.8	✓	✓				
Ghana	5.2	70.9		✓		✓		
Guinea	3.0	54.0	✓					
Guinea-Bissau	0.9	61.4	✓			✓	✓	✓
Guyana	2.1	40.2	✓[4]					✓
Honduras	4.0	55.5	✓				✓	✓
Kenya	6.1	53.7		✓			✓	
Lao People's Democratic Republic	2.2	34.8				✓		
Liberia	1.4	51.2						
Madagascar	3.7	48.4	✓[4]					
Mali	3.0	53.7	✓[4]	✓				

(continues)

TABLE 3.1 (continued)

| | Total External Debt (End-1996)[1] | | Eligible for Paris Club | Debt by Principal Non–Paris Club Creditor Group[3] | | | | | |
| | | | | | | | Multilateral Institutions | | |
	Total (In billions of U.S. dollars)	Of Which: Multilateral (In percent)	Stock-of-Debt Operations on Naples Terms[2]	Debt to Russia	Commercial Banks	IMF	World Bank	Other
Mauritania	2.3	47.1	✓		✓			✓
Mozambique	5.6	32.3	✓	✓		✓	✓	
Myanmar	5.2	25.4	✓	✓	✓			✓
Nicaragua	5.3	30.4	✓	✓		✓		
Niger	1.4	65.2	✓		✓			
Nigeria	28.2	17.9			✓	✓	✓	✓
Rwanda	1.0	86.3				✓	✓	✓
São Tomé and Príncipe	0.3	71.9						
Senegal	3.6	63.8	✓			✓		
Sierra Leone	1.2	56.8	✓		✓	✓✓		
Somalia	2.1	44.7		✓	✓	✓✓		
Sudan[5]	10.7	28.7				✓✓	✓	✓
Tanzania	6.3	50.9	✓					
Togo	1.4	61.6	✓	✓				
Uganda	3.7	77.4	✓[4]	✓	✓	✓	✓	
Vietnam	23.9	4.1	✓[6]	✓				
Yemen, Republic of	5.6	25.7						
Zambia	6.4	54.4	✓			✓		

SOURCES: World Bank Debtor Reporting System; and IMF staff estimates.
[1] Total public and publicly guaranteed debt.
[2] ✓ indicates whether Paris Club concessional rescheduling has taken place.
[3] ✓ indicates significant debt to the respective creditor.
[4] Stock-of-debt operation on Naples terms was agreed to in 1995 or 1996.
[5] Figures for 1993.
[6] Exit rescheduling, no stock-of-debt clause.

key international institutions linked to it. The number and variety of its reschedulings accelerated dramatically over time—from 26 in 1956–1976 to 176 in 1977–1990, well over 200 by the early 1990s, and 308 by the end of 1997 (see Table 3.2).

Since the late 1970s, the Paris Club has become increasingly embedded in a complex web of interactions with other important actors in the international political economy—the IMF, the World Bank, regional development banks, UNCTAD, the Organization for Economic Cooperation and Development (OECD), the Bank for International Settlements, the private debt rescheduling fora of international banks known as the "London Club," the Consultative Groups (country aid consortia), investment bank advisory groups that sometimes represent debtor countries, and, of course, the governments of the debtor countries. These actors take part in the operations of the Paris Club or act as observers and advisers.

Debt rescheduling is one of the easiest and quickest ways to provide badly needed foreign exchange to countries in economic, social, and political trouble, but Paris Club relief is at the center of a complicated set of nested games. Rescheduling is possible only if the debtor country has economic reform programs in good standing with the IMF and the World Bank. In addition, London Club rescheduling is supposed to come only after Paris Club rescheduling, and Consultative Group aid coordination is linked to prior Paris Club rescheduling.

Although Paris Club debt relief was contingent on maintaining economic reform programs with the IMF and the World Bank, the debt owed to these "multilateral" institutions was not reschedulable. This norm was meant to protect the "preferred creditor" status of these institutions. In short, the international debt regime did not cover multilateral debt. Given the high dependence of African countries in particular on loans from the IMF and the World Bank, multilateral debt became an increasingly severe problem throughout the 1980s and a seriously threatening one by the early 1990s.

The structural dilemma has been one important factor driving the evolution of the international debt regime. Far from smooth, generalized, or orderly, and with very interesting politics, this evolution of norms shows the complex interplay of the varied and often shifting interests of the major creditor countries as they interact with their respective legal structures, bureaucratic cultures, and domestic politics—whether electoral, legislative, or special interest. It is fascinating to see why, how, and when some special deals became more generalized norms and others did not. The impact of this evolution on the underlying structural dilemma was minimal, however. As a result, the Western countries that form the core of the Paris Club started proposing more flexible "menus of terms" that

TABLE 3.2   Paris Club Reschedulings, 1956–1997

Albania	1	Jamaica	7
Algeria	2	Jordan	4
Angola	1	Kenya	1
Argentina	8	Liberia	4
Bangladesh	1	Macedonia	1
Benin	4	Madagascar	8
Bolivia	6	Malawi	3
Brazil	64	Mali	4
Bulgaria	3	Mauritania	6
Burkina Faso	3	Mexico	3
Cambodia	3	Morocco	6
Cameroon	5	Mozambique	5
Central African Republic	6	Nicaragua	2
Chad	3	Niger	9
Chile	6	Nigeria	3
Congo	4	Pakistan	4
Costa Rica	5	Panama	2
Côte d'Ivoire	7	Peru	8
Croatia	1	Philippines	5
Cuba	4	Poland	6
Dominican Republic	2	Romania	2
Ecuador	6	Russia	4[1]
Egypt	2	Senegal	11
El Salvador	1	Sierra Leone	7
Equatorial Guinea	4	Somalia	2
Ethiopia	2	Sudan	4
Gabon	7	Tanzania	5
Gambia	1	Togo	10
Ghana	6	Trinidad and Tobago	2
Guatemala	1	Turkey	5
Guinea	5	Uganda	6
Guinea-Bissau	3	Vietnam	1
Guyana	4	Yemen	2
Haiti	1	Yugoslavia	4
Honduras	3	Zaire	10
India	5	Zambia	6
Indonesia	4		

Total countries	73	
Total African countries	36	(49%)
Total reschedulings	308	
Total African reschedulings	175	(57%)

[1] Now a member of the Paris Club (its largest debtor) and now in default.
[2] Includes all reschedulings done under Paris Club rules and personnel.

could be applied to "severely indebted" countries—the Toronto terms of 1988, the London terms of 1991, the Naples terms of 1994, and the Lyons terms of 1996.

NGOs as a Principled-Issue Network on Debt

Over the last two decades several hundred largely religious, humanitarian, labor, and environmental NGOs have focused on the issue of Third World debt and its negative impact on the welfare of millions of people. Their activities evolved largely around a moral discourse that portrays developing country debt as an immoral burden on the backs of the poor. This discourse employs powerful notions of justice, representation, accountability, transparency, and equity. It challenges the notion of who should have authority over such issues in the global community, calls for intervention to rectify injustices and end what is considered to be blatant exploitation, and aims to provide space for debtor representation and agency in the transnational governance processes involving debt. Along the way, the NGOs determine to a large degree who is empowered and who is not, who is represented and who is not.

In 1997, for example, a loose international group of more than fifty NGOs based in Great Britain created the Jubilee 2000 Coalition, which calls for "a one-off cancellation of poor country debt by the year 2000 of the backlog of unpayable debt owed by the world's poorest countries, under a fair and transparent process." Characterizing this as a debt-free start to the next millennium, the network of NGOs portrays itself explicitly as the "New Abolitionists" out to abolish the "slavery of debt":

> Billions of people in the world's poorest countries are enslaved by debt. Debts run up by governments on their behalf. Debts which started as easy credit pushed by rich lenders. Debts which the poor will never be able to repay. Debts which enrich lenders, but leave children malnourished, while families live in desperate poverty.
>
> The Coalition's success will be an irreversible achievement for humanity like that of the abolition of slavery—and is particularly well suited to a Jubilee that will not occur for another 1000 years.[24]

The activities, capabilities, and interests of the NGOs that work on debt vary significantly. These principled-issue networks have some of the characteristics of transnational social movements. Most of the network members are Northern NGOs, but increasingly they help to create, link up with, and foster Southern NGOs interested in debt. Several of the strongest Northern NGOs have a network of offices in poor countries through which they can gather information, work with local governments and social organizations, and interact with the local representatives of the IMF, the World Bank, and the major aid-providing "donor" countries, which, of course, are also the major creditors. Many of the debt NGOs believe that IMF and World Bank structural adjustment is an evil that needs to be abolished.

Two of the most important NGOs on debt are Oxfam International and the European Network on Debt and Development (Eurodad), a coalition of NGOs from fifteen European countries, funded in part by the European Community. These and other NGOs, such as the Debt Crisis Network in the United States and Britain, worked assiduously to collect and analyze information on debt and the operation of the international debt regime, educated themselves and other NGOs, lobbied Paris Club governments and their legislatures for greater debt relief both in general and for specific countries, lobbied hard with the IMF and the World Bank and at each of the annual G-7 summits for broader debt relief and new mechanisms for it, attended the joint spring and annual meetings of the Fund and the Bank, organized public-education and letter-writing campaigns, and worked closely with the media. Coordination increased considerably over time, facilitated by growing fax, Internet, and e-mail capabilities as well as frequent travel and network conferences such as the annual ones organized by Eurodad. Information and documents collected by one organization are shared quickly with others. Above all, as NGO capabilities and sophistication grew, personal ties based on respect (if not always on agreement) developed between NGO representatives and some officials in creditor governments and the Fund and the Bank, thereby significantly improving the exchange of views on growing debt problems, especially multilateral debt. This exchange, in turn, led to significantly more influential position and briefing papers, to special-issue alerts about the functioning of the international debt regime, and to ongoing discussions about what to do about debt.

This process both facilitated and fostered the growing professionalization of the more important NGOs that were working debt. It also promoted increasingly close relations between fragments of a large and amorphous epistemic community on development, rooted to various degrees in neoclassical economics. It remains unclear, however, whether the activities of the debt NGO networks and those on other issues represent the rise of a new global civil society that will foster linkages between various locals and the global community in terms of more representative, effective, just, and accountable webs of transnational governance.

The Rise of the HIPC Debt Initiative

The innovation of the Paris Club debt menus in the late 1980s and early 1990s was a sign that major actors of the international debt regime were beginning to recognize the existence of the underlying structural dilemma, but only in relation to bilateral debt. The emergence of the menus resulted from (1) the quiet lobbying of small European countries on their G-7 colleagues; (2) the important leadership of Britain, Canada, and, to a lesser but still important degree, the United States; (3) the persistent work of the debt-oriented NGOs in encouraging both sets of countries; and (4) ideas that emerged from the epistemic community on debt, both from outsiders and, quietly, from those inside some Paris Club governments, the World Bank, and, to a much lesser degree, the IMF. With each new menu, however, it rather quickly became clear that the Paris Club innovation was not adequate, and pressure built for additional measures—but, again, only within the context of the Paris Club. At the same time, there was a growing realization inside the NGO networks and some parts of the epistemic community that the problem of multilateral debt needed to be confronted, irrespective of cost or the absence of classic geostrategic importance, largely for developmental and normative reasons.

By 1992 the NGOs had geared up their activities in regard to multilateral debt, especially with the G-7, while some of the like-minded smaller creditor countries also quietly lobbied the G-7. At the joint IMF and World Bank annual meetings in Madrid in 1994, the United States and Britain proposed that the two institutions conduct a study of multilateral debt. The issue reemerged at the 1995 spring meetings of the Fund and the Bank and then again at the G-7 summit in Halifax in June of that year.

Although the influence of the NGOs was certainly important, larger factors had come into play, resulting in part from the nature of the structural dilemma and in part from the quiet restructuring of the major powers themselves. For Britain in particular, but also to a lesser degree for the United States and Canada, very real fiscal constraints were cutting into aid budgets—leading to the possible inability to support client states among the HIPCs as the multilateral debt problem grew in importance. This was the case because structural adjustment was having only a marginal effect in most of these countries. As a result, both the Fund and the Bank were extending part of their loans to facilitate the repayment of earlier ones that had been used to launch economic reform efforts. Some of the Paris Club countries helped as well by repaying multilateral debt. Those advocating multilateral debt relief cited Uganda as a way to illustrate the need for it.

A crucial point was reached when American banker James Wolfensohn became the ninth president of the World Bank on June 1, 1995. Wolfensohn was more open to the views of debtor governments and the NGOs, especially after a trip to Africa; he was less worried about the financial market consequences of altering the Bank's preferred creditor status; and he needed major policy initiatives to demarcate his arrival at the head of this powerful international organization. He saw debt relief as one of these initiatives and empowered sympathetic elements of the Bank staff to accelerate its ongoing work on a new debt initiative. Just before the joint Fund-Bank annual meeting in the fall of 1995, a Bank staff report that proposed the creation of an international Multilateral Debt Facility was leaked to the *Financial Times*. Many in the NGO community believed that the report was leaked by Bank and Fund staff opposed to the proposal. The leak had the effect of galvanizing opposition to the plan among more hard-line G-7 governments and some of their legislatures. The primary worries were cost and modality, although they were not always expressed in those terms. Despite earlier support for multilateral debt relief, the United States also expressed some reservations about both concerns. The Paris Club secretariat was very suspicious of the plan, as were many members of the IMF staff.

The more technically capable NGOs such as Oxfam International and Eurodad made important contributions to the design of the HIPC apparatus, not always getting what they wanted but certainly making a difference as advocates of the debtor countries. In fact, it was one of the NGO consultants from the epistemic community who came up with a compromise formula specifying that the IMF and World Bank were to be "preferred but not exempt" creditors. Oxfam in particular had excellent access to key executive directors on the boards of both the IMF and the World Bank, to staff members of each institution, and to finance ministries of key creditor countries. The same held true for some of the academic fragments of the epistemic community interested in debt.

Planning shifted to a proposal that eventually became the complicated Rube Goldberg mechanism of the HIPC Initiative (see Figure 3.2), with the Paris Club continuing to play a central role while allowing the IMF, the World Bank, and the other multilateral creditors to tackle their debt problem with the HIPCs. The IMF was brought on board inasmuch as Michel Camdessus eventually saw the wisdom of trying to steer the design of the mechanism rather than resisting it. The HIPC Initiative was formally approved and announced at the September 1996 Fund-Bank joint annual meeting

The intent of HIPC was to provide an exit from the rescheduling process by reducing debt to "sustainable" levels so that it was not an impediment to growth and poverty reduction. HIPC was billed as a new paradigm for international action, despite the fact that it builds on existing mechanisms in a very complicated way. It was meant only for those countries that demonstrated a very strong commitment to major IMF and World Bank economic reform for at least six years and was conditioned on continued compliance with their dictates. In a complex, multistage process, the Paris Club countries were to provide concessional debt relief and reduction on a case-by-case basis to eligible countries, and the IMF

FIGURE 3.2   The Heavily Indebted Poor Country (HIPC) Debt Initiative

First Stage

- *Paris Club* provides flow rescheduling as per current Naples terms—that is, rescheduling of debt service on eligible debt falling due during the three-year consolidation period (up to 67 percent reduction on eligible maturities on a net percent value basis).
- *Other bilateral and commercial creditors* provide at least comparable treatment.
- *Multilateral institutions* continue to provide adjustment support in the framework of a World Bank/IMF-supported adjustment program.
- *Country* establishes first three-year track record of good performance.

Decision Point

Exit

- *Either*... Paris Club stock-of-debt operation under Naples terms (up to 67 percent present reduction of eligible debt) and comparable treatment by other bilateral and commercial creditors is adequate for the country to reach sustainability by completion point—country not eligible for HIPC Debt Initiative.

Eligible

- *Or*... Paris Club stock-of-debt operation (on Naples terms) not sufficient for the country's overall debt to become sustainable by completion point—country requests additional support under the HIPC Debt Initiative, and World Bank/IMF Boards determine eligibility.

Second Stage

- *Paris Club* goes beyond Naples terms to provide more concessional debt reduction of up to 80 percent in present value terms.
- *Other bilateral and commercial creditors* provide at least comparable treatment.
- *Donors and multilateral institutions* provide enhanced support through interim measures.
- *Country* establishes a second track record of good performance under Bank/IMF-supported programs.

Completion Point

- *Paris Club* provides deeper stock-of-debt reduction of up to 80 percent in present value terms on eligible debt, so as to achieve an exit from unsustainable debt.
- *Other bilateral and commercial creditors* provide at least comparable treatment on stock-of-debt.
- *Multilateral institutions* take such additional measures as may be needed for the country's debt to be reduced to a sustainable level, each choosing from a menu of options and ensuring broad and equitable participation by all creditors involved.

Borderline

- *Or*... for borderline cases, where there is doubt about whether sustainability would be achieved by the completion point under a Naples terms stock-of-debt operation, the country would receive further flow reschedulings under Naples terms.

If the outcome at the completion point is better than or as projected, the country would receive a stock-of-debt operation on Naples terms from Paris Club creditors and comparable treatment from other bilateral and commercial creditors.

If the outcome at completion point is worse than projected, the country could receive additional support under the HIPC Debt Initiative, so as to achieve exit from unsustainable debt.

and the World Bank were to provide important formal debt relief for the first time. In fact, the HIPC apparatus shifted the center of gravity from the Paris Club toward the IMF and the World Bank because the latter were tasked with doing the debt sustainability analyses central to the new process. All non–Paris Club creditor countries and commercial creditors were supposed to provide comparable treatment, although how this would be achieved was not clear. When Russia became a member of the Paris Club in 1997, about $170 billion were brought under the HIPC umbrella. Initial estimates put the cost of HIPC to the creditor countries, the IMF, and the World Bank at about $5.5 billion, with the hope that the initiative would catalyze private financial flows and help reintegrate these countries into the global economy in productive ways. The actual cost is likely to be much higher, however, and the catalytic effect of this version of the implicit bargain much lower than expected.

Although the initiative was likely to help only about twenty countries (and not very quickly at that), it was resisted strongly from the beginning by Japan, Germany, and Italy because of concerns about cost, burden sharing, moral hazard, and issues related to the proposed sale of IMF gold reserves. It was likewise seen to undermine the credibility of the IMF and the World Bank as enforcers of major economic reform. The United States and the IMF have also continued to have doubts along the way.

Uganda became the first country to enter the complicated multistaged HIPC process, but not without considerable controversy. Some actors preferred to avoid starting with Uganda precisely because its case for relief was so strong that they feared making precedent-setting changes in the delicately negotiated framework. Major battles over funding and technical design were fought over Uganda, and the Ugandan government lobbied effectively—in part, by using its own NGOs and international ones to push the country's case over a wide range of issues. Oxfam weighed in with a hard-hitting press release:

> This decision [to delay] will hurt the poor people in Uganda. This year many children, especially girls, will not be going to school, many health clinics will go without basic medicines. The decision also sends the wrong signals to those other countries undertaking painful economic reforms. If Uganda, which is seen as the jewel in the economic reform crown, is so shoddily treated, what incentive is there for other countries?[25]

Uganda freely shared data with the best of the NGOs, Oxfam in particular, and employed its epistemic contacts to good effect. It also sent a high-level delegation to Eurodad's annual conference in January 1997 and, working with the NGOs, actively used major international newspapers to make its case.

In April 1997 Uganda became the first country approved for HIPC treatment after important battles were fought on several fronts. Uganda did not get everything it wanted—but far more than it would have without the efforts of the NGOs and their epistemic community allies. Similar processes played out in the cases of Bolivia, Côte d'Ivoire, and, more contentiously, Mozambique. Clearly, the NGOs and their epistemic community allies played an important role in designing the HIPC Initiative and altering the structure and process of the international debt regime. They continued to be influential with each country case as it came up, helping to defend the debtor's sovereignty and interests in the face of powerful larger forces. Finally, in April 1998, Uganda received its first actual HIPC debt relief. One Western diplomat praised Uganda's proactive approach by "adopting the reforms as their own and not using the IMF and World Bank as scapegoats when the going gets tough."[26]

Serious doubts remained, however. Major NGOs, led by Oxfam and Eurodad, maintained that the Paris Club and the IMF, in particular, lacked the will to achieve serious debt relief. They claimed that IMF conditionality was much too stringent; they challenged the way sustainability, vulnerability, and threshold indicators were assessed; and they pointed to weak comparability mechanisms and commitment to poverty reduction. Oxfam charged the IMF and some of the major countries with systematic attempts to delay and restrict implementation, partly through data manipulation, all the while asserting that industrialized countries could easily afford the cost.

On both the technical knowledge and moral discourse fronts, the battle for greater representation, accountability, and, hence, better global economic governance continued. The NGOs kept up their pressure for greater debt relief by following individual countries as they came before HIPC and, more generally, by lobbying the major Paris Club creditors and the IFIs. As a result, the rules of HIPC began to be stretched and new, more lenient ones were created. The World Bank began to consult outside groups more openly, starting with religious leaders and NGOs in 1998, while the Fund and the Bank conducted internal reviews of HIPC. Then, in February and March 1999, the Bank conducted a series of formal consultations with NGOs, government officials, and civil society groups in Washington, London, Oslo, Lomé, Maputo, and Tegucigalpa. By March, ten countries were formally in the HIPC process, and the number eligible for assistance had been raised to twenty-nine. The Fund and the Bank discussed a major joint review of HIPC at their spring 1999 meetings, which revealed a 30 percent increase in the estimated cost as the process then existed, and they agreed that changes needed to be made. At the same time, major Paris Club creditors committed themselves to greater debt relief under HIPC. A major sticking point remained: Who was going to pay for it? The United States, Britain, and Canada suggested that a portion of IMF gold reserves be sold to finance HIPC relief, and, for the first time, Japan, Italy, and Germany indicated that they might agree to the initiative under certain conditions. Major battles will be fought before these prospects become reality, however. Wolfensohn publicly warned the creditor countries that if they proposed greater debt relief, they had to be willing to pay for it. The Fund, the Bank, and the major creditors were in agreement about tying debt relief very closely to structural adjustment conditionality and performance, whereas the NGOs wanted far greater debt relief that was not tied in any way to structural adjustment.

Although Nigeria is not a HIPC country, the new civilian government there wanted debt relief on HIPC terms. Britain indicated that it would try to facilitate major debt relief under Paris Club auspices but not on HIPC terms; however, Nigeria first had to agree to a structural adjustment program with the IMF and implement it. Gordon Brown, Britain's Chancellor of the Exchequer, then stated: "We will build support for a Paris Club restructuring, including a three-year grace period, which delivers the maximum possible assistance to Nigeria, as soon as a funded IMF programme is established."[27] At its spring meeting, the IMF also created a new mechanism of precautionary defense against contagion for countries engaging in reform, as it had done first for Brazil earlier in the year. One of the first beneficiaries of this mechanism, known as Contingent Credit Lines, was likely to be South Africa, Africa's one nonmarginalized economy. In short, Africa was able to take advantage of new mechanisms of global economic governance and affect the processes that created them, including the Fund and the Bank's new postconflict assistance mechanisms.

Prospects for the Future

Given the enormous constraints discussed in this chapter, what are the prospects that African countries will engage successfully in economic reform and establish more effective linkages to the world economy? The answer appears to be that simultaneous marginalization and dependence are likely to continue, and will probably increase, for most countries. A few—with hard work, propitious facilitating circumstances, and luck—may begin to lessen their marginalization from the world economy and their dependence on the IMF, the World Bank, and the creditor countries. Differentiation among African states, already long evident, will increase as spreading conflict weakens large parts of the continent. A few will stay in the Third World and do relatively better economically, but many will continue to descend into the Fourth and Fifth Worlds.

The trajectory of individual countries will be affected by both internal and external factors. On the internal side, the degree of effective leadership, political will, and, above all, "stateness"—the technical and administrative capabilities to formulate *and* implement proper economic policies—will be crucial. On average, Africa has the lowest level of state capabilities and overall development of any region in the world. As the IMF and the World Bank have begun to realize, it takes a relatively capable state to implement successful neoorthodox economic reform consistently over time. A high degree of stateness is central to positioning a country better in the international political economy and to taking advantage of new mechanisms of global economic governance. Above all, a country needs the ability to bargain and interact with all types of actors—private business groups, states, the IFIs, and, now, the NGOs as well. Whether increased stateness will emerge in many places, however, is very questionable. Certainly political dynamics will play a central role in the arrival at a productive balanced tension between state and market, state and society. Some African leaders have begun to understand this. They know that, at bottom, it is a self-help world and that one should not wait for external miracles. Africa's much-touted "new generation" of leadership was beginning to look quite tattered by 1999, however.[28]

External factors affecting country trajectories are also very important, even in a self-help world. They revolve around two central issues: (1) the degree of openness of the world political economy, and (2) the degree to which the implicit bargain is fulfilled. Prospects for fulfillment of the implicit bargain are not very bright. As private actors in the world economy increasingly pass Africa by, Western countries—even those with declining interest and resources—and the international financial institutions will continue to play central roles. If African countries are to have any chance of making economic progress, such actors must help to fulfill this bargain, primarily through increased aid levels and substantial but careful debt relief. Given the domestic politics of Western industrial democracies, debt relief might be the easier route to take, for it is more politically malleable, though not unproblematic. As resources are scarce, aid and debt relief should be given only to those countries actually undertaking these difficult changes, *and* they should not be tied automatically to political conditionality. It is not clear, however, how many reformist rulers external actors can actually support at the level required for sustained economic change. Since such reform is difficult, stop-go cycles are a fact of life, and external actors need to learn to adjust to them.

Finally, external actors should avoid the "faults of analytic and policy hurry" and not create undue expectations about what can be achieved in Africa over the medium run. Given the enormous obstacles confronting African countries, overly optimistic expectations can be very dangerous. Slow, steady, consistent encouragement and progress are far preferable. There are no shortcuts. Given that change is incremental, uneven, often contradictory, and dependent on the outcome of unpredictable socioeconomic and political struggles, policymakers—both international and

African—must try to bring about important changes, but they need to retain a sense of the historical complexity involved. If they do not, undue expectations can get in the way of making slow but steady progress on difficult obstacles. Today's policy fads can easily become tomorrow's failed initiatives. And adjustment with a human face, capacity building, policy dialogue, good governance, and democratization can easily become just the latest in international passing fancies in the face of hard African realities of failing states, warlords, and the continued informalization and criminalization of much economic activity. As the millennium approaches, Africa is even more caught between a rock and a hard place in regard to the world political economy, and all actors will have to work very hard to alter that fact. But, as Alassane Ouattara indicated, try they must, for not trying could have even worse consequences for Africa's long-suffering peoples.

Notes

1. Alassane D. Ouattara, "Africa: An Agenda for the 21st Century," *Finance and Development* 36, no. 1 (March 1999), p. 2. Note that the term *Africa* is used in this chapter to mean sub-Saharan Africa.

2. Ralph Austen, *African Economic History* (London: James Currey, 1987), pp. 102, 109.

3. The economic and financial data in this chapter have been gathered from the following sources: the 1989–1998 editions of World Bank, *World Development Report* (Washington, D.C.: World Bank); the 1991–1999 editions of World Bank, *Global Economic Prospects and the Developing Countries* (Washington, D.C.: World Bank); World Bank, *Sub-Saharan Africa: From Crisis to Sustainable Growth* (Washington, D.C.: World Bank, 1989); World Bank, *Africa's Adjustment and Growth in the 1980s* (Washington, D.C.: World Bank, 1989); *IMF Survey* 22, no. 19 (October 11, 1993) and *IMF Survey* 28, no. 6 (March 22, 1999); *Financial Times* (London) surveys titled "Africa: A Continent at Stake" (September 1, 1993) and "IMF: World Economy and Finance" (September 24, 1993); Department of Public Information, "African Debt Crisis: A Continuing Impediment to Development" (New York: United Nations, 1993); various issues of *Africa Recovery* (New York: United Nations) and the *Financial Times*; Elliot Harris, "Impact of the Asian Crisis on Sub-Saharan Africa," *Finance and Development* 36, no. 1 (March 1999), pp. 14–17; World Bank, *World Development Indicators* (Washington, D.C.: World Bank, April 1999); World Bank, *Global Development Finance* (Washington, D.C.: World Bank, April 1999); IMF, *World Economic Outlook* (Washington, D.C.: April 1999); and other IMF and World Bank documents.

4. Confidential interview, New York, April 26, 1990.

5. B. A. Kiplagat, quoted in "Africa Fears Its Needs Will Become Secondary," *New York Times*, December 26, 1989.

6. See Thomas M. Callaghy and John Ravenhill (eds.), *Hemmed In: Responses to Africa's Economic Decline* (New York: Columbia University Press, 1993).

7. Quoted in "Ghana: High Stakes Gamble," *Africa News* 31, no. 2 (January 23, 1989), p. 10.

8. Excerpts from this speech are reprinted in *IMF Survey* 19, no. 7 (1990), pp. 108–111.

9. Barber B. Conable, "Address as Prepared for Delivery to the Bretton Woods Conference on Africa's Finance and Development Crisis," Washington, D.C., April 25, 1990, World Bank mimeograph, p. 3.

10. Quoted in Margaret A. Novicki, "Interview with Edward V. K. Jaycox," *Africa Report* 32, no. 6 (November-December 1987), p. 32.

11. World Bank, *Adjustment Lending* (Washington, D.C.: World Bank, 1988), p. 3.

12. World Bank, *From Crisis to Sustainable Growth;* United Nations Economic Commission for Africa (ECA), *African Alternative Framework to Structural Adjustment Programmes for Socio-economic Recovery and Transformation* (Addis Ababa: ECA, 1989).

13. Oxfam, *Africa Make or Break: Action for Recovery* (London: Oxfam, 1993).

14. World Bank, *The East Asian Miracle: Economic Growth and Public Policy* (Washington, D.C.: World Bank, 1993).

15. Quoted in Edward Balls, "Structural Maladjustment and the CFA Franc," *Financial Times*, November 15, 1993.

16. On the "thesis of the perverse effect," see Albert O. Hirschman, "Reactionary Rhetoric," *Atlantic Monthly* 263, no. 5 (May 1989), pp. 63–70.

17. See Richard L. Sklar, "Democracy in Africa," in Patrick Chabal (ed.), *Political Domination in Africa* (Cambridge, Eng.: Cambridge University Press, 1986), pp. 17–29.

18. Daniel Green, "Fast Growth Forecast Targets Asia and Africa," *Financial Times*, January 13, 1997; Johanna and Marguerite Michaels, "Africa Rising: After Decades of Famine and War, Life Is Finally Looking Up for Many Africans," *Time*, March 30, 1999, pp. 34–46; Alassane D. Ouattara, Deputy Managing Director of IMF, "The IMF's Role in the Unfolding African Renaissance," Africa-U.S. Economic Conference, Arlington, Virginia, June 11, 1998; Michel Camdessus, Managing Director of IMF, "Africa: A Continent on the Move," address at the Summit of Heads of State and Government of the Organization of African Unity, Ouagadougou, Burkina Faso, June 9, 1998. For economic and financial data relating to this section, see the sources cited in Note 3.

19. Tony Hawkins, "Renaissance Train Has Been Delayed," *Financial Times*, October 2, 1998.

20. Harris, "Impact," p. 15.

21. By "real income effects" I mean the changes in the nominal trade balance owing to changes in export and import prices, as a percentage of GDP.

22. World Bank, *Global Development Finance 1999*, p. 168; Janet Roitman, "The Garrison-Entrepôt," draft manuscript (1998), and "New Sovereigns? The Frontiers of Wealth Creation and Regulatory Authority in the Chad Basin," in T. Callaghy, R. Kassimir, and R. Latham (eds.), *Transboundary Formations of Authority, Representation and Violence in Africa*, forthcoming; William Reno, "Global Markets and the Political Economy of Local Politics in Weak States," in Callaghy, Kassimir, and Latham (eds.), *Transboundary Formations*, forthcoming.

23. The best treatment of this topic is Barry Eichengreen, *Toward a New International Financial Architecture: A Practical Post-Asia Agenda* (Washington, D.C.: Institute for International Economics, February 1999). (It is a sign of Africa's marginalization that Eichengreen does not mention Africa or the debt relief programs discussed in the present chapter.) This section is based on confidential interviews with current and former officials of the IMF, World Bank, and the U.S. and British governments, as well as with representatives of NGOs working on debt relief conducted in Washington, New York, London, and Brussels between September 1997 and December 1998; it is also based on the research I conducted while a resident at the Woodrow Wilson Center in Washington, D.C., in 1997–1998. See also Thomas M. Callaghy, "Globalization and Marginalization: Debt and the International Underclass," *Current History* 96, no. 613 (November 1997), pp. 392–396.

24. This passage was taken from the Jubilee 2000 website (www.oneworld.org/jubilee2000/) on October 31, 1997.

25. Justin Forsyth, Oxfam International press release, "Oxfam Condemns Delay on Uganda's Debt Relief: A Betrayal of the Commitment to Reduce Poor Country Debt," Washington, D.C., April 23, 1997.

26. Quoted in "Uganda Debt Deal Seen Boosting Investor Confidence," Reuters, April 9, 1998.

27. Quoted in "Britain Offers Nigeria Help for IMF Compliance," Reuters, May 4, 1999.

28. See Marina Ottaway, *Africa's New Leaders: Democracy or State Reconstruction?* (Washington, D.C.: Carnegie Endowment, 1999).

4

Europe in Africa's Renewal: Beyond Postcolonialism?

GILBERT M. KHADIAGALA

Europe will not abandon Africa. Europe is not a fortress. Europe is a bridge. There will be no clash of civilizations. The key parameters for the future of Euro-African relations will be partnership and solidarity.

—*João de Deus Pinheiro*[1]

Introduction

At the start of negotiations between the European Union (EU) and the African, Caribbean, and Pacific (ACP) states for economic arrangements to succeed the Lomé IV Convention in September 1998, the EU commissioner for cooperation and development, João de Deus Pinheiro, heralded the end of the "postcolonial days," which he saw as "a unique strategic opportunity to develop a new partnership based on common interests that adapts to changes in the world."[2] Three months later, forty-nine African countries converged upon Paris for the largest Franco-African summit ever. There, French President Jacques Chirac exhorted them to move toward "a collective architecture of security," since "the reality at the end of 1998 is that a quarter of Sub-Saharan African states are in crisis and, in most cases, spilling over national borders."[3]

Commissioner Pinheiro's celebration of the demise of the postcolonial era and President Chirac's abiding interest in African security capture contrasting images central to Africa's relations with Europe in the late twentieth century. The one is the desire to sever the fledgling institutional links of the postindependence period, and the other is the attempt to preserve a modicum of the leadership role founded on the trappings of postcolonial obligations. In the post–Cold War era, Europe's disengagement from Africa has deepened, but there are enormous challenges to finding new links to replace old ones. Confronted with profound uncertainty, both regions have lurched onto the not-so-novel concept of partnership to describe and prescribe markedly different things: For Europe, partnership denotes the inevitable decline of special relations with Africa amidst globalization and regionalization, whereas for most of Africa, partnership camouflages the persistence of paternalism and, at worst, Europe's economic marginalization.[4]

In this chapter I argue that the potential for a partnership between Africa and Europe that transcends postcolonial economic and political ties hinges on a renewal that is belied by the multiple pressures on the African state. African renewal presupposes meaningful institutional and leadership changes that the current experiments with democratization and economic liberalization have yet to produce. Although Africa's renewal at domestic and regional levels needs to occur to provide the basis for a partnership that promotes greater equality and shared responsibilities, this trend has been stymied by two contrasting trends. First, regional integration in Europe has remarkably altered the nature of the state, enlarging the opportunities for collective decisionmaking. In Africa, state disintegration has threatened the postcolonial order and stymied any serious efforts at regional integration. Second, European integration has generated the momentum for decreasing postcolonial ties at a juncture when Africa is less prepared and capable of building alternative political and economic arrangements.

Although Africa entered the postcolonial era with a heightened sense of purpose and organizational tools for self-determination, the purported end of postcolonialism is occurring against a backdrop of political weakness, with vague visions and programs for the future. In a word, as Europe disengages from Africa because of integration, Africa is fragmenting for lack of both internal integration and viable external approaches to postcolonialism.

The Postcolonial Ties: The Lomé Conventions

Since 1975, the institutional emblems of postcolonialism were the Lomé Conventions, a series of five-year preferential trade and aid agreements between Europe and the ACP countries. As successors to the Yaounde Conventions, which linked former French and Belgian colonies with the European Economic Community (EEC), the Lomé Conventions broad-

ened Europe's growing multilateral ties with former colonies. Even with
the inclusion of Caribbean Commonwealth and Pacific countries, African
states remained Lomé major players and beneficiaries. Despite the asymmetrical relations between the two blocs, the Lomé process was erected
on two fundamental principles: the promise of equality between partners
and of respect for sovereignty, mutual interest, and interdependence; and
the right of each state to determine its own political, social, cultural, and
economic policy options.[5]

The first Lomé Convention established the trade and financial pillars
for future agreements. In trade Europe offered unrestricted, nonreciprocal, and duty-free access for industrial products (including coal, steel, tex-
tiles, clothing); duty reductions; and quantitative access for agricultural
products. Two central components of the trade relationship were the Stabilization of Export Earnings (Stabex), and Stabilization of Minerals (Sysmin), which were created to maintain the revenues of producers against
sharp falls in production or price. In addition, four protocols of the Convention gave free access to EU markets for a fixed quantity of sugar, beef,
veal, rum, and bananas from selected ACP suppliers. Under financial cooperation Lomé provided for massive aid packages channeled through
the European Development Fund (EDF) and the European Investment
Bank (EIB).[6]

Lomé's provisions sprang from a reciprocity in which Africa produced
commodities for export in exchange for European economic assistance.
During the Cold War, these arrangements also afforded Europe considerable influence over aid recipients. The Lomé Conventions were born in
the peculiar international climate of the 1970s when the Third World
flexed its commodity power, threatening the postwar economic applecart
with agitation for a new world order. It is for this reason that framers of
Lomé hailed the arrangements as signaling an innovative "partnership of
equals" that would preempt commodity radicalism. The initial euphoria
about partnership, however, quickly dissipated from the mid-1980s onward as Europe, facing economic hardships, scaled down levels of development assistance and market access. In the Lomé III (1985–1990) and
Lomé IV (1990–1995) negotiations, Europe was reluctant to concede to aid
and trade increases to reflect expanding populations, inflation, and the
addition of new African members.[7]

Coinciding with declining aid levels was the economic malaise that
gripped Africa in the 1980s. Economic stagnation further diminished
Africa's bargaining power. Moreover, there emerged profound pessimism
about the Lomé Conventions from critics charging that generous aid provisions had not produced visible economic gains and that market access
had failed to stimulate economic diversification. Characteristic of the economic problems were crippling debt burdens, falling commodity prices,

and the drastic fall in capital flows. Kevin Watkins summarized this gloomy picture at the end of the 1980s, Africa's lost decade, as follows:

> During [the Lomé] period, not one ACP country has entered the ranks of the newly-industrializing countries, and most are more dependent upon primary commodities than they were in 1975. Not only, it seems, has Lomé failed to stimulate trade dynamism or bring about structural change, it has failed in one of its principal stated aims—promoting the performance of the ACP countries in EC markets. It has been even less successful in protecting the ACP countries from the effects of high-interest rates and slump in external capital flows. Economic growth and living standards in sub-Saharan Africa fell steadily behind those of other regions in the 1980s, with the result that . . . most people in the region are poorer in real terms than they were when Lomé I was signed.[8]

Africa's diminishing bargaining leverage gave Europe the opportunity to abandon the pretenses of equal political partnership. Instead, starting in the mid-1980s, Europe proposed the concept of policy dialogue, giving donors a greater voice in decisions about the utilization of aid and development assistance. Policy dialogue and concerns for human rights were the precursors to external intervention in Africa's political management, policies that found new elaboration under the rubric of governance and democracy-building in the post–Cold War era.[9] Policy dialogue mirrored unresolved but pertinent questions of the postcolonial era, particularly those concerning Europe's role in ensuring the appropriate use of development assistance. Forcing debate on policy was a marked departure from the tendency by most European countries to gloss over the authoritarian practices of African regimes that were contributing to the worsening of the continent's economic crises.

African states categorically rejected policy dialogue and human rights as part of the aid and trade regime, invoking the sovereignty shield. But Europe won the argument, insisting that sustainable development could occur only within a framework encompassing the rule of law, democracy, and respect for human rights. Starting with Lomé III in 1985, Europe made aid conditional upon the recipient countries' observance of human rights. In the midterm review of Lomé IV in 1995, the EU suggested a staggered system of aid disbursement, with only a percentage of the earmarked aid given at the outset; in this way, the EU would be better able to reward countries that used aid efficiently and to penalize those that did not. As part of this policy, the EU obtained the right to curtail aid immediately in cases of violations of human and democratic rights; and, for the first time, there was a clause in the Convention allowing for the suspension of a country on human rights grounds.[10]

Posing the most serious challenge to postcolonial relations was the acceleration of European integration culminating in the Maastricht Treaty on European Union (TEU) in 1992.[11] The treaty's multifaceted goals of economic integration, monetary union, and harmonization of foreign policy left little room for African interests. Building a wall around the EU's expanding membership, Europe shifted the focus on cooperation toward other developed countries, Eastern and Central Europe, the Mediterranean, and the new functional considerations such as illegal immigration and drug trafficking. For Africa, the post–Cold War image of "fortress Europe" was evident in the harmonization of health, environmental, security, and immigration standards, changes that placed Africa at a disadvantage and eroded its previous pyramid of privileges.[12]

Framing Partnership for a Changing Multilateral Order

Despite paltry economic outcomes, two decades of Lomé Conventions created a multilateral context for Europe's gradual disengagement from most of its postcolonial relationships while also contributing to Africa's capacity to manage its own affairs. Europe's belated focus on the political underpinnings of development did not, however, substantially change its overriding goal of gradually reducing its postcolonial commitments. For Africa, the Conventions denoted collective voices for contractual obligations that allowed a measure of economic certainty and stability. Africa's challenge for the post–Cold War 1990s was how to retain a unity of purpose against the background of growing European disinterestedness.

In the mid-1990s, the accelerating momentum for European integration and globalization set the terms of the debate for recasting Europe-Africa relations for the twenty-first century. In January 1995, Commissioner Pinheiro called for a "rebirth" of ACP-EU cooperation, instructing EU's Development Directorate to begin dialogue with ACP states after the expiry of the Lomé IV Convention in 2000. The EU Commission's Green Paper published in November 1996 formed the conceptual backdrop for wide-ranging discussion on past experiences and future options. Nearly a year later, in October 1997, consultations in Europe yielded compromise negotiating guidelines, which became the final mandate for negotiations that began in September 1998. Three broad themes dominated Europe's outlook: (1) the gradual integration of African countries in the global economy, (2) a newfound interest in relating economic and development cooperation to poverty elimination, and (3) a focus on conflict prevention and peace-building as legitimate areas of cooperation. These goals have occasioned intense debates about approaches, timing, and motives—questions that speak to Europe's contribution to Africa's renewal.[13]

The goal of global economic integration reflects Europe's attempt to further multilateralize its African relations largely through the World

Trade Organization (WTO), successor to the General Agreement on Tariffs and Trade (GATT). The WTO's array of free and competitive trade regulations undermine the Lomé Convention's multiple privileges and preferences that allowed Africa's unfettered access to European markets.[14] An ACP report painted a grim picture of Africa's economic conditions under the stringent WTO rules: Trade liberalization threatens Africa's less than 3 percent share of world trade as most of its primary producers lose about $173 million per annum of revenue, or 0.7 percent of the total value of their sales, to the EU. In addition, liberalization would neither ameliorate Africa's severe dependence on the export of a few primary commodities nor make these goods any more competitive. The ACP's overall share of the EU market fell from 4.7 percent in 1990 to 2.8 percent in 1994, as world trade liberalization steadily eroded the advantage afforded by Lomé preferences. As an African economist noted: "The new rules will liberalize access to markets. But, there is no way a country like Zimbabwe can penetrate a major industrial market like Japan. Basically the rules will result in developed countries swamping the fragile economies of the Third World."[15]

In looking for alternative trade arrangements that would not only be "WTO-compatible" but also insulate African economies from the uncertainties of liberalization, Europe proposed the differentiation of the ACP into more developed and least developed countries. As African countries form the majority of the least developed countries, they would continue to have market access with preferential tariffs. The more developed countries would enter into negotiations with the EU for reciprocal Free Trade Agreements (FTAs) that would come into effect in 2015. FTAs, Europe contends, would offer

> more than just market access: they help create a framework which becomes more attractive for private investment by stabilizing ACP's trade and investment policies, enhancing their predictability and credibility in a long-term perspective. . . . The marginalization of the ACP economies can only be overcome by an innovative strategy geared to improving the economic environment and encouraging measures to develop investment and private enterprise.[16]

Regional differentiation dovetails with Europe's long-term goal to promote regional integration in Africa, building chiefly on the experiments of Southern African Development Community (SADC), the Economic Community of West African States (ECOWAS), the Intergovernmental Authority on Development (IGAD), and the East African Cooperation (EAC). These geographic groups are slated to form the future foundations for Regional Economic Partnerships (REPAs) with Europe.

Opposition from African countries and their European sympathizers before the start of the negotiations produced some concessions on market access and the timing of future negotiations for the FTAs. Criticisms by a British Parliamentary Select Committee on International Development underscored the nature of these concerns:

> It is immoral for the EU to misuse its economic strength to dictate clearly un-favorable terms to the ACP. . . . The pace of liberalization should not be forced and to do so could do serious damage to the ACP economies. We do not accept that the negotiations toward FTAs between the EU and ACP proposed by the European Commission are at present either realistic or desirable, since they are not in the interest of the ACP countries.[17]

As a result, the EU modified the initial strategy of prescribing FTAs to all the countries and promised a flexible transition period in which the existing nonreciprocal preferences would continue to allow for national and regional adjustments. Flexibility is warranted, the EU acknowledged, because there are "uncertain prospects of the developing countries in the face of the globalization of trade and ever-tougher international competition [since] the rules currently governing international trade take insufficient account of the difficulties of the transition for developing countries."[18]

Debates about development assistance are undergirded by pessimism about its past role in Africa's economic development. From the EU's standpoint, aid is a glaring symbol of Lomé's failures, a monument to some of the stultifying features of postcolonial dependence. Critics of aid contend that although the EU is still the world's largest aid donor (it donated some $31 billion in aid during 1996), such aid has not significantly helped African states out of poverty.[19] Yet when Europe harps on these failures to demonstrate the importance of "genuine" nondependent relations, it opens itself up to charges of marginalizing Africa[20]—all the more so given that, whereas Africa still accounts for the largest share of EU aid disbursements, it has experienced a sharp decline as a proportion of total allocable EU aid from over 70 percent at the beginning of the 1970s to under 40 percent by the mid-1990s. Moreover, the absolute decline in the quantity of aid has been compounded by slow and complex disbursement procedures. For instance, an EU Commission study revealed that disbursements under the 1976 Lomé I Convention were not completed until 1990, whereas under the 1984 Lomé III Convention only 64 percent of the funds had been disbursed by the end of 1992.[21]

Europe preaches the virtues of replacing the shortfalls of official capital flows with private capital flows. But a United Nations report shows that sub-Saharan Africa's share of the global stock of inward direct investment fell from 21 percent in 1980 to 5 percent in 1997. From 1990 to 1997 Africa's share of the cumulative $470 billion flow of foreign direct investment to all developing countries was only $23 billion—less than half of 1 percent—whereas only a few countries benefited significantly, with 70 percent of foreign direct investment (FDI) going to oil producers (Angola and Nigeria) and to Ghana, Uganda, and South Africa. As a consequence, Africa's FDI represents only 1 percent of GDP compared with 2 percent for developing economies as a whole.[22]

To meet the substantial drop in development assistance, the EU has proposed greater differentiation among the aid recipients on the basis of relative wealth, geography, past use of aid, and commitment to effective reforms. As a departure from the practice of automatic entitlements, aid differentiation targets the objective of poverty alleviation and strengthens the mechanism for aid accountability and conditionality. The EU has also suggested the elimination of the Stabex and Sysmin commodity compensatory schemes as a way of streamlining aid. These programs are unpopular in Europe because they are expensive and have neither stabilized commodity earnings nor contributed to economic diversification. Despite Africa's preferences for their retention, Stabex and Sysmin are less likely to survive in a global climate that shuns economic subsidies.[23]

Another primary concern in the poverty-focused aid policy is social and human development that specifically targets women. Under the catchphrase of "gender mainstreaming," the EU has advanced "a substantial package of support for the empowerment of women through improving literacy, access to primary education, basic health care and reproductive health care, preferably through program aid."[24] Related proposals include direct support for the institution-building of independent women's organizations and establishment of mechanisms for monitoring their performance at all levels. Gender and equity concerns signal the search for a broad-based Lomé that encompasses governments, the private sector, and grassroots organizations, but they also mark the growing political weight of EU NGOs in shaping the discourse on development.[25]

Sectoral targeting of development assistance has expanded the range of interventionist tools available to European donors and, invariably, has bolstered the policy conditionalities that were established in the late 1980s. The basis of new partnership, the EU's negotiating mandate asserts, is mutual commitment to greater dialogue and recognition that a "political environment guaranteeing peace and stability, respect for human rights, democratic principles, the rule of law and good governance is a prerequisite for development." Toward this end, it has proposed that a future Convention would contain an "essential elements clause" reaffirming that the parties' domestic and foreign policies must be informed by respect for these universal principles.[26]

The proliferation of policy conditionalities associated with economic reforms, debt relief, human rights, and good governance is matched by a new preoccupation with conflict prevention and postconflict reconstruction. Conflict prevention as part of development thinking started with

British and French proposals in 1994 for an African peacekeeping initiative. In June 1997, the Dutch presented a "Common Position Concerning Conflict Prevention in Africa," which subsequently influenced discussions for a coherent approach to questions of preventive diplomacy, peacekeeping, and postconflict reconstruction. These efforts led in part to an agreement by European heads of state on a code of conduct on arms transfers into Africa's conflict zones in June 1998.

Commissioner Pinheiro provided a comprehensive outline of the key principles that would guide cooperation in conflict prevention.[27] First is the principle of African ownership, whereby

> it will be up to the Africans themselves to decide to what extent they are determined to engage in conflict prevention, management and resolution, and to what extent they are determined to build the institutions and policy-making structures that make a viable state. This principle of ownership should not serve as a pretext to lean back and leave all initiatives to others. On the contrary, the Union will pursue a pro-active policy on that matter. But ownership means that Europe will not attempt to deliver ready-made solutions.

The second is taken up with the prevention of violent conflicts:

> When I say prevention, I do not merely mean diplomacy or declarations in a situation of tension. . . . I mean first of all peace-building: the prevention of violent conflicts at a very early stage, even at a stage where tensions are not yet obvious. . . . The key challenge for the international community as a whole is to overcome the culture of reaction, and to develop a culture of prevention.

The third concerns the deployment of development assistance for conflict prevention and peace-building, goals that entail the creation of a wider political environment for peace:

> It is not economic growth that counts most: Politics, functioning political systems, is the key for Africa's well-being. State failure, ineffective and illegitimate governance, corruption, imbalances of power and opportunities, the theft of national wealth by a small elite, and the repression of democracy, human rights and freedoms. These are the key problems that need to be addressed. These are root-causes of violent conflict, and our assistance must target them. Assistance must help the people to achieve a state of structural stability. Assistance must strive to reinforce those factors that enable peaceful change. . . . Providing development assistance to ineffective states or rewarding corrupt dictatorships is counterproductive. Only a consistent policy that focuses on the construction of viable states and public institutions, and that is rewarding those countries that are undertaking serious efforts of reform, that pursue policies of power-sharing, and encourage a real democratic process, only such a consistent policy will be credible and will have chances of success.[28]

The final principle envisages Europe's coordination of African peace-building and conflict-prevention initiatives with the United States, the United Nations, and NGOs. Such global coordination would specifically address the strengthening of regional mechanisms for conflict prevention, management, and resolution. Throughout this process, multilateral dialogue would be animated by two questions: "How can we best assist Africans? And what do Africans need most for their well-being, now and in the longer-term?"[29] The EU's framework for dealing with globalization, economic development, and conflict reduction ultimately depends on shared responsibilities and reciprocities between Africa and Europe. "The key approach to partnership between the EU and the ACP countries," Pinheiro conceded, will require "each party taking its share of the initiative and assuming its share of the responsibility. . . . We are seeking a balance between two requirements: on the one hand preserving the Lomé character, whilst on the other hand reforming fundamentally the EU-ACP relationship in order to meet new challenges and to achieve new objectives."[30]

The National and Regional Contexts of Africa's Partnership

Africa's potential contribution to partnership with Europe rests vitally on national and regional renewal. Economic integration and the post–Cold War security environment have afforded most of Europe an exit option out of postindependence burdens, but disintegrative forces in Africa delay Europe's envisaged disengagement. The lack of substantive change in Africa despite the cataclysmic events of the 1990s has conspired to postpone the translation of the paternalism of decolonization into a credible pattern of mutual engagement and burden-sharing. In the uncertain African environment of the late twentieth century, the towering goals of partnership are part mirage, part concealment of Africa's insignificance to Europe. From this perspective, the post-Lomé partnership is even more illusive than the one that heralded the 1975 agreement.

The end of postcolonial despotic order and the inauguration of the democratization wave in the early 1990s seemed to be the organizational framework of African renewal. Proponents of this wave celebrated the liberation from dictatorships, oppression, and economic decay as participation and representation replaced tyranny and autocracy gave way to accountability. African reformers saw democracy and pluralism as avenues for refurbishing political stability and steady economic growth, goals that had eluded the independence generation.[31]

Democracy-building in Africa presented a remarkable opportunity to a Europe poised to shed the postcolonial legacy of engagement with unsavory African leadership. Whether posited as governance, pluralism, or liberalism, Europe embraced democracy as an essential part of the Maastricht's development assistance policy. More pertinent, if democracy would produce effective state structures that stabilized authority and precluded conflicts that often attracted foreign intervention, it would ease Europe's gradual withdrawal from Africa, steadily consigning outstanding postcolonial responsibilities to the impersonal forces of globalization.

Supporting African democratization in the early 1990s, the EU applied diverse pressures on recalcitrant African leaders such as Togo's Gnassingbe Eyadema, Zaire's Mobutu Sese Seko, Kenya's Daniel arap Moi, and Malawi's Kamuzu Banda. In other coordinated measures, the EU suspended cooperation with Somalia, Sudan, Liberia, and the Gambia, owing to either human rights violations or instances in which the standards of good governance were flouted.[32] In imposing sanctions against Eyadema, for instance, the European Parliament condemned the violation of human rights and backed a request from the opposition for a postponement of parliamentary elections. Describing the "regime of president Eyadema [as] one of the most brutal dictatorships in Africa," the report acknowledged that "terror, murder and torture are a daily occurrence."[33] Similarly, when the military regime of Sani Abacha in Nigeria annulled the 1993 democratic elections, the EU decreed sanctions.[34]

Ten years into the democratic transition, however, the momentum seemed to slacken. Although many countries had held elections, few had made any progress toward meaningful participation and accountability. Beyond the procedures of democracy and the rule of law, there was little to show in terms of the contents of such processes. For the most part, remnants of old single-party regimes reverted to their old authoritarian tactics, either by emasculating their power under new electoral mandates or by destroying the feeble opposition parties. Entrepreneurial elites such as Moi, Eyadema, Omar Bongo of Gabon, and Robert Mugabe of Zimbabwe selectively appropriated themes of multiparty elections and constitutional development to wring economic concessions out of Western donors. Cumulatively, at the end of the 1990s, the African political scene was replete with halfhearted pluralism, whereby the wave of democratization had unleashed pent-up pressures for participation that had yet to find room in genuine representative institutions. Adding to this political picture is widespread economic and social decline that has exacerbated ethnic and communal conflicts and discredited the fragile democracies.[35]

The false starts in democratization as predictable avenues for regeneration pointed to the myriad internal problems of building effective authority for order, security, and legitimacy. But Europe also lost the enthusiasm for African democracy as soon as Rwanda degenerated into genocidal violence, Somalia ceased to exist, and Liberia and Sierra Leone descended into civil wars. The rehabilitation of Moi, Mobutu, and Eyadema in the mid-1990s began a process of European skepticism about the course of democracy-building in Africa, culminating in French foreign minister Alain Juppé's dire warning in 1994 about the fallacy of elections: "It's a long, profound process to establish the rule of law, balance of power, transparency and decentralization. . . . There is a collective illusion about elections. They don't settle everything."[36] Gorm Rye Olsen has correctly noted that the EU's promotion of democracy and respect for human rights in Africa lacked serious commitment, primarily because of the lingering security concerns of individual donors. Despite policy declarations, when it came to implementation, the "'non-declared' interests of the donor countries themselves were decisive and not the official ones found in treaties and public statements."[37]

In the place of democratization, Europe, like most of the Western world, lurched toward the concept of generational change as the sliver of hope for African political development. Finding expression in the leadership of Yoweri Museveni in Uganda, Meles Zenawi in Ethiopia, Issayas Afewerki of Eritrea, and Paul Kagame of Rwanda, the new generation seemed to combine stable, albeit semi-authoritarian, rule with the mobilization of a national consensus for difficult economic reforms.[38] As antidotes to the extremes of political chaos of Sierra Leone and the economic decay of Kenya, the new leaders fit the bill of institutional halfway houses toward accountable and transparent governance. The EU's embrace of Pierre Buyoya's military government in Burundi, which overthrew a weak civilian government in July 1997, epitomized the triumph of law and order over the ambiguity of multiparty democracy. The allure of the new leaders in Africa's regeneration did not take long to dissipate, for this regeneration was erected, as in the 1960s, on the weak reed of charisma in the absence of long-term institution-building. The leverage of new leaders as agents of change was limited by domestic constraints, dependence on foreign economic handouts, and potential challengers in their regions. By early 1999, the rhetorical commitment of new leaders to end corruption, cronyism, and instability plaguing postcolonial Africa had collapsed in the welter of civil and regional wars.[39]

Throughout the 1990s, the EU promoted regional integration in Africa, touting its own experience as an example of the benefits of collective efforts and envisioning this experience as a model for future cooperation and dialogue with differentiated geographic regions. Regionalism forms the prop to Europe's grand proposal of Regional Economic Partnership Agreements, which would replace old trade preferences. Regional integration, the EU negotiating framework stated, is "a necessary stepping stone toward a smooth integration of national economies within the global economy."[40] And a report by the European parliament emphasized that regional cooperation in Africa, especially in the areas of energy and transport, would promote economic development and help defuse political crises and wars. Moreover, regionalism seemed to offer the foundation for security cooperation mechanisms.[41]

After decades of faltering experiments at integration, SADC emerged as the most promising regional institution that would combine the objectives of economic prosperity and security. Under postapartheid South African leadership, SADC presented opportunities that Europe sought to develop in its post–Cold War African relationships. South Africa was critical for two reasons: A successful economic agreement with the EU would pave the way for post-Lomé negotiations; and Pretoria, as a political and economic power center, would serve as a source of stability for southern and central Africa.[42] The EU's negotiations with South Africa started in June 1995 with proposals that sought a special contractual relationship respecting its unique social and economic situation. In 1998, South Africa became a partial member of the Lomé Convention, ineligible for nonreciprocal trade preferences and financial assistance because of the structure of its developed economy. Instead, the comprehensive bilateral trade and cooperation agreement was tailored to the needs of South Africa. The EU also proposed the start of a long-term mutual trade liberalization that would lead to the establishment of an FTA after a transitional period of ten years or more.[43] The proposed FTA has occasioned widespread mistrust among the rest of SADC members who see it as the model for the entire region, but the EU has argued that it would be restricted to South Africa:

> On the basis of our current analysis we do not contend that it would be in the interest of the other countries of the region, including the countries that are in a Customs Union with South Africa, to formally accede to a Free Trade Zone with the EU. In the short and medium term these countries would therefore continue to benefit from preferential and non-reciprocal access to the EU market, in line with the current Lomé provisions.[44]

With respect to engaging SADC as a whole, the EU initiated a series of ministerial conferences on vital issues, beginning with the Berlin conference in September 1994. As expressed in the Berlin Declaration, both sides sought to "promote democracy at all levels and the rule of law, respect for human rights, and promotion of social justice and good governance."[45] By the second EU-SADC ministerial conference in Windhoek, Namibia, in 1996, SADC had signed a protocol as a prelude for trade regional liberalization, and in the security realm, it had established the SADC Organ on politics, defense, and security—a comprehensive mechanism for peace-building and peacekeeping. These achievements, Commissioner Pinheiro told SADC,

> represent a positive example for other regions, particularly in Sub-Saharan Africa. The general trend in the region in the last two years confirms our

common endeavors and values of human rights, good governance and rule of law. The regional integration and cooperation process, which is based on your commitment to building free and prosperous societies respectful of human rights and protective of minorities, bodes well for the future. The consolidation of a strong Southern African regional bloc will have an indelible impact not only on your own people but also on the peoples of neighboring countries and beyond the African Continent.[46]

The replication of southern Africa's regionalism as a model for post-colonial partnership is constrained by the persistence of intra-SADC trade disputes—in particular, those between SADC states that are not members of the South African–dominated Southern African Customs Union (SACU).[47] An EU report concluded: "While, in the long run, SADC would be a natural REPA partner for the EU, institutional, political and economic constraints make it difficult, if not impossible, for SADC to conclude a REPA in the time scale envisaged by the EU. The fourteen SADC members have made uneven progress toward trade liberalization, and a lot remains to be achieved before a FTA, let alone a customs union, could be in place."[48] Complaints that most SADC export producers have a more difficult time penetrating the fortress South African market than the EU market indicated the severity of these conflicts. Invariably, trade conflicts have affected other functional areas of cooperation such as labor mobility, water resources, and finance and investment.

Moves toward deeper integration have also slackened with the decline in the consensus over the parameters of security cooperation. SADC was successful in the mid-1990s in forging a security alliance for conflict prevention and democracy-building. In 1997, SADC began regional military training exercises that some analysts described as the bedrock for an indigenous African peacekeeping force. Yet serious differences between South Africa and Zimbabwe have surfaced regarding the nature and mandate of SADC's security structures—differences that originate from competition for regional leadership and that are exacerbated by personal animosities between Mandela and Mugabe. These conflicts came to a head in 1998, when Zimbabwe broke ranks with South Africa over SADC's intervention in the Congo, a new member state in the midst of internal and external threats. Mugabe, backed by Namibia and Angola, invoked SADC's security mechanism to lend military assistance to Laurent Kabila's government, whereas South Africa demurred, opting for a negotiated settlement. Almost coincidentally, South Africa failed to obtain SADC's support in its own botched military intervention in Lesotho in September 1998, when civil violence threatened to topple the elected government. Furthermore, the resurgence of civil war in Angola, growing bilateral tensions between Angola and Zambia, and an unresolved border conflict between Botswana and Namibia have arrested the momentum for peace and prosperity. Mozambique has attempted to bridge the widening political chasms in the region, but SADC faces formidable obstacles in evolving a consistent pattern of security collaboration that might solidify an order that Europe seeks to promote in Africa.[49]

The fragility of regionalism elsewhere in Africa is demonstrated by the performance of Eastern Africa's Intergovernmental Authority on Development, made up of Djibouti, Eritrea, Ethiopia, Somalia, Kenya, Uganda, and Sudan. IGAD became a full-fledged economic integration scheme in 1996, following a decade when its main focus was to alleviate drought and desertification. The EU was a dominant force in the shift in mandate, dangling the carrot of economic assistance for regional infrastructure and development through the Forum of Partners and Financial Backers. Similarly, IGAD ventured into the area of conflict prevention and management, assuming the leadership of mediating civil wars in the Sudan and Somalia. Informal groupings known as the Friends of IGAD and the IGAD Peace Fund, composed largely of European states, provided financial and diplomatic support for the mediation initiatives. By the end of 1998, although the IGAD talks on the Sudan had made progress on principles of a peaceful settlement, these efforts were threatened by a border conflagration between Eritrea and Ethiopia.[50]

West Africa's potential for regionalism was heightened in January 1994 by French devaluation of the African Finance Community (CFA) franc, a vital institution for French monetary exchange and dominance over fourteen countries. The devaluation raised fears about the future of French monetary guarantees, but it also propelled the Francophone countries to set up their own integration mechanisms, both the Economic and Monetary Union of West African States (UEMOA), comprising Burkina Faso, Mali, Niger, Côte d'Ivoire, Senegal, Guinea-Bissau, and Togo, and its central African counterpart, the Economic and Monetary Union of Central African States (UDEAC-CEMAC), made up of Cameroon, the Central African Republic, Congo, Gabon, Chad, and Equatorial Guinea. UEMOA, for instance, was described by the chairman of the European Parliament's Cooperation and Development Commission, Michel Rocard, as one of the best examples of African integration, whereby "everything is done with utmost seriousness."[51]

Amid uncertainties about the impact of a single European currency on the CFA zone, France persuaded the EU to peg it to the Euro after the launching of the single currency.[52] This guarantee nonetheless has not resolved the larger question of indigenous regional institutions in West Africa as a whole. Some critics of the CFA have proposed the creation of national currencies by West African states with fixed but adjustable exchange rates to allow gradual monetary cooperation within the larger West Africa.[53] Although ECOWAS has since 1975 epitomized a much wider integration model that cuts across the Anglophone and Franco-phone divide, its economic goals were imperiled in the 1990s by successive conflicts in Liberia, Sierra Leone, and Guinea Bissau. The twenty-first summit of ECOWAS in November 1998 acknowledged its limited achievements, attributing them to this lack of political will to implement decisions and perennial financial crisis. In the same vein, ECOWAS members recommitted themselves to enhance "collective weight in the search for continental renewal and reconstruction in a new international economic order that better reflects the needs of developing countries and the poor."[54] Reduced essentially to putting out escalating regional fires, ECOWAS, like IGAD, seemed to offer few prospects of sturdy regional structures.

Despite its growing pains, African regionalism was, for most of the postcolonial era, founded on states underwritten by universal principles of territoriality and sovereignty. The Organization of African Unity (OAU) articulated these principles, domesticating them and lending them an African flavor that legitimized the patchy state structures that European colonialism bequeathed. The EU's contemplated conflict mechanisms for Africa correctly recognize the significance of strengthening regional and subregional organizations, but there is a remarkable silence as the doctrines underpinning African states have come under siege. In the 1990s, the upsurge of internal conflicts led to a whittling of the conceptual foundations of some of these norms, as neighboring states took more responsibilities for disintegrating states. Yet the assumption of greater responsibility by a majority of African states has potentially opened the sluice gates for revisions of core OAU principles in uncharted directions. Compounding this problem is the veritable decline of statesmanship, civility, and trust that formed the essential infrastructures for pan-Africanism and institution-building in African interstate relations. As OAU norms weaken, redefined haphazardly by weak states, they pose a bigger threat to Africa's security than do architects of regional organizations for conflict prevention and early warning envision.

This is the dilemma that has surrounded the transition from Zaire to the Democratic Republic of Congo since May 1997. When two of the new leaders, Museveni and Kagame, coalesced into an alliance against the discredited Mobutu regime, Africa and the outside world lauded them for essentially trampling on principles of territorial integrity. But as they intervened again in support of a rebel movement to overthrow the Laurent Kabila government, they faced military opposition from some neighboring states, igniting a direct military conflict of unprecedented regional dimensions.[55] Viewed primarily as a contest by weak states over an equally weak state, the Congo conflagration endangers colonial and postcolonial territorial norms that have lent considerable stability to African interstate relations.

These principles are being remade by weak states (on shoestring budgets) seeking foreign policy victories to shore up fledgling domestic support, a scenario that opens vistas for anarchy and instability. The Congo thus is a metaphor for the breakdown of postcolonial principles of interstate amity and territoriality, rules that may be yearning for improvement but can find neither credible authors nor a definite direction. Contributing to the erosion of African amity was the rising propensity of African states to invade and subvert each other, practices that UN Secretary General Kofi Annan has described as "military adventures": "Divided and conflict-ridden, I don't think Africa stands a chance to move onto economic and social development."[56] Commonwealth Secretary General Chief Emeka Anyaoku sounded a similar warning: "Unless states pursue policies that ensure its peoples have a sense of belonging despite their diverse cultural backgrounds, ethnicity and divisive pluralism will constitute the greatest threat to peace for the twenty-first century."[57]

A Single Europe, Multiple African Policies

The African political context checks the construction of worthwhile external relationships that would erode the ineluctable trend toward marginalization. Africa is weak not just in salvaging remnants of postcolonial privileges but also in defining the future direction of postcolonialism. The multiplicity of Europe's African policies further bedevils the emergence of a consistent future framework. The negotiating blueprint crafted by the Brussels bureaucracy was a collective European effort, but the implementation of its objectives of development and conflict resolution depends on harmonizing the interests of various actors with competing interests. There is more coordination of European foreign and security policy elsewhere than in Africa. As a consequence, African policies are being held hostage to the unilateral interests of European powers, as Belgian Defense Minister Erik Deyrcke complained: "Europe's Africa policy operates in piecemeal. When Congo, Rwanda, and Burundi are discussed, Belgium is listened to. France, when it is the Francophone West Africa. Portugal when it is Angola. That is outdated."[58]

Multiple voices have stymied European complementarity and coordination, one of the pillars of the Maastricht Treaty. In particular, unilateralism still dominates French policies toward Africa. Under both conservative and socialist governments in the 1990s, France reaffirmed its position as Africa's leading Western partner, broadening its relations to include English- and Portuguese-speaking Africa.[59] But although Chirac has tried to shade the negative image of paternalism and intervention, some features of the past persist. An ardent supporter, President Ange-Felix Patasse of the Central African Republic, excoriated French policy: "There is an official France, a thoroughly republican France and an underground and neocolonialist France which sees its relations with Africa in terms of domination. . . . We are asking France to listen to Africa . . . because we are Francophiles."[60]

The November 1998 Franco-Africa summit in Paris, which was devoted to security issues, revealed the continuing problems of French African policy. The record number of African states in attendance presented the inauspicious specter of desperate states searching for economic assistance from a patron bereft of adequate means to meet escalating demands. Purported to show that France appreciated the monumental problems facing Africa and was willing to lend an ear, the summit was long on scoring points but short on tangible results, as unilateral promises distracted attention from the negotiations for a post-Lomé Convention. Further, Chirac's abortive attempt to mediate among the warring parties in the Congo War demonstrated French diplomatic sway, but it worsened the perception of an Africa in disarray, incapable of forging a minimum consensus on inter-African conflicts.

Strong demands by French human rights and civic groups for a transparent African policy have been a constant feature of the 1990s. During the November 1998 summit, these groups decried continued military and economic support for unstable regimes and called for parliamentary scrutiny of military cooperation agreements, including the shifting of African policymaking from the presidency to the foreign ministry. They also demanded that Paris revise its military and security intervention policies in Africa to reflect evolving European norms of peace, democracy, and human rights. Pressure for French transparency and accountability was shown in the appointment of a parliamentary committee to probe extensive links with Rwanda's Hutu-led government, but the committee's blanket exoneration of French policy demonstrates the severe obstacles to change.[61]

In contrast to the expansion of French influence, the other leading European powers—Britain and Germany—would prefer to cede their declining African commitments to NGOs and EU institutions, pursuing an African policy that is defined largely in terms of aid and debt. Germany's policy operates, for the most part, in the shadow of French policy, primarily because of Berlin's limited interests in Africa.[62] For their part, the British have scaled down their diplomatic and political links even within the Commonwealth, as illustrated by dwindling technical, educational, and cultural exchange. The British foreign secretary, Robin Cook, has pledged London's "hard-nosed self-interest in seeing Africa wealthy and prosperous"; but, in reality, Africa is not a core priority.[63] As a stark sign of Africa's declining relevance, a Kenyan parliamentary group visiting London in December 1998 complained that virtually no one in the British parliament had knowledge of recent political developments in Kenya. An editorial reflected on this changing relationship:

> It is a waste of time to complain about the ignorance of British MPs and the lack of understanding of Kenyan affairs. For such understanding will probably get even worse in the new millennium, particularly as the foreign office concentrates even more on European affairs. Until Africa is again of strategic economic and political importance to Britain and forces it to pay attention, it seems certain that future visits by Kenyan MPs are again likely to end in disappointment.[64]

More revealing of the British approach to Africa was the episode over the collusion between the British embassy in Sierra Leone and private arms dealers in breaking the UN arms embargo imposed on Sierra Leone in early 1998. The arms supply bolstered ECOMOG's ouster of the military regime and the restoration of the civilian elected government. At the same time, it embarrassed the British government and raised questions about delegating foreign policy to private groups.[65]

The delegation of roles to nonstate actors is a larger phenomenon of European policy indifference in the context of weak countervailing institutional structures. Without a clear and consistent EU policy on African issues, private agencies and organizations will become more decisive actors, stepping into the yawning vacuum. Since the mid-1990s, African civil conflicts and the accompanying humanitarian emergencies have engendered an interventionary fatigue that has increasingly enhanced NGO actors of every stripe. This trend, however, invariably multiplies the number of actors converging around African policies, muddying the policy-making context and making settlements difficult. One manifestation of this trend is the informal dependence by Europe on humanitarian agencies to determine African policies. Fortuitously, most humanitarian agencies and their civil society allies have utilized their organizational power on the ground to shape the parameters of Europe's Africa policy on development and conflict resolution in a positive direction. For instance, in April 1995, an alliance of eight hundred European NGOs called for the establishment of an "enforceable" European "code of conduct" to make arms sales part of EU legislation. In addition, the NGOs demanded a "coherent arms policy" to enforce policies already adopted by the EU member states against arms sales to human rights abusers. This advocacy culminated in the passage of the European code of conduct on arms control in June 1998.[66]

Devolving security functions pose a more formidable challenge to the coordination of European-African policy, particularly in cases where private militia groups and arms merchants collaborate with established governments. Aldo Ajello, EU special envoy to the Great Lakes Region, observed, for instance, that in the mid-1990s, Africa was "transformed into a volcano on the brink of eruption. . . . Arms are pouring into Africa from every source—arms dealers, mercenaries, security firms, even governments trying to pursue their individual agendas."[67] In addition to the blueprint for the prevention and resolution of conflict in Africa, the EU has made formal efforts to curtail the operations of private arms suppliers by choking their underground circuits. For example, in November 1998, Emma Bonino, EU commissioner for human rights and humanitarian operations, noted that as part of the arms control regime, the EU had submitted to member states a set of criteria for restricting arms exports. In particular, the EU had drawn up a list of military equipment whose export would be monitored and had requested that producers of light weapons take stricter measures with respect to brand names to make it easier to trace weapons. These measures, she noted, were necessary to "prevent the EU from eternally rebuilding schools and dispensaries in Africa that those who benefit from the continent's conflicts destroy by encouraging arms trafficking and the existence of private military groups."[68]

Resource constraints, however, reduce the effectiveness of these policies, precluding the evolution of a policing regime for private armed enterprises working with states and transnational corporations in Europe. However tenuous the links to European governments, security subcontracting legitimizes the roles of private armed groups, as the example of the British government in Sierra Leone demonstrates. Similarly, the military overthrow of the government of Pascal Lissouba in Congo-Brazzaville in 1997 is reported to have been initiated by arms purchased by the French oil giant Elf-Aquitaine in concert with the French government.[69] It is partly because of the proliferation of such links that the Joint EU-ACP Assembly in April 1998 criticized the EU-proposed code of conduct on arms sales in Africa, claiming that it

> is not setting the common standards high enough, as the guidelines leave room for subjective interpretation, provide weak consultation mechanisms, make no reference to parliamentary scrutiny, and contain no provisions for controlling third party brokering and end-use. . . . [T]he Code therefore in its current form risks having weak material impact on arms exports to regions of instability and countries which abuse human rights. . . . An effective conflict prevention policy must be based, among other things, on a transparent and monitored arms trade. Democratic institutions, especially in Africa, are seriously threatened by illegal or obscure arms trade and must be protected by clear and transparent rules.[70]

Africa's peripheralization has elevated sundry groups to dominant positions in decisionmaking, spawning additional obstacles to coordination. Private actors understandably fill the vacuum left by European states that are disengaging from Africa, but they would hardly exist without the escalating internal conflicts. Whether in their humanitarian or military roles, these actors thrive on the vicious cycle of wars and intervention. Thus weak states embroiled in conflicts with their neighbors or domestic challengers attract arms merchants of every stripe, followed closely by humanitarian agencies intervening to save lives. Crises and instability, in turn, increase the pressure on Europe and the rest of the industrialized world to disengage from Africa.[71]

Conclusion

The expiration of the Lomé IV Convention in February 2000 will mark a momentous phase in Europe-African relations, but it will hardly presage a "new partnership." Postcolonial institutions sought to mitigate paternalism through multilateral engagement as Lomé's glaring asymmetries were ameliorated by generous aid and trade packages. Yet that era was equally replete with enormous contradictions, fostering unsustainable dependencies that will take serious efforts to undo. Having squandered the opportunities for economic emancipation and integration behind the stability of the postcolonial Cold War era, Africa now finds a less congenial international environment for redefining its relations with Europe. The frameworks of African renewal are working states with some sense of coherence and direction that can confront the daunting demands of globalization. Such states would lend credence to partnership.

Notes

1. João de Deus Pinheiro, "Six Principles for Conflict Prevention in Africa," speech addressed to the International Peace Academy, New York, June 24, 1997. Deus Pinheiro is the EU commissioner for cooperation and development.

2. Quoted in "Commission Proposes New Partnership with ACP Countries," *The Courier ACP-EU*, no. 167 (January-February 1998), p. 5.

3. Quoted in Ruth Nabakwe, "France Promises to Help End African Conflicts," *Pan African News Agency*, November 28, 1998.

4. For diverse debates on the meaning of partnership, see Okello Duncan, "Partnership: Beyond Terminology," *Journal of the Society for International Development* 41, no. 4 (December 1998); Samie Ihejirika, "The Search for a New Partnership for Global Security and Sustainability," *Journal of the Society for International Development* 41, no. 4 (December 1998); Sadig Rasheed, "The Theory and Practice of African-European Partnership: African Realities Facing Global Challenges," *Journal of the Society for International Development* 41, no. 4 (December 1998); Gordon Crawford, "Whither Lomé? The Midterm Review and the Decline of Partnership," *Journal of Modern African Studies* 34, no. 3 (1996), pp. 503–518; and Gordon Crawford, "Rethinking the Lomé 'Partnership,'" *Lomé 2000*, no. 3 (October 1996).

5. For background analyses on the evolution of this process, see Isebill V. Gruhn, "Eurafrica Reconsidered: The Road Beyond Lomé," *Mediterranean Quarterly* 3, no. 3 (Summer 1992), pp. 60–61; and Enzo Grilli, *The European Community and Developing Countries* (London: Cambridge University Press, 1993).

6. Carol Cosgrove, *A Framework for Development* (London: George Allen and Unwin, 1981); and Michael Lake, "Africa and the European Community," in *Africa South of the Sahara, 1989* (London: Europa Publications, 1991), pp. 63–73.

7. Trevor Parfitt, "The Decline of Eurafrica? Lomé's Midterm Review," *Review of African Political Economy* 23, no. 67 (1996), pp. 53–56; and Karin Arts and Jessica Byron, "The Midterm Review of the Lomé IV Convention: Heralding the Future?" *Third World Quarterly* 18, no. 1 (1997), pp. 73–89.

8. Kevin Watkins, "Africa and the European Community: The Lomé Conventions," in *Africa: South of the Sahara 1991*, 12th ed. (London: Europa Publications, 1990), p. 50.

9. For a summary of the debates on policy dialogue, see Dieter Frisch, "The Political Dimension of Lomé," *The Courier ACP-EU*, no. 167 (January-February 1998); and Lord Plumb, "The Lomé Convention, Human Rights, and Europe," in Marjorie Lister (ed.), *European Development Policy* (London: Macmillan, 1998), pp. 8–11.

10. Crawford, "Whither Lomé?" pp. 5–7.

11. For comprehensive analyses of the provisions of the SEA and Maastricht, see Gita Bhatt, "Europe 1992: The Quest for Economic Integration," *Finance and Development* 26, no. 2 (June 1989), pp. 40–42; Louis J. Emmerij, "Europe 1992 and the Developing Countries: Conclusions," *Journal of Common Market Studies* 29, no. 2 (1990), pp. 243–253; and Andrew Moravcski, "Negotiating the Single European Act," *International Organization* 45, no. 1 (Winter 1991), pp. 19–56. For a discussion of its impact on Africa, see Kwame Boafo-Arthur, "Europe 1992: A Challenge to Sub-Saharan African Development," *Africa Development* 17, no. 2 (1992), pp. 32–42; and C. Owusu Kwarteng, "Africa and the European Challenge After 1992," *International Social Science Journal* 45, no. 137 (1993), pp. 405–412.

12. For a summary of these challenges, see I. William Zartman, *Europe and Africa: The New Phase* (Boulder: Lynne Rienner Publishers, 1993); John Ravenhill, "Dependent by Default: Africa's Relations with the European Union," in John Harbeson and Donald Rothchild (eds.), *Africa in World Politics: Post–Cold War Challenges* (Boulder: Lynne Rienner Publishers, 1995); and Paul Collier, "European Monetary Union and '1992': Opportunities for Africa," *The World Economy* 15, no. 15 (1992), pp. 633–643.

13. European Commission, *Green Paper on Relations Between the European Union and the ACP Countries on the Eve of the 21st Century: Challenges and Options for a New Partnership* (Brussels: EC, November 1996); and "EU Member States Set Out Their Positions," *Lomé 2000*, no. 6 (October 1997). For a discussion of African responses, see Ibrahima Seck, "Contribution to the Analysis of the 'Green Paper on Relations between the European Union and the ACP Countries on the Eve of the 21st Century,'" prepared for the Conference on "Beyond Lomé IV: For Improved Partnership in Future EU-ACP Cooperation," Brussels, April 10–11, 1997; and Rudo M. Chitiga, "Contribution to the Analysis of the 'Green Paper on Relations Between the European Union and the ACP Countries on the Eve of the 21st Century,'" prepared for the Conference on "Beyond Lomé IV: For Improved Partnership in Fu-

ture EU-ACP Cooperation," Brussels, April 10–11, 1997; and Andrea Koulaïmah-Gabriel, Jean Bossuyt, and Peter Gakunu, "Relations between the European Union and the ACP Countries on the Eve of the 21st Century: Synthesis of Comments by ACP Researchers," prepared for the Conference on "Beyond Lomé IV: For Improved Partnership in Future EU-ACP Cooperation," Brussels, April 10–11, 1997.

14. Peter Gakunu, "ACP-EU Trade: Past, Present, and Future," *The Courier ACP-EU*, no. 167 (January-February 1998), pp. 16–18.

15. This report is discussed in Debra Percival, "Development—Europe: ACP Nations Set to Clash with EU over Trade," *Inter Press Service Feature*, July 11, 1994. For a good perspective on the impact of WTO on Africa, see Patrick Watts, "Losing Lomé: The Potential Impact of the Commission Guidelines on the ACP Non–Least Developed Countries," *Review of African Political Economy*, no. 75 (1998), pp. 47–71; Christopher Stevens, "The Post-Lomé Trade Options: Questions Concerning the Feasibility and WTO Compatibility of EU's Preferred Approach," Institute for Development Studies, Sussex, 1997; and Paul Collier et al., "The Future of Lomé: Europe's Role in African Growth," *The World Economy* 20, no. 3 (1997), pp. 307–338.

16. João de Deus Pinheiro, "The Future of the European Union's Development Program," speech to a seminar of chairmen of Parliamentary Committees—Development, London, June 12, 1998. See also Watts, "Losing Lomé," pp. 49–52; "Cooperating with 'Dysfunctional States,'" *Lomé 2000*, no. 5 (May 1997); and "Globalization and Development," *Lomé 2000*, no. 3 (October 1996).

17. Desmond Davies, "U.K. Parliament Unhappy with Proposals for New Lomé Convention," *Pan African News Agency*, June 3, 1998; Tabby Moyo, "Lomé Talks Restart Today," *Mail and Guardian*, September 30, 1998; and Niccolo Sarno, "Development—Trade: Future of Lomé Treaty Still Clouded," *Inter Press Service Feature*, February 8, 1999.

18. European Union, *Guidelines for the Negotiation of New Cooperation Agreements with the African, Caribbean and Pacific (ACP) Countries: Policy Guidelines for Future EU-ACP Relations* (Brussels: EU, December 1997).

19. Stephen Bates, "Aid Groups Attack EU Budget Plans: Third World 'Squeezed' as EU Reaches Eastwards," *The Guardian*, April 21, 1998. See also "Lomé Crossroads," *Financial Times* (London), July 1, 1998, p. 19; "Vulnerable ACP States," *Lomé 2000*, no. 7 (February 1998); and João de Deus Pinheiro, "The Role of Aid: We Must Not Sign Away the Future," *The Courier ACP-EU*, no. 149 (January-February 1995), pp. 3–5.

20. Niccolo Sarno, "ACP Seeks a Common Line in Lomé Talks with EU," *Inter Press Service Feature*, November 9, 1997; and John Madeley, "The Future of EU-ACP Cooperation: The End of a Historical Relationship?" *Development and Cooperation*, no. 3 (May-June 1998), pp. 8–11.

21. European Research Office, "The Question of 'Blocked Resources': A Brief Elaboration of the Lomé Financial Arrangements," *Lomé IV Review Briefing*, no. 2 (December 1993–January 1994).

22. Tony Hawkins, "Survey—African Banking," *Financial Times* (London), June 2, 1998, p. 1; Stephen Bates, "Aid Groups Attack EU Budget Plans: Third World 'Squeezed' as EU Reaches Eastwards," *The Guardian*, April 21, 1998.

23. "Battle Lines Drawn over Future Aid Deal," *Irish Times*, May 23, 1998; and "Where Does the Post-Lomé IV Debate Stand?" *Lomé 2000*, no. 7 (February 1998).

24. Philip Lowe, "Combat Poverty and Help Our ACP Partners to Expand Trade, Investment and Employment: These Are the 21st Century Challenges," *The Courier ACP-EU*, no. 169 (May-July 1998), pp. 2–5; "Putting Poverty Alleviation Up Front," *Lomé 2000*, no. 4 (January 1997); "Local Development and Decentralized Cooperation," *Lomé 2000*, no. 6 (October 1997).

25. George Huggins, "Civil Society, Development and Lomé: Policy Options for EU—ACP Relations," paper prepared for the workshop "Civil Society Participation in a New EU-ACP Partnership," Amsterdam, January 11–12, 1999; and "The EU-ACP Negotiations: Goals and Challenges for 2000," *Eurostep*, September 30, 1998.

26. European Commission, *Green Paper on Relations Between EU and the ACP Countries*; and John Madeley, "The Future of EU-ACP Cooperation: The End of a Historical Relationship?" *Development and Cooperation*, no. 3 (May-June 1998), pp. 8–11.

27. João de Deus Pinheiro, "Six Principles for Conflict Prevention in Africa," speech to the International Peace Academy, New York, June 24, 1997.

28. Ibid.

29. Ibid.

30. Pinheiro, "The Future of the European Union's Development Program."

31. Michael Bratton and Nicholas van de Walle, *Democratic Experiments in Africa: Regime Transitions in Comparative Perspective* (London, Eng.: Cambridge University Press, 1997); and Celestin Monga, *The Anthropology of Anger: Civil Society and Democracy in Africa* (Boulder: Lynne Rienner Publishers, 1996).

32. "Development: EC Considers Corps to Aid Democratization Process," *Inter Press Service Feature*, November 25, 1993. These efforts were wide-ranging, including the monitoring of elections in Malawi, Uganda, Kenya, and Tanzania and the provision of funds for training of parliamentarians in Mozambique.

33. Bob Mantiri, "Europe-Togo: EC Maintains Economic Embargo Against an African State," *Inter Press Service Feature*, December 1, 1994.

34. "Nigeria—Politics: Will EC Sanctions Check Military Extravagance?" *Inter Press Service Feature*, December 3, 1994.

35. Celestin Monga, "Eight Problems with African Politics," *Journal of Democracy* 8, no. 3 (1997), pp. 156–170; and Bruce Baker, "The Class of 1990: How Have the Autocratic Leaders of Sub-Saharan Africa Fared Under Democratization?" *Third World Quarterly* 19, no. 1 (1998), pp. 115–28.

36. Quoted in Debra Percival, "Africa—Europe: EU Seeks to Restore Relations with Zaire," *Inter Press Service Feature*, September 24, 1994. See also Bob Mantiri, "Zaire-Belgium: Brussels Criticized for Resuming Aid to Kinshasa," *Inter Press Service Feature*, August 11, 1994.

37. Gorm Rye Olsen, "Europe and the Promotion of Democracy in Post–Cold War Africa: How Serious Is Europe and for What Reason?" *African Affairs*, no. 97 (1998), p. 345. See also Gordon Crawford, "Human Rights and Democracy in EU Development Cooperation: Toward Fair and Equal Treatment," in Marjorie Lister (ed.), *European Union Development Policy* (London: Macmillan, 1998), pp. 131–178.

38. For laudatory analyses of "new leaders," see Dan Connell and Frank Smyth, "The Heady Politics of Economic Growth, Personal Empowerment and Political

Freedom: A New Africa, Reviving Hope for a Failed Continent," *San Diego Union–Tribune*, March 29, 1998; and Marina Ottaway, *Africa's New Leaders: Democracy or State Reconstruction?* (Washington, D.C.: Carnegie Endowment for International Peace, 1999).

39. For different approaches to "new leaders," see Karl Vick, "Uganda's Glow Fades: Corruption Tarnishes Advances in Economy and Democracy," *Washington Post*, February 7, 1999, p. A23; David Anderson, "Death of the African Dream: Optimism About Africa Has Withered in the Face of Calamities Across the Continent," *The Independent* (London), August 27, 1998, p. 5; and Savid Reiff, "In Defense of Afro-Pessimism," *World Policy Journal* 15, no. 4 (Winter 1998–1999), pp. 10–22.

40. European Center of Development Policy Management (ECDPM), "Towards an ACP Position: Exploring ACP Responses to the EU Proposal for Regional Economic Partnership Agreements," *Lomé Negotiating Brief no. 4* (Maastricht: ECDPM, 1998); and ECDPM, *The EC's Impact Studies on Regional Economic Partnership Agreements*, Lomé Negotiating Brief no. 5 (Maastricht: ECDPM, 1999). African countries reject REPAs because regional economic integration and partnerships among them are still limited, even in the subregions identified by the EU. For a discussion of this position, see "Negotiations to Open for New Lomé Convention," *Pan African News Agency*, February 7, 1999.

41. For a discussion of regionalism, see João de Deus Pinheiro, "Introductory Statement on Regional Integration and Cooperation," Windhoek, Namibia, November 15, 1996; and Guy de Jonquie'res, "Regionalism: Blocking Moves," *Financial Times* (London), May 18, 1998, p. 6.

42. Martin Holland, "South Africa, SADC, and the European Union: Matching Bilateral and Regional Policies," *Journal of Modern African Studies* 33, no. 2 (1995), pp. 263–273; and Martin Holland, "Bridging the Capability-Credibility Gap: A Case Study of the CFSP Joint Action on South Africa," *Journal of Common Market Studies* 33, no. 4 (1995), pp. 555–572.

43. Lynda Loxton, "Tough Trade Test Ahead: Spain's Acceptance of South Africa to the Lomé Convention," *Mail and Guardian*, March 27, 1997; and Martin Walker, "New EU Deal for Developing Nations," *Mail and Guardian*, February 23, 1999.

44. João de Deus Pinheiro, "Southern Africa the Challenge to Europe: Building a New Framework for Trade and Co-operation with South Africa and the Other Countries in the Southern African Region," speech delivered at the European Conference on Southern Africa, Maastricht, April 17, 1997; Deborah Percival, "EU–South Africa Negotiations: What Consequences for South Africa's Neighbors?" interview with Jean Claude Boidin, head of the Task Force for Negotiations with South Africa," *Inter Press Service Feature*, November 20, 1997.

45. Debra Percival, "Europe-Africa: 'New Chapter in Relations' Begins in Berlin," *Inter Press Service Feature*, September 6, 1994.

46. João de Deus Pinheiro, "Opening Statement at the 2nd SADC-EU Ministerial Conference," Windhoek, November 14, 1996. See also João de Deus Pinheiro, "Opening Address at the EU-SADC Ministerial Conference," Vienna, November 3–4, 1998.

47. "South Africa's Neighbors Wary of an EU Trade Deal," *Mail and Guardian*, November 24, 1997.

48. ECDPM, *The EC's Impact Studies on Regional Economic Partnership Agreements*.

49. For a discussion of the mounting security problems in the region, see Susan Willet, "Demilitarization, Disarmament, and Development in Southern Africa," *Review of African Political Economy*, no. 77 (1998), pp. 409–430.

50. Gilbert M. Khadiagala, "Reflections on the Ethiopia-Eritrea Conflict," *Fletcher Forum* (Summer 1999); and Marc Michaelson, "The Eritrean-Ethiopian Border Conflict," *Institute of Current World Affairs Letters* (November 1998), pp. 1–10. See also Lionel Cliffe, "Regional Dimension of Conflict in the Horn of Africa," *Third World Quarterly* 20, no. 1 (1999), pp. 89–111.

51. Quoted in Toby Helm, "EU Proposes Linking Single Currency to Africa's Franc," *Daily Telegraph*, July 6, 1998, p. 10.

52. Celestin Monga, "A Currency Reform Index for Western and Central Africa," *The World Economy* 20, no. 1 (1997), pp. 103–125; and "Call to CFA Franc Zone to Have Trust in the Euro," *Pan African News Agency*, December 28, 1998.

53. Felix Machi Njoku, "Should French African Countries Abandon the Franc?" *Mail and Guardian*, June 10, 1998.

54. Quoted in Paul Ejime, "ECOWAS Still Bogged Down by Politics and Conflict," *Pan African News Agency*, November 4, 1998. See also James Rupert, "West Africa's Bumbling Behemoth," *Washington Post*, June 10, 1998; and "EU Commends ECOMOG's Role," *Pan African News Agency*, January 13, 1999.

55. Ian Fisher and Norimitsu Onishi, "Congo's Struggle May Unleash Broad Strife to Redraw Africa," *New York Times*, January 12, 1999.

56. Quoted in "Secretary-General Says Conflicts in Africa Overshadow Economic Gains," *UN Department of Public Information*, February 11, 1999; "UN Blames African Leaders for Conflicts," *Addis Ababa Tribune*, October 2, 1998. For a discussion of European efforts in the Congo, see "EU Offers to Help Rehabilitate DRC," *Pan African News Agency*, February 22, 1999.

57. Quoted in Ruth Nabakwe, "Conflicts Leading Africa to Self-Destruction," *Pan African News Agency*, February 23, 1999.

58. Quoted in "Belgian Defense Minister, Erik Deyrcke, Comments on Great Lakes," *Foreign Broadcast Information Services–Africa*, October 15, 1998. For broader accounts of European decisionmaking, see Christopher Hill, "The Capability-Expectation Gap, or Conceptualizing European International Role," *Journal of Common Market Studies* 31, no. 3 (1993), pp. 305–328; João de Deus Pinheiro, "Can EU Development Assistance Contribute to Peace and Security?" speech at the CESD-ISIS Conference on "The Future of the EU's Common Foreign and Security Policy," Brussels, September 24, 1998; Friedrich Hamburger, "An Overview of EU Development Policy," in Marjorie Lister (ed.), *European Union Development Policy* (London: Macmillan Press, 1998), pp. 12–16; and "How Does the EU Make Decisions?" *Lomé 2000*, no. 4 (January 1997).

59. Robert Graham, "Chirac Looks to Africa's Non-Francophone States," *Financial Times*, July 2, 1998, p. 4.

60. Quoted in Jules Souleymane Gueye, "Patasse Calls for Sincere Partnership with France," *Pan African News Agency*, November 23, 1998. Another supporter, Gabonese Omar Bongo, criticized the French policy of broadening relations beyond the Francophone, charging that it amounted to allowing Africa's Common-

wealth countries to "drink out of two troughs." See Graham, "Chirac Looks to Africa's Non-Francophone States," p. 4. For a discussion of previous policies, see Barbara Borst, "France-Africa: New President, But Old Policies Will Remain," *Inter Press Service Feature*, May 8, 1995; and Angeline Oyog, "France-Africa: Investigators Urged to Look Elsewhere for Corruption," *Inter Press Service Feature*, November 15, 1994.

61. Ruth Nabakwe, "Planned Demonstrations Could Mar France-Africa Summit," *Pan African News Agency*, November 17, 1998; Angeline Oyog, "France-Africa: NGOs Call for Parliamentary Review of Arms Sales," *Inter Press Service Feature*, September 5, 1994.

62. Gorm Rye Olsen, "The Marginalization of Africa in the New International System: European Interests and European Concerns," paper prepared for ECPR-ISA Joint Conference, Vienna, September 16–19, 1998.

63. Quoted in Michael Holman and Michela Wrong, "Continental Drift Could Put Cook Under Pressure," *Financial Times*, May 12, 1998, p. 11.

64. "Waning UK Interest in Kenya Not Surprising," *Daily Nation*, December 21, 1998.

65. Chris Allen, "Britain's Africa Policy: Ethical, or Ignorant?" *Review of African Political Economy*, no. 77 (1998), pp. 405–407; Jon Hibbs, "Arms-to-Africa Envoy Stands by His Decision," *Daily Telegraph*, November 4, 1998.

66. Debra Percival, "Africa-Development: NGOs Set Task of Defining New EU Partnership," *Inter Press Service Feature*, April 27, 1995; "Europe-Africa: EU NGOs Search for New Partnership with Africa," *Inter Press Service Feature*, April 29, 1995; and Debra Percival, "Trade-Arms: Europe's NGOs Seek Controls on Trade to South," *Inter Press Service Feature*, May 11, 1995.

67. Quoted in Al Venter, "Arms Pour into Africa," *New African* (January 1999).

68. Quoted in Thomas Hiren, "Africa's Donors Want Crackdown on Mercenaries," *Mail and Guardian*, December 22, 1998.

69. *New African* (May 1998), pp. 12–13.

70. "The ACP-EU Joint Assembly Meeting, Port Louis (Mauritius), 20 to 23 April 1998," *The Courier ACP-EU*, no. 170 (May-June 1998).

71. See, for instance, Marina Ottaway, "Keep Out of Africa," *Financial Times*, February 25, 1999.

5

Africa and Other Civilizations: Conquest and Counter-Conquest

ALI A. MAZRUI

Introduction: Cultural Receptivity

As we enter the new millennium let us examine Africa's cultural balance-sheet.

One of the most intriguing aspects of the historical sociology of Africa in the preceding century has been the continent's remarkable cultural receptivity. For example, Christianity has spread faster in a single century in Africa than it did in several centuries in Asia. European languages have acquired political legitimacy in Africa more completely than they have ever done in formerly colonized Asian countries like India, Indonesia, and Vietnam. Indeed, whereas nobody talks about "English-speaking Asian countries" or "Francophone Asia," African countries are routinely categorized in terms of which particular European language they have adopted as their official medium (Lusophone, English-speaking, and Francophone African states).

Examining the preceding millennium, we find not only that North Africa and much of the Nile Valley were converted to the Muslim religion but, indeed, that millions of the inhabitants were linguistically transformed into Arabs. Elsewhere in Africa the Muslim faith has continued to make new converts despite the competitive impact of Euro-Christian colonial rule following the Berlin conference of 1884–1885.

Linguistic nationalism in favor of indigenous languages in postcolonial Africa has been relatively weak. Only a handful of African countries allocate much money toward developing African languages for modern needs. On the other hand, most African governments south of the Sahara give high priority to the teaching of European languages in African schools.

No African country has officially allocated a national holiday in honor of the gods of indigenous religions. All African countries, on the other hand, have a national holiday either in favor of Christian festivals (especially Christmas) or Muslim festivals (such as Idd el Fitr) or *both* categories of imported festivals. The Semitic religions (Christianity and Islam) are nationally honored in much of Africa; the indigenous religions are at best ethnic occasions rather than national ones.

Toward Conquering the Conquerors

Africa's readiness to welcome new cultures is both its strength and its weakness. There is an African preparedness to learn from others; but there is also the looming danger of Africa's dependency and intellectual imitation.

What has so often been overlooked is the third dimension of this equation. Africa's cultural receptivity can over time make others dependent on Africa. There is a cyclic dynamic at play. Those who have culturally conquered Africa have, over time, become culturally dependent upon Africa. The biter has sometimes been bitten; the conqueror has sometimes been counter-conquered. The present chapter is about this boomerang effect in acculturation and assimilation. Africa has sometimes counterpenetrated the citadels of its own conquerors.

This process of Africa's counterpenetration has sometimes been facilitated by Africa's political fragmentation in the egalitarian age. The majority of the members of the nonaligned movement are from Africa. Almost half the members of the Organization of the Islamic Conference are also members of the Organization of African Unity. Much of the agenda of the Commonwealth since the 1960s has been set by its African members— inasmuch as they have used the "Britannic" fraternity to help liberate southern Africa and dismantle apartheid. Although African countries are only a third of the fifty-four members of the Commonwealth, they have been by far the most influential regional group in shaping its agenda and its decisions. In the 1990s African influence was for a while enhanced by the election of the first African secretary-general of the Commonwealth, Chief Eleazar Emeka Anyaoku of Nigeria. South Africa's readmission under majority rule brought the whole story full circle. And when Mozambique was admitted in 1995, the Commonwealth ceased to be an exclusively Anglophone club.

Countries from Africa were also almost a third of the total global membership of the United Nations, until the Soviet Union and Yugoslavia collapsed and Czechoslovakia split into separate UN members. Africa's fragmentation in an egalitarian age had for a while helped Africa's voting power in the General Assembly. Africa's percentage of the total membership has declined in the 1990s.

On the other hand, Africa has had two successive secretaries-general of the United Nations—Boutros Boutros-Ghali and Kofi Annan—partly as a result of the wider rivalries of world politics. On the negative side, the United States and Great Britain also succeeded in hounding out of power the first African director-general of the United Nations Educational, Scientific, and Cultural Organization (UNESCO), Amadou-Mahtar M'Bow of Senegal. Even in this relatively egalitarian age in human history, real power continues to be decisive—when there is enough at stake to invoke it. Early in the twenty-first century, will Africa provide another director-general of UNESCO? Ismail Serageldin of Egypt has been widely discussed as a serious candidate.

Even Africa's weakness has—on other occasions—been a source of power. As indicated, Africa's territorial fragmentation has translated into voting influence even in UNESCO, notwithstanding what happened to Dr. M'Bow. And the General Assembly of the United Nations continues to take into account the liberation concerns of the African group.

Similarly, Africa's cultural receptivity—though often excessive and a cause of Africa's intellectual dependency—has sometimes become the basis of Africa's counterinfluence on those who have conquered her. This report about Africa's counterpenetration is supposed to be illustrative rather than exhaustive. We shall examine Africa's relationship with two interrelated civilizations—*Arab* and *Islamic*. We shall then examine the *French* connection as an illustration of Africa's potential in counterinfluencing the Western world. We then examine Africa's interaction with *India*—with special reference to the legacies of Mahatma Gandhi and Jawaharlal Nehru. We shall conclude with Africa's conquest of Africa—the full circle of autocolonization.

The Arab factor in Africa's experience is illustrative of the politics of *identity*. The Islamic factor is illustrative of the politics of *religion*. With the French connection we enter the politics of *language*. And with the Afro-Indian interaction we examine the politics of *liberation*. Finally, we examine the future politics of *self-conquest*. Let us now turn to these five case studies (Afro-Arab, Afro-Islamic, Afro-French, Afro-Indian, and Afro-African) in greater detail.

Africa Conquers the Arabs

In the seventh century C.E. parts of Africa were captured by the Arabs in the name of Islam. Three factors speeded up the Arabization of North

Africa and the Lower Nile Valley. One factor was indeed Africa's cultural receptivity—a remarkable degree of assimilability. The second factor that facilitated Arabization was the Arab lineage system and the way it defined the offspring of mixed marriages. The third factor behind Arabization was the spread of the Arabic language and its role in defining what constitutes an Arab.

At first glance the story is a clear case of how the Arabs took over large chunks of Africa. But on closer scrutiny the Afro-Arab saga is a story of both conquest and counter-conquest. It is comparable to the role of the British in colonizing North America. Much later, imperial Britain was being protected and led by its former colonies, the United States of America.

But there is one important difference in the case of reciprocal conquest between the Arabs and the Africans. The actual creation of *new Arabs* is still continuing. Let us more closely examine this remarkable process of "Arab-formation" in Africa across the centuries.

The Arab conquest of North Africa in the seventh and eighth centuries initiated two processes: Arabization (through language) and Islamization (through religion). The spread of Arabic as a native language created new Semites (the Arabs of North Africa). The diffusion of Islam created new monotheists, but not necessarily new Semites. The Copts of Egypt are linguistically Arabized but they are not of course Muslims. On the other hand, the Wolof and Hausa are preponderantly Islamized—but they are not Arabs.

The process by which the majority of North Africans became Arabized was partly biological and partly cultural. The biological process involved intermarriage and was considerably facilitated by the upward lineage system of the Arabs. Basically, if the father of a child is an Arab, the child is an Arab—regardless of the ethnic or racial origins of the *mother*. This lineage system could be described as ascending miscegenation—since the offspring ascends to the more privileged parent.

This is in sharp contrast to the lineage system of, say, the United States, where the child of a White father and a Black mother *descends* to the less privileged race of that society. Indeed, in a system of descending miscegenation like that of the United States, it does not matter whether it is the father or the mother who is Black. An offspring of such racial mixture descends to Black underprivilege. The American system does not therefore co-opt "impurities" upward across the racial barrier to high status. It pushes "impurities" downward into the pool of disadvantage.

It is precisely because the Arabs have the opposite lineage system (*ascending* miscegenation) that North Africa was so rapidly transformed into part of the Arab world (not merely the Muslim world). The Arab lineage system permitted considerable racial co-optation. "Impurities" were admitted to higher echelons as new full members—provided the father was an Arab. And so the range of colors in the Arab world is from the Whites of Syria and Iraq to the Browns of Yemen, from blonde-haired Lebanese to the Black Arabs of Sudan.

Within Africa the valley of the White Nile is a particularly fascinating story of evolving Arabization. The Egyptians were of course not Arabs when the Muslim conquest occurred in the seventh century C.E. The process of Islamization in the sense of actual change of religion took place fairly rapidly after the Arab conquerors had consolidated their hold on the country.

On the other hand, the Arabization of Egypt turned out to be significantly slower than its Islamization. The Egyptians changed their religious garment from Christianity to Islam more quickly than they changed their linguistic garment from ancient Egyptian and ancient Greek to Arabic. And even when Arabic became the mother tongue of the majority of Egyptians, it took centuries before Egyptians began to call themselves Arabs.

But this is all relative. When one considers the pace of Arabization in the first millennium of Islam, it was still significantly faster than average in the history of human acculturation. The number of people in the Middle East who called themselves "Arabs" expanded dramatically in a relatively short period. This was due partly to the exuberance of the new religion, partly to the rising prestige of the Arabic language, and partly to the rewards of belonging to a conquering civilization. Religious, political, and psychological factors transformed Arabism into an expansionist culture that absorbed the conquered into the body politic of the conquerors. In the beginning there was an "island" or a peninsula called "Arabia." But in time there were far more Arabs outside Arabia than within. At the end of it all there was an "Arab world."

Along the valley of the White Nile, Northern Sudan was also gradually Islamized—and more recently has been increasingly Arabized. Again, a people who were not originally Arabs have come to see themselves more and more as Arabs.

The question that arises is whether there is a manifest destiny of the White Nile—pushing it toward further Arabization. It began with the Egyptians and their gradual acquisition of an Arab identity. The Northern Sudanese have been in the process of similar Arabization. Are the Southern Sudanese the next target of the conquering wave of Arabization within the next hundred to two hundred years? Will the twin forces of *biological mixture* (intermarriage between Northerners and Southerners) and *cultural assimilation* transform the Dinkas and Nuers of today into the Black Arabs of tomorrow?

It is not inconceivable, provided the country as a whole holds together. As intermarriage increases, Northern Sudanese will become more Black in color. As acculturation increases in the South, Southerners will become more Arab. Biological Africanization of the North and cultural Arabization of the South will reinforce each other and help to forge a more integrated Sudan, provided peace is restored to the country. Without peace the country will break up sooner or later.

Southern Sudanese are the only sub-Saharan Africans who are being Arabized faster than they are being Islamized. They are acquiring the Arabic language faster than they are acquiring Islam. This is in sharp contrast to the experience of such sub-Saharan peoples as the Wolof, the Yoruba, the Hausa, or even the Somali—among all of whom the religion of Islam has been more triumphant than the language of the Arabs. This rapid Arabization of the Southern Sudanese linguistically has two possible outcomes in the future. The Southern Sudanese could become Sudan's equivalent of the Copts of Egypt—a Christian minority whose mother tongue would then be Arabic. Or, the Arabization of the Southern Sudanese could be followed by their religious Islamization—in time making Southern and Northern Sudanese truly intermingled and eventually indistinguishable.

Meanwhile, the Swahili language has been creeping northward toward Juba from East Africa as surely as Arabic has been creeping southward from the Mediterranean. The Swahilization of Tanzania, Kenya, Uganda, and eastern Zaire has been gathering momentum. With Arabic coming up the Nile toward Juba and Kiswahili coming down the same valley, Southern Sudanese will find themselves caught between the forces of Arabization and the forces of Swahilization. Historically, these two cultures (Arab and Swahili) have so easily reinforced each other. It is because of this pattern of trends that the manifest destiny of the Valley of the White Nile appears to be a slow but definite assimilation into the Arab fold over the next century or two. Ironically, the Arabization of Southern Sudan may continue even if the South breaks away and forms a separate country.

Nevertheless, racial ambivalence will maintain a linkage with Africanity. Indeed, the Southern Sudanese are bound to be the most negritudist (having pride of blackness) of all Sudanese—even if they do become Arabized and do not secede. There is a precedent of Black nationalism even among Northern Sudanese. It is not often realized how much "Negritude" sentiment there is among sectors of Northern Sudanese opinion. Muhammad al-Mahdi al-Majdhub has been described as "probably the first Sudanese poet to tap the possibility of writing poetry in the Arabic language with a consciousness of a profound belonging to a 'Negro' tradition."[1]

The poet al-Mahdi has indeed affirmed:

> In the Negroes I am firmly rooted though the Arabs may boastfully claim my origin. . . . My tradition is: beads, feathers, and a palm-tree which I embrace, and the forest is singing around us.[2]

Muhammad Miftah al-Fayturi is another Arab negritudist. Information about his ancestry is somewhat contradictory. His father was probably Libyan and his mother Egyptian but of Southern Sudanese ancestry. In his words:

> *Do not be a coward*
> *Do not be a coward*
> *say it in the face*
> *of the human race:*
> *My father is of a Negro father,*
> *My mother is a Negro woman,*
> *and I am black.*[3]

In some notes about al-Fayturi's early poetic experiences there is the anguished cry: "I have unriddled the mystery, the mystery of my tragedy: I am short, black and ugly."

Then there are the Arab negritudists who sometimes revel in the fact that they are racially mixed. They can also be defiant and angrily defensive about their mixture. Salah A. Ibrahim, in his piece titled "The Anger of the Al-Hababy Sandstorm," declared:

> *Liar is he who proclaims:*
> *"I am the unmixed". . . Yes, a liar!*[4]

In the Sudan of the future there may be even less room for such "lies" than there is at present. After all, Arabization is, almost by definition, a process of creating mixture—and its relentless force along the White Nile is heading southward toward Juba and beyond.

How has the boomerang effect worked in relation to the Arabization of Africa? In what sense has there been an Africanization of the Arab world? In what way has the whole process been *cyclic?*

It is worth reminding ourselves that the majority of the Arab people are in Africa. Over 60 percent of the population of the Arab world is now west of the Red Sea on African soil. The largest Arab country in population is Egypt—which in 1989 and 1993 became the presiding country in the Organization of African Unity, while its president was at the same time seeking a resolution of the Palestinian-Israeli impasse during both years.

The headquarters of the Arab League is in Africa. From 1979 to 1989 it was located in Tunis, having previously been in Cairo. In 1990 the decision was made to return the League to Cairo. If the headquarters of the Arab League symbolizes the capital of the entire Arab world, then the capital of the Arabs in the second half of the twentieth century has been located on the African continent.

When the Palestine Liberation Organization and its warriors were expelled from Lebanon by the Israeli military invasion of 1982, the headquarters of the Palestinian movement also moved to Africa. Major decisions about the Palestinians, including the declaration of the Palestinian state in exile, were now made on African soil—from Tunis. Partly because of this evolving Afro-Palestinian solidarity, Yassir Arafat was in Lusaka in 1990 to embrace Nelson Mandela when the latter made his first trip outside South Africa in thirty years.

The largest city in the Arab world is located on its African side. The population of Cairo is larger than the population of Saudi Arabia as a whole.

Cairo also has become the cultural capital of the Arab world. The greatest singers and musicians of the Arab world—including the incredible Umm Khulthum, affectionately known as "the Star at Sunrise"—used to mesmerize the Middle East from the studios of the Voice of the Arabs Broadcasting System in Cairo. Israelis even invented one more anti-Arab joke—"O yes, the Arabs have at last found unity—every Thursday night when they all tune in to listen to the voice of Umm Khulthum." Her funeral in 1975 was second only to President Nasser's burial in 1970 in terms of the largeness of the crowds and the passions and public grief displayed.

The most famous Arab musical composer of the twentieth century has also come from the African side of the Arab world. Al-Ustadh Muhammad Abdul Wahab was in his younger days primarily a singer and instrumentalist. His musical compositions were initially modest, though they suited his vocal power. After deeper study of Western classical music—with special reference to Beethoven—Muhammad Abdul Wahab took Egyptian music into new levels of cross-cultural complexity. He developed new styles of Arab orchestral and even symphonic music. He was doing all this innovative work from the African side of the Arab world.

Culture has its technological and professional infrastructure—a significant part of which is supplied by Egypt, by far the most important filmmaking country in both Africa and the Arab world. Egyptian shows feature prominently on cinema screens and television programs on both sides of the Red Sea.

There are other skills of the Arab people that also disproportionately emanate from the African side. Dr. Boutros Boutros-Ghali, when he was Egypt's minister of state for foreign affairs, estimated that Egypt's technical assistance to other Arab countries is sometimes as high as 2 million Egyptians scattered in the region.[5] Boutros-Ghali later became secretary-general of the United Nations, as I indicated.

All this is quite apart from the importance of Egypt in the Arab military equation in at least four of the Arab-Israeli wars. Until the 1973 war the Arab armies were no match for the Israelis. And even in 1973 Arab triumphs occurred mainly at the beginning of the conflict. What is clear is that the nearest thing to an Arab military credibility against Israel came from the African side of the Arab region. This is why the United States invested so heavily in the Camp David Accords and in the neutralization of Egypt as a "confrontation state" against Israel.

In the year 639 C.E. the Arabs crossed into Africa and conquered Egypt. By the second half of the twentieth century Egypt had become the most important pillar of the military defense of the Arab world. History has once again played its cyclic boomerang game in the interaction between Africa and its conquerors. The ancestral home of the Arabs in Asia is now heavily dependent culturally and militarily on the African side of the Arab nation.

In His infinite wisdom Allah has so far permitted the ancestral home of Islam—Saudi Arabia—to retain a preponderance of oil reserves and petro-power. Perhaps only the petro-factor has prevented the African side of the Arab nation from attaining complete preponderance. Arabized Africa now leads the way demographically, culturally, technologically, militarily, and artistically. Allah has permitted the birthplace of the Prophet Muhammad to lead the way in petro-power for the time being.

Africa: The First Islamic Continent?

Why are Islam and Christianity continuing to spread so fast in sub-Saharan Africa? Why has *religious* receptivity in Africa been so remarkable?

The spread of Christianity during Africa's colonial period was particularly spectacular. The Christian gospel spread faster in a single century in Africa than it did in several centuries in places like India and China.

When we turn to Islam, there is just the chance that Africa will become to Islam what Europe has been to Christianity—the first continent to have a preponderance of believers. Europe was the first continent to have a majority of Christians. Is Africa becoming the first continent to have a majority of Muslims?

Since independence, two issues have been central to religious speculation in Africa—Islamic expansion and Islamic revivalism. Expansion is about the spread of religion and its scale of new conversions. Revivalism is about the rebirth of faith among those who are already converted. Expansion is a matter of geography and populations—in search of new worlds to conquer. Revivalism is a matter of history and nostalgia—in search of ancient worlds to reenact. The spread of Islam in postcolonial Africa is basically a peaceful process of persuasion and consent. The revival of Islam is often an angry process of rediscovered "fundamentalism."

In Arab Africa there is little expansion taking place—although some Egyptian Muslim militants regard the Coptic Church as a historical anachronism that ought to end. For North Africa as a whole, Islamic revivalism is the main issue. It probably cost President Anwar Sadat his life in 1981 and has sometimes threatened the ruling regimes of Tunisia, Algeria, and Morocco. Indeed, Algeria has been plunged into an ugly civil war ever since the military aborted an election that the Islamists were set to win in 1992.

Outside Arab Africa the central issue concerning Islam is not merely its revival—it is also the speed of its expansion. We are back to the issue of receptivity. Not often realized is the fact that there are more Muslims in Nigeria than there are Muslims in any Arab country, including Egypt. Muslims in Ethiopia are nearly half the population. Islam elsewhere in Africa has spread—however unevenly—all they way down to the Cape of Good Hope. Islam in South Africa is three hundred years old, having first arrived not directly from Arabia but from South East Asia with Malay immigrants.

The largest countries in Africa in population are Nigeria, Egypt, Ethiopia, and Zaire. Between them, these four countries account for more than 160 million Muslims. (The Islamic part of Zaire is mainly in the east.) Virtually half the population of the continent is now Muslim.

But religion in Africa does not of course exist in isolation. The world of religious experience in Africa is rich in diversity.

Indigenous religions are of the *oral tradition* and tend to be more receptive to other religious influences. African traditional religions, in particular, are especially ecumenical. The same African individual may combine either Islam or Christianity with his or her ethnic religion. This is what so-called syncretism is all about. However, whereas an African may be both a Muslim and a follower of a traditional creed, the African is unlikely to be both a Muslim and a Christian. One religion of sacred text (e.g., Islam) can be combined with a religion of oral message (e.g., Yoruba religion). But it is rare to find two religions of sacred text (Sunni Islam and Roman Catholicism) adhered to by the same individual. Religions of sacred text tend to be mutually exclusive. Shiite Muslims are unlikely to be simultaneously Methodists or Greek Orthodox.

Of the three principal religious legacies of Africa (indigenous, Islamic, and Christian) the most tolerant on record is the indigenous tradition. It is even arguable that Africa did not have religious wars before Christianity and Islam arrived. Indigenous religions were neither *universalist* (seeking to convert the whole of the human race) nor *competitive* (in bitter rivalry against other creeds). Christianity and Islam, on the other hand, were both universalist and competitive—perhaps especially in Black Africa. In that arena south of the Sahara, Christianity and Islam have often been in competition for the soul of the continent. Rivalry has sometimes resulted in conflict.

Indigenous African religions, by contrast, are basically communal rather than universalist. Like Hinduism and modern Judaism—and unlike Christianity and Islam—indigenous African traditions have not sought to convert the whole of humankind. The Yoruba do not seek to convert the Ibo to Yoruba religion—or vice versa. Nor do either the Yoruba or the Ibo compete with each other for the souls of a third group like the Hausa. Because they are not proselytizing religions, indigenous African creeds have not fought with each other. Over the centuries Africans have waged many kinds of wars with each other—but hardly ever *religious* ones before the universalist creeds arrived.

But what has this to do with cultural receptivity in contemporary Africa? Indigenous toleration today has often mitigated the competitiveness of the imported Semitic religions (Christianity and Islam). Let me illustrate with Senegal, which is over 90 percent Muslim. The founder president of this predominantly Islamic society was Leopold Sedar Senghor. He presided over the fortunes of postcolonial Senegal for two decades (1960–1980)—in basic political partnership with the Muslim leaders of the country, the Marabouts.

Contrast this phenomenon with the history of the United States as a predominantly Protestant society. In spite of a constitution that ostensibly separated church from state beginning in the eighteenth century, it was not until 1960 that the American electorate was ready to elect a Roman Catholic as president. When will the United States elect a Jew to that highest office? Although U.S. Jews have occupied some of the highest offices of the land (and have been represented on the Supreme Court), it seems unlikely that there will be a Jewish president of the United States in the near future.

Muslims in the United States may now equal the Jews in numbers (although not in influence and power). Although the constitution still insists on separating church from state, for the time being the prospect of a *Muslim* president of the United States remains mind-boggling.

And yet newly independent Senegal could in 1960 calmly accept a Roman Catholic to preside over the fortunes of a basically Muslim country. Not just a fellow Muslim, Senghor was from a different denomination (as Kennedy was a fellow Christian to most Americans, but from a different sect). Senghor belonged to a faith entirely different from that of most Senegalese. And yet he was president of a stable Muslim country for some twenty years.

His successor as president (partly sponsored by him) was Abdou Diouf, a Muslim ruler of a Muslim society at last. But the tradition of ecumenical tolerance continued in Senegal. The first lady of the country—Madame Elizabeth Diouf—was Roman Catholic. And several of the ministers of the new president have from time to time been Christian.

To summarize the argument so far: Predominantly Muslim countries south of the Sahara have sometimes been above average in religious toleration. The capacity to accommodate other faiths may even be part of the historical Islamic tradition in multireligious empires. But far more religiously tolerant than either Islam or Christianity have been indigenous African traditions—especially since these do not aspire to universalism and are not inherently competitive. In Black Africa this indigenous tolerance has, as I indicated, often moderated the competitive propensities of Christianity and Islam.

When we place Islam in the context of the African continent as a whole, the cultural cyclic boomerang effect is once again discernible. The most influential Islamic university in the world—Al-Azhar University—is on the African continent. Al-Azhar in Cairo is credited with some of the most important *fatwas* under the Shari'a (legal opinions under Islamic law) in the last six hundred years.

Al-Azhar was founded by the Fatimids in C.E. 970. This makes it one of the oldest and most durable universities in the world. The basic program of studies through the ages has been Islamic law, theology, and the Arabic language. Other subjects have more recently been added, especially since the nineteenth century. Women have been admitted since 1962. The university has continued to attract Muslim students from as far afield as China and Indonesia. It is widely regarded as *the* chief center of Islamic learning in the world.

Islamic modernism has also been led from the African side of the Muslim world. Muhammad Abduh (1849–1905) is still widely acclaimed as the chief architect of the modernization and reform of Islam. Born in the Nile Delta, he was later influenced by the great pan-Islamic revolutionary Jamal al Din al-Afghani, who had settled in Cairo before being expelled for political activity in 1879. Abduh himself also suffered exile more than once. He lived to become the leading jurist of the Arab world, a professor at Al-Azhar University, and eventually *Mufti* of Egypt (chief Islamic chancellor). His doctrinal reforms included freedom of will in Islam, the harmony of reason with revelation, the primacy of ethics over ritual and dogma in religion, and the legitimacy of interest on loans under Islamic law.

A much more recent disciple of Abduh and al-Afghani was the Sudanese scholar, Mahmoud Muhammad Taha. Taha's own version of Islamic modernism in Sudan earned him a punishment more severe than what Abduh and al-Afghani suffered in nineteenth-century Egypt. Under the presidency of Jaafar el-Nimeiry in Sudan, Mahmoud Muhammad Taha was executed in his old age in January 1985 on charges of apostasy and heresy.[6]

Although this history of Islamic modernism includes personal tragedy as well as intellectual originality, there is no doubt about Africa's role in the reformation of Islam. Africa has often been the very vanguard of Islamic innovation and doctrinal review.

Africa's remarkable presence in the global Islamic equation includes the scale of the continent's membership in the Organization of the Islamic Conference (OIC). Almost half of the members of this global Islamic organization are also members of the Organization of African Unity. And Africa has produced some of the leaders of the OIC. The late Ahmed Sekou Toure of Guinea (Conakry) was chairman of the organization when he attempted to mediate between Iraq and Iran in the earlier phases of their war.

In distribution, Islam is indeed an Afro-Asian religion. Almost all Muslim countries are either in Africa or in Asia. In a television address to the American people in August 1998, President Bill Clinton estimated that Muslims were already a quarter of the world's population. The president's estimate was close.

The fastest rate of increase of the Muslim population of the world is currently in Africa. One reason is that Africa is undergoing the fastest rate of Islamic conversion of any major region on earth. Another is that natural fertility rates in Africa are higher than anywhere else—and Muslims in Africa are reproducing at a faster rate than most other Africans. As one study has demonstrated:

> The single most remarkable demographic aspect of Islamic societies is the nearly universal high level of fertility—the average of childbearing in Islamic nations is 6 children per woman. . . . Fertility rates are highest for those Islamic nations in sub-Saharan Africa—an average of 6.6 births per woman. Furthermore, African Islamic nations south of the Sahara have higher fertility on average than do other developing nations in that region.[7]

There is evidence not only that Muslim women are married significantly earlier than other women in developing countries, but also that Muslim women aspire to have more children.

Although Asia still has many more millions of Muslims than Africa, the demographic indicators show that the African continent is narrowing the gap dramatically. In the twenty-first century Africa may already have become the only continent in the world with an absolute Muslim majority. This second-largest continent on earth geographically may have become the first in terms of Muslim preponderance.

History is in the process of playing out a remarkable prophetic destiny. The first great Muezzin of Islam was a Black man—the great Bilal, son of Rabah of Ethiopian extraction. Today we might compare his great voice with that of Paul Robeson. Bilal called Muslim believers to prayer in seventh-century Arabia.

Symbolically, Bilal's Islamic call to prayer has echoed down the centuries. In the twentieth century has Bilal been heard particularly clearly in his ancestral continent of Africa? Perhaps the cultural boomerang effect has now taken the form of echoes of an African Muezzin reverberating back across the centuries. What of the echoes from that other great civilization in Africa's destiny—the Western heritage? Our case study here concerns the French version of the idea of "Eurafrica." Let us explore this area.

Eurafrica: The French Connection

France invented the concept of "Eurafrica"—asserting an organic relationship between Europe and Africa. How does this concept relate to the French language?

Although the majority of French-speaking people in the world are in the West—mainly in France itself—the majority of French-speaking *states* are in Africa. More than twenty members of the Organization of African Unity are French-speaking in the sense of having adopted French as an official language.

Without Africa the French language would be almost a provincial language. If Congo (Kinshasa) succeeds in stabilizing itself, and in assuming effective control over its resources, it may become France's rival in influence and power in French-speaking Africa as a whole.

Looking at the global scene overall, we find that the French language is shrinking in usage in the Northern Hemisphere. On the other hand, French is still spreading and gaining in influence in the Southern Hemisphere, especially in Africa. Let us consider each of these propositions in turn. Why is French declining in Europe and the North as a whole?

The most important challenge to the French language in the Northern Hemisphere has been the vast expansion of American influence in the twentieth century. The language has of course been English. Whereas the spread of the English language in Africa has been mainly due to the impact of imperial Britain, the spread of the English language in Europe, and its expanding role in international affairs, has been largely due to the new American hegemony in the Northern Hemisphere. The triumph of the English language globally has ranged from increasing usage in diplomacy to its preeminent role as the supreme language of aviation and air-traffic control.

A related reason for the shrinkage of French in the Northern Hemisphere concerns the computer revolution and the Internet. The amount of information circulating in English is so much greater than what is transmitted in French that English is gaining even further ascendancy. The old adage that "nothing succeeds like success" has now been computerized. The global influence of American computer firms like IBM and Microsoft has reinforced this Anglo computer revolution.

The third factor behind the decline of French in the Northern Hemisphere was Britain's entry into the European Economic Community, later known as the European Union. This made English more decisively one of the official languages of the community. The new language became increasingly influential in the affairs of the European Union, both written and oral. Smaller members of the Union have more frequently turned to English than to French in the post-Gaullist era of European affairs.

Turning to the Scandinavians, we find that they are greater linguists than average. Their schools are still sensitized to the importance of French and German as well as English. But linguistic priorities have indeed changed in the Nordic syllabi and curricula—and in class enrollments. The English language has definitely been the main beneficiary of the decline of German—whereas the French language has sustained a decline in educational emphasis.

Japan is also part of the Northern Hemisphere. It too has experienced shifts in emphasis that have demoted German and French—and raised the role of English in educational and linguistic priorities.

The United States' continuing special relationship with Japan after the postwar occupation consolidated Japan's cultural reorientation. The confirmation of the English language as Japan's first Western language in the postwar era has been part of this American phase of Japan's transformation. The decline of French and German languages in Japanese priorities was an inevitable consequence of the Americanization of Japan.

If these have been the main factors resulting in the decline of the French language in the Northern Hemisphere, which factors have contributed to its expansion in the South?

What must be emphasized in the first instance is that the Southern expansion has mainly occurred in Africa. On the whole the distribution of the French language is *bi-continental*—entailing a large number of French-speaking *individuals* in *Europe* and a large number of French-speaking *states* in *Africa*. Europe and Africa are by far the primary constituencies of the French language.

Factors favoring expansion in Africa have included the type of states that French and Belgian imperialism created during the colonial period. These were often multiethnic countries that needed a lingua franca. Colonial policy had chosen the French language as the lingua franca—and the entire educational system and domestic political process consolidated that linguistic choice.

A related factor was the assimilationist policy of France as an imperial power. This created an elite mesmerized by French culture and civilization. A surprising number of people retained dual citizenship with France even after independence. If President Bokassa was anything to go by, some African heads of state may secretly still be citizens of France. Annual holidays in France continue to be part of the elite culture of Francophone West and North Africa.

With some subsidies and technical assistance, the French language is also being increasingly featured in classrooms throughout Anglophone Africa. Before independence, British educational policymakers were more committed to the promotion of indigenous African languages than to the promotion of the rival French legacy in British colonies. Nor was there any welcome for French offers of language teachers for schools in British colonies.

The global French fraternity of Francophonie now has a Secretariat in Paris partly headed by an African: Boutros Boutros-Ghali. Membership of the Francophonie club now includes countries that have not adopted French as a national language but can be persuaded to teach more French in their schools.

The difference that Africa's independence has made partly consists in the greater readiness of Anglophone governments to accept France's offers of teachers of the French language. Many an African university in the Commonwealth has been the beneficiary of technical assistance and cultural subsidies from the local French Embassy or directly from France.

France's policy in Africa is consolidated partly through an aggressive cultural diplomacy. Considerable amounts of money are spent on French-style syllabi and curricula in African schools, and on the provision of French teachers, advisers, and reading materials. A residual French economic and administrative presence in most former French colonies has deepened Africa's orientation toward Paris.

In addition, every French president since Charles de Gaulle has attempted to cultivate special personal relations with at least some of the African leaders. There is little doubt that French-speaking African presidents have greater and more personalized access to the French president than their Anglophone counterparts have had to either the British prime minister or the British head of state, the queen, in spite of Commonwealth conferences.

Here again is a case of reciprocal conquest. There is little doubt that the French language and culture have conquered large parts of Africa. Many decisions about the future of Africa are being made by people deeply imbued with French values and perspectives.

Moreover, French is expanding its constituency in Africa, at least outside Algeria. It is true that the postcolonial policy of re-Arabization in Algeria is designed to increase the role of Arabic in schools and public affairs at the expense of the preeminent colonial role of the French language. The rise of Islamic militancy in Algeria may pose new problems to aspects of French culture. It is also true that the late Mobutu Sese Seko's policy of promoting regional languages in Zaire (Lingala,

Kikongo, Tchiluba, and Kiswahili) was partly at the expense of French in Zairean (now Congolese) curricula. Since 1994 French has also suffered a setback in Rwanda, led by Anglophone Tutsi originally educated in Uganda. But such setbacks for French in Africa are the exception rather than the rule. On the whole French is still on the ascendancy in Africa, though the pace of expansion has drastically declined.

However, when all is said and done, France's aspiration to remain a global power requires a cultural constituency as well as an economic one. It seems likely that the 1990s will continue to signify a change in France's *economic* priorities in favor of the new pan-European opportunities and against the older investments in Africa. But it seems equally certain that a more open Europe after the end of the Cold War will favor the English language at the expense of the French language, even within France itself. As custodian of the fortunes of French civilization, France could not afford to abandon the cultural constituency of Africa entirely in favor of the more open Europe. The collapse of the Soviet Empire has been a further gain for the English language. France may need Africa more *culturally*, but less *economically*.

Its cultural constituency in Europe has been declining; its cultural constituency in Africa becomes more valuable than ever. A remarkable interdependence has emerged—still imperfect and uneven, but real enough to make Africa indispensable for the recognition of France as a truly global power and the acceptance of the French language as a credible *world* language. "Eurafrica" as a concept gets its maximum meaningfulness in the destiny of the French language. But is there also a concept of "Afrindia" worth exploring? And how does this relate to the legacies of Gandhi and Nehru?

Afrindia: Between Gandhi and Nehru

Quite early in his life Mahatma Mohandas Gandhi saw nonviolent resistance as a method that would be well suited for the African as well as the Indian. In 1924 Gandhi said that if the Black people "caught the spirit of the Indian movement their progress must be rapid."[8]

In 1936 Gandhi went even further. And to understand his claim one should perhaps link it up with something that was later said by his disciple Jawaharlal Nehru: "Reading through history I think the agony of the African continent . . . has not been equaled anywhere."[9]

To the extent, then, that the Black man had more to be angry about than other men, he would need greater self-discipline than others to be "passive" in his resistance. But by the same token, to the extent that the Black man in the last three centuries had suffered more than any other, passive but purposeful self-sacrifice for the cause should come easier to him. And to the extent that the Black man had more to forgive the rest of the world for, that forgiveness, when it came, should be all the more weighty. Perhaps in response to adding up these considerations, Gandhi had concluded by 1936 that it was "maybe through the Negroes that the unadulterated message of non-violence will be delivered to the world."[10]

And so it was that in America the torch came to be passed to Martin Luther King, Jr. And in South Africa, where Gandhi first experimented with his methods, it passed to Albert Luthuli and, later, to Desmond Tutu. In Northern Rhodesia (Zambia after independence) Kenneth Kaunda became a vigorous Gandhian: "I reject absolutely violence in any of its forms as a solution to our problems."[11]

In the Gold Coast (Ghana before independence) Nkrumah had translated *satyagraha* (soul force) into a program of "Positive Action"—a program that he himself defined as "non-cooperation based on the principle of absolute non-violence, as used by Gandhi in India."[12] In 1949 the *Morning Telegraph* of Accra went so far as to call Nkrumah the "Gandhi of Ghana."[13]

African conceptions of dignity now seemed very different from what was implied by that old ceremonial affirmation of young Kikuyu initiates that Kenyatta once told us about—the glorification of the spear as "the symbol of our courageous and fighting spirit." But these new conceptions of dignity could now also be differentiated from the submissive virtues of early missionary teachings.

Yet one question remained to be answered: Could passive resistance survive the attainment of independence? Would Gandhism retain political relevance once its immediate objective of liberation from colonialism was achieved?

It is perhaps not entirely accidental that the two most important Indian contributions to African political thought were the doctrines of nonviolence and nonalignment. In a sense they were almost twin-doctrines. Gandhi contributed passive resistance to one school of African thought; Nehru contributed nonalignment to almost all African countries. We should note how Uganda's President Milton Obote put it in his tribute to Nehru after his death in 1964. Obote said: "Nehru will be remembered as a founder of nonalignment. . . . The new nations of the world owe him a debt of gratitude in this respect."[14]

However, Gandhi and Nehru both taught Africa and learned from it.

But how related are the two doctrines in their assumptions? For India itself Gandhi's *nonviolence* was a method of seeking freedom, whereas Nehru's *nonalignment* came to be a method of seeking peace. And yet nonalignment was, in some ways, a translation into foreign policy of some of the moral assumptions that underlay passive resistance in the domestic struggle for India's independence.

As independent India's first prime minister, Nehru called for an *armed* ejection of Portuguese colonialism from *Goa* in 1961—a move that had a different impact on Africa. India's Foreign Minister Khrishna Menon in the United Nations described colonialism as "permanent aggression." Particularly "permanent" was the colonialism of those who regarded their colonies as part of the metropole—as Portugal had pretended to do. In such a situation, when colonialism threatened to be more durable than "permanent," the military solution was a necessary option.

Nehru's use of armed force against the Portuguese set a grand precedent for an Africa still shackled by Portuguese imperialism in Angola, Mozambique, and Guinea-Bissau. Had Gandhi's *satyagraha* been replaced in 1961 by Nehru's *satya-Goa?* Was there a Hegelian negation of the negation? Was Nehru's negation of nonviolence a legitimation of the violence of liberation?

If Gandhi had taught Africa civil disobedience, had Nehru now taught Africa armed liberation? Had the armed ejection of Portugal from the Indian subcontinent strengthened Africa's resolve to eject Portugal from Angola, Mozambique, and Guinea-Bissau?

Africa's Reverse Impact on Gandhi and Nehru

What has seldom been adequately examined is the reverse flow of influence *from* Africa *into* both Gandhi's vision of *satyagraha* and Nehru's concept of *nonalignment.* Experience in the southern part of Africa must be counted as part of the genesis of Gandhi's political philosophy. And the 1956 Suez War in the northern part of Africa was probably a major influence on Nehru's vision of nonalignment.

South Africa was the *cradle* and threatened to be the *grave* of passive resistance as a strategy of Africa's liberation. Gandhi first confronted the problem of politicized evil in the context of racism in South Africa. He lived in South Africa from 1893 to 1914. Racial humiliation in that part of the continent helped to radicalize him—and therefore helped to prepare him for his more decisive historical role in British India from 1919 onward.

Gandhi's political philosophy developed from both the world of ideas and the world of experience. Moreover, in the realm of ideas he relied heavily on both Western liberalism and Indian thought. But what helped to radicalize Gandhi's own interpretation of those ideas was the power of experience. And within that crucible of experience we have to include Gandhi's exposure to sustained segregation in South Africa—a deeper form of racism than even the racist horrors of British India at that time.

If Gandhi's *satyagraha* was a response to the moral confrontation between good and evil, Nehru's nonalignment was a response to the militarized confrontation between capitalism and socialism. If Gandhi's political philosophy was originally a response to racial intolerance, Nehru's nonalignment was originally a response to ideological intolerance. The regime in South Africa became the symbol of racial bigotry for Gandhi. The Cold War between East and West became the essence of ideological bigotry for Nehru.

South Africa as an inspiration for Gandhi is well documented. North Africa as an inspiration for Nehru's nonalignment has been less explored.

Two wars in North Africa in the 1950s were particularly important to the Afro-Asian interaction. The Algerian war from 1954 to 1962 took African resistance beyond the passive level into the militarized active domain. African Gandhism was in crisis. Had *satyagraha* been rejected as no longer relevant for the struggle against colonialism?

The second great war in North Africa in the 1950s was the Suez conflict of 1956. If the Algerian war marked a possible end to *satyagraha* as a strategy for African liberation movements, the Suez war marked a possible *birth* of nonalignment as a policy of the postcolonial era. Gamal Abdel Nasser of Egypt was economically punished by the United States, Britain, and the World Bank for purchasing arms from the Communist bloc. Washington, London, and the Bank reneged on their commitment to help Egypt build the Aswan Dam. Nasser's nationalization of the Suez Canal was an assertion of self-reliance. Revenue from the canal was going to help Egypt construct the Great Dam. Egypt's sovereign right to purchase arms from either East or West was not for sale. In retrospect, Nasser's nationalization of the Suez Canal was a kind of unilateral declaration of nonalignment. This was before the nonaligned movement itself had been formally constituted.

Before the actual outbreak of the Suez hostilities, the diplomatic division at the level of the Big Powers was indeed East/West. Socialist governments were also neatly in support of Nasser, whereas the capitalist world was alarmed by his nationalization of the canal. However, when Britain, France, and Israel actually invaded Egypt, the Western world was divided. The United States was strongly opposed to the military action taken by its own closest allies, although Washington was also very hostile to Nasser.

The Soviet Union helped Egypt by providing pilots and engineers to operate the canal after the nationalization, until Nasser could train his own engineers. And in the wake of the West's reneging on the commitment to build the Aswan High Dam, the Soviet Union stepped into the breach—and became the builder of the dam.

Jawaharlal Nehru helped to mobilize Third World opinion on the side of Gamal Abdel Nasser during the whole crisis. Although there was not as yet a nonaligned movement in world politics, the Suez conflict was part of the labor pains of its birth—and Jawaharlal Nehru was the leading midwife in attendance.

It is these factors that have made the Suez crisis part of the genesis of Pandit Nehru's diplomatic thought and vision—just as racism in South

Africa remains part of the genesis of Mahatma Gandhi's principle of *satyagraha,* or soul force.

Suez was the most dramatic test of a Third World country—when invaded by two members of NATO (France and Britain). Never before had a Third World country been the subject of aggression by *two* members of NATO—and yet with the United States as the leader of NATO, protesting against its allies. Nehru was both a teacher over Suez and a learner from its experience.

Forty years later—in the mid-1990s—South Africa had its first multiracial election and Nelson Mandela became president. When the new Republic of South Africa joined the nonaligned movement, the heritage of Gandhi and the legacy of Nehru were at last fused on the very continent where they were once separately born. Morally, "Afrindia" was about to be vindicated.

South Africa is indeed the last testing ground. If India was the brightest jewel of the British crown, Africa is now the richest source of all jewels.

And five Black men influenced by Gandhi have won the Nobel Prize for Peace:

Ralph Bunche (1950)
Albert Luthuli (1960)
Martin Luther King, Jr. (1964)
Desmond Tutu (1984)
Nelson Mandela (1993)

Two were Black Americans and three Black South Africans. By a strange twist of fate, Mahatma Gandhi himself never won the Nobel Prize. His Black disciples did. Mandela's prize was shared by F. W. de Klerk, a former white adversary.

Africa's capacity to turn weakness into a form of influence has found a new arena of fulfillment. Fragmentation and excessive cultural receptivity are weaknesses. And weakness is not an adequate currency in the marketplace of power.

But quite often the power of the weak is, in human terms, less dangerous than the weakness of the powerful—their arrogance and all.

And yet, when all is said and done, the ultimate conquest is Africa's conquest of itself. The ultimate colonization is *self-colonization* under the banner of *Pax Africana.* It is to this ultimate *full circle* that we must now turn.

Toward an African Conquest of Itself

Is the process of Africa's decolonization *reversible?* As we approach the twenty-first century, the question has seriously arisen as to whether

Africa is creating conditions that will sooner or later result in some kind of *recolonization*. And who will be the new colonizer?

In the 1990s a thousand people a day were dying in the Angolan civil war from time to time. Somalia is torn between *chaos* and *clanocracy* (rule on the basis of clans). Burundi has a long history of brutal *ethnocracy* (rule by a particular ethnic group). Rwanda collapsed into genocide and civil war in 1994. Liberia and Sierra Leone had a tumultuous decade in the 1990s.

Is *recolonization* feasible? Indeed, could colonization itself be part of yet another cycle rather than a unilinear experience? Could colonialism have different *incarnations*—a kind of transmigration of the imperial soul?

The imperial soul had previously resided in separate European powers—Britain, France, Portugal, Belgium, and so on. Has the imperial soul transmigrated to the United States? Or is the soul trying to decide whether to settle in the bosom of the United States or to become part of the United Nations? Is this a period of cosmic imperial indecision between the United States and the United Nations as voices of "the world community"?

The next phase of colonialism can be *collective,* through individual powers. This phase may indeed entail the transmigration of the soul of the United Nations Trusteeship Council to some new UN decisionmaking machinery. Will Africa play a role both as guardian and as ward?

Although colonialism may be resurfacing, it is likely to look rather different this time around. A future trusteeship system will be more genuinely international and less Western than it was under the old guise. Administering powers for the trusteeship territories could come from Africa and Asia, as well as from the rest of the membership of the United Nations. For example, might Uganda be officially invited to the United Nations to administer a fragile Rwanda? Might Nigeria be officially invited to administer Sierra Leone for a while on behalf of the United Nations or on behalf of a reconstituted Organization of African Unity?

However, regional hegemonic power can lose influence as well as gain it. Just as there is *sub-colonization* of one African country by another, there can be sub-*de*colonization as the weaker country reasserts itself.

This is part of what has happened between Egypt and Sudan in the 1990s. Sudan, under the Bashir Islamic regime, started asserting an independence of Egypt that is greater than anything that has happened since the Mahdiyya movement under Seyyid Muhammad el Mahdi in the nineteenth century.

Relations between Somalia and Egypt in the era after Siad Barre may also be a case of *sub-decolonization*—the reassertion of the weaker country (Somalia) against the influence of its more powerful brother (Egypt). When Boutros-Ghali was UN secretary-general, his problems with

Muhammad Farah Aideed were perhaps part of the same story of sub-decolonization. Boutros-Ghali was seen more as an Egyptian than as the chief executive of the world body.

If *sub-colonization* of one African country by another is possible, and *sub-decolonization* has also been demonstrated, what about sub-*re*coloniza-tion? Will Egypt reestablish its Big Brother's relationship with Sudan and Somalia? Will there be another full circle? As the Arabs would affirm: *Al-lahu Aalam* (only God knows).

In West Africa the situation is especially complex. Nigeria is a giant of over 100 million people. Its real rival in the region was never Ghana un-der Kwame Nkrumah, or Libya under Muammar Qaddafi or distant South Africa. The real rival to postcolonial Nigeria has all along been France. By all measurements of size, resources, and population in West Africa, Nigeria should rapidly have become what India is in South Asia or South Africa has been in southern Africa—a hegemonic power. Nigeria was marginalized not only by civil war in 1967–1970 but also by its own chronic incompetence and by the massive French presence in West Africa, mainly in its own former colonies but also in Nigeria itself.

In the twenty-first century France will be withdrawing from West Africa as it gets increasingly involved in the affairs of Eastern and West-ern Europe. France's West African sphere of influence will in time be filled by Nigeria—a more natural hegemonic power in West Africa. It will be under those circumstances that Nigeria's own boundaries are eventu-ally likely to expand to incorporate the Republic of Niger (the Hausa link), the Republic of Benin (the Yoruba link), and, conceivably, Cameroon (part of which, at any rate, nearly became Nigerian in a refer-endum in 1959).

The case of postapartheid South Africa also raises questions about a re-gional hegemonic power. On the positive and optimistic side, this will make it possible to achieve regional integration in southern Africa. Re-gional unification is easier where one country is more equal than others—and can provide the leadership.

On the negative side, postapartheid South Africa could be a kind of sub-imperial power—and questions of sub-colonization, sub-decoloniza-tion, and sub-recolonization may become part of the future historical agenda of southern Africa. Another full circle.

If I have presented some frightening possibilities, it is because some African countries may need to be temporarily controlled by others. The umbrella of *Pax Africana* is needed—an African peace enforced by Africans themselves. Africa may have to conquer itself.

A thousand lives a day were indeed being lost in the civil war in An-gola at one time. If South Africa was already Black-ruled, South Africa could have intervened: Benevolent sub-colonization could have been attempted for the greater good. It would have been comparable to India's intervention in East Pakistan in 1971, when the Pakistani army was on the rampage against its own Bengali citizens. India intervened and created Bangladesh. But India had a vested interest in dividing Pakistan— whereas a postapartheid South Africa could intervene in a civil war in Angola for humanitarian and pan-African reasons, and still preserve the territorial integrity of its smaller neighbors. South Africa's intervention in Lesotho in 1998 was bungled and inept, but the basic principle of *Pax Africana* behind it was sound!

New possibilities are on the horizon. We may yet learn to distinguish between benevolent intervention and malignant invasion in the years ahead. Africa could conquer itself without colonizing itself.

Conclusion

I have sought to demonstrate in this chapter the paradox of counterpenetration and the cyclic boomerang effect in Africa's interaction with other civilizations. Africa's cultural responsiveness to its Arab conquerors has now tilted the demographic balance and changed the Arab cultural equation. The majority of the Arabs are now in Africa—and the African side of the Arab world has become the most innovative in art and science.

Africa's receptivity to Islam may make Africa the first truly Islamic continent. What Europe was to Christianity may turn out to be what Africa becomes to Islam—the first continent to have a preponderance of believers.

Africa's responsiveness to the French language and culture has already made Africa the second most important home of French civilization after France itself. The majority of "French-speaking" countries are already in Africa. And Congo (Kinshasa) stands a chance of one day becoming a rival to France in leading the French-speaking part of the world; indeed, it is in the process of closing the population gap and the resource gap with France.

Africa's response to Gandhian ideas, reinforced by Christian pacifism, has already given Africa more Nobel Prizes for peace than India. Gandhi himself had once predicted that the torch of *satyagraha* would one day be borne by the Black world. As I indicated, Mahatma Gandhi himself was never awarded the Nobel Prize.

The result of Africa's response to Nehru's ideas of nonalignment is that a majority of the nonaligned countries are now from Africa. Africa was in fact the first continent to become almost completely nonaligned. If nonalignment once penetrated Africa, Africa has now truly penetrated the nonaligned movement.

But in the future, Africa's *cultural receptivity* has to be more systematically moderated by *cultural selectivity*. Counterpenetrating one's conquerors may be a worthy trend. But at least as important for Africa is a reduced danger of being excessively penetrated by others.

Perhaps one day the sequence of cultural penetration will be reversed. Instead of Africans being Arabized so completely that the majority of Arabs are in Africa, some other *Asians* will be Africanized so completely that they are indistinguishable from native Africans. Instead of Zaire being the largest French-speaking nation after France, some other *European* nation will become the second heartland of Yoruba civilization after West Africa.

Meanwhile, Africa has to conquer itself, if it is to avoid further colonization by others. Africa needs to establish a *Pax Africana*—an African peace promoted and maintained by Africans themselves. One day each African person will look in the mirror—and behold the fusion of the guardian and the ward rolled into one. Amen.

Notes

1. See Muhammad Abdul-Hai, *Conflict and Identity: The Cultural Poetics of Contemporary Sudanese Poetry*, African Seminar Series No. 26 (Khartoum: Institute of African and Asian Studies, University of Khartoum, 1976), pp. 26–27.

2. al-Mahdi, *Nar al Majadhib* (Khartoum: Dar al-Jil and Shariakat al-Muktabah al-Ahliyah, 1969), pp. 195, 287. See also p. 24.

3. Cited by Abdul-Hai, *Conflict and Identity*, pp. 40–41.

4. Salah A. Ibrahim, *Ghadhbat al Hababy* (Beirut: Dar al Thaqafah, 1968). See also Abdul-Hai, *Conflict and Identity*, p. 52.

5. Dr. Boutros Boutros-Ghali, interviewed by Ali A. Mazrui in Cairo, 1985.

6. See Mahmud Muhammad Taha's book, *The Second Message of Islam* (Evanston, Ill.: Northwestern University Press, 1987).

7. John R. Weeks, "The Demography of Islamic Nations," *Population Bulletin* 43, no. 4 (December 1988), p. 15. (*Population Bulletin* is a publication of the Population Reference Bureau, Inc.)

8. This statement, made on August 21, 1924, is cited in Mahatma Gandhi, *Young Indian* (Madras: S. Ganesan, 1927), pp. 839–840. See also Pyarelal, "Gandhiji and the African Question," *Africa Quarterly* 2, no. 2 (July-September 1962). For a more extensive discussion by Gandhi on nonviolence, consult Mahatma Gandhi, *Non-Violence in Peace and War*, 2nd ed. (Ahmedabad: Navajivan Publishing House, 1944).

9. Jawaharlal Nehru, "Portuguese Colonialism: An Anachronism," *Africa Quarterly* 1, no. 3 (October-December 1961), p. 9. See also Jawaharlal Nehru, "Emergent Africa," *Africa Quarterly* 1, no. 1 (April-June 1961), pp. 7–9.

10. Mahatma Gandhi, *Harijan* (October 14, 1939). The present chapter is also indebted to Ali A. Mazrui, *The Africans: A Triple Heritage* (New York: Little, Brown/London: BBC Publications, 1986).

11. See Colin M. Morris and Kenneth D. Kaunda, *Black Government? A Discussion Between Colin Morris and Kenneth Kaunda* (Lusaka: United Society for Christian Literature, 1960).

12. Kwame Nkrumah, *Ghana: The Autobiography of Kwame Nkrumah* (New York: International Publishers, 1957), p. 112.

13. *Morning Telegraph*, June 27, 1949.

14. Quoted in *Uganda Argus*, May 29, 1964. See also Ali A. Mazrui, *Africa's International Relations: The Diplomacy of Dependency and Change* (London: Heinemann Educational Books/Boulder: Westview Press, 1977), pp. 117–121.

PART THREE

Conflict Management and the African State

6

Inter-African Negotiations and State Renewal

I. WILLIAM ZARTMAN

In inter-African relations, two's a conflict, three is company, and fifty-odd is a crowd of free riders. African negotiations over conflict and cooperation are a highly developed exercise, with their own characteristics and patterns, strengths and limitations. In dealing with conflict, bilateral negotiations and broad multilateral negotiation tend to be ineffective in producing outcomes; in between, mediation is frequently needed to bring negotiations among conflicting parties to fruition. In cooperation, multilateral negotiations have a high record of success, although the impact of the outcome has its own limitations and characteristics. This chapter presents the characteristics of that process as practiced in Africa, with examples, and seeks explanations for those characteristics.

In assessing these results and in analyzing the process by which they are achieved, we should remember that conflict is an inevitable—and sometimes functional or even desirable—condition of interstate relations and that negotiation is a means of limiting it, whereas cooperation—although desirable and sometimes functional—is by no means inevitable, and negotiation is the means of achieving it. As a result, the playing field has different slopes according to the subject, imparting different types of difficulties to the negotiation process. Across this distinction runs another, related to the size of the teams. At one end of the spectrum stand conflicts and cooperations that are highly personalized in the head of state, with little interest and involvement by society; at the other are conflicts and cooperations that are national causes, affecting society deeply and arousing deep popular sentiments, often making heads of state and other actors prisoners of larger dynamics.[1] This dichotomy has its impact on negotiations, although the distinction contains a large gray area between the two clear extremes. Personalist leaders speak in the name of their societies and mobilize societal interest behind their positions; yet states and societies do not negotiate—only people do.

Bilateral Conflict Negotiations

Direct bilateral negotiations are not an effective way of ending conflict in Africa. Nor are large-scale multilateral negotiations in regional or subregional organizations, although these organizations do play an important role in setting the norms and parameters for terminating conflicts—either by victory or by reconciliation. It is "trilateral" or mediated bilateral negotiations that are most effective.[2] These characteristics call for an explanation.

Four reasons suggest themselves. First, because of the engrossing nature of African conflicts and their often functional aspects, African states or leaders in conflict are so taken up with the unilateral pursuit of the dispute that they are unable to conceive of bi- or multilateral solutions on their own; they need help. Whether the conflict is a personal dispute between heads of state or the result of a societal feeling of personal right or neighboring hostility, it becomes an emotional and political cause of high importance, leaving little leeway for creative thinking about alternative solutions. In the conflict in central Africa in the late 1990s, the personal animosity between Zimbabwean and South Africa Presidents Robert Mugabe and Nelson Mandela, between Congolese and Ugandan Presidents Laurent Kabila and Yoweri Museveni, and between Kabila and Mandela intractably framed the dispute. This characteristic is reinforced by the absence of other elements that would serve to enlarge the space for the consideration of foreign policy issues: the small size of foreign policy establishments, the often impetuous nature of decisions, and the absence of a loyal opposition and of public political debate.

Second, until the 1990s, African conflicts were the occasion for a competitive race for allies, first within the continent and then outside. Bilateral conflicts generally did not remain bilateral but engaged factions within the continent and, later, European powers and superpowers. This characteristic prevented bilateral settlements but, paradoxically, facilitated mediation.[3] The search for allies can be turned into an invitation to mediation when the level of assistance sought finds a foreign policy opportunity in reconciliation rather than reinforcement. Since the end of the Cold War, the possibility of finding allies within the superpower competition has vanished and, with it, external interest in either restraining or mediating among the conflicting parties. With less interest and influence from external parties, African states tend to find themselves locked in their conflicts, unable to reach for a solution. Thus, the post–Cold War conflicts in the Horn, the center, and the west coast of Africa all remained primarily African conflicts without much outside control, but they escalated into competitions among African coalitions that were impervious to effective mediation. This may not be a durable feature; however, while it lasts, external disinterest in taking sides in a conflict will continue to be paralleled by a lowered interest and leverage in mediating.

Third, there is usually little incentive for African states to reduce, let alone resolve, their conflicts, just as there is little pressure to push them toward bilateral accommodation. Conflicts, as noted, are popular and useful, particularly when kept at a low, less costly level; they can then be revived at any time for purposes of national gain and national unity. Somalia's, Libya's, and Morocco's long irredentist claims on their neighbors are extreme cases in point, but so are the various other border disputes, structural rivalries, and recurrent involvements in neighboring politics that make up much of African conflict. For the parties involved, there is little to gain in making peace and much face to save in pursuing conflict.[4]

Finally, since few unmediated bilateral negotiations had any significant effect on their conflict, precedent gives little incentive to negotiate. A few examples are illustrative. The border dispute that has troubled relations between Morocco and Algeria since their independence was initially and occasionally the subject of direct negotiations.[5] As early as the first three years of the 1960s, the Moroccan kings met with the presidents of the Provisional Government of the Algerian Republic (GPRA) to discuss the problem between sovereign states, among others; when independence came to Algeria in 1962, the agreements to settle this problem were pushed aside since they were unwitnessed and considered nonbinding. Instead, war broke out and the dispute was taken up by the newly created Organization for African Unity (OAU). After further mediation, King Hassan II and President Ahmed Ben Bella met at Saidia in April 1965 and renewed the GPRA's commitment. Ben Bella was overthrown by his army three months later, with the Saidia agreement cited as one of the specific grievances.

Once again, the OAU provided the framework for a reconciliation between King Hassan and the new Algerian ruler, Colonel Houari Boumedienne, in 1968—leading to bilateral summits in the following two years and then to a final border treaty in the context of the OAU. The implementation of the Rabat border agreement of 1972 was interrupted by the eruption of the Western Saharan issue, which destroyed all chances of an effective bilateral negotiation. As the war moved beyond initial expectations of duration and toward an apparent stalemate and division of the territory, preparations began for a bilateral summit at the end of 1978. Boumedienne's death canceled these plans; Hassan expected the new president to be more flexible, whereas the new president, Colonel Chadli BenJedid, had to consolidate his own position before any of his purported flexibility could be shown.

It took another five years and a new stalemate more favorable to Morocco—with many intervening failed mediations—to produce a bilateral summit in February 1983. Despite high hopes and an agreement, the mutual understanding fell apart almost immediately, specifically because there was no third party present to "hold the bets" and witness the agreement. Instead, each party soon felt betrayed by the other. A second summit was held in May 1987 under the auspices of Saudi King Fahd, followed by multilateral summit meetings a year later in Algiers among the Arab heads of state and then in February 1989 in Marrakesh to inaugurate the regional Maghrib Arab Union (UMA). Whatever agreements emerged from these meetings have shown the necessity of witnesses and active mediation. The lesson from this lengthy conflict, still unended, is not that mediated and trilateral negotiations are ipso facto assured of success but, rather, that bilateral negotiation is ipso facto assured of failure. As in other cases, the presence of one or more third parties to midwife and witness an agreement is the necessary but not sufficient condition of success.

There are many other examples in the negative. Conflicts between Angola and Zaire, Somalia and Ethiopia, Sudan and Ethiopia, Eritrea and Ethiopia, Mali and Burkina Faso, and Senegal and Mauritania, among others, were not settled by their bilateral summits; when settlement or progress toward settlement was made, it was in meetings that included parties other than the principals. Even in internal wars, which in principle are particularly difficult to mediate, settlements when reached have been the result of third-party assistance, as in Angola in1990 and 1994, Liberia between 1991 and 1996, Ethiopia in 1991, Mozambique in 1992, Rwanda in 1993, Sierra Leone in 1996, Burundi in 1998, Lesotho in 1994 and 1998, and so on. As bilateral failure is so pervasive, it is pointless to look for other necessary ingredients; rather, one must turn to mediation to find out what else is necessary to make that condition sufficient.

Mediation

Africa does not lack mediators. Whether from a continental cultural tradition[6] or from a conscious interest in maintaining the African state system, African heads of state do more than stand ready to be of assistance—they rush forward in numbers, often competing to bring good and even better offices to the resolution of their colleagues' conflicts to the point where there is a confusion of marriage counselors trying to restore domestic tranquility in the African family. At least this profusion of mediators permits some conclusions on the characteristics of success—whether contextual, tactical, or personal.[7]

Mediators have their own interests in supporting their activities; African mediators have an overriding interest in preserving the African state system and, hence, in maintaining acceptance of the status quo. They therefore also have a framework within which to seek to place their mediated resolutions, reinforcing their efforts and facilitating acceptance of them.[8] But like any other mediators they have their own state interests as well—interests in maintaining or improving relations with the conflicting states, in ending a conflict that strains relations in their region, and, sometimes, in achieving a particular outcome.

African mediators tend to come from neighboring states, from within the same subregion if not from contiguous states; indeed, contiguous states often have enough of their own problems with their immediate neighbor to be disqualified or at least handicapped in mediation. There is a major exception: When the conflict is an internal dispute between a government and an insurgency in which a neighboring state serves as the insurgents' sanctuary, the neighbor can be a useful mediator if it "delivers" the agreement of the insurgents.[9] Mediators also tend to come from states of the same colonial background as the disputants when both of the conflicting parties are French- or English-speaking, illustrating the importance of both personal political ties and communications.

Mediation is a personal affair, conducted personally by African heads of state among other heads of state. It does not lend itself easily to practice by lesser officials—a point that is crucial to understanding the stillbirth in 1964 of the OAU Commission of Mediation, Arbitration and Conciliation, which mandated respected jurists and civil servants but not heads or former heads of state.[10] Even the respected Special Representative of the Secretaries-General (SRSG) of the OAU and the United Nations, Mohamed Sahnoun, allied himself with the president of Gabon in his mediations in Congo (Brazzaville) in 1993 and 1997.[11] Of the three roles available to the mediator—communicator, formulator, manipulator—African heads of state operate primarily in the first two, overcoming obstacles to communications between the conflicting parties and helping them find and formulate mutually acceptable ways out of their conflict.[12] Accordingly, an adjunct function of the personal mediator is to reduce the risks and mistrust that impede the parties' agreement to reconciliation. Since the conflict not only bears on the issue at hand but also colors the whole tone of relations between the disputants, they do not trust each other's word and do not know how much risk is involved in their agreement; the mediator is needed as the agent of trust and the assessor of risk.

The condition for effective mediation to begin is the mutually hurting stalemate, which makes it possible for the mediator to be welcome in his offer of a way out.[13] The stalemate makes the mediation possible; the mediator makes the stalemate fruitful. Without the mutually hurting stalemate, the parties have no interest in being saved from their conflict by meddling outsiders. The first war in southern Sudan was successfully ended following a stalemate in 1972 by layers of mediation, beginning with the World Council of Churches and the All-African Council of Churches, backed by OAU Assistant Secretary General Sahnoun, with Emperor Haile Selassie acting as mediator of last resort at a crucial juncture. When the Addis Ababa Agreement was dismantled ten years later by its author, President Jaafar Numeiri, and war broke out again, mediation became more difficult, first, because of the active support of the new Marxist government of Ethiopia behind the Sudan People's Liberation Army/Movement (SPLA/M) and then, after 1989, because the northern Sudanese government became intransigent when replaced by a Muslim fundamentalist military junta. The shift in fortunes blocked mediated resolution throughout the 1980s and 1990s, and turned the rebellion from a movement to reform the entire Sudanese political system into a secessionist movement. Many mediators tried to resolve the conflict but none succeeded; the stalemate never existed and the situation was not ripe.

The same judgment bears on the Eritrean conflict, which resisted repeated attempts at mediation throughout its thirty-year history, until Eritrea finally overthrew the Ethiopian government in 1991 and seceded. The USSR, East Germany, the Italian Communist Party, and President Jimmy Carter of the Carter Center at Emory University all tried their hands at mediating between the Eritrean rebels and the Ethiopian government between 1978 and 1989, but the conflict was never ripe.[14] After Eritrea then achieved independence, war broke out over the common border in mid-1998; the United States and Rwanda nearly succeeded in mediating an agreement, but subsequent attempts by the United States and by SRSG Sahnoun over the next twenty months were not able to close the gap. Although militarily stalemated, both sides still believed in victory and refused to see the cost. In the ongoing civil war in Chad, an interesting set of mediations was conducted by the current OAU presidents as well as by the presidents of Togo and Nigeria and, later, a large number of African heads of state—both during the period of General Felix Malloum in 1975–1979 leading to the establishment of the Transitional Government of National Unity (GUNT) under Goukouni Weddei in 1980 and after the final takeover in 1982 by Hissene Habre leading to the return of nearly all the former dissidents into the new government fold. Like the Eritreans, the Chadian rebels correctly saw no stalemate and then, after their victory, saw no gain in individual holdouts.[15] The mediation attempted by

Zairean President Mobutu Sese Seko in the Angolan civil war at Gbadolite and some lesser venues in 1989 suffered from the absence of a mutually hurting stalemate (which occurred a year later in the battle for Mavinga) and of a capable mediator (who appeared two years later in Portugal). It was further muddied by the attempts of Zambian and Zimbabwean Presidents Kenneth Kaunda and Robert Mugabe to save the situation later in the same year at Lusaka as the Gbadolite démarche was collapsing. But the agreements signed at Bicesse in 1991 under Portuguese mediation after the Mavinga stalemate collapsed in the ensuing elections the following year, and the more careful agreements mediated by the United States and the United Nations in l994 in Lusaka also broke down by 1998.

Particularly striking are the War of the Zairean Succession and its regional extensions, which began in 1996. In May 1997, as the Alliance of Democratic Forces for the Liberation of the Congo (ADFL), backed by Rwanda and Uganda, approached the gates of Kinshasa, South Africa, backed by the United States, tried to mediate a cease-fire and smooth transition from Mobutu Sese Seko to Laurent Kabila. The effort was particularly ill-conceived, since there was no stalemate and each of the parties was most reluctant to engage in negotiations with the other! A year later, in August 1998, many of the parties of ADFL, now alienated from Kabila, launched a new rebellion under the name of the Rally for a Democratic Congo (RDC) with the support of the same neighbors; Zimbabwe, Namibia, and Angola (and, to a lesser extent, Chad, Libya, and Sudan) rushed to save the Kabila government. The Southern African Development Community, which backed the intervention by the three member-states, also tried to mediate a cease-fire throughout the end of 1998 and early 1999, under the chairmanship of Zambian President Frederick Chiluba. But both sides clung to the expectation of victory, the mediating body clung to its partisan involvement, and the Congolese government refused to meet the rebels. The conflict was not ready for mediation and the war worsened, hurting but unstalemated, until a truce of fatigue was finally signed in Lusaka in July–September 1999. Stalemates determined which moments were ripe to begin the peacemaking, but the behavior of the parties following the negotiations can destroy the stalemate and the agreement.

The African mediator's primary weapon is persuasion, which reinforces the personal nature of the task and reflects the need for the perception of a mutually hurting stalemate. The mediator's main leverage lies in his ability to help his brothers out of the bind into which their conflict has led them. There are unfortunately not enough studies of the actual mediatory exchanges among heads of state to permit a detailed analysis of actual mediation behavior, but all available evidence indicates an exercise in pure persuasion.[16] Together, the cases indicate that, rarely, promises of side payments and, more frequently, threats to withdraw from mediation or support are used when available, but also that it is the unavailability of leverage, not any fraternal inhibitions on its use, that keeps inter-African mediation in the realm of persuasion.

Some cases have already been mentioned. The three successful moments of agreement between Algeria and Morocco—whatever the problems of renewed conflict brought by new events later on—were the result of mediation, either third party or institutional. The war of 1963 was ended through the good offices of Emperor Haile Selassie and Malian President Modibo Keita; the border treaty of 1972 was prepared by the mediation of Tunisian President Habib Bourguiba and then by the context of the OAU summit of 1968, when King Hassan made his first trip to Algiers; and the agreement to set aside the Saharan conflict, proceed with Maghrib unity without a Saharan participant, and resolve the dispute by a referendum on terms favorable to Morocco came out of the border summit of 1987 chaired by King Fahd.[17] The recurrent Mali-Burkinabe (Voltaic) border dispute was mediated, first, by an OAU ad hoc commission composed of French-speaking states of the region, bringing a cease-fire in July 1975; next, by a series of mediators from Libya and Algeria, who failed at the end of 1985; and, then, by mediators from Senegal and Ivory Coast within the framework of the French-speaking West African Economic Community (CEAO), who succeeded in January 1986.[18]

Mediators also abounded in the Horn of Africa, until conflict overtook the states themselves in the 1990s and defied all attempts to bring it under control. President Ibrahim Abboud of Sudan stepped into the 1963–1964 border war between Somalia and Ethiopia to bring about a cease-fire and other conflict management measures. President Julius Nyerere of Tanzania attempted the same in the "bandit" war between Somalia and Kenya the following year but was hindered by his approach and his own problems with Kenya; in 1967–1968 he was succeeded by President Kenneth Kaunda of Zambia, who was able to get the parties talking as a new stalemate weighed in on them. When the agreed-upon conflict management arrangements did not produce the next step of conflict resolution, Somalia invaded Ethiopia. No one was able to mediate, although the United States did successfully press the Soviet Union to guarantee that Ethiopia would not cross the border as it threw back the Somali invaders in 1978.[19] Eight years later, Somalia offered Ethiopia a new round of conflict management measures; the secretary-general of the Inter-Governmental Agency on Drought and Development (IGADD) and Djibouti, the IGADD host, served as mediators to bring the two heads of state together in January 1986 and finally, in April 1988, to win Ethiopian agreement to the proposals. Ironically, withdrawal of Ethiopian support and control of the Somali rebels left them free to overthrow their own government in

1990, at the same time as the Ethiopian government fell to its own ethnic rebellions. Many mediators—Egypt, Ethiopia, the SRSG of the United Nations, and the United States, among others—have tried throughout the 1990s to mediate the ensuing conflict in the collapsed state of Somalia, but to no avail.

In internal conflicts—increasingly the predominant type of African conflict—the key to effective mediation seems to be the mediator's ability to guarantee fair treatment and a share in the new political system for all parties, rather than any tangible side payments. In Liberia, first the Liberian Council of Churches and then fellow members of the Economic Community of West African States (ECOWAS) tried again and again between 1990 and 1996 to mediate a cease-fire that would last between the factions; agreements were finally reached in August of 1995 and 1996 when the mediation was taken over by Nigerian dictator General Sani Abacha, whose military contingents made up the bulk of the Economic Community Monitoring Group (ECOMOG).[20] The Abuja agreements finally gave the remaining combatants a stake in the outcome, ending in the election of Charles Taylor as president in July 1997. Another three-year civil war, in Rwanda, was temporarily brought to a mediated agreement in August 1993 at Arusha under the auspices of the OAU and Tanzania, made possible by the introduction of a UN peacekeeping force; the Arusha agreement was then destroyed in the 1994 genocide by Coalition for the Defense of the Republic (CDR) extremists excluded from Arusha.[21]

There are a few exceptions to the pure persuasion characteristic, but none of these are very clear, given the nature of the subject. King Fahd, host of the 1987 summit between King Hassan and President BenJedid, was operating as Morocco's past funding source and Algeria's potential funding source of the future, whether specific financial arrangements were mentioned or not.[22] When the World Council of Churches moved the government of Sudan and the Southern Sudanese Liberation Movement (SSLM) toward Addis Ababa, where an agreement to end the war was eventually signed in 1972, it threatened on occasion to withdraw from mediation and resume humanitarian supplies to the SSLM if its efforts were rejected.[23] After a complex stalemate, President Samora Machel of Mozambique, who served as one of the several mediators in the Lancaster House negotiations in 1979 leading to Zimbabwean independence, threatened to close down the Patriotic Front's bases in Mozambique if its leader, Robert Mugabe, did not go along with the settlement being negotiated.[24] Similarly, the Frontline States, particularly Angola, threatened the SouthWest African People's Organization (SWAPO) with loss of support and sanctuary if it did not stay in the Namibian negotiations.[25] Following a gradual stalemate reinforced by a drought, the October 1992 Mozambican peace settlement negotiated in Rome by the Sant'Egidio Community in the presence of a number of interested states contained a provision of $15 million for the Mozambican National Resistance (RENAMO) to facilitate its transformation from a guerrilla to a political organization.[26] There may be other examples as well.

In general, failed attempts at mediation did not benefit from the conditions and tactics that caused success—effective perception of stalemate on the part of all parties, skillful persuasion by the mediator, and a convincing formula for a way out minimally satisfactory to all. At best, one is able to conclude that the mediator can pull an agreement on a salient solution out of a propitious context—that is, accomplish a negotiation that over-commitment to the conflict prevents the parties from doing by themselves—but he cannot create a ripe moment and a winning solution out of thin air, among peers in Africa anymore than anywhere else.

Multilateral Conflict Negotiation

The OAU has been the major multilateral African forum for the conduct of negotiations to deal with conflict,[27] although it has increasingly shared its role with subregional organizations, the most active of which are the Intergovernmental Authority on Development (IGAD) in the Horn of Africa; the Economic Community of West African States (ECOWAS); the French-speaking West African Economic Community (CEAO), which became the Economic and Monetary Union of West African States (UEMOA) in 1994; and the Southern African Development Community (SADC). Most of these subregional organizations were not created for conflict reduction at all but, rather, provided a ready forum where heads of state could meet primarily for economic reasons and work out differences in the corridors; conflict reduction became a necessary precondition for carrying out their other, primary business. Two different types of multilateral negotiation need to be distinguished: One is the activity of ad hoc multilateral committees established to deal with specific conflicts, whereas the other is the business of the plenary of summit meetings of the multilateral organizations themselves.

There is no need to spend time on the major African committee envisaged to reduce conflict among African states: the Commission for Mediation, Arbitration and Conciliation. Created by the OAU Charter, it never came into existence, since it conflicted with the rapidly established characteristic of inter-African relations as the domain of heads of state. Instead, the OAU appointed ad hoc committees to deal with conflicts as they arose on the summit agenda, with membership carefully allocated to language, ideological, regional, experience, and other interest groups. Their record was not good—given successful outcomes in only one out of three cases in some two dozen instances in the first two decades of the organization.[28] In addition, many of the successes were only temporary, with conflict breaking out in another form later on (and requiring a new committee). After the mid-1980s, however, ad hoc commitees were rarely used by the OAU. Very often conditions were not propitious, and, more frequently still, the purposes of the mother organization were other than conflict resolution (as discussed below); these purposes therefore overrode the efforts of the committees. In a few other cases, conflict management—the reduction of the means (often leading to a reduction of the ends) of conflict—was the outcome of committee efforts rather than of the settlement of basic issues. Unfortunately, it is impossible to calculate a similar batting average reflecting the incalculable private efforts at mediation, to see whether OAU committees did better than individual heads of state.

Committee mediation has been a more important function of the OAU than its record might indicate, however. It has overcome one major defect of private mediation, in that it has provided coordination where private mediators often competed among themselves. This competition has then allowed the parties to the conflict to sit by and wait—or even actively campaign—for better terms to come along in the hands of other private mediators. In OAU committees, many of the members have been passive, overlooking and legitimizing the activities of the few members who actively perform the mediation. Furthermore, OAU committees have been constrained by the guidelines of the organization and its summits; they cannot seek just any terms for agreement, yet they are at the same time the standard-bearers of OAU principles. That dual role has sometimes made it impossible to find terms of agreement to which both sides could subscribe. It is difficult to fault either the OAU committees or the private mediators in such conflicts as the Somali-Ethiopian dispute or the Western Sahara; the two contestants' positions were simply irreconcilable, and resolution had to await a change in the cost of holding out for one or both that would lead them to soften their positions.

Thus, an OAU committee was named to mediate the Somali-Ethiopian border problem at the 1973 summit, and when it failed another was named at the 1976 summit. As they operated under the 1964 OAU resolution affirming the sanctity of colonial boundaries, they had little leeway in which to meet Somalia's grievances; instead, they reaffirmed the principle. But an OAU committee extracted a promise (false, as it turned out) from Ghana not to practice subversion against the Ivory Coast, Upper Volta, and Niger in 1965, in accordance with OAU Charter principles; and another intervened to free Guineans held in Ghana on the way to the OAU summit in the following year. In such cases, OAU committees, acting within charter principles, made it possible for transgressing states to return to behavioral norms without loss of face, a task for which multi-membered OAU committees were even better suited than private mediators. Since the establishment of the Mechanism for the Prevention, Management and Resolution of Conflicts within the OAU in 1993, the Special Representative of the Secretary-General (SRSG) has come into use, replacing the committees.

In these situations, risk, trust, persuasion, and stalemate are the ingredients of success. The actual negotiations are accomplished by skillfully luring the erring party back from the limb on which he has crawled, while the mediator gives assurances on risk and trust and provides an atmosphere of unity and fraternity that prevents the other party from crowing. Since the conflicting parties usually have no dispute with the mediator, it becomes difficult for them to refuse his assurances and reject his atmospherics.

The OAU itself, in its biennial ministerial and annual presidential meetings, is not a conflict resolution mechanism. It provides corridors and committees that operate as described, and principles that provide the guidelines for solutions. But a body of more than fifty members is not a mechanism for resolving disputes. If it does come to the point of decreeing a solution, either the conflict on the ground has changed or a lot of negotiation has taken place beforehand to make that solution acceptable. Otherwise, the conflict goes on. This has been the fate of the major conflicts that have torn the OAU apart—namely, the second (1964) Congo crisis, Biafra, the dialogue with South Africa, Sahara, Chad, Angola, Rwanda, Burundi, and the fourth (1998–1999) Congo crisis.

Yet in the OAU's handling of each of these conflicts, there has been some important and even skillful negotiation. A prime example that shows the possibilities of negotiation within the organization versus the political stance of its summits is the Western Sahara. The OAU revived the 1964–1967 committee to investigate the causes of the Saharan war as a committee of Wisemen to resolve the Western Saharan issue in 1978. This committee was diligent and creative in trying to bridge the positions of Algeria and Morocco. Then, at the 1981 summit, under pressure from an impending recognition of the Sahrawi Arab Democratic Republic (SADR), Morocco agreed to a referendum and the Wisemen were transformed into an Implementation Committee of the OAU. It met three times and, through painstaking negotiation with the parties, established guidelines for a referendum that were essentially still in place as the parties moved toward a vote under UN auspices a decade later, while at the same time holding back the efforts of various parties at various times to undo previous aspects of the evolving agreement. However, at the close of the third meeting ("Nairobi III") in February 1982, the OAU Council of Ministers disavowed its committee by admitting the SADR to membership, and, curiously, the heads of state on the committee lacked the commitment to put their decisions into effect nonetheless.

Other cases of OAU negotiations show similar characteristics. The work of the non-OAU committee on Chad that met in Kano and Lagos in 1979, and set up the GUNT, was followed by an OAU committee on Chad and then by the 1981 summit in Nairobi; intense negotiations produced a plan for a multinational peacekeeping force and a timetable for negotiations between the Chadian factions, elections, and the withdrawal of the African troops. Yet for all its coherence, the plan was unrealistic: Funding, mission, sanctions, and contingency plans were not provided.[29] Some skillful negotiations bringing the conflicting parties close to agreement were undercut by the lack of political commitment within the OAU to carry the project to fruition.

Thus the OAU summit—as distinguished from its committees—plays a number of roles in regard to conflict negotiations. It sets principles, appoints committees, and provides a forum and corridors; however, because of its own political divisions and the fear of offending other heads of state, it has been unable to take forthright positions of reconciliation in African disputes. The 1989 summit assiduously avoided the bitter dispute between Senegal and Mauritania; earlier summits were unable to follow through in their own conflict management and resolution mechanisms in the Saharan and Chadian conflicts.

Under the pressure of criticism for its inability to rid Africa of its recurrent and intermittent conflicts, particularly as expressed in the articulate and visionary call for a Conference on Security, Stability, Development and Cooperation in Africa (CSSDCA) launched by former Nigerian President Olusegun Obasanjo in Kampala in May 1991, the OAU voted in its 1993 summit to create a new division of the secretariat on conflict prevention, management, and resolution.[30] The Kampala Document also called for the constitution of a Council of Elders, former heads of state who could serve as mediators and peacemakers; former Presidents Leopold Senghor of Senegal, Julius Nyerere of Tanzania, Aristide Pereira of Cape Verde, and Obasanjo volunteered their services, but the OAU did not adopt the proposal, preferring its own ad hoc elders. The organization also undertook a more proactive role in preventive as well as resolving mediation, eliciting invitations to provide good-office missions in Togo, Congo (Brazzaville), Congo (Zaire), Rwanda, and Liberia, both to forestall and to end violence. In so doing, the African universal organization took a major step toward formalizing its personal and ad hoc efforts to reduce conflict and facilitate negotiation among—and within—its member-states.

Negotiation for Cooperation

Negotiation means overcoming conflict with agreement, but many negotiations lead to agreement on new cooperation rather than simply termination of old conflict. All the regional and subregional organizations in Africa, including the OAU itself, were established through negotiation, and a major multilateral set of cooperation agreements of the postwar world—the Yaounde series and then the Lomé series between the European Communities (EC) and the African and other states[31]—also involved repeated negotiations within the African side. As in conflict negotiations, there is little that is uniquely or specifically African in these experiences; but at the same time it is clear that African statesmen are negotiating, and are developing a broad experience that, when successful, underscores some important universal lessons and characteristics of the process.

In African multilateral negotiations for cooperation, as in multilateral negotiations over conflict, the political purposes of the negotiating session override the technical commitments of the negotiated outcome. Indeed, cooperative negotiations can be divided into diplomatic and integrative cooperation; in the former, it is the declaration of the moment, attendance at the meeting, and announcement of joining or not joining that matters, whereas in the latter, it is the long-term engagement that is important. In the first case, the substance of the negotiations is needed as an occasion or a cover for the diplomatic event of the moment, but its coherence, feasibility, and reality are less important. In the second, the substance is the event and parties do not leave the table before they have agreed to something that will work.

In 1968, for example, Zaire negotiated an Economic Union of Central Africa (UEAC) to win the Central African Republic (CAR) and Chad away from the Customs Union of the Central African States (UDEAC) of former French Equatorial Africa, including the rival state of Congo.[32] The goal was a diplomatic event in which the important matter was to see who would attend "Mobutu's party"; the substance of the Economic "Union" was secondary, and the negotiations did not waste time over its details. The CAR soon left UEAC to return to UDEAC, leaving the remaining members not even contiguous. Although this example is particularly striking, it is typical of a large number of cooperative negotiations and is present as a consideration even in those cases where integrative cooperation is also present. The supposedly biennial summit meetings of the Maghrib Arab Union (UMA), the regional organization of North Africa, provide an example from the 1990s.[33]

In the substance of cooperation, the technical expertise often comes from outside, since African states' technical resources are sometimes limited. The Mano River Union of Liberia, Sierra Leone, and Guinea was based on a 1972–1973 United Nations Development Program (UNDP) mission report, and the subregional economic organizations—ECOWAS, the Preferential Tariff Area (PTA) of East and Southern Africa (which in

1997 became the Common Market for East and Southern Africa [COMESA]), and the Economic Union of the States of Central Africa (CEEAC)—were based on studies of the Economic Commission for Africa (ECA).[34] The fact that the Mano River Union as well as CEAO conflicted with provisions of ECOWAS, which had been negotiated with the same members and others at about the same time, was an instance of political decision bypassing the technical engagements. In the case of African negotiations with the EC, the external source of expertise has particularly difficult implications for Africa. European states are able to coordinate their political and technical diplomacy into an agreed proposal for aid and other aspects of their relationship with associated African states under the Yaounde conventions and with the African, Caribbean, and Pacific (ACP) states under the subsequent Lomé conventions—a proposal that can be presented as a take-it-or-leave-it offer.[35] Only in 1975, in the negotiation of the first Lomé convention, did the African states develop enough solidarity among themselves under the political clout of Nigerian leadership and coordinate their own technical and political inputs to be able to make their own proposals as a basis for discussion and finally for agreement.[36]

At the same time, when the two inputs operate together, they play a crucial role in African negotiations for cooperation, and the fact that some states effectively integrate political and technical components of their diplomacy while others do not gives the former a clear edge in specific negotiations. A country that provides a proposed text has a clear edge over the others, and African cooperative negotiations frequently proceed on the basis of a single negotiating text. The examples represented by the Lomé I negotiations and the external proposals for subregional economic communities are echoed on the intra-African level by a case such as the Maghrib Arab Union negotiated at Marrakech in 1989. Morocco and Algeria had minimalist and diplomatic notions of cooperation, and Libya and Mauritania were less precise in their expectations. But Tunisia came with a well-prepared draft that served as the basis of the agreement. (At an earlier time of bilateral cooperation, it was Libya that came to Jerba with a political draft for a union in 1974—a draft that Tunisia signed but then repudiated on closer examination.)[37] The same characteristic marked the negotiation of the OAU itself in Addis Ababa in 1963, when Ethiopia proposed its own draft, elaborated by experts on the basis of the Rio Treaty of the Organization of American States in conjunction with the Monrovia-Lagos Group of African states; in this case, the similar Ethiopia and Monrovia-Lagos texts were confronted by a very different draft for a tighter union proposed by the Casablanca Group of African states. Specifically, the latter draft offered an alternative that could be rejected as individual provisions were selected.[38]

Once the single negotiating text is in hand, African multilateral diplomacy generally proceeds, in a classical fashion, by amendment and consolidation. Amendment involves the addition of proposals not contained in the main draft. An example is Tunisia's detailed proposal for the Commission for Mediation, Arbitration and Conciliation added to the OAU Charter at Addis Ababa. The degree to which additional proposals are integrated into the main proposal is an indicator of the primacy of integration over the simple diplomatic cooperation involved in negotiations. Consolidation is often more characteristic, referring to a watering down of proposals to the lowest common denominator in order to achieve the necessary consensus. Since consensus rather than coherence is required for diplomatic cooperation, consolidation by watering down is a frequent characteristic. It is also a common feature in the negotiation of OAU resolutions.

In multilateral cooperative negotiations, African state representatives behave as other negotiating parties do, but with some characteristics exhibited more strongly than others. The main emphasis in this analysis has been on the distinction between diplomatic and integrative cooperation, and the history of resulting regional and subregional organizations of cooperation bear out the point. Yet such organizations do exist, even if inefficacy is often the price paid for their continued existence. More strikingly, when they die, they have to be reinvented, as the experience of north, west, east, central, and southern Africa all show. Their creation, maintenance, and reinvention all take negotiation, whether of the diplomatic or the integrative kind.

Conclusions

African states are becoming increasingly experienced in negotiation, and their negotiating often errs in the direction of overaccommodation rather than overintransigence. They know how to make a deal, more than they know how to keep one. Negotiations are more successful in dampening or managing the current rounds of conflict, or in providing frameworks for the current rounds of cooperation, than in devising lasting resolutions or durable integration. Even that, however, is no mean achievement, for it not only provides limits to conflict and experience in cooperation but also reinforces the nature and rules of the ongoing African system of international relations.

Such behavior may be pervasive because it finds its roots in cultural traditions, which in turn are perhaps more accurately described as exaggerated cultural determinism. The tradition of blood money in some areas and the absence of a negotiating tradition at all in others may be just as characteristic. More important has been the role that negotiation has played in achieving independence.[39] All formerly colonial African states (with the possible exception of Guinea Bissau) achieved independence through some degree of negotiation, in most cases after only minimal violence; and in those cases where violent struggle was prolonged, such as Algeria, Zimbabwe, Namibia, Angola, and Mozambique, negotiation was all the more important. Such experience and conditioning have been crucial to the establishment of contemporary political cultures and behaviors. In that sense, Africa can be said to have a culture of negotiation, as contrasted, for example, with the culture of violence that some observers have described as increasing within Latin American countries.

Africa's culture of negotiation faces important challenges well into the future. It promises a degree of hope for overcoming the major conflict over sociopolitical integration in South Africa, where the experiences of neighboring states contributed to counterbalancing the absence of a negotiating tradition within South Africa itself. In a situation that by many counts is prerevolutionary, the specter of bloodbath for both sides brought a change from a winning to a conciliating mentality at the beginning of the 1990s and opened up the long process of negotiating a new constitutional regime in South Africa. The negotiated solution is a major achievement in the avoidance of violence and the peaceful achievement of African goals.[40] Colonial training in negotiation is also absent in the Horn of Africa, where a negotiated solution to the problems of empire, in connection with Ethiopia, Somalia, Eritrea, and Sudan, also poses a challenge to African practices of peaceful change. Limited negotiations that have taken place in the conflicts of the Horn, with some results for conflict management if not for full resolution, give way to continuing and renewed conflict.

Because the challenge is ongoing, it is more important than ever to end with the traditional call for more research. So little has been done regarding the actual practice of negotiation in Africa (as noted at several points above), and yet the field of examples is rich. The challenge of finding out "who said what to whom with what effect," so necessary to a deep understanding of negotiating behavior, is probably no greater in Africa than elsewhere and may actually be lessened by the value given to the practice. The few studies that do exist have shown that the challenge can be overcome. Ultimately, a better grasp of the African process will expand an understanding of the methods and potentialities of that process, and reinforce the culture of negotiation itself.

Notes

1. On state-society relations, see Jean-François Bayard, *L'État en Afrique* (Paris: Fayard, 1989); Donald Rothchild and Naomi Chazan (eds.), *The Precarious Balance*

(Boulder: Westview Press, 1989); Jean-François Bayard, Stephen Ellis, and Beatrice Hibou, *Criminalization of the State* (Bloomington: Indiana University Press, 1997); and Christopher Clapham, *Africa and the International System* (New York: Cambridge University Press, 1996), esp. Part I.

2. See I. William Zartman, "Conflict Prevention, Management and Resolution," in Francis Deng and I. William Zartman (eds.), *Conflict Resolution in Africa* (Washington, D.C.: Brookings Institution, 1991).

3. On Cold War efforts to limit African conflicts, see the chapters by I. William Zartman, Crawford Young, and Daniel Kempton on the Horn and on North, central, and southern Africa, respectively, in Roger Kanet and Edward Kolodziej (eds.), *The Cold War as Cooperation* (New York: Macmillan, 1991).

4. For a discussion on the causes of African conflict, see I. William Zartman, *Ripe for Resolution: Conflict and Intervention in Africa*, 2nd ed. (New York: Oxford University Press, 1989), ch. 1. On the Somali and Moroccan irredenta, see Zartman, *Ripe for Resolution*, chs. 2 and 3. On Libya, see René Lemarchand (ed.), *The Green and the Black* (Bloomington: Indiana University Press, 1988). And on the stability of the status quo over settlement outcomes in the Western Saharan conflict, see Khadija Mohsen-Finan, *Sahara occidental: Les enjeux d'un conflit régional* (Paris: CNRS, 1997).

5. On the Moroccan-Algerian case, see Zartman, *Ripe for Resolution*, ch. 2; Nicole Grimaud, *La politique extérieure de l'Algérie* (Paris: Karthala, 1984); John Damis, *Conflict in Northwest Africa* (Stanford: Hoover, 1983); and Khadidja Mohsen, *Le Sahara occidental: Les enjeux d'un conflit régional* (Paris: CNRS, 1987).

6. See Robert G. Armstrong et al., *Socio-Political Aspects of the Palaver in Some African Countries* (Paris: UNESCO, 1979); and Sally Engle Merry, "Mediation in Non-Industrial Societies," in Kenneth Kressel and Dean G. Pruitt (eds.), *Mediation Research* (San Francisco: Jossey-Bass, 1989). But cf. Laura Nader and Harry Todd (eds.), *The Disputing Process: Law in Ten Societies* (New York: Columbia University Press, 1978), where the argument is made that mediation appears only in non-African cases; and I. William Zartman (ed.), *African Traditional Conflict "Medicine"* (Boulder: Lynne Rienner Publishers, 1999). For divergent African attitudes toward negotiation and conflict management, see the sections on conflict resolution in Zartman, *Ripe for Resolution*, chs. 2–5.

7. For some recent studies of mediation, including African applications, see Kressel and Pruitt (eds.), *Mediation Research*; Saadia Touval and I. William Zartman (eds.), *International Mediation in Theory and Practice* (Boulder: Westview Press, 1985); Christopher Mitchell and Keith Webb (eds.), *New Approaches to International Mediation* (Westport, Conn.: Greenwood, 1988); Jacob Bercovitch and Jeffrey Rubin (eds.), *Mediation in International Relations* (New York: St. Martin's, 1992); Jacob Bercovitch (ed.), *Resolving International Conflicts* (Boulder: Lynne Rienner Publishers, 1996); Marieke Kleiboer, *International Mediation* (Boulder: Lynne Rienner Publishers, 1997); Stephen John Stedman, "Negotiation and Mediation in Internal Conflict," in Michael Brown (ed.), *The International Dimensions of Internal Conflict* (Cambridge, Mass.: MIT Press, 1996); I. William Zartman (ed.), *Elusive Peace: Negotiating to End Civil War* (Washington, D.C.: Brookings Institution, 1995); and Jacob Bercovitch, "Mediation in International Conflict," in I. William Zartman and Lewis Rasmussen (eds.), *Peacemaking in International Conflict* (Washington, D.C.: U.S. Institute of Peace, 1997).

8. See I. William Zartman, "Africa as a Subordinate State System," *International Organization* 11, no. 3 (1967): 545–564; Yassin el-Ayouty and I. William Zartman (eds.), *The OAU After Twenty Years* (New York: Praeger, 1984), esp. chs. 2 and 7.

9. I. William Zartman, "Internationalization of Communal Strife: Temptations and Opportunities of Triangulation," in Manus Midlarsky (ed.), *Internationalization of Communal Strife* (New York: Routledge, 1993).

10. C.O.C. Amate, *Inside the OAU* (New York: St. Martin's, 1986), ch. 5.

11. I. William Zartman, "Prevention Gained, Prevention Lost: Collapse, Competition and Coup in Congo," in Bruce Jentleson (ed.), *Opportunities Missed, Opportunities Taken* (New York: Rowman and Littlefield, 1999).

12. On the three roles, see I. William Zartman and Saadia Touval, "International Mediation in the Post–Cold War Era," in Chester Crocker, Fen Hampson, and Pamela Aall (eds.), *Managing Global Chaos* (Washington, D.C.: U.S. Institute of Peace, 1996).

13. I. William Zartman, *Ripe for Resolution*, ch. 6.

14. As shown by Marina Ottaway, "Eritrean and Ethiopia: A Transitional Conflict," in I. William Zartman (ed.), *Elusive Peace*, pp. 112–118.

15. I. William Zartman, "Conflict in Chad," in Arthur Day and Michael Doyle (eds.), *Escalation and Intervention* (Boulder: Westview Press, 1986).

16. For two exceptional accounts, see John Stremlau, *The International Politics of the Nigerian Civil War* (Princeton: Princeton University Press, 1977), chs. 6 and 7; and Saadia Touval, *The Boundary Politics of Independent Africa* (Cambridge, Mass.: Harvard University Press, 1972), ch. 9.

17. Zartman, *Ripe for Resolution*, ch. 2.

18. Jean-Emmanuel Pondi, "The Burkinabe-Malian Border War," in I. William Zartman and Jeffrey Z Rubin (eds.), *Power and International Negotiation* (Ann Arbor: University of Michigan Press, 1999).

19. Zartman, *Ripe for Resolution*, ch. 3.

20. Jeremy Armon and Andy Carl, *The Liberian Peace Process 1990–1996* (London: Conciliation Resources, 1996).

21. Gerard Prunier, *The Rwanda Crisis* (New York: Columbia University Press, 1995); Howard Adelman and Astride Suhrke, *The Rwandan Genocide* (New Brunswick, N.J.: Transaction, 1999).

22. Zartman, *Ripe for Resolution*, p. 68.

23. Hizkias Assefa, *Mediation of Civil Wars* (Boulder: Westview Press, 1987), pp. 128ff.

24. Jeffrey Davidow, *A Peace in Southern Africa* (Boulder: Westview, 1984); Stephen John Stedman, *Peacemaking in Civil War* (Boulder: Lynne Rienner Publishers, 1988). I am grateful to Robert Lloyd for bringing this case to my attention.

25. Zartman, *Ripe for Resolution*, ch. 5.

26. Chris Alden, "The UN and the Resolution of Conflict in Mozambique, *Journal of Modern Africa Studies* 33, no. 1 (1995): 103–128 at 105, 114.

27. On the evolving role of the OAU in general, see Yassin El-Ayouty (ed.), *The OAU After Ten Years* (New York: Praeger, 1975); Michael Wolfers, *Politics in the Organization of African Unity* (New York: Barnes and Noble, 1976); El-Ayouty and Zartman (eds.), *The OAU After Twenty Years;* Yassin El-Ayouty (ed.), *The OAU After Twenty-Five Years* (New York: Greenwood, 1990); R. A. Akindele, "The Organi-

sation of African Unity 1963–1988," *Nigerian Journal of International Affairs* 14, no. 1 (special issue, 1988); Maurice Kamto, Jean-Emmanuel Pondi, and Laurent Zang, *L'OUA: Rétrospective et perspectives africaines* (Paris: Economica, 1990); I. William Zartman, "Mediation in Africa: The OAU in Chad and Congo-B," in Jacob Bercovitch (ed.), *Studies in International Mediation* (New York: St. Martin's, 1999); and Edmond Keller and Donald Rothchild (eds.), *Africa in the New International Order* (Boulder: Lynne Rienner Publishers, 1996). See also Olusegun Obasanjo (ed.), *The Kampala Document* (New York: African Leadership Forum, 1991).

28. These figures were calculated on the basis of annex 6 (mediation efforts), in El-Ayouty and Zartman (eds.), *The OAU After Twenty Years*. See Mohamed Abdirizak, "Conflict Resolution in the OAU," (Mimes, Washington: Johns Hopkins University).

29. On the Chadian peacekeeping operation, see the chapters by Dean Pittman and Henry Wiseman in El-Ayouty and Zartman, *The OAU After Twenty Years;* and Nathan Pelkovits, "Peacekeeping: The African Experience," in Henry Wiseman (ed.), *Peacekeeping: Appraisals and Proposals* (New York: Pergamon, 1983). Cf. the experience of ECOWAS in Liberia, discussed in Margaret Vogt (ed.), *The Liberian Crisis and ECOMOG* (Lagos: Gambumo Publishing, 1992).

30. Obasanjo, *The Kampala Document*.

31. See I. William Zartman, *The Politics of Trade Negotiations between Africa and the European Communities* (Princeton: Princeton University Press, 1971); John Ravenhill, *Collective Clientelism: The Lomé Convention and North-South Relations* (New York: Columbia University Press,1985); Frans Alting von Geusau (ed.), *The Lomé Convention and a New International Economic Order* (Leyden, Md.: Sijtof, 1977); I. William Zartman (ed.), *Europe and Africa: The New Phase* (Boulder: Lynne Rienner Publishers, 1993).

32. Cf. I. William Zartman, *International Relations in the New Africa* (Lanham, Md.: University Press of America, 1987), esp. pp. 147ff.

33. I. William Zartman, "The Ups and Downs of Maghrib Unity," in Michael Hudson (ed.), *Middle East Dilemma: The Politics and Economics of Arab Integration* (New York: Columbia University Press, 1999).

34. Peter Robson, *Integration, Development and Equity* (London: Allen & Unwin, 1983).

35. Zartman, *The Politics of Trade Negotiations*, p. 225 et passim; I. William Zartman, "Lomé III: Relic of the 1970s or Model for the 1990s?" in C. Cosgrove and J. Jamar (eds.), *The European Community's Development Policy* (Bruges: College d'Europe, de Tempel, 1986).

36. Ravenhill, *Collective Clientelism;* Joanna Moss, *The Lomé Conventions and Their Implications for the United States* (Boulder: Westview Press, 1982); I. William Zartman, "An American Point of View," in von Geusau (ed.), *The Lomé Convention*, pp. 141ff.; John Ravenhill, "Evolving Patterns of Lomé Negotiations," in Zartman (ed.), *Europe and Africa*.

37. Nicole Grimaud, *La Tunisie à la recherche de sa sécurité* (Paris: Presses Universitaires Françaises, 1995).

38. Boutros Boutros-Ghali, *The Addis Ababa Charter* (New York: Carnegie Endowment, International Conciliation Series 546, 1964); T. O. Elias, "The Charter of

the OAU," *American Journal of International Law* 59, no. 2 (1965): 243–276; Lawrence Martinelli, *The New Liberia* (New York: Praeger, 1964), pp. 138–140.

39. See Donald Rothchild, "Racial Stratification and Bargaining: The Kenyan Experience," in I. William Zartman (ed.), *The 50% Solution* (New Haven: Yale University Press, 1987); Davidow, *A Peace in Southern Africa;* Stedman, *Peacemaking in Civil War;* and Chester Crocker, *High Noon in South Africa* (New York: Norton, 1992). Unfortunately, similar studies—even historical accounts—do not exist for most African countries.

40. Patti Waldmer, *Anatomy of a Miracle* (New Brunswick, N.J.: Rutgers University Press, 1997); Allister Sparks, *Tomorrow Is Another Country* (New York: Hill and Wang, 1995); I. William Zartman, "Negotiating the South African Conflict," in Zartman (ed.), *Elusive Peace;* I. William Zartman, "Negotiating the South African Conflict," in Louise Nieuwmeijer and Fanie Cloete (eds.), *The Dynamics of Negotiation in South Africa* (Pretoria: Human Sciences Research Council, 1991).

7

The Impact of U.S. Disengagement on African Intrastate Conflict Resolution

DONALD ROTHCHILD

In 1996 alone, fourteen of Africa's fifty-three countries were plagued by armed conflicts, most of them civil wars that pitted states (often ethnic-led) against an opposition that combined ethnic, ideological, and person-alistic dimensions.[1] The outcomes have been devastating, particularly for the civilians trapped by these encounters. The armed conflicts caused millions of deaths and grave destruction of property, undermined political stability, hindered economic development, and resulted in the internal displacement of more than 8 million persons and refugees.

External intervention, which can play an indispensable role in coping with intense ethnic-based conflict, takes place when the internal routes to conflict management are viewed as no longer reliable. As internationally accepted norms on human rights are violated, powerful states within or outside the region may decide upon some form of noncoercive or coer-cive intervention to raise the costs of abusive or obstructive behavior. They may enforce the peace, thus making credible commitment to agreements possible, or they may utilize a variety of pressures and incentives to alter the local parties' calculations on the distribution of gains from current policies.[2]

Although many African and non-African countries, individually or in coalition with others, have interceded in internal conflict situations on the continent, the United States stands out as a key actor in such undertakings in the contemporary period. This circumstance reflects the U.S. government's command of substantial material resources, extensive military and logistical capacity, and perception of global interests in a stable political environment. When it brings pressure to bear on a conflict, it can change the incentives of local actors to break peace accords. The overall effect is to reduce uncertainty about the transition to a durable peace.

However, the United States is, in Richard Haass's terms, a "reluctant sheriff," a risk-averse country that lacks overriding incentives to become embroiled in large-scale overseas interventions.[3] American leaders and the general public seem torn between their commitments to the objectives of political stability, human rights, democracy, and conflict management, on the one hand, and their reluctance to assume the role of global peace enforcer, on the other. The reality of a U.S. government divided between the executive and legislative branches is an additional limit on assertiveness and the pursuit of interests in Africa, especially as many members of Congress deny the existence of a significant U.S. interest there. It is important that we keep this general U.S. aversion to high-risk interventions in mind when considering the extent to which the U.S. commitment to conflict management appears to have altered in response to different African challenges in the post–Cold War period.

To assess the extent of U.S. preparedness to engage in noncoercive and coercive humanitarian interventions in the post–Cold War period, I analyze the American foreign policy approach in terms of three broad macro-analytical trends. These trends coincide broadly but not absolutely with different time periods. Thus, the fact that the U.S. military engaged in limited relief efforts in Rwanda after the genocidal fury had been consumed does not in itself counter the broad pattern of events taking place. What I seek to understand in this context is not a picture of rigidly precise and undeviating time periods but, rather, the unfolding dynamic of conceptualization and implementation practices at work in U.S. foreign policy on intrastate conflicts in Africa.

I begin by focusing on the classic American approach to humanitarian intervention, an approach I describe as the *cautious engagement stage*. During this stage, the American foreign policy establishment was a hesitant proponent of selective involvement in African conflict situations, ever intent upon avoiding the potential losses from involvement in Africa's intrastate conflicts.[4] Then, in the *disengagement stage*, American officials and the public at large, fearful of "mission creep" and unwilling to accept the potential losses from further humanitarian engagements in Africa, recoiled from major peacekeeping initiatives following a brief but bitter firefight in Somalia. The question at this moment is whether President Clinton's 1998 trip to Africa signaled the beginning of a *re-engagement stage*. By 1998, the painful memories of Somalia seemed to be receding somewhat, and the guilt of standing on the sidelines as a genocidal fury swept Rwanda appeared to be causing people in the Clinton administration to recommit themselves, rhetorically at least, to the process of managing these tensions. In reality, however, there was—and is—little firm evidence that U.S. policymakers are prepared to make a credible commitment to assume the risks of intervening directly or through the United Nations in Africa's intense ethnic conflicts.

Although the president directed the government to prepare for future genocide by updating the use of early warning mechanisms and by reorganizing the African Crisis Response Initiative to make it more acceptable to African opinion, the Clinton team seemed less effective in other areas, such as maintaining existing aid levels under the (FY99) foreign operations appropriations bill. Moreover, with memories of the impeachment proceedings still strong and the Republicans intent on a substantial tax cut, there appeared to be very little that the administration could do to alter congressional priorities on these matters. In light of these mixed signals, it seems pertinent to ask at this juncture: What is the trajectory likely to be in terms of U.S. or UN intervention in intrastate conflicts in the years immediately ahead?

I argue that because of domestic pressure against extensive overseas commitments, the two-level political process will likely result in a partial disengagement by the United States and, consequently, the United Nations from multidimensional peacekeeping efforts. In the words of James Woods, the deputy assistant secretary for African Affairs at the Department of Defense from 1986 to 1994, Rwanda was a watershed event because it "confirm[ed] that those who are against intervention would, at least, for the next decade, I suspect, or generation, generally prevail when the issue is raised."[5] U.S. policymakers will likely pursue risk-averse strategies, avoiding losses rather than taking extensive risks to promote peace.[6] By default, this approach will increase the likelihood of U.S. support for ad hoc interventions, bolstered by UN legitimation, in preference to backing for new multidimensional peacekeeping efforts.[7] Such external disengagement by the United States and the United Nations is likely to subject a sizable number of African minorities to serious risk.

Stage 1: Cautious Engagement

It is more and more accepted as doctrine that states have a right to intervene in the domestic affairs of other states to pursue humanitarian objectives. Sovereignty must not act as a screen for political elites engaging in destructive acts of ethnic cleansing, systematic rape, and mass murder. It must be exercised responsibly.[8] When a state launches an attack on a section of its citizenry or formulates and carries out a genocidal program, the international community is adversely affected and cannot remain aloof, justifying inaction in terms of the domestic jurisdiction principle. This was a lesson learned during the struggle against apartheid in South Africa and a lesson that had to be relearned during the Rwanda genocide in 1994, when the international community stood on the sidelines as some 800,000 Tutsis and moderate Hutus were slaughtered. As President Clinton told an audience of genocide survivors in Rwanda: "We in the United States and the world community did not do as much as we could have and should have done to try to limit what occurred in Rwanda in 1994." He then somberly warned that "we're still not organized to deal with it."[9]

U.S. involvement in Africa's intrastate conflicts has taken many forms, ranging from relatively low-cost and easy-to-operationalize noncoercive incentives to relatively high-cost rescue and peacekeeping operations and military interventions. To gauge American and UN commitment to intervene in intense intrastate conflicts, I will concentrate on such key areas of initiative as exhortation, diplomatic pressure, political and military alignment, sanctions, and the facilitation of peace accords.

Exhortation and Diplomatic Pressure

It is not surprising that a powerful international actor such as the United States, alone or in coalition with other states or international organizations, has interceded in the cautious engagement stage to exhort cooperative behavior and to protest abusive actions. Such interventions have long been recognized as representing "a legitimate exercise of the law of humanitarian intervention."[10]

The U.S. Senate took a strong stand on human rights violations in the Sudan, forcefully criticizing the Sudanese government for engaging in a campaign of "ethnic cleansing" against the Nuba people in Kordofan Province; it went on from such criticism to oppose the extension of further World Bank or IMF loans while this situation persists.[11] It also criticized Sudanese government policies on human rights issues. Thus, in 1997, during a visit to Uganda, U.S. Secretary of State Madeleine Albright pointedly met with Sudanese rebel leaders and blamed Sudanese government officials for the continuing civil war in that country.[12]

Four years earlier, in September 1993, the United States and the European Community countries had urged an end to the Kenyan regime's practices of ethnic cleansing in the Rift Valley, at times linking this appeal to the issue of resuming multilateral economic aid.[13] In February 1998, as ethnic clashes in the Rift Valley forced thousands of Kikuyus to flee their homes, the violence received international exposure when U.S. special envoy Jesse Jackson toured the scene of the bloodshed and called upon President Daniel arap Moi to end the violence.[14]

American foreign policy practitioners readily resort to exhortation and diplomatic pressure because they are relatively easy to invoke and low in cost. Little in the way of costs was incurred when in 1998 U.S. Ambassador to the United Nations Bill Richardson expressed the outrage of the international community over the massacres taking place in Algeria.[15] By exhorting African countries to abide by international standards of behavior or by making use of noncoercive pressures, U.S. administrations can at times raise the costs on governments that abuse the civil and political rights of their citizens. Important as such efforts are, their capacity to alter the policies and preferences of target-country governments should not be overestimated. Unless these exhortations are linked to other, more coercive forms of action, their ability to change practices in the target states remains doubtful. Where the target country's political elite is firmly ensconced in power and civil society is relatively ineffective, these noncoercive measures are inevitably limited in their impact.

Political and Military Alignment

Cold War alignments by the superpowers during the cautious engagement stage had an enormous impact on the nature and levels of intrastate and interstate conflict. In the way that the United States joined forces with Haile Selassie's Amharic-dominated state and built up and equipped his armed forces, it strengthened state power at the expense of other nationalities in the country. Bereket Habte Selassie, the former attorney general of Ethiopia and professor of law at various universities, has noted that between 1953 and 1977, the United States extended $279 million in military aid to Ethiopia and trained more than 3,500 Ethiopian military personnel in the United States. The defense pact made between the United States and the Haile Selassie government "bolstered" the Ethiopian army, enabling it to occupy Eritrea and other minority regions. In Bereket Habte Selassie's words, the U.S.-Ethiopian alliance "entailed support . . . of Haile Selassie's imperial ambitions in Eritrea."[16]

A similar dynamic was at work in Liberia, where U.S. foreign policymakers strengthened the political center against challenges coming from the periphery. In the 1980s, U.S. military assistance to the government of Samuel Doe in Liberia nearly doubled, and for a time Liberia became the largest (per capita) recipient of U.S. aid of all the states in sub-Saharan Africa.[17] By aligning himself with the United States and using its aid to build up his army at the political center, Doe was in a position until late 1989 to brutally suppress opposition challenges to his rule. Then Charles Taylor, with the support of the Gio and Mano peoples in Nimba county, attacked the government's (largely Krahn) army and began a new bout of fighting and atrocities. The United States avoided a direct peacekeeping role in this conflict; however, true to its cautious engagement orientation, it did provide financial support for the Economic Community of West African States (ECOWAS) initiative in Liberia.

In contrast to this pattern of support for the government, U.S. policymakers also aligned themselves with insurgent forces against the central authorities. For example, by extending economic and military assistance to the Ovimbundu-based National Union for the Total Independence of Angola (UNITA) insurgency in the 1980s, the United States helped Jonas Savimbi to survive military assaults from the Angolan army and also weakened the capacity of the Luanda government to penetrate and regulate its society. Such alignments were not without political cost for the United States, for it came to be perceived as inspired by its Cold War interests and, therefore, as highly partisan. In the post–Cold War world, military assistance and political alignments remain in evidence. For example, the United States has reportedly supplied military assistance, though not arms, to Uganda, Eritrea, and Ethiopia, which in turn have given weapons to the Sudan People's Liberation Army.[18]

Sanctions

When exhortations and moderate diplomatic pressures fail to induce a change of preferences on the part of leaders in target states, U.S. foreign policymakers often turned during the cautious engagement stage to economic, political, or military sanctions to instill a sense of urgency. Sanctions indicate strong disagreement with the policies of a state or movement and put into effect specific punitive (i.e., coercive) measures if the targeted actor refuses to change its practices.[19] Provided that sanctions are backed by a wide coalition of states inside and outside the region, they can raise the costs of trade and investment. Kofi Annan comments that "[t]he multilateral threat of economic isolation may help to encourage political dialogue, while the application of rigorous economic and political sanctions can diminish the capacity of the protagonists to sustain a prolonged fight."[20] Certainly, the imposition of sanctions on Rhodesia and South Africa did increase their costs of doing business, particularly with respect to acquiring the latest technology and importing petroleum products. Less obvious but also highly important, however, was the psychological impact of belonging to a pariah community and not being able to compete in internationally organized sporting events.

South Africa represents a dramatic American use of the economic sanctions weapon. American pressure was directed mainly at South Africa's white ruling establishment, seeking to raise the costs of its further inaction in coming to the negotiating table and to ensure that no backsliding took place in its commitment to a negotiated settlement. By the time the

Reagan administration took office, the struggle for progressive change in South Africa had emerged as a domestic issue in American politics. Despite the Reagan team's resistance to placing sanctions on South African trade and on its access to certain technology and services, Congress passed the 1986 Comprehensive Anti-Apartheid Act into law. This act made the South African government's acceptance as a legitimate member of the world community conditional upon its reevaluation of the need for political reform. The ban on new loans and investments was damaging to South Africa's economy, as was the denial of access to world markets for certain goods, technology, and services. Real growth had slackened, leading to a continuing rise in unemployment (some 2 million people were out of work by 1991) and an estimated fall in average incomes of some 15 percent.[21]

Although the Bush team did continue to press for all-party negotiations,[22] it seemed ambivalent about utilizing the sanctions weapon. Restrictions were eased in 1990 on iron and steel and the sale of Boeing 747s. Then, in an effort to provide incentives for a further dismantling of the apartheid state, Bush declared himself convinced in 1991 that the transition process was irreversible and terminated federal economic sanctions. Pressures were maintained at the state or local level, however. The period after the new Clinton administration took office actually witnessed a more activist orientation. President Clinton, determined to use his influence to spur negotiations, made clear that his administration would relax the remaining sanctions only when "it bec[ame] clearer that the day of democracy and guaranteed individual rights [was] at hand."[23] Only when President Nelson Mandela assumed power in South Africa and appealed for an end to sanctions did the Clinton team dismantle the existing sanctions legislation. In brief, sanctions did make a difference in the South African case, largely because there was a vocal, domestic community in the United States (and elsewhere) prepared to insist on a firm stand in support of negotiations and racial equality.

Sanctions are a blunt instrument, however. It is not easy to organize a coalition of states prepared to bear the costs of implementing a sanctions policy. Sanctions can also be difficult to apply without hurting the very peoples whose interests they seek to advance. To act as a meaningful incentive, the means of compliance, and therefore the termination of sanctions, must be specified at the outset.[24] Thus, the invocation of sanctions by governments involves complicated relations with their publics at home. Unless sanctions carry with them a dynamic of change, enabling the political elites in the initiating states to tighten or reduce their effects, they are likely to prove static and consequently ineffective.

Sanctions policies have also been invoked, though with limited effect, against Uganda, Libya, Sudan, UNITA, and Burundi. The American government publicly protested the Amin regime's harassment of its Asian citizens and subsequently went beyond this to invoke a wide range of measures. These measures included the closure of the American embassy, the temporary cessation of bilateral aid projects, and the termination of programs by such U.S. government agencies as the Export-Import Bank and the Overseas Private Investment Corporation.[25] The 1978 trade embargo on coffee imports was a congressional initiative that sought to protest Uganda's human rights violations against disadvantaged African groups as well as Uganda's Asian community.

In Burundi, following a Tutsi-led military coup headed by Major Pierre Buyoya, nine countries in the Great Lakes region imposed economic sanctions in an effort to encourage the new regime to negotiate its differences with Hutu leaders. Western governments, including the United States, were reported to be considering a more active role in pushing the peace process ahead in the 1996–1997 period.[26] By late 1998, this initiative had lost momentum, however. Kenya, Ethiopia, and Zambia, three of the original participants, abandoned the effort, and Rwanda, Uganda, and Tanzanian leaders increasingly regarded the undertaking as futile. In this case, the appropriateness of economic sanctions as an incentive for possible constructive change is yet to be demonstrated. Sanctions have been the cause of an economic devaluation; nevertheless, embargo violations are widespread and the Buyoya regime shows few signs of making significant concessions to the militant elements in the opposition. Meanwhile, military engagements between the government army and the Hutu militia forces continue to occur.[27]

The Clinton administration and the U.S. Congress have reportedly backed away from using sanctions in the post–Cold War period, regarding them as an ineffective way of designing a foreign policy program. In part, this situation reflects the pressures of powerful American farm and business organizations concerned over the potential loss of economic opportunities in the target countries. As Bill Lane, the chair of USA Engage (a coalition of 676 companies), declared: "Unlimited sanctions only make foreign rivals stronger and taint us as unreliable suppliers."[28] In the face of such sentiments, the Clinton team has become increasingly cautious about employing the sanctions weapon abroad.

Facilitation of Peace Accords

Mediation of internal wars by the United States or other states, international organizations, or private actors during the cautious engagement stage seemed logical, but the difficulties of achieving such negotiated settlements should not be underestimated. According to data on civil war termination gathered by Stephen Stedman, the general prospects of resolving Africa's civil wars by means of negotiation and mediation are limited. Nevertheless, where certain circumstances have prevailed (such as the emergence of identifiable bargaining parties, a mutually hurting stalemate, leaders determined to rely upon a political solution, or external pressures to reach agreement), third-party intervenors have at times succeeded in facilitating negotiations.[29] In particular, Stedman's data reveal that in twenty out of sixty-eight civil wars in the twentieth century, negotiations between state and opposition interests have resulted in a political settlement; and in eight of these twenty cases, mediation played a significant role in bringing about an agreement.[30] The difficulty of mediating civil wars becomes even more apparent when the civil wars involve an ethnic dimension. Such conflicts reflect the high level of emotion surrounding these encounters and the great reluctance that state authorities have for dealing with the leaders of ethnic-based, guerrilla movements; they fear that such diplomatic contacts may accord the insurgents a measure of international respectability, even legitimacy.[31] Moreover, the room for maneuver in a state-ethnoregional conflict is circumscribed by the nature of the "two-level" bargaining process: Not only must the negotiators deal with each other, but they must negotiate and maintain the backing of their communal members.[32] Yet despite these unpropitious bargaining conditions, third parties have sometimes managed to establish communications, overcome misperceptions, set agendas for the discussion of divisive issues, and even facilitate successful negotiations.

One of the key variables that distinguishes great-power mediators from others is their high status and command of political and economic resources. Access to extensive resources places the great powers in a better position to influence their adversaries by offering or withholding inducements. On some occasions, various African leaders, singly or jointly, have undertaken successful mediatory initiatives in African state-substate conflicts. Indeed, despite the lack of material resources at his disposal, Emperor Haile Selassie proved himself to be an effective arbiter of key disputes in the 1972 Sudanese peace negotiations; ECOWAS mediators contributed to the process of returning Liberia to stable relations; and, in what proved to be only a short-lived success, Foreign Minister Amara Essy of Côte d'Ivoire in 1996 mediated an agreement between the government of Sierra Leone and the insurgent opposition, the Revolutionary United Front.

However, other African leaders have been less successful. Although Kenya's President Daniel arap Moi displayed considerable skill in bringing Uganda's rivals to the bargaining table in 1985 and then hammering out a logical plan of action, he was constrained from the outset by the unwillingness of the negotiating parties to shift their preferences and perceptions to the extent necessary. President Mobutu Sese Seko's peacemaking initiative for Angola in 1989 and the various attempts by Moi, President Robert Mugabe, and President Hastings Banda to intercede in the ongoing civil war in Mozambique softened the perceptions that the adversaries held about one another but produced little decisive change.[33] In Burundi, a formal diplomatic track (the so-called Arusha process), organized by former Tanzanian President Julius Nyerere and backed by the countries in the Great Lakes region as well as U.S. special envoy Howard Wolpe, has been linked with an unofficial track led by the Roman Catholic lay organization Sant Egidio. Although the regional leaders unanimously resolved to maintain their sanctions on Burundi at their sixth summit on the conflict in Kampala, Uganda, in February 1998, their efforts to bring about negotiations between the Tutsi-dominated government and the Hutu rebels have so far remained inconclusive.[34]

By contrast, where the great powers cooperated with each other and mediated *directly* between the parties (as in Angola in 1988), or *indirectly* backed middle powers in their efforts to mediate intrastate disputes (as in Angola in 1991 and Mozambique in 1992), the prospects for successful conflict management were greatly enhanced. The ability of strong third-party actors to alter the choices of conflicting parties was not always sufficient (recall Jonas Savimbi's renewal of the Angolan civil war in 1992), but there is little doubt that such measures often made a critical difference.

In line with this distinction between direct and indirect mediation initiatives, I emphasize here the shift in American policy preferences in the post-Somali intervention period toward indirect mediatory activity. With the end of the Cold War struggle and the weakening of the superpowers' hegemony over their African allies, the international stakes at play have declined and the difficulty of coping with intrastate strife in Africa has increased noticeably. As a consequence, the tendency to become directly involved in highly consuming diplomatic initiatives, as in the case of Angola, has gradually given way to a preference for conflict resolution efforts under the auspices of regional and international organizations or friendly powers.

Direct Mediation. The urge to intervene directly ebbed as the Cold War passed and the United States became aware of the moral responsibilities and costs of implementing peace settlements. Even so, the temptation to become involved directly in facilitating the management of internal conflicts remains. Therefore, it is important for us to note some of the forms that such direct interventions can take.

First, there is considerable scope for linkage between public and private U.S. initiatives. An example of such linkage is ex-President Jimmy Carter's efforts to promote an Ethiopian-Eritrean dialogue in 1989. Certainly Carter, as a past president of the United States, had exceptional entrée to people in high places as well as an aura of power associated with his former office. In addition, his attempt to bring the main protagonists together took place with the tacit approval of the U.S. government and against a backdrop of increasing superpower cooperation on regional issues.[35] Despite their very different conceptions of the negotiating process, the Ethiopian government and Eritrean Peoples' Liberation Front (EPLF) delegations did come to the Carter Center in Atlanta prepared to talk about internal issues. The results represented a hopeful beginning, for agreement was reached on ten out of thirteen points, including the agenda for the follow-up meeting, the nature of the delegations, and the official languages to be used at the meetings. However, several substantive issues on the role of the chair and the nature and composition of the observers were left unsettled, and these contributed to the ultimate breakdown of the dialogue when the follow-up conferees assembled in Nairobi.

Second, prominent U.S. officials, often retired from the State Department, have mediated African conflicts under the auspices of the United Nations. In the South African case, a UN mission led by former Secretary of State Cyrus Vance did engage in August 1992 in some quiet mediatory activities between African National Congress (ANC) Secretary-General Cyril Ramaphosa and Minister of Constitutional Development Roelf Meyer. Moreover, former Secretary of State James A. Baker III, acting under the auspices of the United Nations, mediated on the Western Sahara issue between representatives of Morocco and the Frente Popular para la Liberacion de Saguia el-Hamra y Rio di Oro (the Polisario Front). In meetings at Houston in September 1997, the parties reached agreement on the size of the Electoral College to be used in the upcoming referendum on the territory's self-determination.[36]

Third, officials of the U.S. government have from time to time acted as direct mediators in Africa's internal conflicts. In May 1991, as the insurgent Ethiopian People's Revolutionary Democratic Front (EPRDF) forces approached the perimeters of Addis Ababa and President Mengistu Haile Mariam fled the country, the United States interjected itself into the unfolding Ethiopian crisis. At the request of the caretaker government and the opposition movements in the field (the EPRDF, the EPLF, and the Oromo Liberation Front), Assistant Secretary Herman Cohen convened a meeting of these parties in London on May 27 to work out a cease-fire and transition to a new regime. The situation on the ground was deteriorating rapidly. EPRDF troops remained on the outskirts of Addis Ababa, honoring a pledge to Cohen that they would not enter the city prior to the commencement of negotiations. Upon learning that the interim government was losing control of its troops, and anxious to spare the city the destruction that accompanies house-to-house combat (as in Somalia),

Cohen seized the initiative and publicly recommended that the EPRDF be allowed to move into the capital "in order to reduce uncertainties and eliminate tensions." The interim government, unable to prevent the occupation of the city by EPRDF troops, watched helplessly during the night of May 27–28 as the insurgents took charge. By sanctioning the EPRDF takeover, Cohen contended that he acted as the "conscience of the international community," sparing Addis Ababa from certain havoc.[37]

Cohen also made proposals to the Sudanese government and the Sudan People's Liberation Movement and Sudan People's Liberation Army (SPLM/SPLA) concerning a cease-fire, disengagement of forces, and the adoption of federalism in March 1990, but to no avail.[38] He did succeed in mediating an agreement in Zaire between President Mobutu Sese Seko, Archbishop Laurent Monsengwo (the president of the High Council of the Republic), and Prime Minister Etienne Tshisekedi wa Mulumba on a sharing of power during the 1992–1994 transition period, but this effort also proved disappointing, for Mobutu, after accepting the compromise, refused to abide by its terms.[39]

Nevertheless, it was the *international* negotiations over Angola and Namibia that showed that U.S. initiatives can sometimes result in enduring settlements. From independence in November 1975 to the signing of the Angola/Namibia agreements in December 1988, the conflict among the Angolan nationalist movements—UNITA, the Popular Movement for the Liberation of Angola (MPLA), and, until the early 1980s, the National Front for the Liberation of Angola (FNLA)—was a civil war exacerbated by the ties that these nationalist movements had to various external powers. Whereas the MPLA government was bolstered by Soviet military equipment and Cuban combat troops, UNITA and, for a time, FNLA received Chinese military equipment following decolonization, U.S. military assistance around independence and after 1985, and South African military assistance and combat support during all phases of the war. As the civil war continued into the 1980s, and the MPLA and UNITA forces, backed by their external allies, became locked into a costly stalemate, the various local and international actors showed themselves to be increasingly responsive to proposals for international—but not internal—negotiations. By late 1987, the time seemed ripe to make a new concerted effort to settle outstanding regional differences.[40] The opportunity for a serious peace initiative was greatly advanced by the change from adversarial to cautiously cooperative relations that took place in the mid-1980s between the great powers.

With U.S. Assistant Secretary of State for African Affairs Chester A. Crocker acting as mediator, the representatives of Angola, Cuba, and South Africa met in secret in London in May 1988 to explore the Angolan proposal for a four-year withdrawal of Cuban forces. This was followed by sessions in Brazzaville, Cairo, and New York, where persistent behind-the-scenes Soviet and American communications and pressures on their allies resulted in the acceptance of general principles on Namibia's independence, a phased Cuban withdrawal, verification, and formal recognition of the U.S. role as mediator.

Then, in the Geneva talks that followed, the conferees issued a joint statement announcing a de facto cessation of hostilities and proposed dates for Namibia's independence and the exit of Cuban and South African troops from Angola. At successive meetings in the fall, the parties narrowed the gaps between them on the issue of Cuban troop withdrawal, agreeing that the pull-out would take place over a twenty-seven-month period and that two-thirds of these soldiers would leave during the first year, with the remainder being redeployed by stages to the north.

Although the MPLA government and the various external intervenors remained antagonists, they had nonetheless managed to act in a pragmatic manner with respect to the issue of regional peace in southern Africa. However, this pragmatism did not carry over to the related task of reconciling the internal war between the MPLA and UNITA. Only as the great powers came to recognize the urgency of reaching an *internal* agreement, and, under the auspices of a Portuguese mediator, to exert significant influence on their respective allies, did a fragile and largely ineffective peace agreement materialize.

Indirect Mediation.   With U.S. leverage circumscribed in the post–Cold War period, it is not surprising that the Clinton administration has turned increasingly to indirect forms of mediating Africa's internal conflicts. Indirect mediatory activity, as the phrase is used here, refers to U.S. backing for a formal mediatory effort mounted under the auspices of another actor. This approach can involve U.S. support either for a private, informal mediator (as in former President Jimmy Carter's 1989 attempt to mediate between the Ethiopian government and the EPLF) or for a formal third-party undertaking led by another state, regional, or international organization (as in U.S. special envoy Howard Wolpe's support of the Nyerere-led mediation effort in the negotiations between the Great Lakes countries and Burundi in the late 1990s, and in the U.S. backing of South Africa's mediation efforts in the Congo in 1997 and 1998). Yet the line between indirect mediatory activity and direct mediation can sometimes be blurred. In Somalia following the U.S. humanitarian intervention in 1992–1993, for example, American diplomats mediated certain local conflicts on their own. However, in the critical negotiations of March 1993, where the fifteen factional leaders agreed in Addis Ababa to set up a Transitional National Council, UN and Ethiopian government leaders played a prominent third-party role, facilitated by a behind-the-scenes American diplomatic effort.

There are numerous instances of U.S. indirect mediatory action. In the case of Rhodesia (Zimbabwe), where Britain was still recognized the world over as the colonial power, U.S. diplomats appropriately played a supporting role during the Lancaster House peace negotiations in 1979. At one critical juncture when the future constitutional arrangements were being discussed, it became necessary for the British to try to overcome the Patriotic Front's objections by offering to grant financial assistance for land resettlement and redistribution to an independent Zimbabwe. At this time, U.S. diplomats, who had been observing the procedures closely, came to the support of the British mediators, offering financial grants to an independent Zimbabwe for such broad purposes as agriculture and education. By enabling the Patriotic Front negotiators to save face, the American side-payment helped to keep the conference from breaking down over the land issue.[41]

Although U.S. mediators played the central role in promoting an Angolan peace settlement among the international actors in 1987–1988, they followed the lead of two middle-power mediators and the United Nations during negotiations for an internal agreement between the MPLA government and UNITA. The first such peacemaking effort was undertaken by Zaire's President Mobutu Sese Seko, with the quiet backing of the Soviet Union and the United States. Mobutu organized an African summit initiative at Gbadolite, Zaire, in June 1989, attended by eighteen African heads of state. After meeting separately with Angolan President José Eduardo dos Santos and UNITA leader Savimbi to work out an agreement on the summit declaration, Mobutu presented the rivals before a gathering of Africa's respected leaders, securing a handshake between the arch adversaries as well as a sketchy agreement on a cease-fire and on plans to move toward national integration. Given the hasty way in which the agreement was hammered out and the vagueness of the resulting principles, it was not surprising that the accord proved extremely hard to implement. Though supportive in principle of the Gbadolite peace process, U.S. policymakers did not put sufficient pressure on Savimbi to ensure that he would appear at the Kinshasa mini-summit or move toward a compromise agreement.

When it became apparent that the Gbadolite process had stalled, dos Santos called for the acceptance of a new third-party intermediary. Portugal, the former colonial power, stepped into the situation and from mid-1990 to 1991 chaired a series of talks between representatives of the Angolan government and UNITA. This time, the two great powers took a very active stance in support of the Portuguese mediators. Because they continued to supply their local allies with extensive military aid, they had considerable leverage in the negotiations.

In seeking to buttress the Portuguese mediation effort, U.S. Secretary of State James Baker met publicly in December 1990 with the Angolan foreign minister, whereas Soviet Foreign Minister Eduard Shevardnadze conferred with Savimbi. Then the two great powers jointly sponsored a meeting in Washington, D.C., attended by the Angolans and the Portuguese, that produced the so-called Washington Concepts Paper, a conceptual framework for the Portuguese-mediated talks. Under the terms of this paper, the coming into effect of a cease-fire would be followed by a cessation of exports of lethal materiel to the parties by the United States, the USSR, and all other countries (the so-called triple zero option); an amendment of the constitution to provide for multiparty democracy; free and fair elections; the creation of a national army; and the installation of an international monitoring force. The Washington agreement on basic negotiating principles gave a new impetus to the flagging Portuguese-led deliberations. With U.S. and Soviet observers in attendance, the negotiators at Bicesse came to an agreement on such knotty issues as the formation of a national army, the setting of dates for the cease-fire, the timing of multiparty elections, and the international monitoring process (including great-power participation).

Following the first round of the presidential elections in 1992, it became apparent to Savimbi that he was unlikely to win the runoff election, and, claiming fraud, he withdrew the UNITA units from the new Angolan army and renewed the civil war. At the outset, UNITA successfully occupied some 70 percent of the country, but neither the capital city nor the oil-producing enclave of Cabinda. Then, as the Angolan government purchased new arms from abroad and hired the services of Executive Outcomes (a South African security firm), the tide of war changed and the UNITA forces were put on the defensive.[42] Savimbi realized that it was time to return to the negotiating table.

The turn to peace was facilitated by the existence of ongoing negotiations between the Angolan government and UNITA at Lusaka, under the auspices of a UN special representative, Alioune Blondin Beye. In 1994, Beye, assisted by U.S. special envoy Paul Hare and other diplomats, carefully negotiated what became known as the Lusaka Protocol. This protocol reaffirmed the Bicesse accords. It reestablished formal control by central authorities over the whole country, while at the same time providing UNITA with confidence-building measures: terminating Angolan army offensives; repatriating mercenaries; releasing political prisoners and captured soldiers; providing for UN monitoring of demobilization, including UNITA personnel in the police and army; and appointing UNITA party officials to high executive and administrative positions. Implementation of the protocol proved extremely difficult, mainly because Savimbi and his lieutenants appeared to engage in delaying tactics. Nevertheless, in April 1997, the new government of national unity was installed. It was an ominous sign, however, that Savimbi did not attend the opening ceremonies and that fighting was still occurring in contested areas.

Indirect mediatory action was also evident on the part of U.S. officials during the critical phase of the 1992 Mozambican negotiations. In seeking to reconcile the Mozambican government and the Mozambique National Resistance (RENAMO), U.S. diplomats worked with the major regional leaders to facilitate a settlement of the civil war. An abortive effort by Kenya's President Daniel arap Moi and Zimbabwe's President Robert Mugabe to mediate the conflict in August 1989 soon lost its impetus as RENAMO demanded recognition as a condition for negotiations while the Mozambique Liberation Front (FRELIMO) government sought recognition as the country's valid ruling authority.[43] In these circumstances, a new intermediary acceptable to both sides became essential. The rival parties agreed, in the summer of 1990, to begin direct talks in Rome under the joint mediation of the Italian government, the Roman Catholic Lay Organization Sant Egidio, and the Roman Catholic Archbishop of Beira.

The United States, as Assistant Secretary of State for African Affairs Herman J. Cohen testified, "played a prominent facilitative role": It advanced the agenda of the talks, encouraged the parties to go to the bargaining table, and consulted with the mediators and rival interests over a two-year period.[44] In its capacity as an official observer, the United States sent legal and military experts to Rome to help iron out the details, and it consulted regularly with the contending parties over the cease-fire and military-related issues.[45] After sixteen years of war and an estimated 1 million deaths, the peace treaty signed by President Joaquin A. Chissano and RENAMO leader Afonso Dhlakama represented a major achievement. The timetables set for demobilization, disarmament, and the unification of forces proved to be somewhat unrealistic, requiring further negotiations. Nevertheless, a successful consolidation of this shaky agreement through externally facilitated monitoring and supervision added significantly to the constructive outcome.

In sum, the stage of *cautious engagement* in Africa's internal conflicts showed the United States to be actively facilitating the management of disputes in a variety of ways. With the possible exceptions of such high-profile issues as South African sanctions and the 1988 mediation in Angola, these U.S. initiatives involved a limited commitment of effort and resources. The credibility of the United States was not at stake, and public opinion was not mobilized effectively to create a sense of urgent change on the part of government officials. Because of the limited American commitment, involvement in regional or global multilateral coalitions was more likely to produce constructive results than higher-profile, unilateral engagements. Moreover, indirect mediation tended to be more useful than direct mediation in the context of negotiating and implementing peace accords than direct mediation—an outcome that may have been disappointing to well-intentioned observers determined upon creating shortcuts to peaceful outcomes.

Stage 2: Disengagement

In line with the trajectory of cautious engagement described above, the Somali humanitarian intervention assumed limited objectives at its outset. Prior to the American involvement, agriculture was in disarray, many hospitals were unable to function, and each day more than one thousand people were dying from starvation.[46] With a situation of anarchy existing in many parts of the country, relief organizations were unable to distribute desperately needed goods, making some form of external military intervention vitally important.

Elated over its military victory in the Gulf War and prodded on by scenes of starvation and suffering in Somalia (the so-called CNN-effect), the Bush administration, with UN endorsement, dispatched a 25,000-person U.S. military force to Somalia in 1992 to ensure a stable and safe environment for the delivery of relief supplies and to begin the process of national reconciliation.[47] Overwhelming force was deemed necessary by U.S. policymakers so that there would be no doubts among factional leaders about the need to cooperate.[48] This force proved sufficient to enable relief agencies to distribute supplies, reopen schools, reactivate hospitals, and begin economic rehabilitation; however, the U.S. military resisted appeals from the UN secretary-general to disarm the rival militias.[49]

The Somali intervention diverged from the normal pattern of cautious engagement in that U.S. policymakers were prepared to intercede in situations where the state had failed, something they had been reluctant to do elsewhere. From the outset, it was unclear what would represent a successful outcome or when it would be possible to disengage. There were nagging questions early on about the mission's ability to disarm the militias and restore order in Mogadishu, to cope with the threat of national disintegration, and to undertake the diplomatic initiative necessary for political healing. The U.S. military could not be expected to impose political legitimacy on a divided society with its clan-based rivalries and ethnoregional antagonisms (e.g., the Isaak rebellion and separatism in northern Somalia).[50] All that could reasonably be expected of it was to utilize the momentary opportunity of its overrule to create the conditions for internal negotiations. The military did secure the main transportation routes, pacified a sizable area of the country, and, to a limited extent, began the process of putting an administrative and security system in place.

However, the peace talks that took place under the aegis of the United Nations Task Force (UNITAF) proved to be a tenuous basis for peace. Instead of encouraging the development of civil society (traditional leaders and authorities, religious leaders, professionals, women's organizations, and intellectuals), the American and UN diplomats, intent on a quick and cost-effective solution, promoted negotiations among the powerful warlords on the scene. The route of negotiating a pact among warlords was attractive to American authorities because it was quicker and easier to put into effect. John Hirsch and Robert Oakley, describing this strategy as "pragmatic," argue that it "reduced the level of confrontation with the faction leaders and minimized the risk of casualties, it put heavy weapons out of circulation, and it quickly broke through obstacles to the delivery of food and medicine in south-central Somalia."[51] On the downside, such a pact among militia leaders meant cautious efforts to promote disarmament and entailed dealing with the very people who had been the source of the breakdown.[52]

The diplomatic process that followed the U.S. military intervention represented a cautious effort to contain the most destructive elements of the conflict. Although the American team did mediate some of the local conflicts on its own, the main task of negotiating a nationwide agreement fell to Ethiopian leader Meles Zenawi and the United Nations, with the Americans playing a supporting role.[53] In March 1993, the fifteen main factional leaders met in Addis Ababa under UN sponsorship. They agreed to establish a seventy-four-member Transitional National Council that would have included the various clan leaders plus three representatives (one of whom had to be a woman) elected by each of the eighteen regional councils. The Transitional National Council would have served as a legislative body, and it would have set up an independent judiciary as well as provided for the establishment of elected and regional councils.[54] All this appeared to come apart in the ensuing months as violence flared up anew, and the UN high command declared this provisional framework null and void.[55]

As the security environment improved and relief convoys encountered less difficulty in delivering supplies to those requiring help, the American government pressed the UN secretary-general for a transition to United Nations authority. The UN secretary-general not surprisingly resisted assuming this costly and difficult assignment, even though the United States gave assurances of continued operational support during the transition phase. With Somalia lacking an effective government and an integrated army, and with weaponry spread widely throughout the country, the new force—the United Nations Operation in Somalia (UNOSOM II)—

found itself in a precarious situation from the beginning. Partly to compensate for UNOSOM II's apparent frailty, the Security Council authorized UN commanders to use force if necessary under Chapter VII of the UN Charter.

By failing to disarm the militia factions and to set a realizable political agenda, the initial UNITAF mission left UNOSOM II in an imperiled position as the transition came into full effect in May 1993.[56] These problems were compounded by the gap between the new, ambitious mandate the UN set for itself and its perceived lack of capabilities to achieve its objectives. Under Security Council Resolution 814, the member-states emphasized "the crucial importance" of disarmament and went on to request that UNOSOM II "assume responsibility for the consolidation, expansion and maintenance of a secure environment throughout Somalia."[57] Such goals might be logical, but they were exceedingly difficult to apply in the context of a failed state. The United Nations, which lacked the necessary military and civilian personnel and equipment to achieve such tasks, was thinking in terms of lofty principles, but not strategically.

This deficiency soon became apparent. In June 1993, Somali National Alliance (SNA) militiamen attacked a UNOSOM II inspection team, killing twenty-four Pakistanis and three Americans. UN Secretary-General Boutros Boutros-Ghali, pinning the responsibility for this attack on General Mohamed Farah Aidid, launched a series of raids to capture him. These forays culminated in a disastrous battle in Mogadishu on October 3 that left eighteen American soldiers and one Malaysian soldier dead; ninety U.S., Malaysian, and Pakistani soldiers wounded; and many hundreds of Somalis killed or injured. The October confrontation, as Boutros-Ghali noted, was "a turning-point in the international community's involvement in Somalia."[58] As William Schneider observed, American support for a "nonself-interested" foreign policy had declined noticeably in the post–Cold War period.[59] This interpretation received support in public opinion surveys, held immediately following the October battle, that showed a significant segment of the American public favoring a withdrawal of American troops from Somalia in six months.[60]

Americans generally regarded the Somali intervention as a humanitarian undertaking that did not advance U.S. national interests. Therefore, when SNA militiamen killed a number of American servicemen and dragged one of their bodies through the streets of Mogadishu, the incident triggered widespread public demands for withdrawal from Somalia. The American political elite was most outspoken on the need to disengage. Republican Senator Trent Lott stated unambiguously that "[u]nder no circumstances should the United States remain in Somalia."[61] On the Democratic side, Senator Sam Nunn opposed military support for an expanded UN mission and declared: "Our role is too important in areas of the world that are significant to United States military interests, security interests, and economic interests to allow our military effectiveness to be dissipated in places where we have no economic and no security interests."[62] Faced with this strong opposition, President Clinton took the pragmatic course and announced America's intention to withdraw its forces by March 1994. The UN soon followed this lead, with UNOSOM II's mandate being terminated by the Security Council. The final withdrawal of UN forces occurred in March 1995.

The upsurge of U.S. demands for a withdrawal of American forces from Somalia had broad ramifications. In April 1994, as the killings began in Rwanda, the U.S. government decided against taking action of a preventative nature, fearing, according to President Clinton, that the risks outweighed the potential rewards.[63] As a frenzy of genocide swept Rwanda, the United States justified its inaction by questioning whether the killings in fact constituted a genuine case of genocide.[64] By downplaying the nature and extent of Rwanda's planned murders, the United States was avoiding its obligation to take action under the Genocide Convention. Moreover, the U.S. government, determined to avoid involvement in peacekeeping exercises, was not supportive of efforts to mount a strong military response at the United Nations. Three days into the crisis, an American delegate at an informal and secret meeting of the UN Security Council reportedly cast serious doubts on whether the small force of UN peacekeepers then in the country should remain there and, on April 12, declared that the peacekeeping mission did not look viable "under current circumstances."[65] On April 21, with full American backing, the Security Council voted to withdraw the main body of peacekeepers from Rwanda, leaving behind a token force of 264.[66] Although Presidential Decision Directive (PDD) 25, which urged that both U.S. and UN involvement in peacekeeping be selective and more effective, was not finalized until May 1994, U.S. officials were already using its criteria to argue against peace operations in Rwanda in April of that year.[67] As Kofi Annan commented in regard to the impact of this international failure of political will: "[T]he inability of the United Nations to restore peace to Somalia soured international support for conflict intervention and precipitated a rapid retreat by the international community from peacekeeping worldwide."[68]

The following month, this decision was codified by the Clinton administration in PDD 25. Although it recognized that "UN and other multilateral peace operations will at times offer the best way to prevent, contain or resolve conflicts that could otherwise be more costly and deadly," PDD 25 emphasized the need to take into consideration such factors as American interests, the existence of a significant threat to international peace and security, the specific objectives of an intervention, and the means to carry out the mission before supporting a UN undertaking.[69] In line with this policy direction, some members of Congress proposed legislation during the following year to make significant cuts in U.S. contributions to international peacekeeping and to bar U.S. troops from serving under foreign commanders except in specific circumstances.

Clearly, American policy had shifted from cautious engagement to disengagement. In practice, U.S. policymakers appeared most reticent about engaging in new, multidimensional peacekeeping operations in Africa, whether on their own or in support of an active UN or regional organization involvement. Thus, the U.S. government stood on the sidelines as intrastate conflicts wreaked havoc not only in Rwanda but also in Sudan, Burundi, and the Democratic Republic of the Congo.

Stage 3:
Re-engagement—Rhetoric or Reality?

Although it seems doubtful that the pendulum in American thinking on humanitarian intervention has begun to swing back toward re-engagement, there are some signs, rhetorically at least, of some new American thinking on this matter. During his visit to Rwanda in March 1998, President Clinton seemed to signal a new American concern over coping with threats of genocide. He noted the international community's failure to call the crimes by their rightful name, genocide; to act quickly once the killing had begun; and to prevent the refugee camps from becoming safe havens for the murderers. Clinton then spoke about actions to counter future threats of this sort. He ordered his administration to improve early warning mechanisms and commented that the international community must have the ability to act when the possibility of genocide arises.[70] Such statements have raised African expectations of a stronger U.S. commitment in the future.

Clinton's call for the capacity to act in the event of an emergency gained substance as plans for some type of rapid reaction force were pushed ahead. There was considerable disagreement over the relative roles of the United States and the UN and on the question of whether the force would have a standing core and chain of command or be composed of units drawn from African armies after a crisis surfaced.[71] In 1996, when the Clinton administration initially proposed the idea of an African Crisis Response Force, the reaction in the U.S. Congress and a number of European and African countries was skeptical, even hostile.[72] Subsequently, the proposal was revamped and renamed the African Crisis Response Initiative (ACRI). The more modest ACRI scheme, coordinated by an Interagency Working Group headed by Ambassador Marshall McCallie, avoids the standing military force approach and instead seeks to enhance the capacity of African partner states to respond to peacekeeping challenges on the continent. "Our objective," stated Ambassador McCallie, "is to assist in developing rapidly-deployable, interoperable battalions and companies from stable democratic countries that can work together to maintain peace."[73] The initiative seeks to develop the capacity of African peacekeepers to respond rapidly and effectively to evidences of violence. It has begun training African contingents, using common doctrine and procedures, and leaving open the possibility for future coordination of these African military units should an emergency arise.

In sponsoring ACRI, the United States has edged away from disengagement. It trains African military units for peacekeeping, but leaves until later the demanding task of coordinating these units for rapid deployment. Although this initiative is pro-active, it thus far seems to have fallen short of a credible commitment. In training Africans to take on the military tasks that the United States and the international community are not prepared to assume, ACRI could be interpreted as an undertaking that has the long-term effect of enabling the United States to remain on the sidelines as new crises surface. Clearly, the scope of the challenge is complex and enormous, and unless the international community is itself prepared to quickly project sufficient force into an armed conflict, it is unlikely to have the leverage to enforce peace.

Activity on the part of the Congress to enhance Africa's trade opportunities with the United States may also be a sign of a mood to re-engage. The new bill on enhanced trade opportunities shifts the American approach from one based on aid to one concentrating on trade and private-sector investment. Despite Clinton's assurances while in South Africa that increased U.S. trade would not mean decreased U.S. economic assistance, and despite his pledges to raise American assistance to Africa to historic U.S. levels, the new (FY99) foreign operations appropriation bill shows Africa receiving less than it had previously.[74] Thus, current aid levels point to a continuing mood of disengagement, and, with the Clinton administration weakened following its impeachment ordeal, it is apparent that this administration has squandered much of its political capital and is not in a position to reverse these trends. Clearly, therefore, it is too early to conclude that the Clinton rhetoric during his trip to Africa and the modest follow-ups afterward are tantamount to a serious American re-engagement with Africa.

Conclusion:
The Selectivity of Ad Hoc Interventions

At the outset, I noted the uncertainty of the United States about using the capacity at its disposal to facilitate an end to civil wars and thereby protect Africa's vulnerable minorities. The United States sought to advance its interests both by actively promoting a stable international environment and by avoiding the risks and costs of overseas military engagements. The dilemma is further compounded by the limits of American power. Although the United States does not always have the power attributed to it by observers at home and abroad, it can at times exercise more leverage to influence outcomes than its foreign policy establishment assumes. The upshot is a dilemma of political will and commitment that can have substantial implications for advancing peace.

In the 1980s and early 1990s, U.S. leaders dealt with these dilemmas by adopting a policy of cautious engagement, taking the fewest of risks to promote peaceful intrastate relations in Africa. They were not, as some critics imply, completely neglectful of the peacemaking potential at their disposal. Ever cautiously, these policymakers did exert diplomatic pressures and mediated directly or indirectly to encourage rival interests to change their preferences on the issues at hand. During this period, the anti-apartheid legislation directed at the government in South Africa represented something of a high point in the effort to induce a change of behavior.

However, when the military-diplomatic intervention in Somalia stalled and the search for General Aidid led to a bitter firefight, such forms of engagement proved unacceptably risky to many members of Congress and the public, and a policy of strategic withdrawal was deemed politically prudent by the Clinton administration. At this point, the administration ranked the avoidance of potential losses higher than taking substantial risks for peace. The disengagement from Somalia triggered a new reticence, as Congress resisted appropriations for other peacekeeping efforts, and the international community stood on the sidelines as tragic civil wars produced lengthy casualty lists in Rwanda, Burundi, Sudan, and elsewhere.

Finally, during Clinton's visit to Rwanda in 1998, the American president momentarily held out hope of a renewed engagement of the United States with African peacekeeping. However, this rhetoric of re-engagement was soon overtaken by the continuing reality of a mood of disengagement. Clinton pledges notwithstanding, increased African trade opportunities came at a time of decreasing aid levels, making it extremely difficult for Africa to compensate for the effects of economic globalization. Behind the statements of American concern over Africa's economic and human rights dilemmas, then, is evidence as well of a hesitant pragmatism that shuns intervention whenever possible.

The consequences in terms of human rights are potentially quite grave. It appears that the UN-approved (and, in part, U.S.-financed) ad hoc intervention initiatives that are currently being mounted by states and regional organizations are likely to prove highly selective, involving concerted attempts to deal with specific crises. Other genocidal actions or threats to the peace, however, may fail to attract sufficient concern on the part of possible interveners and be left to burn themselves out (as recently occurred in eastern Congo, where some 180,000 Hutu refugees were killed during the civil war).[75] Thus, U.S. and UN engagement seems likely to provide rather selective safety nets for highly vulnerable peoples in the twenty-first century—a failure on the part of the world community to meet its commitments under the Genocide Convention and the UN Charter.

Notes

I wish to express my appreciation to Timothy Sisk, John Harbeson, Matthew Hoddie, and Edith Rothchild for their comments on the first draft of this chapter.

1. Kofi Annan, *The Causes of Conflict and the Promotion of Durable Peace and Sustainable Development in Africa* (New York: United Nations, April 21, 1998), p. 3. See also the website located at http://www.unorg/ecosocdev/geninfo/afrec/sgreport/report.htm.

2. Donald Rothchild, *Managing Ethnic Conflict in Africa: Pressures and Incentives for Cooperation* (Washington, D.C.: Brookings, 1997).

3. Richard N. Haass, *The Reluctant Sheriff: The United States After the Cold War* (New York: Council on Foreign Relations, 1997).

4. Michael J. Smith, "Humanitarian Intervention: An Overview of the Ethical Issues," *Ethics and International Affairs* 12 (1998), p. 66.

5. James Woods interview with *Frontline*, "The Triumph of Evil." For further information, see the website at http://www.pbs.org/wgbh/pages/frontline/shows/evil/interviews/woods.html.

6. Jack S. Levy, "An Introduction to Prospect Theory," in Barbara Farnham (ed.), *Avoiding Losses/Taking Risks: Prospect Theory and International Conflict* (Ann Arbor: University of Michigan Press, 1994), pp. 7–22.

7. On the increasing use of ad hoc peacekeeping initiatives, see Timothy D. Sisk and Donald Rothchild, "Beyond United Nations Peacekeeping: Changing International Responses to Intrastate Conflicts," paper delivered at the annual meeting of the American Political Science Association, Washington, D.C., August 28–31, 1997.

8. Francis M. Deng, Sadikiel Kimaro, Terrence Lyons, Donald Rothchild, and I. William Zartman, *Sovereignty as Responsibility: Conflict Management in Africa* (Washington, D.C.: Brookings, 1996), p. 172.

9. Quoted in James Bennet, "Clinton Declares U.S., with World, Failed Rwandans," *New York Times*, March 26, 1998, p. A1.

10. Ernst B. Haas, "Human Rights: To Act or Not to Act?" in Kenneth Oye, Donald Rothchild, and Robert Lieber (eds.), *Eagle Entangled: U.S. Foreign Policy in a Complex World* (New York: Longman, 1979), p. 181.

11. Senate Resolution 94, *Congressional Record—Senate*, vol. 139, no. 46 (April 3, 1993), p. S4508; and House Concurrent Resolution 131, 103rd Congress, 1st Sess. (August 3, 1993), pp. 5–6.

12. Ed Warner, "Can Sudan Break Up?" *Voice of America*, no. 5-39444 (April 1, 1998).

13. "Kenya: A difficult courtship," *Africa Confidential* 34, no. 20 (October 8, 1993), p. 4.

14. Sonya Laurence Green, "Kenya President," *Voice of America*, no. 2-226577 (February 11, 1998).

15. "Editorial: Richardson on Algeria Rights Abuses," *Voice of America* (April 1, 1998). See also the website at Gopher.voa.gov:70/00/newswire/tue/EDITOR-IAL%3A__RICHARDSON_ON_ALGERIA_RIGH.

16. Bereket Habte Selassie, *Conflict and Intervention in the Horn of Africa* (New York: Monthly Review Press, 1980), pp. 63, 170. See also B. Selassie, "The American Dilemma on the Horn," in Gerald J. Bender, James S. Coleman, and Richard L. Sklar (eds.), *African Crisis Areas and U.S. Foreign Policy* (Berkeley: University of California Press, 1985), p. 170.

17. Yekutiel Gershoni, "War Without End and an End to a War: The Prolonged Wars in Liberia and Sierra Leone," *African Studies Review* 40, no. 3 (December 1997), p. 58.

18. Ed Warner, "Can Sudan Break Up?" *Voice of America* (April 1, 1998), p. 1. See also the website at Gopher.voa.gov/00/newswire/wed/CAN_SUDAN_BREAK_UP%3f.

19. Rothchild, *Managing Ethnic Conflict*, pp. 104–105.

20. Annan, *The Causes of Conflict*, p. 8.

21. "Sub-Saharan Africa," *Foreign Broadcast Information Service (FBIS)*, vol. 92, no. 238 (December 10, 1992), p. 20; Donald Rothchild and John Ravenhill, "Retreat from Globalism: U.S. Policy in the 1990s," in Kenneth A. Oye, Robert J. Lieber, and Donald Rothchild (eds.), *Eagle in a New World* (New York: HarperCollins, 1992), p. 399.

22. Herman J. Cohen, "South Africa: The Current Situation," *U.S. Department of State Dispatch* 3, no. 30 (July 27, 1992), pp. 587–588.

23. Bill Clinton, "A Democrat Lays Out His Plan: A New Covenant for American Security," *Harvard International Review* (Summer 1992), p. 62.

24. Carnegie Commission on Preventing Deadly Conflict, *Preventing Deadly Conflict: Final Report* (Washington, D.C.: Carnegie Commission on Preventing Deadly Conflict, 1997), p. 54.

25. Donald Rothchild, "Africa's Ethnic Conflicts and Their Implications for United States Policy," in Robert I. Rotberg (ed.), *Africa in the 1990s and Beyond: U.S. Policy Opportunities and Choices* (Algonac, Mich.: Reference Publications, Inc., 1988), pp. 277–278.

26. "Burundi: U.S. Ponders Sanctions," *Africa Research Bulletin* (Political, Social and Cultural Series), vol. 34, no. 12 (December 31, 1997), p. 12936.

27. "Burundi Sanctions Likely to End," *Electronic Mail & Guardian*, December 22, 1998. See also the website at http://www.mg.co.za/mg/news/98dec2/22dec-burundi.html.

28. Quoted in Eric Schmitt, "Sanctions Don't Work, U.S. Realizes," *International Herald Tribune* (Frankfurt), August 1–2, 1998, pp. 1, 8.

29. On these variables, see Donald Rothchild and Caroline Hartzell, "The Peace Process in the Sudan, 1971–72," in Roy Licklider (ed.), *Stopping the Killing: How Civil Wars End* (New York: New York University Press, 1993), pp. 68–77.

30. Stephen John Stedman, *Peacemaking in Civil Wars: International Mediation in Zimbabwe 1974–1980* (Boulder: Lynne Rienner Publishers, 1987), pp. 5–9.

31. Daniel Frei, "Conditions Affecting the Effectiveness of International Mediation," *Papers of the Peace Science Society* (International), vol. 26 (1976), p. 70. Highlighting the intensity of civil wars, Paul Pillar's data indicate that nearly twice as many interstate wars ended with negotiations as did civil wars. See Paul R. Pillar, *Negotiating Peace: War Termination as a Bargaining Process* (Princeton: Princeton University Press, 1983), pp. 5–7.

32. Robert D. Putnam, "Diplomacy and Domestic Politics: The Logic of Two-Level Games," *International Organization* 42 (Summer 1988), pp. 433–435.

33. I am indebted to Monila Kuchena of the University of Zimbabwe for her helpful comments on the impact of these mediation initiatives (Thika, Kenya, July 21, 1993). For other examples, see I. William Zartman, "Testimony to the House Foreign Affairs Africa Subcommittee," March 31, 1993, p. 8. (Typescript copy.)

34. "Burundi: Sanctions to Stay," *Africa Research Bulletin* (Political, Social and Cultural Series), vol. 35, no. 2 (February 28, 1998), pp. 13012–13013.

35. "Ethiopia: Talks start at last," *Africa Confidential* 30, 17 (August 25, 1989), p. 3.

36. "Morocco/Western Sahara: Good Conduct Accord," *Africa Research Bulletin* 34, no. 9 (September 30, 1997), p. 12833.

37. Quoted in Terrence Lyons, "The Transition in Ethiopia," *CSIS Africa Notes*, no. 127 (August 27, 1991), p. 5.

38. On the Cohen initiative, see Deng et al., *Sovereignty as Responsibility*, pp. 187–188.

39. Georges Nzongola-Ntalaja, "The Zairian Tragedy: A Challenge for the Clinton Administration," *Africa Demos* 3, no. 1 (February 1993), p. 9.

40. Rothchild and Hartzell, "The Case of Angola," p. 185; and Michael McFaul, "The Demise of the World Revolutionary Process: Soviet-Angolan Relations Under Gorbachev," *Journal of Southern African Studies* 16 (1990), pp. 182–183.

41. Rothchild, *Managing Ethnic Conflict*, pp. 177–178.

42. Ibid., pp. 134–141.

43. Interview, Nairobi, March 1, 1991. See also Witney W. Schneidman, "Conflict Resolution in Mozambique: A Status Report," *CSIS Africa Notes*, no. 121 (February 28, 1991), p. 6.

44. "Testimony by Assistant Secretary of State for African Affairs, Mr. Herman J. Cohen, Before the House Foreign Affairs Subcommittee on Africa", October 8, 1992, p. 4. (Typescript copy.)

45. Ibid., p. 7.

46. David Shinn, testimony on Somalia before the House Subcommittee on Africa, Washington, D.C., March 16, 1994, p. 1. (Mimeo.)

47. Raymond W. Copson and Theodros S. Dagne, *Somalia: Operation Restore Hope* (Washington, D.C.: Congressional Research Service, January 19, 1993), p. 1.

48. Robert Oakley, "Remarks" to the Subcommittee on Africa of the House Committee on Foreign Affairs, Washington, D.C., March 31, 1993, p. 3. (Mimeo).

49. United Nations, *The United Nations and Somalia 1992–1996* (New York: United Nations, 1996), p. 41. On the military's efforts to place larger weapons in quarantine, however, see U.S. Institute of Peace, *Restoring Hope: The Real Lessons of*

Somalia for the Future of Intervention (Washington, D.C.: U.S. Institute of Peace Press, n.d.), p. 9.

50. See Hussein M. Adam, "Somalia: Militarism, Warlordism or Democracy?" *Review of African Political Economy*, no. 54 (1992), p. 18; and Rakiya Omaar, "Somalia: At War with Itself," *Current History* 91, no. 565 (May 1992), p. 233.

51. John L. Hirsch and Robert B. Oakley, *Somalia and Operation Restore Hope* (Washington, D.C.: U.S. Institute of Peace Press, 1995), p. 104.

52. Ken Menkhaus and Terrence Lyons, "What Are the Lessons to Be Learned from Somalia?" *CSIS Africa Notes*, no. 144 (January 1993), p. 7.

53. Robert Oakley, "Remarks," p. 1.

54. "Sub-Saharan Africa," *FBIS*, vol. 93, no. 058 (March 29, 1993), p. 1. On this issue, I have also benefited from discussions with Professor Abdi I. Samatar (Berkeley, April 24, 1993).

55. Abdullah A. Mohamoud, "Somalia: The Futility of Peace Talks," *West Africa* (June 28–July 4, 1993), p. 1112.

56. Walter Clarke, "Failed Visions and Uncertain Mandates in Somalia," in Walter Clarke and Jeffrey Herbst (eds.), *Learning from Somalia: The Lessons of Armed Humanitarian Intervention* (Boulder: Westview Press, 1997), p. 4.

57. United Nations, *The United Nations and Somalia*, pp. 262–263.

58. Quoted in ibid., p. 61.

59. William Schneider, "The New Isolationism," in Robert J. Lieber (ed.), *Eagle Adrift* (New York: Longman, 1997), p. 27.

60. Steven Kull and Clay Ramsay, *U.S. Public Attitudes on Involvement in Somalia* (College Park, Md.: Program on International Policy Studies, Center for International and Security Studies, University of Maryland, October 26, 1993), p. 3.

61. *Congressional Record—Senate*, vol. 139, no. 133 (October 5, 1993), p. S13043.

62. *Congressional Record—Senate*, vol. 139, no. 134 (October 6, 1993), p. S13146.

63. Bennet, "Clinton Declares U.S., with World, Failed Rwandans," p. A1.

64. Quoted in Gerard Prunier, *The Rwanda Crisis: History of a Genocide* (New York: Columbia University Press, 1995), p. 274.

65. "How the World Failed to Save Rwanda," *Electronic Mail & Guardian* (December 9, 1998). See also the website at http://www.mg.co.za/mg/news/98dec1/9dec-rwanda.html.

66. Ibid.

67. I am grateful to Timothy D. Sisk for this observation.

68. Annan, *The Causes of Conflict*, p. 4.

69. "The Clinton Administration's Policy on Reforming Multilateral Peace Operations" (May 1994), p. 4. (Typescript copy.)

70. "Clinton's Tour Renews Relations," *Africa Research Bulletin* (Political, Social and Cultural Series), vol. 35, no. 3 (March 31, 1998), p. 13028.

71. On support of an integrated force under the authority of the UN Security Council, see Carnegie Commission, *Preventing Deadly Conflict*, pp. 65–67.

72. Dan Henk and Steven Metz, *The United States and the Transformation of African Security: The African Crisis Response Initiative and Beyond* (Carlisle, Pa.: Strategic Studies Institute, U.S. Army War College, 1997), pp. 23–24.

73. Marshall F. McCallie, "The African Crisis Response Initiative (ACRI): America's Engagement for Peace in Africa," speech delivered at the "Emerald Express" Symposium, Camp Pendleton, California, April 8, 1998, p. 1.

74. Deborah Tate, "Clinton/Africa Econ," *Voice of America* (March 28, 1998), p. 2. See also the website at Gopher.voa.gov:70/00/newswire/sat/Clinton_ _AFRICA_ECON.

75. Regarding the Democratic Republic of the Congo, the U.S. government reportedly embraced President Laurent-Desire Kabila at the same time that it chided him for failing to allow a search for the remains of the Hutu refugees who were apparently murdered. See Howard W. French, "Congo Not Alone in Blocking Search for Killers of the Hutu," *New York Times*, May 7, 1998, p. A1.

8

From ECOMOG to ECOMOG II: Intervention in Sierra Leone

ROBERT MORTIMER

Had any doubt ever existed that the Economic Community Monitoring Group (ECOMOG) was primarily an instrument of Nigerian foreign policy, it was dispelled by Nigeria's decision to mount an offensive against the junta in Sierra Leone in February 1998. Employing the banner of ECOMOG to cover an essentially unilateral operation, Nigeria moved to restore its regional ally Ahmed Tejan Kabbah to power. Victor in the 1996 presidential election, Kabbah had been ousted in May 1997 to virtually universal disapprobation. Yet the lack of any international support for the military junta did not overcome the reservations of several regional states to this unilateral display of Nigerian power. On the contrary, it enhanced long-standing fears of a Nigerian quest for hegemony in West Africa— fears already raised by its role in Liberia.

The concept of regional approaches to peacekeeping and conflict resolution is an attractive one to many theorists of international relations. Regional organizations like the Economic Community of West African States (ECOWAS) seem potentially well suited to the task of mediating local disputes in their own zones. They have an immediate interest in regional stability, especially in preventing spillover of civil strife from one country to another, and they have a considerable knowledge of the proximate environment. The UN Charter itself recognizes the role that regional organizations might be expected to play in the management of collective security within their respective regions. The creation of ECOMOG in August 1990 as a mechanism to halt the bloodshed in Liberia's civil war was widely hailed as a promising model of regional peacekeeping. Yet it soon become apparent that regional peacekeepers faced all the same political dilemmas that UN peacekeepers had confronted in the context of conflicting national interests that so often surrounds civil and interstate war. In the specific case of Liberia, ECOMOG became as much a party to the struggle for power in that warlord-ridden land as anything else. This was because Nigeria, always the dominant military power within ECOMOG, had strong preferences about who should wield power in Liberia—preferences that clashed with those of other regional actors such as Côte d'Ivoire and Burkina Faso. As John Inegbedion wrote in 1994, "Nigeria was, and remains, the backbone of ECOMOG";[1] this was no less true in 1997–1998 when Nigeria decided to project ECOMOG into Sierra Leone, where a military junta had unseated a staunch ally of the Nigerian regime. This chapter analyzes the extension of ECOMOG's mission into Sierra Leone against the backdrop of its role in Liberia: The preeminence of Nigeria in the battle for Freetown confirms the unilateral essence of a nominally multilateral force and explains why ECOMOG's victory has intensified the search for an alternative model of African peacekeeping.

The Sierra Leone Connection

Sierra Leone has been enmeshed in ECOMOG and the Liberian civil war from the outset. In July 1990 Freetown hosted the first meeting of the Standing Mediation Committee (SMC) that ECOWAS had only recently instituted at its May summit meeting. Even though it was not a member of the SMC, which took the decision to send an interventionary force into Liberia early in August, Sierra Leone decided to contribute soldiers to ECOMOG; moreover, Freetown served as the staging ground for the August 24 deployment of ECOMOG to Monrovia. Sierra Leone's apparent eagerness to participate stemmed from two related factors. Charles Taylor's insurrection was driving refugees across the border into Sierra Leone; and, even more important, Sierra Leonean President Joseph Momoh was fearful of the effects that a National Patriotic Front of Liberia (NPFL) victory might have upon his own fragile regime.

ECOMOG may well have been Momoh's best bet for containing the Liberian crisis's impact upon his country. In the stalemate that ensued between ECOMOG and the NPFL, however, Sierra Leone was inexorably drawn deeply into the conflict. Little inclined to respect conventional territorial boundaries in any case, Taylor sent his NPFL across the border, offering "his support to an assortment of renegade politicians, army commanders, and illicit traders, in Sierra Leone."[2] Taylor encouraged the formation of the Revolutionary Unity Front (RUF), which attacked the Pujehun and Kailahun districts in southeastern Sierra Leone in March 1991; indeed, many of the Sierra Leoneans involved in the RUF incursion reportedly first fought in the ranks of the NPFL in return for a promise of aid in their bid to unseat the Momoh regime. Some NPFL troops (and possibly some Burkinabe) served in the RUF invasion, and the movement enjoyed a safe rear base in "Taylor-land."[3] As William Reno has pointed out, Taylor displayed his scorn of traditional borders by proclaiming RUF leader Foday Sankoh "governor of Sierra Leone."[4] This "transnationalization" of the Sierra Leonean internal conflict contributed to the coup against Momoh in April 1992, carried out not by Sankoh but by junior army officer Valentine Strasser, who had served both with ECOMOG in Liberia and at the front against the RUF.

Throughout the years of the ECOMOG operation in Liberia, Freetown remained a rear base for the Nigerian military command, and Nigeria sent fresh troops and supplies to the capital following the first NPFL incursions into Sierra Leone in 1991. Likewise, the Momoh government sponsored meetings that contributed to the emergence of other Liberian factions. For example, the United Liberation Movement for Democracy (ULIMO) was organized in Freetown and fought against the RUF before challenging the NPFL in Liberia. The head of ULIMO was a Mandingo intellectual and former Doe minister, Alhaji Kromah, who formed the movement in order to protect traders who operated across the borders of Liberia, Sierra Leone, and Guinea. Although Kromah's transnational ties were primarily with Malinke-speakers in Guinea—another secondary actor in ECOMOG—he was prompted into action by the NPFL's cross-border activities all along the Liberia/Sierra Leone/Guinea boundary. ULIMO-J, a primarily Krahn faction led by Roosevelt Johnson, who had been close to former president Samuel Doe, was also organized in Freetown, in mid-1992. The emergence of alternative factional leaders or warlords such as Kromah, Johnson, and George Boley of the misnamed Liberian Peace Council (LPC) provided ECOMOG with additional instruments to confront its nemesis, Charles Taylor. Using fire to fight fire, ECOMOG increasingly adopted a sort of warlord/counter-warlord strategy in order to keep its own costs down.[5] Moreover, various Nigerian officers commanding ECOMOG units were not averse to using their position for economic gain, much as the Liberian warlords were doing. As François Picard reported in *Le Monde*, ECOMOG "had often been accused of engaging in the same racketeering and pillaging activities as the Liberian militias."[6] Nigerian soldiers trafficking in diamonds got caught up in the rivalries between ULIMO factions late in 1995—for example, when ULIMO-J captured some 130 peacekeepers at

Tubmanburg, accusing them of trading weapons and diamonds with Kromah's branch of ULIMO.

The collapse of Liberia into warlord zones engulfed Sierra Leone, thus making it ripe for what would eventually become ECOMOG II. Strasser's 1992 takeover hardly stemmed the breakdown of state authority associated with the RUF insurrection in the south. By 1995, RUF forces were threatening Freetown itself, compelling Strasser to call in the private security force known as Executive Outcomes (EO). The latter collaborated with the Sierra Leonean armed forces to push the RUF back, aided as well by a new paramilitary militia known as the Kamajors. EO provided modern arms and rudimentary training to these traditional hunters, recruited largely from Mende initiation and hunting societies, converting the Kamajors into a relatively effective irregular military force against the RUF. Strasser, meanwhile, faced external pressure to restore the electoral process; resisting this call, he was removed by his second-in-command, Brigadier Julius Bio, who proceeded to organize elections that brought Ahmed Tejan Kabbah to office in March 1996. It was the overthrow of Kabbah in May 1997 that set the stage for ECOMOG II. Yet Nigeria's decision to define a new mission for the ECOWAS peacekeeping force was a consequence of the evolution of the operation in Liberia, especially in the time since Nigeria's mid-1985 turnabout with regard to Charles Taylor.

The Latter Phases of ECOMOG in Liberia

Punctuated by major armed operations against the NPFL shortly after the force's arrival in 1990, in the fall of 1992, and in the siege of Monrovia during the spring of 1996, the ECOMOG peacekeeping process was generally much more diplomatic than military. Because ECOMOG, even with its warlord associates, was incapable at its existing force level of defeating the NPFL militarily, and because the sixteen member-states of ECOWAS were not unanimously behind the Nigerian-led intervention, the regional organization sponsored a long series of diplomatic initiatives designed to reach a negotiated settlement. The first phase—orchestrated by Ivoirian President Felix Houphouet-Boigny, who was not unsympathetic to Taylor's cause—was known as the Yamoussoukro Process and lasted from mid-1991 to mid-1992.[7] A second phase coincided with the period of Benin's chairmanship of ECOWAS and led to the Cotonou Accord of July 1993; the OAU and the United Nations became more prominently involved during this stage. Delays in implementing the Cotonou agreement, and second thoughts about Ghana's participation in the force, prompted Ghana's President Jerry Rawlings to initiate a further round of negotiations when he in turn assumed the chairmanship of ECOWAS in 1994. Rawlings's diplomacy produced a new agreement signed in Akosombo that, according to François Prkic, "set in motion the dynamic that led some three years later to the end of the conflict."[8]

Rawlings, weary of a war in which his forces had been deployed from the outset, was at once critical of Nigeria's mode of leading the ECOMOG operation and convinced that a settlement in Liberia was a precondition for the kind of economic integration that he hoped for in the ECOWAS region. Rawlings had concluded that the Cotonou Accord could not be applied without an accommodation with the NPFL, an arrangement that Nigeria had consistently blocked. As his foreign minister Mohamed Ibn Chambas put it, "As chairman of ECOWAS, it was imperative for President Rawlings to make the peace process move forward by dealing with those who controlled the situation on the ground. But that meant those who had the arms."[9]

Toward this end Rawlings invited Taylor, Kromah, and General Hezekiah Bowen, head of the Armed Forces of Liberia (the remnants of the national army), to participate directly in talks in Ghana, which led to their signing the Akosombo Agreement on September 12, 1994. Although the other factional leaders and the head of the transitional government set up after Cotonou were also present, they were not signatories to the agreement. The terms stipulated that these three leaders would become the members of a new Council of State. The logic of Rawlings's plan was to engage those who controlled the largest number of combatants directly in the peace process. Not surprisingly, the scheme was criticized as the creation of a military junta, but it represented a pragmatic accommodation with reality that had heretofore been lacking. In fact, the Akosombo plan proved impossible to implement promptly because of changes in the military situation on the ground, notably setbacks to all three of the primary actors designated. Yet Rawlings's initiative opened the door to power that Charles Taylor eventually crossed.

Rawlings's activism prompted Nigeria's dictator General Sani Abacha to hold direct talks with Taylor in June 1995. Indicating his desire for cooperation, Taylor declared that "Nigeria holds the key to peace in Liberia."[10] The contact eventually led to yet another peace agreement—actually the eleventh in a string reaching back to November 1990—signed under ECOWAS auspices in the Nigerian capital Abuja on August 19, 1995. Abacha's rapprochement with Taylor was a grudging acknowledgment that Rawlings's approach had to be tried. As a result, Taylor joined the new governing council inaugurated in September of that year. Still the relationship between Nigeria—and hence ECOMOG—and the headstrong leader of the NPFL remained prickly all the way up to Taylor's eventual victory in national elections finally conducted in July 1997.

Like previous agreements, the Abuja accord called for ECOMOG to disarm the rival factions as a prelude to national elections. Yet ECOMOG's

7,000 men hardly had the means to disarm some 60,000 soldiers of seven competing warlords, who engaged in frequent violations of the presumed cease-fire—usually directed at other factions but sometimes directed at ECOMOG itself. The governing council, of which Taylor was a prominent member, made calls for signature of an agreement on the very status of ECOMOG as a precondition to disarmament. Hence it was clear that the faction leaders remained wary of ECOMOG's role in the country and sought to assert their authority over the multilateral force. Meanwhile, ECOWAS Secretary-General Edouard Benjamin announced that Burkina Faso would for the first time provide troops to ECOMOG to participate in the task of disarming the factions. As Burkina Faso had been one of Taylor's firmest supporters, this was yet another effort to increase his confidence in dealing with ECOMOG. In April 1996 another round of interfactional fighting broke out, once more generating hostilities between the peacekeepers and the warlords.

Monrovia was devastated as ECOMOG was incapable of restraining the violence between the warlords. On April 6, Taylor attempted to have Roosevelt Johnson arrested. Johnson's Krahn loyalists resisted and took control of the Barclay barracks; teenage militia members roved the streets of the stricken capital for two weeks before a cease-fire took hold. Some 1,500 people died during the fighting. Overwhelmed by the hostilities, ECOMOG appealed via the voice of Nigerian Foreign Minister Tom Ikimi for U.S. logistic support. Eventually Deputy Assistant Secretary of State William Twaddell stated that Washington was prepared to spend $30 million to shore up ECOMOG capabilities, but the whole episode demonstrated the peacekeepers' extremely tenuous grasp of the situation. In effect, the warlords already controlled Monrovia, but Taylor had not yet established his own supremacy over the situation and needed to work through ECOMOG to legitimize his power. This, however, implied redefining the statute of ECOMOG. For his part, President Abacha sent Major-General Victor Malu, victor in the 1992 struggle for Monrovia, back to lead ECOMOG, replacing General John Inienger whose forces had been overwhelmed in the April carnage.

In the aftermath of the bloodshed in Monrovia, the following ECOWAS summit once again took up the Liberian problem. Meeting again with warlords Taylor, Kromah, Boley, and Johnson, the heads of state brokered a new agreement dubbed Abuja II. It called for Ruth Perry, a former senator, to head a new interim government charged with the preparation of elections in 1997. The faction leaders pledged their cooperation, agreeing to turn over their weapons to a newly beefed-up ECOMOG and to dissolve their militias by January 1997. The agreement called on member-states to prevent the flow of arms from their territories into Liberia and gave ECOMOG the right to search anyone in the country, including members of the transitional body; a number of measures designed to ensure compliance—such as freezing the assets of any violators of the accord—were enacted. Referred to as Liberia's "last chance" by the Nigerian government, Abuja II was sustained less because of the strength of ECOMOG than because the chief warlords finally saw the opportunity to come to power via the electoral process. Taylor and Kromah had in effect forged an alliance against both Roosevelt Johnson, whose depleted forces retreated to Tubmanburg, and Boley, who had no real power base in Monrovia.

In the months following Abuja II, ECOMOG finally carried out the assignment of disarming the factions that it had been given in 1991. Taylor's rapprochement with Abacha gave him sufficient confidence that he would not be deprived of the fruits of victory if he abided by the electoral process. The long-awaited elections took place in July 1997: Exhausted from seven and a half years of war, Liberians gave Taylor more than 70 percent of the vote. Although the inauguration of Taylor as president on August 2, 1997, might have been anticipated to bring ECOMOG's mission to a close, the situation in Sierra Leone dictated otherwise. The overthrow of the Kabbah government two and a half months earlier reconfigured the situation in the subregion.

ECOMOG and the Restoration of the Kabbah Government

The disgruntled officers who overthrew the Momoh government in April 1992 formed a military government that they called the National Provisional Ruling Council (NPRC). For some two and a half years, this military regime conducted operations against the RUF without seriously seeking to end the unstable conditions in the diamond-rich part of the country: Under cover of rebel-caused insecurity, Strasser and his military colleagues enriched themselves in the illegal diamond trade.[11] Nevertheless, the NPRC did face international pressure for a return to civilian rule; in April 1995, Strasser announced that his government would restore the electoral process by the end of the year. When the young captain—too young to satisfy the constitutional age requirement to serve as president—reneged on his pledge, Brigadier Bio removed Strasser from office. The election then went forward quite rapidly, with a first round at the end of February and a runoff on March 15, 1996. The winner campaigned as the candidate of the old Mende-based Sierra Leone People's Party, defeating an even older political veteran, eighty-year-old John Karefa-Smart.

Ahmed Tejan Kabbah had been a civil servant until his departure from Sierra Leone in 1968 for a career in the UN secretariat. Having returned to his homeland in 1992, he was named to head the body set up by the NPRC to write a new constitution and restore the country to multiparty democracy. Absent from the country throughout the Siaka Stevens–Joseph Momoh years of single-party rule, Kabbah did not have a strong political base despite his comfortable victory (with 59.5 percent of the vote) in the March election. He faced a dual threat to his power: the RUF, which continued to wreak destruction in the south and the east, and the Sierra Leone Army (SLA), which was far from reconciled to the elected civilian government. Kabbah moved on both fronts at once, opening negotiations with the RUF and initiating a policy of downsizing the army whose ranks had become swollen under the NPRC regime. His ally in this process was the largely Mende militia, the Kamajors—trained, as noted earlier, by Executive Outcomes. He came also to rely increasingly on a second ally, the Nigerian forces that had been posted to Freetown ever since the creation of ECOMOG.

Nigeria's stake in the Kabbah government was twofold. On the one hand, supporting "democracy" in Sierra Leone was a public relations asset for the much-condemned Abacha regime. On the other, Nigeria remained wary—despite its accommodation with Charles Taylor—of the Liberian warlord's close links with the RUF. Having accepted the prospect of Taylor's accession to power in Liberia, Nigeria had no desire to see the RUF take over Sierra Leone. All things considered, the internationally approved Kabbah government seemed the best route to containing Taylor and to maintaining a Nigerian presence in this part of the West African region. Thus anticipating Taylor's eventual victory in the Liberian elections, Nigeria made itself indispensable to the insecure Kabbah government. Only months into his term, Kabbah faced an attempted coup by soldiers loyal to the previous military regime in September. Foiled with the aid of the Nigerian forces already present, the threat prompted the government to call in a team of Nigerian investigators; in the succeeding months, the Nigerian presence in Freetown continued to expand. Although there were also small numbers of Ghanaian and Guinean forces present in Sierra Leone under ECOMOG auspices (replicating the situation in Liberia), the Nigerian assistance was the most prominent and critical resource for the beleaguered government.

President Kabbah did strengthen his position by successfully negotiating a peace accord with the RUF. Brokered by the Ivoirian government, the agreement was signed on November 30, 1996, in Abidjan.[12] The accord called for the creation of "a Neutral Monitoring Group (NMG) from the international community" to report any violations of the cease-fire, and it specified that Executive Outcomes would withdraw from the country "five weeks after the deployment of the Neutral Monitoring Group."[13] Nowhere does the document refer to ECOMOG; on the contrary, it stipulates that "Government shall use all its endeavors, consistent with its treaty obligations, to repatriate other foreign troops no later than three months after the deployment of the Neutral Monitoring Group."[14] It is apparent that part of the RUF's price for ending the war was to remove Nigerian troops from the scene. The final article of the agreement states that "the Government of Côte d'Ivoire, the United Nations, the OAU and the Commonwealth shall stand as moral guarantors that the Peace Agreement is implemented with integrity and in good faith by both parties."[15] Again, Côte d'Ivoire was bidding to replace Nigeria as a guarantor of peace and stability in Sierra Leone.

Although Kabbah did dismiss Executive Outcomes in January 1997— he was under International Monetary Fund pressure to cut these expenses as well—he did not move to repatriate the Nigerians. Nor did the RUF hasten to meet its obligations under the Abidjan Accord. Much like the scenarios of the many agreements negotiated during the Liberian civil war, the Abidjan deal did not stick, as Foday Sankoh refused to cooperate either with the Peace Commission or with UN representatives seeking to set up the neutral monitoring group, and the president remained reliant on the Kamajors as well as on the Nigerians who had taken direct responsibility for presidential security. Kabbah was able to make little headway on any front: trimming the army, implementing the agreement with the RUF, or restoring Sierra Leone's severely battered economy. In May the army and the RUF, both of which felt threatened by the Kamajors, made common cause against the elected government.[16]

The coup began at dawn on May 25, 1997, with an attack on a Freetown prison where many of the leaders of the previous coup attempt were being held. The rebels released Major Johnny Paul Koromah, who took power as head of the Armed Forces Revolutionary Council (AFRC). While Kabbah fled to Guinea (with American protection), Koromah invited Foday Sankoh (who was in detention in Nigeria) to join in the new military government. By all reports the takeover was particularly bloody. There were severe clashes between the forces engaged in the coup and the Nigerian soldiers guarding the State House; the Nigerians took some casualties and then moved quickly to reinforce their ranks by bringing in soldiers from the ECOMOG contingent in Liberia. Rumors flew that the Nigerians were ready to reinstate the government by force, but President Abacha decided to work first through ECOWAS in his capacity as chairman of the regional organization.

The ensuing situation was eerily akin to the one in Liberia. The Nigerian—and other foreign—forces around Freetown had always nominally been part of ECOMOG. They continued to occupy their positions while confronting a hostile national force in the AFRC that included elements of Taylor's RUF allies. ECOWAS decreed economic sanctions that the ECOMOG contingent was supposed to enforce. It also created a Committee of Four (Côte d'Ivoire, Ghana, Guinea, and Nigeria, renamed the Committee of Five when Liberia was invited to participate as well) to negotiate with the new military junta over a return to civilian rule under the elected president. At the end of July, however, AFRC leader Koromah broke off the talks, declaring that he "would not be stampeded into a return to civilian government."[17] At this point, ECOMOG announced that it would tighten the blockade around Freetown, warning all ships and aircraft away from the country. ECOMOG lacked the means fully to enforce the blockade, but it exercised some control over access to the port of Freetown; beyond this, Nigerian planes unilaterally carried out bombing missions similar to operations that had been conducted in Liberia. These operations did not sit well with all the member-states of ECOWAS. Meanwhile, it should be added, the new Taylor government in Monrovia was trying to renegotiate the status of ECOMOG forces there.

These concerns were largely addressed at the subsequent ECOWAS summit meeting held in Abuja at the end of August 1997, which Taylor attended triumphantly in his long-sought capacity as the elected president of Liberia. Well aware of the ironies involved, Taylor expressed Liberia's "appreciation for the many sacrifices which our brothers of the subregion have made" to restore peace to his country.[18] At the same time, he argued that parliament had mandated him to negotiate a status of force agreement regarding ECOMOG with ECOWAS. The mandate of the peacekeeping force should be redefined to one of assistance in restructuring Liberia's army and police so as to provide Liberia with the capacity to ensure its own national security. Taylor agreed to include the commander of ECOMOG in a new nine-member National Security Council. The summit concluded that ECOMOG, reduced in size, should stay on in this capacity, but only as mutually agreed and as financed by Liberia itself. The date of February 2, 1998, was fixed as an end point for the original peacekeeping mission and the nominal transition to capacity-building of the Liberian security forces. The August summit likewise introduced a formal distinction between the force in Liberia and ECOMOG II; the latter's mandate remained limited to monitoring the situation in Sierra Leone and enforcing the embargo.

While Taylor renegotiated the status of ECOMOG, the parent organization addressed the problem in Sierra Leone. The Committee of Five held talks in Conakry, where Kabbah had taken refuge, with representatives of the junta. These led to an agreement, signed on October 23, 1997, that foresaw the return of Kabbah at the head of a reconstituted government by April 22, 1998.[19] This outcome represented a pragmatic concession by Koromah, who earlier had spoken of staying on at least until the year 2001. Thus there appeared to be some progress toward a compromise, yet clashes between the Nigerians outside Freetown and the forces of the junta continued.

Uneasiness with Nigeria's conduct of the ECOMOG mandate in Sierra Leone was evident at the December 1997 extraordinary ECOWAS summit in Lomé. ECOWAS had indeed imposed economic sanctions upon the AFRC regime, but it had not authorized the use of force against the junta. Although the discussions were not public, the delegates heard from General Malu as commander in chief of ECOMOG; the secretariat revealed that the ECOMOG experience had "fed the debates."[20] Abacha declined to attend the Lomé session; Foreign Minister Ikimi, however, defended Nigerian policy with the broad argument that West African regional peacekeeping was better than initiatives that came from elsewhere. Senegal's foreign minister indicated that his government had reservations about the manner in which the regional force was being employed in Sierra Leone.

The final communiqué handled these differences with diplomatic tact. It indicated that the heads of state "explored the ways and means aimed at preventing, managing, and settling conflicts as well as maintaining and strengthening peace, security, and stability in the region"; that they renewed their support to the committee dealing with Sierra Leone and expressed their "appreciation" of the role of ECOMOG there (after heated debate over whether to use the word *satisfaction*); that they hailed the positive action of ECOMOG in Liberia; and that they reaffirmed the role of ECOWAS (not ECOMOG) in settling the Sierra Leone crisis.[21] Close reading reveals that the communiqué was a rebuff to Nigeria and a warning not to act unilaterally: The full membership of ECOWAS had the authority to define the group's policy toward the junta. Nigeria alone did not have the right to expand the mission of the peacekeepers. ECOWAS invited President Kabbah to attend the summit, making perfectly clear that it did not recognize the junta and that it considered the deposed president to be the legitimate head of state. Support for Kabbah was not intended to give Nigeria a free hand, however.

The outbreak of hostilities between ECOMOG and the junta on February 6, 1998, thus took many of the members of ECOWAS by surprise. Nigeria claimed that junta troops carried out an attack on its peacekeepers east of Freetown, but there were some indications that the Nigerians may have been planning an offensive for some time.[22] The UN Security Council unanimously called for a cease-fire on February 11, "implicitly blaming" (in the view of *Le Monde*) "the ECOMOG forces."[23] ECOMOG reinforcements crossed the Mano River bridge from Liberia, bringing in heavy weaponry as the Nigerian forces closed in on Freetown. Whatever the initial provocation may have been, the Nigerian forces under the banner of ECOMOG launched a generalized offensive to restore Kabbah to power. Within a week, the Nigerians took Freetown while the junta leaders fled into the countryside. Nigeria thereby reestablished a kind of military protectorate over Sierra Leone at just the moment that it was significantly reducing its presence in Liberia. With President Kabbah beholden to Abuja (which he visited in February, well before returning to Sierra Leone on March 10), Nigeria retained the capacity to project its power into the subregion. It remained well positioned to assist other regional allies such as Guinea, which was concerned about Liberian subversion. It also averted the need to repatriate some seven thousand war-hardened and not altogether satisfied troops back to Nigeria. Having discovered means of earning income in Liberia, these soldiers might find comparable opportunities in the diamond fields of Sierra Leone. Nigeria was able to accomplish these tactical and strategic goals while marching under the banner of restoring an elected leader to office.[24]

The tight interlocking between the Sierra Leonean and Liberian situations was evident during the hostilities as well. Nigerian commanders accused Taylor of sending NPFL troops across the border to help the junta. Taylor in turn was irate that ECOMOG planes forced down two helicopters carrying junta officials in Liberian airspace and that Nigerian alpha-jets buzzed over the presidential residence in an obvious act of intimidation. He called upon ECOMOG to withdraw the armored vehicles that it was deploying in Monrovia during the Sierra Leonean campaign. Despite these protests, Taylor did not have the means to counter the Nigerian fait accompli, nor did other governments have the will.

Only Taylor's longtime backer, President Blaise Compaoré of Burkina Faso, publicly expressed reservations about Nigeria's unilateral decision to convert ECOMOG II into an enforcement operation. In particular, Compaoré questioned "just what might be the intentions of those who have employed force for the restoration of President Kabbah."[25] Although other states were reluctant to criticize the outcome openly, the weekly *Jeune Afrique* commented that the Nigerians reinforced their position in the region "with the silent approbation of ECOWAS (which in reality betrayed the disapproval of certain of its members)."[26] Elsewhere in the francophone press, it was clear that the intervention rekindled longstanding suspicions of Nigerian hegemonic aspirations. For example, *Sud-Quotidien* in Dakar questioned Nigeria's "eternal quest for leadership" and perceived a strong element of "opportunism" in the reconversion of ECOMOG.[27]

The adverse reaction of the Senegalese government became evident in the months following the Nigerian campaign, notably at the meeting of the ministers of foreign affairs of the ECOWAS member-states held in Yamoussoukro in March 1998. A debate erupted at this meeting between Foreign Minister Ikimi of Nigeria and his Senegalese counterpart, Moustapha Niasse, concerning regional peacekeeping. Ikimi lauded the achievements of ECOMOG, declaring that "[w]e have an instrument which has proved that it works. Our subregion is the envy of the world's other regions." He went on to criticize "foreign countries [that were] working to weaken our inter-African organizations by dividing us along anglophone-francophone lines."[28] More specifically, he singled out a multilateral military training exercise carried out during the last week of February in the Senegal River valley.

The exercise, known as Guidimakha '98 (after the name of a former province situated at the borders of contemporary Mali, Mauritania, and Senegal), represented an alternate track to regional peacekeeping. Financed largely by France at a cost of some $6 million, Guidimakha brought together a multinational battalion called RECAMP (an acronym in French for Reinforcement of African Capabilities for Peacekeeping) with national units from Senegal, Mali, and Mauritania and a smaller support force of primarily French but also U.S. and British soldiers. Five other ECOWAS governments (Cape Verde, Gambia, Ghana, Guinea, and Guinea-Bissau) also sent observers to the exercise. The Guidimakha war game was planned well in advance of the ECOMOG II operation in Sierra Leone as part of a broad international effort to upgrade peacekeeping capacities in Africa.[29] There is no question, however, but that it took on greater significance in the aftermath of the unilateral Nigerian initiative in Sierra Leone.

Senegal's foreign minister was quick to reply to Ikimi's barely veiled criticisms of Guidimakha: Nigeria could not tell Senegal how to conduct its national security policy. "No one," declared Niasse, "can prevent Senegal or any other state from organizing such military maneuvers as it wishes . . . nor can anyone prevent states from training their police, gendarmerie, and army or freely choosing their partners as a function" of their own defense needs. The Ivoirian prime minister also welcomed the training exercise as an "innovative initiative" in regional peacekeeping.[30] For its part, Burkina Faso announced that it would prefer a humanitarian interventionary corps based upon small pretrained national units that would come together in emergencies. However much Ikimi deplored anglophone-francophone divisions, the ECOWAS meeting revealed unambiguously that there was no regional consensus on the means for peacekeeping. The meeting ended on a vague compromise allowing that ECOMOG would remain the bare-bones framework of regional peacekeeping while calling for a thorough reassessment of the legal and political ground rules under which the force should operate. The heated debates at Yamoussoukro revealed that Nigeria had squandered what credit it had earned for its long engagement in Liberia by its cavalier march on Freetown—at least in the judgment of several of its partners in ECOWAS.

Over the following months, Nigeria sought new legitimization of its involvement in Sierra Leone. ECOWAS defense ministers and chiefs-of-staff met in Accra in May, but only half of the member-states actually attended the meeting. Nigeria's chief-of-staff and future head of state Abdulsalam Abubakar appealed for reinforcements to shore up the Nigerian contingent. Although a few governments had expressed their intention to participate in ECOMOG II, they were slow to deliver such troops. Moreover, Ghanaian Foreign Minister Victor Gbeho, while praising ECOMOG in principle, asserted that the primary task of the Accra meeting was to elaborate "a clear definition of the status of ECOMOG in Sierra Leone: its objectives, its rules of engagement, its force levels and the necessary resources, as well as a withdrawal strategy."[31] Nigeria did not receive the concrete support that Abubakar had appealed for out of the Accra session and, instead, found itself bogged down in Sierra Leone, where the RUF and the deposed junta continued their resistance to the restored Kabbah regime. By the summer of 1998, the situation of ECOMOG II in Sierra Leone was bleakly reminiscent of the early days of ECOMOG in Liberia.

Another severe round of violence occurred in January 1999. Against a backdrop of continuing ECOWAS appeals for a cease-fire and dialogue between the rebels and the ECOMOG-backed government, the RUF carried out another ruinous offensive against Freetown. ECOMOG employed Nigerian jets to attack the rebels in the immediate environs of the capital. As a Western journalist observed, the city was a horror of "death, despair, and devastation. Nigerian forces shell the hilly outskirts of eastern Freetown, where the rebels have fled for now, retreating from their latest offensive, launched January 6, to retake this skeleton of a city."[32] Although ECOMOG and the Nigerian government were reluctant to release casualty figures, reports circulated that as many as several hundred Nigerians may have been lost in combat.[33] These costs raised serious questions about ECOMOG in Nigeria, where a transition from military to civilian rule was under way. Likewise, the continuing criticism of such regional leaders as President Compaoré—who declared in February that the Nigerian soldiers "conduct themselves quite simply like an army of occupation . . . ECOMOG is going well beyond the mandate that was entrusted to it"—undermined public support for the mission in Nigeria.[34] The prospect that the new government of Olusegun Obasanjo would terminate Nigeria's almost nine-year expedition into regional peacekeeping seemed plausible in the spring of 1999.

Hegemons and Peacekeepers

In crossing the formal border between Liberia and Sierra Leone, the Nigerian forces merely repositioned themselves in the transnational war that has wracked this part of West Africa since Christmas Eve 1989. The arrival in power of Charles Taylor, definitively sanctioned by the July

1997 election, was a setback for Nigeria's broad strategy of influence in the ECOWAS region. In forming ECOMOG in the first place in August 1990, Nigeria had sought to prevent Taylor's NPFL from toppling an ally, Samuel Doe. Taylor's own indiscriminate use of violence allowed Nigeria to enlist at least the tacit support of most of the other members of ECOWAS in its pursuit of a Nigerian national interest—namely, the maintenance of a friendly regime in an anglophone enclave (Liberia/Sierra Leone) surrounded by francophone states. Taylor's accession to power forced Nigeria to redeploy the bulk of its regional presence to Freetown, where the civilian government needed whatever protection it could find.

Of the francophone states, only Guinea aligned itself squarely with Nigerian policy. The reason was straightforward: President Lansana Conte was also fearful of Taylor's political intentions. The Conte regime has appeared particularly vulnerable since the nearly successful coup of February 1996. Taylor was as capable of supporting opposition movements in Guinea (for example, Alpha Condé's Rassemblement du Peuple de Guinée) as in Sierra Leone. Indeed, Guinea has contributed a small number of troops to ECOMOG since the beginning, thus heightening the antipathy between Monrovia and Conakry. Now Guinea is maintaining troops inside Sierra Leone (in the border regions rather than in Freetown)—troops that are officially under ECOMOG II command. Thus one of Nigeria's reasons to keep its forces deployed in the subregion is to prevent the overthrow of the Conte regime, its only reliable ally among the francophone states and a partner in containing Taylor.

The literature about ECOMOG has appropriately treated the operation as a multilateral initiative that constituted an innovation in regional peacekeeping. Even if Foreign Minister Ikimi's "envy of the world" was exaggerated, there was a reasonably large consensus in the region; and beyond that, ECOMOG was carrying out a valuable mission under difficult circumstances. The ECOWAS governments generally supported ECOMOG as a bulwark of the general principle that incumbents should not be overthrown by insurgent movements and as a stabilizing force in a chaotic environment. Governments and international organizations beyond the region—with the exception of France—were content to let the Nigerians bear the brunt of the responsibility for coping with Liberia's political crisis. Nigerian diplomacy was largely successful in presenting the state as a provider of the collective good of benevolent regional leadership. Yet with the passage of time—and the ephemeral coming and going of non-Nigerian participants like Senegal, Tanzania, and Uganda—the predominantly Nigerian character of the operation has increasingly become a bone of contention in the region itself.[35]

For some time, the other member-states of ECOWAS acquiesced in Nigerian predominance for several reasons. In addition to those suggested above—the incumbency principle and collective goods—another was the lack of a viable alternative. ECOMOG was the only available cop on the block. This situation, however, was changing by the time of ECO-MOG II. Another more cynical reason was that Nigeria appeared to be bogged down in Liberia with no apparent place to go. The latter perception changed radically, however, when the force found a new place to go. Much more blatantly than was the case in the desperate situation of Monrovia in August 1990 did the advance upon Freetown appear to be a unilateral projection of Nigerian power and national interest.

Despite the fact that Nigeria had intervened to restore an incumbent government, thus giving the operation some measure of legitimacy, there was implicit criticism of ECOMOG II's fait accompli at the Yamoussoukro and Accra meetings in the spring of 1998. States find themselves in an ambivalent relationship with real or potential hegemons. Hegemonic states can supply collective goods, and weaker states may need the protection of the stronger state. At the same time, smaller states are vulnerable to possible interference in their domestic affairs or to local ambitions by the hegemon. Initially most West African states saw more benefits than costs in Nigeria's projection of its power—seconded by small contributions from others—into the explosive situation in Liberia. Although states likewise perceived some benefits in the restoration of the Kabbah government, the costs outweighed the benefits for several states.

A primary factor permitting states like Senegal to register objections to ECOMOG II was the availability of other options. France, itself a rival for influence in the West African region (notwithstanding its initiatives over the past few years to improve its bilateral relations with Nigeria), provided a potential alternative to ECOMOG in its RECAMP project. By the same token, the United States has mounted an alternative framework via the African Crisis Response Initiative (ACRI). Senegal is among the states receiving training under the program.[36] Neither RECAMP nor ACRI was explicitly directed against ECOMOG, but they both provide additional resources for future defense and/or peacekeeping missions. In this way, they allow states to distance themselves from the need to turn to a regional hegemon. Nigeria's essentially unilateral operation against the AFRC junta increased the incentive to develop alternative mechanisms for peacekeeping.

One of the perceived virtues of ECOMOG was its regional nature. Yet one can see that states may be more comfortable with extraregional support—from France, the United States, and the European Union more broadly—than with a regional hegemon. The same incentives that make a regional power more likely to act render that actor more threatening than a more distant patron. U.S. training and material support to ACRI do not entail direct American control over future decisions to deploy the African peacekeepers. Even the Guidimakha/RECAMP maneuvers, in which French (and even small numbers of British and U.S.) forces were involved, ultimately strengthen African autonomy and genuine multilateralism.

No doubt the nature of the Nigerian regime needs to be factored in. From late 1993 to mid-1998, Nigeria was governed by a particularly unpalatable dictator, Sani Abacha. The disappearance of Abacha and the character of the longer-term successor regime will make some difference in how other states view Nigeria. Yet one can assume that Nigeria will continue to pursue its own national interest in the region. More important than the Abacha regime *per se* is the perception that Nigeria used ECOMOG for its own purposes in launching the February 1998 offensive on Freetown. In this instance, the hegemon abused the trust that other member-states of ECOWAS had vested in it by imposing its own "solution" on the situation a couple of months in advance of the April deadline that had been negotiated at Conakry. This solution has ensconced Nigerian troops in the capital, but it has not ended the violence in Sierra Leone.

States pursue their national interest. Sometimes they do so via regional forces under multilateral mandates. Most member-states, though never all, of ECOWAS saw their national interests being served in Liberia under ECOMOG even as the operation dragged out over a prolonged period. Yet each was likewise attentive to the trade-offs between relying primarily upon Nigeria for regional stability and confronting a hegemonic actor. ECOMOG II has resulted in a revised estimate of the trade-off, and regional peacekeeping is evolving in a direction designed to ward off hegemony.

The formation of ECOMOG in August 1990 occurred during a period of widespread optimism about the capacity for international cooperation in the post–Cold War era. It coincided with a flourish of ambitious new peacekeeping operations under UN auspices.[37] Yet in a world of sovereign states, multilateral peacekeeping is an intrinsically hazardous activity, for there are generally competing interests at stake in the outcome of both interstate and civil wars. As a regional subsystem, West Africa is a microcosm of the larger state system. Over time other regional states became wary of Nigeria's dominant role inside ECOMOG and began to balance against it. Just as there has been a retrenchment regarding UN peacekeeping since the heyday of the early 1990s, there has been a reevaluation of how to implement regional operations in West Africa—not because peacekeeping capabilities are any less urgently needed there but because genuine multilateralism is so difficult to achieve in the state system. No less a practitioner than UN Secretary-General Kofi Annan has observed that peacekeeping must above all be conducted in such a manner as to uphold the legitimacy and credibility of the intervening party.[38] ECOMOG has demonstrated that this axiom is as true for regional as for global peacemakers.

Notes

1. E. John Inegbedion, "ECOMOG in Comparative Perspective," in Timothy M. Shaw and Julius Emeka Okolo (eds.), *The Political Economy of Foreign Policy in ECOWAS* (New York: St. Martin's Press, 1994), p. 231. For a good overview of the early years of the operation, see Karl P. Magyar and Earl Conteh-Morgan (eds.), *Peacekeeping in Africa: ECOMOG in Liberia* (London: Macmillan/New York: St. Martin's Press, 1998).

2. William Reno, "Sierra Leone: Weak States and the New Sovereignty Game," in Leonardo A. Villalón and Phillip A. Huxtable (eds.), *The African State at a Critical Juncture: Between Disintegration and Reconfiguration* (Boulder: Lynne Rienner Publishers, 1998), p. 98. See also William Reno, *Warlord Politics and African States* (Boulder: Lynne Rienner Publishers, 1998), especially chapters 3 and 4. Mark Huband reports that Taylor was "determined to have his revenge on Momoh" for having refused to allow Taylor to launch his planned invasion from Sierra Leone; see Huband's *The Liberian Civil War* (London/Portland, Oreg.: Frank Cass, 1998), p. 59.

3. Paul Richards, "Rebellion in Liberia and Sierra Leone: A Crisis of Youth," in Oliver Furley (ed.), *Conflict in Africa* (London: I. B. Tauris Publishers, 1995), pp. 139–141.

4. Reno, *Warlord Politics*, p. 98.

5. Yekutiel Gershoni sees the proliferation of factions as one of the major factors prolonging the wars in both countries. See his "War Without End and an End to a War: The Prolonged Wars in Liberia and Sierra Leone," *African Studies Review* 40, no. 3 (December 1997), pp. 59–60.

6. Quoted in *Le Monde*, January 14–15, 1996. During the looting of Monrovia in April 1996, a UN worker asserted that "the best cars, the best video players, the best air conditioners went to Ecomog officers" (*New York Times*, April 30, 1996).

7. For an account of the diplomatic process through 1994, see Robert A. Mortimer, "ECOMOG, Liberia, and Regional Security in West Africa," in Edmond Keller and Donald Rothchild (eds.), *Africa in the New International Order* (Boulder: Lynne Rienner Publishers, 1996), pp. 149–164.

8. François Prkic, "Le Ghana dans la gestion de la crise libérienne," paper presented at the Colloquium on Ghana organized at the Centre d'Etude d'Afrique Noire, Bordeaux, May 29–30, 1998, p. 13.

9. Interview with Mohamed Ibn Chambas, cited in ibid., p. 13.

10. Quoted in *Africa Research Bulletin* 32, no. 6 (June 1995), p. 11891.

11. Such at least is the argument of the secretary of state for education in the NPRC government. See Arthur Abraham, "War and Transition to Peace: A Study of State Conspiracy in Perpetuating Armed Conflict," *Africa Development* 22, no. 3/4 (1997), pp. 101–116. Abraham concludes that "once the NPRC had set themselves to plundering the resources of the state to enrich themselves, they had to keep the war going in order to stay in power and thus maintain the opportunity to plunder" (p. 109).

12. Foreign Minister Amara Essy strongly pressured the RUF, which Côte d'Ivoire had tacitly supported for much the same reasons that it supported Taylor's NPFL, to sign the agreement. He was at the time a French-sponsored candi-

date for the secretary-general's post at the United Nations. Thus do global stakes (the rivalry between France and the United States over the secretary-generalship) filter down to local conflicts in unexpected ways. See Yusuf Bangura, "Reflections on the Abidjan Peace Accord," *Africa Development* 22, no. 3/4 (1997), p. 224.

13. The text of the Abidjan Accord appears in *Africa Development* 22, no. 3/4 (1997), pp. 243–252.

14. Ibid., p. 247.

15. Ibid., p. 252.

16. According to Steve Riley, the root cause of the coup is the "conflict between the Kamajors and the army." See his "Sierra Leone: The Militariat Strikes Again," *Review of African Political Economy* 72 (June 1997), p. 290.

17. Quoted in *Africa Research Bulletin* 34, no. 8 (August 1997), p. 12798. For a good account of these early negotiations, see Lansana Gberie, "The May 25 Coup d'Etat in Sierra Leone: A Militariat Revolt?" *African Development* 22, no. 3/4 (1997), pp. 163–165.

18. Quoted in *Africa Research Bulletin* 34, no. 9 (September 1997), p. 12808.

19. The text of the Conakry communiqué appears in *Africa Development* 22, no. 3/4 (1997), pp. 253–258.

20. *Africa Research Bulletin* 34, no. 12 (December 1997), p. 12921.

21. Ibid., p. 12922.

22. Early on February 6, a pro-Kabbah clandestine radio station warned Freetown residents to stay inside "because Ecomog had decided to get rid of the junta for good," and captured Nigerian soldiers told journalists that the march on Freetown had been planned well in advance. See *Africa Research Bulletin* 35, no. 2 (February 1998), p. 12992. Agence France-Presse reported that the assault bore the code name "Operation Sandstorm."

23. *Le Monde*, February 13, 1998.

24. There are reports that the mercenary outfit, Sandline International, was involved in the shipment of weapons to Sierra Leone just before the overthrow of the junta. Sandline appears to have been primarily involved with the Kamajors (who were also pro-Kabbah) rather than with ECOMOG. See Philippe Vasset, "Grande Bretagne: Les 'Chiens de Guerre' de Sa Majesté," *Jeune Afrique* 1949 (May 19–25, 1998), pp. 30–32; and David Shearer, "Outsourcing War," *Foreign Policy* (Summer 1998), pp. 77–78.

25. Quoted in *Sud-Quotidien*, February 18, 1998.

26. "The Liberian Syndrome," *Jeune Afrique* 1938 (March 3–9, 1998).

27. *Sud-Quotidien*, February 18, 1998. For its part, *Le Monde* (February 13, 1998) wrote that Nigeria was "seeking to impose its law on the region."

28. Quoted in *Sud-Quotidien*, March 12, 1998.

29. For a thorough account of Guidimakha, see François Gaulme, "Opération Guidimakha: Et si un état africain était menacé . . . ," *Jeune Afrique* 1939 (March 10–16, 1998), pp. 34–37. See also *Le Monde*, January 18–19, 1998; and *Sud-Quotidien*, March 4, 1998.

30. Quoted in *Wal Fadjri* (Dakar), March 13, 1998.

31. Quoted in *Le Soleil* (Dakar), May 5, 1998.

32. Norimitsu Onishi, "What War Has Wrought: Sierra Leone's Sad State," *New York Times*, January 31, 1999.

33. This according to the Nigerian press, as reported in *Le Monde*, February 20, 1999. The figures were accompanied by reports that ECOMOG soldiers had engaged in summary executions of Sierra Leonean civilians.

34. Interview with Blaise Compaoré, "Je ne suis pas un fauteur de troubles!" *Jeune Afrique* 1988 (February 16–22, 1999), p. 18.

35. On the Senegalese attempt to "de-Nigerianize" the force, see Robert Mortimer, "Senegal's Role in ECOMOG: The Francophone Dimension in the Liberian Crisis," in Magyar and Conteh-Morgan (eds.), *Peacekeeping in Africa*, pp. 123–137.

36. During his spring 1998 tour of Africa, President Clinton visited the base in Senegal where American instructors were training Senegalese troops to participate in the ACRI.

37. On the expansion and subsequent retrenchment of UN peacekeeping, see Olara A. Otunnu and Michael W. Doyle (eds.), *Peacemaking and Peacekeeping for the New Century* (Lanham, Md.: Rowman and Littlefield Publishers, 1998).

38. Kofi Annan, "Challenges of the New Peacekeeping," in Otunnu and Doyle (eds.), *Peacemaking and Peacekeeping for the New Century*, p. 186.

9

Africa in World Affairs

CAROL LANCASTER

Foreign Aid in Sub-Saharan Africa

The end of the Cold War and the new millennium are occasions for reflection and retrospection. One of the major issues worthy of such consideration is the role of foreign aid in Africa. In no other major world region have foreign transfers of concessional resources played so large and influential a role. Now, as it appears that the era of high aid flows to Africa is ending with the downward trend in those flows since 1993, it is appropriate to ask some probing questions: What have been the motivations of governments, international organizations, and, increasingly, nongovernmental organizations (NGOs) for providing aid to Africa? What have been the motivations of Africans seeking and receiving the aid? What has the impact of the aid been on politics and development in Africa? What are the future prospects for aid to Africa?

I address these questions in four sections of the chapter. First, I examine the facts of aid in Africa; next, I review the motivations both of the donors and the recipients of aid; then, I assess the economic and political impact of aid in the region; and, finally, I examine the probable future of aid in Africa, with discussions concerning the size, use, and management of the aid. As will become clear, the motivations of aid donors have been multiple, among which promoting development is only one—and, even then, not always the most prominent one. Indeed, although aid in Africa has had some outstanding development successes, on the whole its impact has been disappointing in terms of promoting African development. The domestic fiscal pressures on aid donors, the declining enthusiasm among several of the major ones (including the United States and Japan), and the problems of aid effectiveness in Africa will likely lead to further reductions in aid there as well as efforts to reform the way aid is delivered and managed in the future. The motivations behind aid have long been highly political; but the political goals of aid in Africa have lessened (though not vanished), as have the levels of the aid itself. There is now a chance for more effective aid for development, but it is almost certainly to be considerably smaller in the future.

The Facts of Foreign Aid in Africa

The story of overall aid flows to sub-Saharan Africa is a straightforward one. Beginning with modest levels during the 1960s, foreign aid[1] to the region rose rapidly starting in the first half of the 1970s, at a time of oil price shocks and collapse of the prices of many primary commodities. Aid levels continued to increase significantly, particularly in the 1980s, as significant quantities of concessional resources were transferred to African countries in support of structural and sectoral adjustment programs. Aid to Africa peaked in the early 1990s and has declined steadily since 1994. The level of aid to Africa in 1997 was equal in real terms to the level of aid in 1983 (see Table 9.1).

As noted earlier, despite the falling levels of aid to African countries, the region is still, on average, the most aided of major world regions. In 1997, net disbursements of concessional resources to sub-Saharan Africa amounted to $16.4 billion. Foreign aid as a percentage of the gross national product (GNP) of the countries of sub-Saharan Africa averaged 5 percent in 1996–1997, down from 10 percent in the 1980s but still the highest of any major developing region.[2] Foreign aid was also equal to half or more of the total level of investment in many African countries. These relatively high levels of aid have continued over several decades or more. The percentage of total aid worldwide allocated to African countries has also risen over the past two decades, from an average of 23 percent in 1981–1982 to 30 percent in 1997 (although this percentage had crept downward from a high of just over 31 percent several years earlier). Yet in 1998, sub-Saharan Africa represented only 13 percent of the population of the developing world.[3]

Which countries in Africa have benefited from this aid, and where has it come from? Table 9.2 lists the major recipients of foreign aid in 1993 and 1997, and Table 9.3 shows the principal sources of aid to Africa from 1980 to 1996.

Table 9.3 also shows some interesting trends among the bilateral and multilateral sources of aid to Africa. Whereas aid from both types of

TABLE 9.1   Aid to Africa, 1970–1997 (in billions constant 1997)

Year	Amount
1970	6.3
1971	6.7
1972	6.3
1973	6.7
1974	8.5
1975	10.0
1976	9.3
1977	10.4
1978	11.8
1979	13.2
1980	14.0
1981	14.9
1982	16.5
1983	16.3
1984	17.5
1985	19.7
1986	19.2
1987	18.8
1988	19.9
1989	21.4
1990	21.9
1991	21.1
1992	21.3
1993	19.9
1994	20.9
1995	18.5
1996	17.2
1997	16.3

SOURCE: Organization for Economic Cooperation and Development (Paris: OECD, various years).

TABLE 9.2   Major Recipients of Foreign Aid (in $millions)

1993		1997	
Mozambique	$1183	Mozambique	$963
Ethiopia	$1094	Tanzania	$963
Tanzania	$953	Zambia	$840
Kenya	$911	Madagascar	$838
Somalia	$890	Ethiopia	$637

SOURCE: Development Assistance Committee (Paris: OECD, 1998), p. A53.

TABLE 9.3   Net Disbursements of Overseas Development Assistance to
Sub-Saharan Africa, by Donor ($millions at 1995 prices and exchange rates)

	1980	1986	1993	1994	1995	1996
DAC Bilateral						
Australia	30	40	59	69	60	55
Austria	21	25	85	81	76	97
Belgium	501	496	263	240	196	207
Canada	294	376	287	263	275	266
Denmark	237	369	414	411	367	458
Finland	66	165	109	104	79	82
France	1686	2678	3555	3550	2700	2448
Germany	1257	1488	1568	1366	1268	1268
Ireland	11	20	30	42	62	75
Italy	97	1434	582	407	359	292
Japan	692	879	1154	1258	1352	1253
Luxembourg	–	–	17	20	–	31
Netherlands	628	782	612	605	695	709
New Zealand	2	1	2	5	4	4
Norway	194	419	360	411	380	386
Portugal	–	–	211	242	155	147
Spain	–	–	82	120	79	209
Sweden	426	608	604	491	388	433
Switzerland	126	319	232	227	219	201
United Kingdom	659	500	530	662	601	619
United States	1024	1161	1503	1490	1050	623
Total DAC	7952	11762	12259	12062	10366	9865
Multilateral						
AtDF	186	448	752	614	549	590
CEC	1219	1376	1900	2275	1736	2073
Nordic Dev. Fund	–	–	–	9	12	28
IBRD	75	2	–	–	–	–
IDA	816	2349	2464	3064	2276	2525
IFAD	8	161	45	42	65	80
UNTA	17	81	95	70	125	60
UNICEF	110	191	351	362	310	294
UNDP	378	443	371	306	274	334
UNHCR	310	309	376	569	427	386
WFP	340	384	1004	836	617	579
Total above	3458	5744	7358	8138	6389	6920
Other UN	164	183	147	140	153	142
Arab agencies	290	148	–11	27	–	–
Other multilateral	754	–200	140	507	1543	161
Total Multilateral	4666	6074	7494	8315	6542	7091
Arab countries	1048	767	45	15	11	38
Other	321	783	9	–	–	–
Overall totals	13987	19185	19947	20900	18463	17150

NOTE: These figures have been deflated by individual DAC country deflators.
SOURCE: Developmental Assistance Committee, (Paris: OECD, 1997).

donors has declined, aid from bilateral donors—especially from the largest donors, such as France, the United States, Japan, and Germany— has decreased most dramatically. Aid from the two principal multilateral sources—the International Development Association of the World Bank and the European Union—has actually risen slightly. These figures suggest a declining interest and engagement on the part of significant world powers in Africa and a resulting shift to multilateral organizations in the burden of aiding the region.

As for the recipients of aid in Africa, every country (including failed states like Somalia or Sierra Leone) received some aid, if only relief assistance. As noted, the countries receiving the largest aid flows in 1993 and 1997 are listed in Table 9.2.

What is missing from this table are the names of several major recipients of foreign aid in the 1980s—in particular, the Democratic Republic of the Congo (the former Zaire) and Sudan. It is also interesting to note that Kenya is not on the list for 1997. We shall examine the reasons for these changes later in the chapter, when we consider the motives of aid donors in providing assistance to Africa.

One more fact is worth mentioning: Countries receiving the largest amounts of aid relative to the size of their economies are not usually the same as those receiving the largest overall aid flows. In 1997, the African countries with the largest aid-to-GNP ratios were São Tomé and Principe (117 percent), Guinea Bissau (71 percent), Rwanda (49 percent), Mozambique (43 percent), and Cape Verde (29 percent). These ratios confirm that smaller countries in Africa and elsewhere tend to receive larger amounts of aid relative to the size of their economies, reflecting the tendency on the part of aid donors to provide aid to countries above certain minimum amounts regardless of the size of the country's population.

With regard to the form that aid in Africa takes, there are several alternatives. Aid can be provided as cash grants or as concessional loans. It can be provided in the form of food aid or other types of aid in kind. Grants or credits may finance the purchase of goods, such as equipment and materials for road construction, or the purchase of services, such as publicly funded research. It can also fund training and technical assistance to recipient governments or organizations. Finally, aid can be provided to governments or to nongovernmental organizations, foreign or indigenous.

Unfortunately, there are few aggregate data available that break down these types of aid by major world region. We can nevertheless make some informed guesses regarding the types of aid provided to the region based on worldwide data and what is known about aid in Africa generally. First, most bilateral aid to African countries and a significant proportion of multilateral aid (especially from the European Union and various

United Nations organizations) is in grant form. Aid from the World Bank and the African Development Bank and Fund is in the form of credits provided on highly concessional terms. Further, a portion of aid to Africa is in the form of food aid. In 1997, food aid worldwide as a proportion of total aid was only 2 percent (not counting food for emergencies), and this proportion has been declining over the past decade. The proportion in Africa may have been somewhat higher, given the food import needs there, but it is unlikely to have been a significant proportion of total aid flows.[4]

Aid in the form of technical assistance continues to constitute a high and rising proportion of aid worldwide (equal to one-third of bilateral aid in 1996). It seems likely that the proportion of technical assistance to total bilateral aid in Africa is considerably higher than one-third, given the feeling among donors that the weak capacity of many African organizations justifies large amounts of such assistance. (Technical assistance as a proportion of multilateral aid is likely to be less than one-third, especially in aid from the World Bank.) Finally, most aid to Africa goes to African governments, but a small and rising amount is provided to NGOs, primarily Northern NGOs. In 1997, roughly 3 percent of total bilateral aid worldwide was channeled to NGOs. Aid to NGOs in Africa is likely to be close to this proportion.

How is the aid used in Africa? Again, we do not have data by region, but the worldwide data give some indication of how aid is likely to have been used in Africa. Roughly a third of bilateral and multilateral aid is used to fund social and administrative infrastructure (including education, health, water supply, and sanitation) as well as government, civil society, and other services. Just under 15 percent of aid is used to fund projects and programs involving economic infrastructure, such as transport and communications and energy. And just under 15 percent is used to fund activities in agriculture, industry, mining, construction, trade, and tourism. The remainder funds a variety of activities, including multisector programs and projects, program assistance, debt relief, and emergency aid. It seems likely that the proportion of aid in Africa that funds social and administrative infrastructure is higher than the worldwide average, and that the proportion of aid for agriculture, industry, mining, trade, and tourism is somewhat lower. Program aid, tied to sectoral and structural adjustment programs, may also be higher in Africa than elsewhere.

Aid-Donor Motives in Africa

In any given year, there are typically thirty to forty governments and international organizations providing foreign aid to individual African countries.[5] They include European, North American, and Japanese governments; the governments of Arab oil-producing countries; former socialist bloc countries (which were important sources of aid during the Cold War but today provide relatively little if any assistance); a group of "new" aid donors such as Korea, Turkey, and other formerly poor countries; and, finally, a host of development banks and international organizations. Each has its own mix of motives, which in turn influence the three key decisions it must make regarding the allocation of aid: Which countries will be aided? How much will they receive? And what will the aid be used for?

The purposes for which aid is given fall into five major categories. One is to promote *development* in recipient countries. Ideas of what development is and how it is to be promoted often vary among donors; they have also changed over time, particularly in terms of the emphasis given to promoting growth versus reducing poverty. During the 1960s, the focus was on promoting growth by using aid to relieve the budgetary and balance-of-payments constraints on growth, especially through funding the expansion of infrastructure and social services such as education and health. The 1970s saw a shift toward using aid to benefit the poor directly, by funding projects in rural areas that addressed "basic human needs" such as primary education, health care, clean water, and sanitation, and by promoting "integrated rural development" with a mix of activities that would enable small farmers to expand their production and income.

The debt crisis and collapse in growth rates of the 1980s shifted the focus of foreign aid yet again, toward funding economic reforms regarded as essential to restoring growth in developing countries. These included exchange rate devaluations and reductions in fiscal deficits. In the 1990s, the emphasis on structural and sectoral adjustment reforms gave way to a focus on "governance" and democratization, together with a number of other concerns that had been peripheral to development during much of the past several decades: protection of the environment, capacity building, engaging and strengthening civil society, and postconflict rehabilitation. Toward the end of the 1990s, major aid donors, such as the World Bank, returned to emphasizing poverty reduction. This time, however, there did not appear to be a specific "policy paradigm" governing programs and projects designed for this purpose.

The promotion of development has played a prominent role in the aid programs and projects of most aid donors, though its prominence has varied among them and over time. Not surprisingly, international and regional organizations and development banks have tended to place the greatest emphasis on this goal. A group of smaller countries with relatively limited diplomatic or commercial interests in Africa—dubbed by some observers as the "humane internationalists"—have also made development their primary goal. This group includes most prominently the Nordic countries, the Netherlands, and Canada.

A second major purpose for which foreign aid has been provided to Africa is *diplomatic* in nature. As a tool of foreign policy, foreign aid is frequently deployed to promote particular diplomatic goals. During the Cold War, competition between the USSR and its allies, on the one hand, and the Western countries, on the other, was a major motivating purpose behind aid to Africa. This purpose was important not only in terms of the aid allocations of the major competitors in this war, but also because it generated mini–Cold Wars of its own, drawing an unlikely set of donor governments into the business of aiding Africa: the two Chinas, the Arabs and Israelis, Cuba, and even the two Koreas.

The Cold War was an important motivator of aid to Africa, but it was not the only source of the "high politics" of aid-giving. Another set of diplomatic purposes was related to postcolonial relationships. The French government viewed its former territories in Africa as part of its "pré carre," or natural sphere of influence, intended to boost France's international status and influence. Aid was a key element in preserving these relationships. The U.K. took a different approach: It wanted to reduce its engagement and exposure in Africa while preserving its economic interests, the well-being of its settler populations, and a modicum of influence there. Indeed, aid was a useful tool to ease London's withdrawal from active engagement in the region.

For most aid-giving governments, there were also the "low politics" of aid—providing aid in exchange for particular benefits from the recipient government. This category might include, for example, votes in the United Nations or simply enhanced access to prominent political figures. The fact that most governments with diplomatic representation in African countries also have aid programs in those countries (even if the programs are small) is a manifestation of the politics of access.

A third category of purposes is *commercial*, in that it entails the providing of aid, often in a package of mixed credits (e.g., with export credits on relatively hard terms), as an inducement for African governments to purchase goods and services from enterprises in the donor country. These packages of mixed credits have often been tied to particular projects, such as the construction of a dam or airport or the import of large-scale equipment such as trains or aircraft. The most avid practitioners of aid for commercial advantage have been the Italians and the French governments, though they were never entirely alone. Another commercial purpose in aid-giving has been the assurance of donor governments' continued access to the markets of African countries, particularly in cases where the donor needed to import certain primary products that it did not produce at home. In its early years of aiding African countries, Japan was strongly motivated by this purpose.

A fourth purpose is *cultural*, including the spread of particular languages, religion, and values. The French have been the most prominent practitioners of tying aid to the maintenance and spread of the French language and culture, but they are not the only ones. The Portuguese and Italians have shown the same motivation, eager to fund educational and other activities that involve the use of Portuguese or Italian. And Arab governments and multilateral organizations have deployed aid in support of mosques and other organizations and activities related to Islam. One is tempted to view the U.S. emphasis on democracy as an expression of U.S. cultural values, as much as one of political and developmental goals.

Last but far from least is the collective *humanitarian* purpose of foreign aid: to relieve suffering, to promote rehabilitation and recovery in the wake of natural or manmade disasters, and to help improve the lives of the least advantaged, if only for a time. Nearly all donors of foreign aid in Africa have provided a portion of their aid for this purpose—one that, typically, their publics support strongly.

It is very important to recognize one further influential force on the aid policies and practices of all aid donors: the politics within aid agencies and governments. The motivations described above may determine whether a government has an aid program and affect many of the policy and allocative decisions involving that aid. But aid agencies, whether bilateral or multilateral, are political entities, embedded in political institutions and environments. These institutions and environments often play a significant role in influencing and constraining aid decisions. Indeed, it is difficult to understand many of an aid agency's policies without taking bureaucratic politics, legislative influences, political party preferences, interest groups, societal characteristics, and public opinion in donor countries and organizations into account. We shall return to this point presently.

What factors determine how individual donors are motivated by the above-mentioned purposes in their allocation and use of aid? One approach is an "agency-centered" one, focusing on aid agencies and the institutions and political environments in which they are embedded. Let us assume that a government's aid agencies are committed to promoting development (however defined) and, further, that they are the major voice within governments supporting that goal. There is plenty of evidence that this is usually the case, even if factions within aid agencies differ on which aspects of development to emphasize. But aid agencies are almost never autonomous; indeed, they tend to be relatively weak compared to other government agencies. (For example, they are rarely elevated to cabinet-level rank, and they are often part of other agencies—usually ministries of foreign affairs.) In cases where several aid agencies are involved, the voice within government for development is usually further weakened—as in Japan and France, whose aid organizations are highly fragmented. All aid agencies appear to share one thing in common: the circumstance of being pressured to spend available funds within whatever time frames those funds are made available. This pressure derives from the incentive structure within which bureaucrats typically function: Monies not expended are seen by legislatures, budget offices, and others as a sign that less funding is required. But public officials almost always strive to expand rather than contract spending. As a result, a failure to spend all available monies is usually seen as a career-limiting failure. Clearly, the pressure to spend is greater when agencies are attempting to expand their budgets and less compelling when budgets are falling. This pressure constrains the bargaining power of aid officials in relation to foreign recipients and can lead to hasty allocative decisions on the part of those agencies.

Other agencies within governments have their own missions and goals and typically attempt to influence the allocation and use of aid resources to promote those goals. We can begin to understand the allocative and policy decisions made by aid agencies when we examine their relationships with other bureaucratic actors. Where ministries of foreign affairs are powerful (and this is usually the case with governments that are pursuing foreign policy goals linked closely to national security or high-priority diplomatic concerns), they frequently have significant influence over the allocative decisions of aid agencies. (They also become advocates of aid with other parts of their governments or publics.) Ministries of Trade and Commerce also attempt to influence the allocation of aid to support their goals abroad. Where ministries of foreign affairs have few compelling national goals or are weak, and where economic ministries are strong, aid allocations often emphasize commercial purposes. This appears to have been the case in the Soviet Union at the end of the 1980s, when the Soviet aid agency was merged with the Ministry of Foreign Trade and Soviet aid was increasingly tied to Moscow's commercial interests.

A key bureaucratic actor is the presidency. Where presidents or prime ministers become involved in aid decisions, they do so almost always for high-priority political reasons; they usually preempt all other interests and wield significant influence, diverting aid from developmental purposes. This scenario has been evident in Washington at times when there was a presidential interest in allocating aid for particular purposes (e.g., peacemaking in the Middle East). It has also been evident in Paris, where the presidency has long viewed aid (especially that managed by the Ministry of Cooperation) as an important tool to support French political interests in France's former African territories—including those involving individual African presidents and officials. The late, formidable Jacques Foccart, long an adviser to French presidents on Africa, once termed these types of aid relationships as "cousinage et copainage" (relations among cousins and mates).

Outside of the bureaucracy, one must examine the influence of the legis-lature on aid policies and allocations. For the most part, national legisla-tures have little to say about their government's foreign aid. Parliamentary systems discourage legislators' interference in aid decisions. In contrast, the fragmented political system of the United States, where members of Con-gress are elected independently of presidents and party discipline is weak, allows the legislature to play a major role in influencing not only the levels and country allocation of foreign aid but also, increasingly, the use of such aid. In appropriations bills, Congress includes "earmarks" and directives indicating how and where it wants much of the aid spent. These have in-creased in recent years as the concept of what can fairly be called "develop-ment" has broadened (and blurred), and, in turn, as the decline of the Cold War has diminished the interest and engagement of the Department of State in promoting and influencing foreign aid.

Ministries of finance and budgetary agencies (where they are separate) can also have a major influence on aid levels, reflecting broader macro-economic and fiscal concerns. Such influence has affected the outcome of efforts to reduce the fiscal deficit in the United States and in Europe—in the latter case, to meet the Maastricht criteria for participation in the new monetary union of the European Union.

Outside of legislatures, one must likewise consider private organized and unorganized interests that attempt to influence the allocation and use of aid. Nongovernmental organizations have become an increasing voice in favor of development in recent years in most aid-giving countries, but they have also attempted to influence the ways in which aid is used to promote development, typically calling for a greater focus on poverty re-duction. In addition, some have succeeded in increasing the focus and size of resources devoted to particular purposes—population control, family planning, environmental protection, and so on—including the channeling of increasing amounts of aid through NGOs themselves. The influence of NGOs is most evident in the fragmented political system of the United States, but NGOs have also been influential in Sweden, Canada, and elsewhere. In particular, they have managed to influence the allocation and use of aid by several multilateral aid agencies, including the World Bank, by working directly with the banks and through the leg-islatures of major funding countries, including the United States, Canada, and several European countries. The influence of NGOs in Japan, France, and Italy has remained weak—because of the nature of the political insti-tutions in those countries and, possibly, because of the strength of other interests in influencing aid decisions—the presidency in France and the business sectors in Japan and Italy.

Political parties affect aid allocations in a number of countries. Those with strong social democratic ideologies often support generous allocations of aid to governments with similar ideologies in Africa and else-where. One reason that Tanzania under Julius Nyerere received so much aid was that governments like those in Ottawa and Stockholm regarded him as a political soul mate. Other influences on aid allocations can de-rive from the ethnic makeup of donor countries (often reflected in the constituencies of particular political parties), as in Belgium, where Walloons tended to support President Mobutu's Zaire and Flemish tended not to (with aid allocations to Zaire changing according to which group was in control of aid decisions). Similarly, in Canada, the interests of French- and English-speaking populations led to the maintenance of roughly equal levels of aid to the Francophone and Anglophone countries of Africa.

Finally, one must look at public opinion in aid-giving countries. Such opinion tends to be passive and permissive, except when an economic or political disaster provokes demands for more aid (i.e., as a response to disasters and human suffering in Africa and elsewhere) or when political disasters involve the aid program. For example, the revelation of perva-sive corruption in Italian aid agencies at the beginning of the 1990s led to a public outcry as well as to a collapse in Italian aid to Africa that shows no signs of recovering.

What would a snapshot of aid donor motivations tell us today about aid in Africa? The Cold War is no longer a motivating force in the aid pro-grams of major donors. The elimination of this purpose has had two con-sequences. First, it has undoubtedly contributed to falling levels of aid to Africa in countries, such as the United States, where traditional economic and political interests are limited and there is no longer a simple, com-pelling reason to provide significant amounts of aid. Second, it has per-mitted aid donors to be more selective about the countries they aid. Soon after the end of the Cold War, most donors cut off aid to the corrupt and incompetent government of Mobutu Sese Seko of Zaire. Aid to Kenya has dropped significantly since the early 1990s for the same reason.

France continues to provide significant amounts of aid to its former ter-ritories, but even this aid is decreasing; in fact, the influence of these countries in Paris appears to be diminishing. This change is related far less to the Cold War than to changes in the French political elites, dissatis-faction among certain elements of the informed public over France's shady relationships with corrupt African leaders, and the falling commer-cial interest in France's former colonies, which now offer French business relatively few attractive opportunities. Perhaps it is the case, as one for-mer senior French aid official said several years ago, that "l'Afrique du papa est fini."

Also evident is the deconcentration of aid to Africa: Aid donors have fewer favored partners now that the Cold War is over and economic growth is yet to take off. As a result, many donor countries are reducing their aid but spreading it more widely. For example, Japan has an aid program—often very small—in virtually every African country. The same is true of the United States. These governments—and, more particularly, their ambassadors in Africa—want access. (And Japan wants votes in support of its bid for a permanent seat on the UN Security Council.)

Moreover, aid for commercial purposes in Africa is likely to remain relatively small until broad economic recovery occurs in the region. But the hoped-for African renaissance is yet to appear, and circumstances may get worse before they get better given the decrease in primary product prices at the end of the 1990s and the spread of civil and interstate conflict in central, northeast, and West Africa.

However, the decrease in the diplomatic and commercial importance of Africa to major donors has not yet led to a major drop in aid to the region—only to a slow decline. This fact suggests that the development purpose is real and continues to support relatively high levels of aid, despite the increasing discomfort of aid donors with the past ineffectiveness of their aid in Africa—a discomfort compounded by uncertainty as to how to make aid more effective in the future.

The Motives of African Aid Recipients

African officials actively sought and almost always accepted foreign aid, and they continue to do so. What have been their motivations?

Like political officials anywhere, Africans have put a high priority on protecting their national security and independence. Foreign aid has helped them in this regard in two ways. First, it provides additional resources to governments that can free up domestic resources to be used for security purposes. In a number of cases (e.g., Sudan during the 1980s), aid donors provided governments with economic assistance for precisely this purpose—to enable those governments to spend more funds on military equipment. We do not know how many African governments on their own exploited the "fungibility" (i.e., substitutability) of foreign aid for domestic resources to fund additional military expenditures or other activities related to national security.[6]

Foreign aid can be useful in strengthening the national security of African countries in a second way as well. Often overlooked is the fact that aid is not just a transfer of resources from one government to another. It also often carries important symbolic significance. As a voluntary gift from one government to another, it reflects the donor's approbation of the recipient. Rising levels of aid typically symbolize increasing approbation, whereas declining levels or the elimination of aid are seen as reflecting disapproval of recipients on the part of donors. (Similarly, a recipient's acceptance or rejection of aid is a manifestation of approbation or disapproval of the donor on the part of the recipient.) The symbolic significance of aid is evident in the efforts by aid donor governments to initiate or increase aid at the time of state visits, as with President Clinton's recent trip to various African countries. Ambassadors of donor countries frequently plead for a continuation or increase in aid for the countries to which they are accredited, arguing that cutting aid would "damage the foreign policy interests" of their governments—meaning that it would be taken by recipients as a symbol of disapproval.

African officials find the approbation associated with aid programs from major powers useful in signaling to their populations and their neighbors that they have powerful friends, implying that the same friends might come to their aid if their security is threatened. It is quite clear that President Mobutu of Zaire sought, received, and presented the aid he received from the United States, France, and even Belgium in this light. Once that aid was terminated, Mobutu's enemies at home and abroad began to take heart in attacking him and his government, no longer fearing the protective intervention of his powerful official friends.

Foreign aid also serves a purpose that is important to African leaders: preserving their rule. Here, too, the symbolic functions of aid can play a role in several ways. First, as with external threats to national security, aid can be presented or perceived as a reflection of the approbation of donors, thereby strengthening the status and power of the recipient government and its leadership.[7] Second, aid can help leaders to consolidate their power. Most African leaders have, at least rhetorically, placed national economic development at the top of their political agendas. As a result, they and their regimes have often been judged in terms of their success or lack thereof in bringing about an improvement in the conditions of the lives of their peoples. But development is at best a long-term process, with the benefits of today's decisions likely to be apparent only years or decades later. So African leaders have sought to present to their peoples the symbols of development; and, apart from visible, showcase projects, these symbols have relied on the promises of aid or the initiation of aid-funded activities. Consider the words of Julius Nyerere, former president of Tanzania:

> Our Government and different groups of our leaders never stop thinking about methods of getting finance from abroad. And if we get some money, or even if we just get a promise of it, our newspapers, our radio, and our leaders, all advertise the fact in order that every person shall know that salvation is coming, or is on the way. If we receive a gift we announce it, if we receive a loan we announce it, if we get a new industry, we make an announcement of the promise. Even when we have merely started discussions with a foreign government or institution for a gift, a loan or a new industry, we make an an-

nouncement—even though we do not know the outcome of the discussions. Why do we do all this? Because we want people to know that we have started discussions which will bring prosperity.[8]

Aid was and is a symbol of development—or, at least, of the promise thereof—and thus very important to the many African governments whose legitimacy and support rest on the promise of prosperity.

Perhaps even more important for domestic political purposes is another use of aid: the provision of resources that can be used for patronage, which in turn is the glue that has kept many an African government (whether democratic or authoritarian) from falling apart. African leaders recognized this use of foreign aid early on, and so did many outside observers. It is not that the aid is simply transferred to the bank accounts of the clients of political leaders (or to their own bank accounts). This happens, though probably much less than is generally assumed, given the existence of auditors from donor governments who keep an eye on how the aid funds are used. Aid can provide patronage, indirectly through its ability to free up domestic resources and directly in terms of the activities it funds. Aid funds training and attendance at conferences outside the country (with comfortable per diems for participants). It funds vehicles and equipment that expatriate technical assistants leave behind. It funds local improvements—roads, schoolhouses, and clinics, for example—and it can create local jobs (at least temporarily while the aid project is under way) that function as forms of patronage for the residents of favored localities. Even though as much as three-quarters of foreign aid is spent on goods and services purchased outside of recipient countries (the proportion of U.S. aid that is tied to the purchase of U.S. goods and services is reportedly around 80 percent), the goods and some of the benefits of the services eventually end up in African hands. In the cash- and commodity-starved countries of the region, aid is still a welcome gift that political leaders can use to bolster their support at home.

All African leaders make rhetorical commitments to promote the development of their countries. And many (apart from the most corrupt or repressive leaders) implement policies and programs intended to realize this purpose. Aid can be an important source of additional resources toward the same end, and African leaders, heading the governments of some of the least developed and poorest countries in the world, realize that their countries are unlikely to make rapid economic progress in the absence of additional resources provided by aid. This is especially the case in African countries where private foreign and domestic investment remains very low.

In seeking and accepting large amounts of aid from foreign governments and international institutions, African leaders have faced a difficult problem. Their status as leaders of independent countries (only recently emerging from colonialism) and their freedom to make decisions on foreign policy, economic policy, and political issues at home require them to protect that independence (including the appearance of independence). But receiving large amounts of aid, especially when that aid is provided by a few powerful foreign governments or organizations, can appear to compromise a leader's independence and, in fact, circumscribe that independence in key areas. How can African officials benefit from aid without losing or even appearing to lose their freedom to act as the leaders of independent countries?

During the Cold War, African governments adopted a number of tactics to preserve their independence from aid donors. We can observe three principal ones: (1) "switching" or threatening to switch sides in the Cold War in order to keep major donors from attempting to exert control over key policies, (2) "balanced benefaction,"[9] and (3) "reliance/penetration." Let us examine each of these briefly.

"Switching" is the best-known but in reality the least employed tactic used by Africans to protect their independence from aid donors. Kwame Nkrumah of Ghana, Sekou Toure of Guinea, and Siad Barre of Somalia have all used this tactic. It led both to distrust on the part of the United States and the USSR and to relatively low levels of aid for the African governments. Mobutu Sese Seko used more subtle tactics, often threatening to switch among his major funders (the United States, Belgium, and France) and, at times, hinting at his intention to look for support from socialist countries as well. He long benefited from playing off major funders against one another and received large flows of aid over an extended period of time, with relatively little effective influence exerted by donors over policies he considered important (e.g., how government revenues were spent).

Many African governments, ruling relatively small and poor countries with little strategic value or diplomatic influence, did not have the option of switching and, hence, adopted the tactic of "balanced benefaction." Specifically, they sought aid from a wide variety of governments but avoided becoming excessively reliant on any one of them so that if they had to reject aid because of efforts on the part of donors to influence their policies, they would not suffer serious consequences. These countries tended to be ex-British colonies—Tanzania and Kenya, in particular— where multiple aid donors felt comfortable operating.

The third tactic—"reliance/penetration"—is used when a country relies heavily on a single aid donor but attempts to influence that donor's decisions and policies through penetration of its political system. This is the tactic employed by Francophone African countries in relation to France, which has remained the principal source of aid for most of these countries. The Africans, in turn, have developed or maintained their personal relations with French officials and political elites (including contributions to French political parties) and have acted singly or together to fend them off or to pressure them to adopt particular policies favored by the Africans. The Côte d'Ivoire, Gabon, and, to a lesser extent, Senegal have all used this tactic to good effect—at one point, successfully blocking a reorganization of French aid, ensuring French opposition to a devaluation of the CFA franc for many years, and hastening the departure of French officials involved with African or aid policies they did not like. The influence of Africans in Paris (which may well be declining) should not be exaggerated, but neither can it be ignored. In no other donor country is the political influence of African leaders greater or more a part of domestic politics than France.

With the end of the Cold War, Africans have lost the ability to engage in or even credibly threaten switching. Increasing concerns among aid donors over the developmental effectiveness of their aid in Africa (or the increasing evidence of its past failures), combined with the collaboration among donors on structural adjustment programs, have also undermined the ability of Africans to play one donor off against another or to reject the pressures of one donor without losing the support of all. Thus balanced benefaction no longer works very well. However, they have adopted a new tactic that has worked effectively to reduce donor pressures for economic reforms: "promise/avoidance." It is well established that many African officials have agreed reluctantly to economic reform programs urged on them by aid donors—only to fail to implement them, or to reverse them once they have been implemented.[10] They have learned that pressures to spend prevent donors from cutting Africans off (except temporarily) when promised reforms do not materialize. President Mobutu (surely Africa's most accomplished manipulator of other governments throughout much of his career, until he overplayed his hand in the early 1990s) was able to develop this approach into an art form, with successive stabilization and adjustment programs negotiated, partially disbursed, and then canceled for nonperformance on the part of his government, only to be renegotiated with the same consequences. This approach continues today.

The Developmental Effectiveness of Aid in Africa

Thus far, we have examined foreign aid and the governments that provided it and received it in the diverse political environments in which they all functioned and continue to function. Foreign aid in Africa and elsewhere cannot be well understood in any other way.

However, with the decline in diplomatic motives for providing aid, combined with the relatively high levels of aid on which many African economies and governments have come to depend, aid donors have seriously begun to examine the impact of that aid on development in the region. The results of the research on aid effectiveness in Africa are not reassuring. In one study, for example, Craig Burnside and David Dollar of the World Bank found that (1) there was little systematic relationship between aid and development (this had been observed in other econometric studies of aid and development as well); (2) aid was effective where good policies (defined primarily in terms of fiscal and monetary policies) were in place; and (3) aid was not effective in persuading governments to adopt good economic policies.[11] Applied to aid in sub-Saharan Africa, these findings suggest that aid had relatively little impact on development in most of the region where economic policy environments were poor as well as little impact on improving those policy environments.[12] (See Table 9.4 for a summary of net aid flows to sub-Saharan Africa.)

In another approach to examining aid effectiveness, the present author[13] looked at the evaluations of eight major aid donors (the United States, the U.K., France, Italy, Sweden, Japan, the World Bank, and the European Union) and found the following pattern: (1) Aid to Africa tended to be the least effective of any aid worldwide; (2) it also tended to be the least sustainable, often with fewer than half of aid-funded projects surviving after aid was terminated; (3) the least effective types of projects and programs were those involving "complex interventions" requiring the management of multiple activities and organizational actors and/or social or political changes within African societies to be effective and sustained. Aid donors had seized the major role in the aid relationship with African governments in deciding not only which governments were to be aided and with how much but also what the uses of that aid would be. It is interesting to note here that whereas African officials were often very reluctant to give in to (or even to appear to give in to) pressures from donors for particular diplomatic, economic, or political decisions, they happily ceded to those same donors much of the responsibility for making decisions on how aid monies would be spent in their countries. This anomaly has much to do with the weak capacity and confidence on the part of African governments to take the leadership in managing aid donors as well as the aid they provided. It also may reflect the excessive eagerness on the part of Africans to get as much aid as possible, making it difficult for them to reject the aid offered by donor governments (whether it fit their economic priorities or not).

On their part, the donors, having claimed (or accepted) the major responsibility for designing and implementing aid programs and projects in Africa, found that their capacity was also limited. They frequently lacked the ability to design and manage effectively the large amounts of aid and large numbers of aid-funded activities involving complex and of-

TABLE 9.4   Net Aid Flows to Sub-Saharan Africa (in $billions)

Year	Current $	Constant 1995 $
1970	1.2	6.3
1971	1.3	6.7
1972	1.4	6.3
1973	1.8	6.7
1974	2.5	8.5
1975	3.3	10.0
1976	3.2	9.3
1977	3.9	10.4
1978	5.2	11.8
1979	6.5	13.2
1980	7.5	14.0
1981	7.6	15.9
1982	8.0	16.5
1983	7.7	16.3
1984	8.1	17.5
1985	9.4	19.7
1986	11.4	19.2
1987	13.0	18.8
1988	14.8	19.9
1989	15.5	21.4
1990	18.2	21.9
1991	17.9	21.1
1992	19.2	21.3
1993	17.3	19.9
1994	18.9	20.9
1995	18.5	18.5
1996	16.7	17.2
1997	16.4	16.8

SOURCE: Develoment Assistance Committee (Paris: OECD, various years).

ten experimental interventions. Indeed, the donors had relatively little knowledge of local conditions, little "technical" expertise in the areas in which they were working (e.g., in "building civil society" or even in the highly important political dimension of making structural-adjustment programs effective and sustainable), little flexibility, and few bureaucratic incentives for gaining this knowledge and expertise.

Further, both aid donors and Africans were beginning to worry about the secondary effects of aid dependence—namely, the "Dutch disease" of aid inflows pushing up the value of a country's currency or domestic price levels and thus distorting economic incentives and dampening growth; the "soft budget" constraints that large aid flows can cause, lessening the incentives for governments to implement needed reforms or to make a serious effort to mobilize their own resources for development; the tendency of high levels of technical assistance (typically spent on expatriate consultants) to weaken the capacity of African governments to manage their own economies; the impact of high aid levels on the accountability of African governments to their own people rather than to aid donors (especially in the case of governments that depend on that aid to fund a large proportion of their expenditures); and the potentially corrosive impact of large aid levels over a long period of time on the attitudes of African officials, reducing their sense of responsibility and initiative. Finally, the impact of the thirty or forty aid-giving governments and international organizations (not to mention the often hundreds of foreign NGOs) operating in their countries has taxed the abilities of the most capable African governments to manage their budgets, their policies, their investments, and the aid donors themselves, most of whom have separate purposes, administrative requirements, and operating styles—and who typically send periodic delegations of their own aid officials to observe their projects and to meet with already-overburdened African officials.

As the strategic importance of Africa diminishes, and as its commercial attraction declines or stagnates, both Africans and aid donors are becoming more concerned about development in the region and the benefits (and problems) that aid can bring about in the region.

Aid and Development in Africa in the Twenty-First Century

Eight trends, now evident, are likely to shape foreign aid in Africa in the twenty-first century. First, the aid will be less politicized in that aid donors will have fewer high-priority political or diplomatic goals that influence the allocation or use of the aid. No major international political issue has surfaced to replace the Cold War as a driving force in the diplomacy of major powers, nor is one likely to do so. In the absence of such an issue, relationships with African governments—to gain their support internationally, their votes in the United Nations and elsewhere, or their diplomatic collaboration—are far less important to major powers that are already less willing to channel their concessional resources to the region in pursuit of their own diplomatic interests. African countries have not been able to substitute commercial attractions for diplomatic ones in their relationships with external actors. They are even more diplomatically marginalized in global terms than they were during the Cold War and likely to become more so in the years ahead.

This important fact has significant implications for the future of foreign aid in the region, some of which are already evident in existing aid programs. For one thing, there will be less aid with the elimination of the security justifications for high aid levels. Security justifications for aid tend to override objections to that aid posed by budget cutters, effectiveness-wallahs, and isolationists in donor governments. Aid to Africa is no longer protected from those who tend to oppose it, and, as a result, it has begun a decline that is likely to continue.

Also reflecting this change is the shift of importance in aid-giving from bilateral governments to multilateral institutions—principally the World Bank and the European Union. This shift is already evident in the data on aid-giving, and it, too, is likely to continue. Aid from these organizations may also begin to diminish eventually (especially to the extent that it depends on continual replenishment by member-governments); but that decrease will continue to lag behind the decline in aid from individual governments, since these organizations are dedicated primarily to promoting development and thus do not have the competing purposes that governments have for the allocation and use of their resources.[14]

Competing purposes for aid in coming years are another factor likely to affect aid to Africa. There is little doubt at the time of this writing (mid-1999) that very large amounts of aid will be required for the foreseeable future to provide relief for the refugees from crises in the Balkans and support for the countries hosting them, and, eventually, to help reconstruct those parts of the Balkans badly damaged by bombing and destruction by various armies. And additional conflicts, unforeseen now, could well break out in other parts of the world (e.g., between India and Pakistan or between North and South Korea or almost anywhere in the Middle East), making further demands on increasingly scarce aid resources. The trend toward using aid for relief, reconstruction, and peacemaking in postconflict situations is likely to continue and to draw additional funds away from promoting development in Africa.

If the bad news is that aid to Africa is declining (and not all observers see this as bad news) and is likely to continue to do so, the good news is that it may be freed from the political constraints of the past to address issues of development in the region more consistently and efficiently. One is reminded of Greta Garbo's famous line in the film *Ninochka;* when asked about the impact of the purges of the 1930s on Soviet life, she replies: "Yes, there will be fewer Russians. But better ones."

Perhaps that will also be the case with aid to Africa in the coming century. Several other trends, made possible both by the end of the Cold War and by declining aid levels, are suggestive in this regard. One such trend involves the focus on "selectivity," a strategy much emphasized by the World Bank. Past efforts to bring about fundamental economic and political change in Africa through conditioning aid on those changes are increasingly regarded as having failed. The idea now is to provide significant amounts of aid only to governments that have adopted effective economic policies, especially those involving fiscal and monetary management.

Yet there are difficult questions to be addressed in operationalizing this idea in Africa or anywhere else. First, what criteria are to be used in selecting the governments eligible to receive large aid flows? (And who decides on the criteria, and how is the decision made?) The tighter the criteria, the more likely the aid is to be effective in promoting development in the recipient country—but, also, the fewer the recipients. Restrictive criteria are still very much the case in Africa, especially if problems of governance and capacity in recipient countries are taken into account. Declining aid levels make it easier for donors to refuse to aid Africans. But there are still pressures to spend that make a strict interpretation of selectivity as an approach to aid allocation difficult to implement.

A second question is whether any aid should be provided to poorly performing African governments—and, if so, how much, for what, and through which vehicles. The United States and other governments can aid African countries without aiding odious African governments. U.S. aid to apartheid South Africa, to corrupt and repressive Nigeria under President Abacha, and to corrupt Kenya under President Moi has gone almost entirely to nongovernmental organizations. However, multilateral development banks (which primarily provide loans, not the grants that NGOs need) find it especially difficult to take this approach, owing to both the terms of their assistance (which limit the amount they can provide to NGOs) and the nature of their governance. They cannot easily refuse all lending to poorly performing governments, among which are the governors of the institutions themselves. These are difficult issues to resolve, especially if a policy of true selectivity is to be maintained. More fundamentally, it is likely that the greater the reliance on NGOs as recipients of aid and its implementing agencies, the smaller the overall aid flows will be. It is not possible to provide these organizations billions of dollars in aid without overwhelming their capacity to effectively manage funding and undercutting their legitimacy and accountability to their own members and missions. Significantly more aid to NGOs, if the aid is to be responsibly and effectively used, means lower overall aid levels—a fact that many aid advocates (who themselves often regard the overall level of aid as *the* key symbol of the commitment by donors to, and the prospects of recipients for, development) are very unwilling to acknowledge.

Another trend increasingly emphasized at the rhetorical level by officials from aid agencies and African governments alike is "ownership." This category is a vague one, but at its core is the notion that where the beneficiaries of aid do not support what the aid is being used for or do not feel responsible for its success, the aid is unlikely to be effective. Emphasis on this notion grew out of the disappointing impact of structural adjustment programs in which aid was conditioned by donors on recipients reluctant to undertake desired reforms. Indeed, there are plenty of cases in Africa of "donor-driven" aid projects, designed, managed, and implemented by donor agencies or their agents in African countries with little engagement on the part of Africans in their design and management—projects that collapsed as soon as the donor agencies withdrew.

How is a sense of ownership created? Some aid agencies have emphasized the importance of "participation" by officials and citizens in recipient countries in discussions of aid activities. Indeed, "participation" became something of a mantra in many aid agencies in the 1990s, with donor officials convoking indigenous NGOs and citizen groups to discuss aid strategies and projects. We do not yet know how real these consultations have been or whether they have produced useful ideas for aid donors or improved the effectiveness of their aid. After all, many experts from developed countries, NGOs, and aid-receiving countries have "participated" in perfunctory consultations involving aid officials who had long before made up their minds about what they were going to do and, like radio announcers, were only transmitting rather than receiving during such sessions.

At the heart of the ownership issue is not consultation but control. If aid donors truly wish to transfer greater responsibility for managing their aid to their recipients, they must be willing to cede a measure of control over key decisions involving that aid. This is not to say that they need only write checks to recipients with no strings attached; that would be foolish, as has been demonstrated in the past in Africa and elsewhere. But they do have to be willing to step back from the highly interventionist posture they have assumed in the region, to wait for African governments and NGOs to put together workable proposals, and to accept the risks of failure that are involved with new activities by new or relatively weak and inexperienced organizations. Note that this approach, too, may imply decreased transfers of aid while African organizations are gaining the experience needed to handle significant amounts of funding effectively and efficiently.

A move in this direction is being made by the World Bank and several donor governments, but it is likely to become controversial in coming years. The World Bank has argued that because aid to governments is unlikely to promote development unless good policies are in place, and because aid is highly fungible, it makes sense for donors to identify governments that are good performers and to provide those governments with aid for budget support (untied to particular projects, reform programs, or other specific activities). Aid to good governments will support the programs and projects chosen by those governments as having high national priority. In this case the governments, not the donors, will make the choice as to how the aid is used (within whatever constraints of accountability are required by the donors). Moreover, if donors act together in this way, the coordination problem among them will diminish. There are lots of potential difficulties associated with this approach—such as deciding on which governments are eligible, judging the efficacy of their proposed public expenditure and investment programs, getting donors to collaborate, measuring meaningful results, and managing the process so that donors can be accountable for the expenditure of their funds to their own publics. Yet there have also been several experiments involving donors who have collaborated to support the sectoral or budgetary priorities of African governments. The jury is still out on the question of whether the approach has worked as hoped and with what impact.

This approach may potentially conflict with another trend in aid-giving in Africa, one that is also likely to accelerate in coming decades: channeling aid through NGOs, both from donor and recipient countries. A rising amount of aid over recent years has, in fact, been channeled by most donors through such organizations, though that aid does not yet exceed 10 percent of any donor's overall program, according to the Development Assistance Committee (DAC) of the OECD. However, the emphasis on strengthening civil society, encouraging grass-roots development, achieving poverty reduction through direct delivery of assistance to the poor, attaining social justice, and engaging Africans more centrally in their own betterment is likely to support continuing increases in aid to NGOs. The increasing importance of NGOs as constituents in donor countries for aid for development is also likely to lead to increases in aid channeled through them.

This trend can create tensions between NGOs and governments over the division of aid between them. After the end of the apartheid government in South Africa, donors began to shift their aid away from NGOs and toward the new government of Nelson Mandela—provoking criticism from NGOs that they were being cast aside and equal and opposite criticism from governments that now that a responsible government was in place, more aid should be channeled to it to support reconciliation and development. These tensions have appeared in other countries as well. If the above-mentioned approach whereby donors fund the budgets of African governments expands, the tensions among NGOs and aid-giving and aid-receiving governments could heighten.

There is another issue involving NGOs that is waiting to erupt: the tension between Northern NGOs and NGOs indigenous to African (and other) recipient countries. Thus far, much of the aid delivered by NGOs has been delivered by Northern NGOs, which are known to aid-giving governments, often constitute an important part of their political constituencies, and usually have the experience and capacity to program the aid in a reasonably effective manner. And NGOs in recipient countries, albeit often only recently formed, are understandably in favor of shifting the funding and responsibility for managing aid activities to them, arguing that as their capacity strengthens, they should take the lead in promoting development while Northern NGOs take the lead in advocacy for development with their own governments. This argument may be logical, but it overlooks human nature. Northern NGOs are often reluctant to cede control and funds to indigenous NGOs: Like most organizations, they wish to protect their budgets and their *raison d'être*. In addition, if Northern NGOs cut back on their direct development activities in poor countries, they may also begin to lose the contributions from their publics that partly fund those activities. They cannot just become advocates and survive intact. The balance of funding, specializations, and focus between Northern and Southern NGOs is yet to be worked out.

Two other aid issues are likely to gain prominence in Africa in the coming century: postconflict recovery and African debt. With the problems of civil war in Africa come the problems of recovery from civil war—not just the relief provided to refugees and displaced persons but also the retraining, reequipping, and returning of refugees to their homes, the demining so often necessary after a prolonged conflict, and the reconstruction of physical infrastructure, political institutions, and social trust. Aid donors—both bilateral and multilateral—have become involved in all of these activities and will continue to do so in the future. This is an important area of learning and experimentation.

The other issue that must be addressed is African debt. It is well known that African countries tend to be among the most heavily indebted in the world. The bulk of that debt is owed to other governments or to multilateral institutions such as the International Monetary Fund, the World Bank, and the African Development Bank and Fund. Creditor governments have been hesitant to wipe out this debt. Some, like the Japanese, are uncomfortable with eliminating debt at all. Others run into budgetary problems when doing so; an example is the United States, which has to offset debt relief against new aid flows. Finally, most governments have concerns about the "moral hazard" of encouraging future irresponsible behavior by forgiving that behavior on the part of African governments in the past. Up to now, governments have committed themselves to generous debt relief, but, somehow, a large bilateral public debt overhang continues in Africa. Some debt relief has been provided to individual countries, but this has often involved rescheduling or canceling payments due, rather than reducing or eliminating the overall stock of bilateral debt.

Multilateral development banks have resisted debt relief, debt rescheduling, or debt cancellation, arguing that they must be "preferred lenders," with their debts always serviced, if they are to protect their credit ratings in world money markets that permit them to borrow and on-lend to developing countries. For some time, in fact, the World Bank and IMF have effectively been rolling over their debts, through funding new loans that are used to service old ones. (Bilateral aid agencies have also effectively been funding the repayment of loans to these organizations.) Several years ago, the World Bank and IMF agreed to institute a new debt reduction initiative for Heavily Indebted Poor Countries (HIPCs)—many of which were in Africa. However, the stringency of the qualifying criteria and the length of time it typically takes to implement HIPC arrangements have meant that very little African debt has been reduced.

The creditors have a point: African officials borrowed funds from foreign governments and international organizations, used the funds poorly from an economic standpoint, or, in some cases, were so incompetent and corrupt in their economic management that any borrowed funds were wasted. If creditors simply write down those credits, current and future leaders will take the credit terms less seriously and have little incentive to use future loans responsibly. Moreover, it makes no sense to write down the credits of the more corrupt or incompetent African officials in power today.

However, this approach puts all of the responsibility for failed aid-lending decisions on the Africans, particularly on the populations of countries that have been or are now led by irresponsible or rapacious officials—populations who must directly or indirectly help repay those debts. (The African populations themselves cannot be blamed for putting those leaders in place. Some of that blame rests with the very governments that gave them such generous loans.) Aid donors, as we observed earlier, decided which governments got their loans and grants. They could have refused to lend in cases where governments were inappropriate partners; but they did not, for the reasons earlier described. So who is responsible for the continuing debt? In any case, the large debt overhangs can discourage the private investment necessary to spur future growth, defeating the ultimate purpose of the loans and grants of aid in the first place.

This issue, fraught with moral and practical problems on both the creditor and debtor sides, will continue to occupy a central place in aid debates in the coming decades—until it is resolved.

What is the promise for aid and development in Africa in the coming century? It seems likely that there will be less aid, but unlikely that the aid will diminish drastically or disappear entirely (an outcome that would cause major problems, given the dependence on the aid by the Africans). It is also possible that both Africans and their aid donors are at a point where, together, they can try to make their aid more effective, such that either side can reject it if it is seen as inappropriate. The discourse on how to do a better job with the aid is just now beginning between the two sides. That fact alone gives hope.

Notes

1. *Foreign aid* is generally defined as a transfer of concessional resources (i.e., with at least a 25 percent grant element) from one government or international organization to another government or nongovernmental organization in a poor country with the goal of promoting development in that country.

2. For Oceania, the average aid-to-GNP ratio is higher, at 27 percent; for Latin America and Asia, it is less than 1 percent; and for the Middle East and North Africa, it averaged just over 1 percent in 1996–1997. See Development Assistance Committee, *Development Cooperation 1998* (Paris: OECD, 1999), tables A55 and A56.

3. Ibid.

4. The data from the Development Assistance Committee of the OECD, on which this chapter is based, do not include a breakdown of food aid by world region.

5. The material in this section is drawn from Carol Lancaster, *Aid to Africa* (Chicago: University of Chicago, 1999).

6. "Fungibility" refers to a situation where foreign aid is spent on activities that governments would have funded even in the absence of aid, thus freeing up the domestic resources planned for those activities to be used for other purposes. Under these circumstances (which many economists believe are common in Africa and elsewhere), aid is in effect financing not the apparent projects or programs to which it is tied but, rather, other activities, such as military expenditures or luxury imports, that range far from the purposes for which the aid was intended.

7. Another symbolic aspect of aid—that the receiving government is a puppet of the donor—was one Africans were very aware of and sought to counter with a number of stratagems, of which more presently.

8. Julius Nyerere, *Freedom and Socialism* (New York: Oxford University Press, 1968), p. 238.

9. This term was coined by Ali Mazrui, "Socialism as a Mode of International Protest: The Case of Tanzania," in Robert Rotberg and Ali Mazrui (eds.), *Protest and Power in Black Africa* (Oxford: Oxford University Press, 1970), p. 152.

10. See, for example, Jane Harrigan, Paul Mosley, and John Toye, *Aid and Power: The World Bank and Policy-Based Lending*, 2 vols. (New York: Routledge, 1991).

11. Craig Burnside and David Dollar, *Assessing Aid: What Works, What Doesn't and Why*, World Bank Policy Research Report (Washington, D.C.: Oxford University Press, 1998).

12. Ibid.

13. See Lancaster, *Aid to Africa*.

14. One possible exception to this generalization involves the African Development Bank and Fund, which was deeply troubled by serious problems of mismanagement and corruption in the past and now faces the problem not only of fundamentally changing its staff and the way it operates but also of dealing with a large number of nonperforming credits made to nonperforming African governments. Outside observers are hopeful about the Bank's reforms and its ability in the future to play a role in development in Africa. But we may be well into the next century before the Bank is able to play the role within the region that many had hoped it would.

10

Externally Assisted Democratization: Theoretical Issues and African Realities

JOHN W. HARBESON

In the post–Cold War mushrooming of industrial country assistance to democratic transitions in African and other less developed countries, policy and practice have opened or reopened extensive new and still largely unexplored theoretical frontiers. In the literature devoted to post–Cold War external promotion of democratic reform in less developed countries, very little attention has centered on the theoretical significance of these initiatives. Although external involvement in the emergence and consolidation of democracy has become almost routine, the contemporary empirical theoretical literature on democracy and democratization has given little consideration to the concept of an externally assisted democracy.[1] How, if at all, can the pervasive reality of externally assisted transitions find legitimacy in theories of democracy and democratization?

The question certainly includes, but is nonetheless considerably larger than, the matter of political conditionality. Beyond overt diplomatic and economic pressure on leaders of nondemocratic regimes to permit multiparty elections lie less dramatic but no less potentially significant interventions in support *inter alia* of furthering constitutional development, strengthening civil society, reforming electoral processes, ensuring civic political education, training legislators, improving adherence to the rule of law, and reforming executive branches.

At the same time, industrial countries' assistance to the birth of democracy in African and other less developed countries has represented a near-revolutionary change in thinking about international relations. Largely if not wholly ignored in the heyday of realist and neorealist theories of international relations spawned by the Cold War, the Kantian and Wilsonian belief that democracy *per se* is a key to peace has gained substantially revived credibility in both the intellectual and policymaking arenas.[2] A significant branch of international relations theory and many of the dominant voices in policymaking arenas now at least tacitly accept that institutionalized belief systems have an important bearing upon the character and management of power relations among nations.[3] The most arresting and empirically supported hypothesis of this theoretical approach has been that democracies do not fight one another. However, the question of *why* and/or *how* democracy promotes peace has continued to perplex political science analysis despite, or perhaps because of, the relatively sophisticated methodological tools employed. This democratic peace literature has been in general agreement that if democracies do indeed refrain from going to war with one another, the reasons have to do with some combination of *domestic* democratic structures and/or democratic political culture. An important corollary to this proposition has scarcely been investigated at all: If domestic features of democracy secure peace *internationally* between pairs of democracies, should not those same features produce similar results *domestically,* and, if so, why and how?

The theoretical frontiers have been further enlarged by the fact that theories of democracy and democratization continue to rest on two-legged stools. Democratic peace theory, like other schools of international relations theory, is built almost entirely upon the experience of European countries since 1815, and contemporary theories of democracy and democratization implicitly claim global reach on the foundation of an only slightly less constricted empirical foundation—namely, the countries of the Americas as well as of Europe. The proposition that any scientifically legitimate claims to universality or global reach in those theories must remain tentative and provisional until validated by truly global arrays of data has generally been accorded lip service at best. Nowhere is this more the case than with respect to sub-Saharan Africa. Africa's continuing, even deepening, marginalization in the political economy of international relations has been mirrored in academic discourse on theories of democracy and of international relations and their applications in post–Cold War circumstances.

My purpose in this chapter is to discern possible implications for contemporary theories of democracy and of international relations in the context of U.S. assistance to sub-Saharan African democratic initiatives. Toward that end I examine such assistance from the perspectives of the (1) origins, (2) underlying theory, (3) objectives, (4) implementation, and (5) initial indications of outcomes and prospects for U.S.-assisted sub-Saharan democratic transitions.

Origins

U.S. assistance for democratization initiatives has been a bipartisan response to powerful, emerging post–Cold War realities, an initiative begun during the latter half of the Bush administration and continued during the Clinton era. Its true historical roots lie much deeper, however, in a multilateral response in the 1970s by industrial countries to the twin realities of Cold War detente and lagging postcolonial development in much of the Third World, especially sub-Saharan Africa. Detente fostered a degree of relaxation in alliance discipline, permitting subtle but significant shifts in priorities by Warsaw and NATO alliance partners away from collaboration on military security and toward more unilateral pursuit of economic development.[4] Detente also permitted a fundamental multilateral rethinking of development strategy to address the disappointing results of the preceding "development decade."[5]

During Robert McNamara's tenure as its president, the World Bank became somewhat alarmed that the preceding postcolonial development decade, the 1960s, had yielded not only limited but also grossly unequal progress, enlarging the gap between poorer and richer countries and between what it termed the poor majority and the fortunate few in Latin America, Asia, and especially sub-Saharan Africa. Under McNamara's bold and determined leadership, the Bank fundamentally refashioned its development strategy on the premise that, by seeking to reach more directly the Third World's poor majority countries, donors could facilitate both growth and equity. In what became known as the "new directions" strategy, the United States rewrote its own foreign assistance legislation, joining other industrial-country bilateral donors in following the Bank's new vision.

Central to this new strategy was the contention, based upon a wealth of empirical research, that (1) small producers who constituted the poor majority in most countries were more efficient (if somewhat more risk-averse) users of scarce resources than those operating on a larger scale, and (2) only by enabling those small producers to participate actively in designing and managing development initiatives intended to benefit them would poor countries in sub-Saharan Africa realize their economic potential and diminish domestic economic inequalities. In essence, the strategy defined a new political economy of democracy in calling for the political empowerment of the poor majority in order to achieve growth with equity.

Even before the era of structural adjustment commenced in the 1980s, the United States was in the forefront among bilateral donors in targeting inefficient and unresponsive national governments as major obstacles to realizing the new political economy of democracy at the grass roots. It initiated the implementation strategy of working increasingly through partnerships of international private voluntary organizations (PVOs) and host-country nongovernmental organizations (NGOs) rather than through national governments that were seen as both captives and instruments of evolving political and economic oligarchies.

An array of small, potentially replicable and sustainable success stories under the new strategy of seeking "development from below" were swept aside early in the 1980s by a burgeoning international debt crisis, sparked by the threat of default by some of the largest debtor nations— none of which were sub-Saharan African. Supported by new, very conservative governments in the United States and Europe, the World Bank and the International Monetary Fund initiated what continues to be the era of structural adjustment—an era that reversed the "new directions" strategy, substituting macro-level reform of economic policy for multisectoral, grass-roots participatory development.[6] This transformation coincided with renewed escalation of the Cold War contestation as the Western democracies increasingly undertook to link progress in reducing military confrontation with the Soviet Union to evidence of Soviet behavior consistent with that objective in its relationships with its perceived surrogates in sub-Saharan Africa.

However, if structural adjustment may have fit somewhat awkwardly with the simultaneous reintensification of Cold War competition, ironically it served as much to reinforce as to contradict important thrusts of the development strategy it replaced. Economic liberalization opened new entrepreneurial opportunities for the communities whose participation in development initiatives had been encouraged under the previous "new directions" strategy. In demanding that African and other governments privatize large sectors of their economies, the Bank, the Fund, and industrial-country donors sought explicitly to afford economic legitimacy to pervasive revolts by small- as well as larger-scale producers against counterproductive "management" by overextended bureaucracies.[7] Their escape into second economies (i.e., black markets, informal economies, or economies of affection) helped to fiscally strangle governments, drive civil servants themselves into second economies, and force governments to capitulate to reform. In ways that deserve more research than they have received, this economic liberalization appears to have released much new human energy and financial resources for the growth of civil society, some of whose participants' aspirations escalated to include political liberalization and then democratization.[8]

In the estimation both of donor agencies and of those pressing for economic liberalization in host countries, democratization became *inter alia* an important means to this end.[9] It is important to emphasize that the impetus for external encouragement for democratization was as much a recognition of democracy as a *means* to economic ends, and it was an *end* in itself. This relative underemphasis on democracy as an end in itself appears to have carried significant consequences for U.S. strategies for assisting democratic initiatives overseas, at least with respect to sub-Saharan Africa. Among the most important of these, as examined below, has been an underemphasis on the political context within which democratization is to take place. As the scope of government began to shrink under structural adjustment dictates, recognition grew regarding the continuing, even increased importance of legitimate remaining governmental roles. But here the focus appeared to be principally upon those roles most likely to facilitate an anticipated economic renaissance—roles such as those played by institutions of accountable, transparent public administration and the rule of law.[10]

Thus, post–Cold War external demands and support for political liberalization and democratization in sub-Saharan Africa emanating from industrialized countries melded with growing, *preexisting internal* African pressure for a similar political renaissance. Meanwhile, in complicated, not fully explicated ways, a dramatic evolution in prevailing academic orthodoxies synchronized with, and helped legitimize, what Samuel Huntington has termed democracy's "third wave."[11] A new academic wave of research on democracy and democratization received stimulation from the overthrow of long-established dictatorships in southern Europe and Latin America that included an Eastern European, empirically inspired rediscovery of the venerable but long-eclipsed concept of civil society in political philosophy.[12] Renewed intellectual attention to the importance of even shrunken governments in helping to stimulate economic development reinforced the importance of the democratization agenda.[13] Meanwhile, the ideological dimension of reinvigorated Cold War contestation during the 1980s spurred new interest in the global promotion of democracy, especially in the United States. Among its most enduring fruits in the United States has been formation of the National Endowment for Democracy along with its component organizations, the National Democratic Institute and the International Republican Institute. These organizations have continued to be major partners of the U.S. Agency for International Development (USAID) in implementing democratization assistance in sub-Saharan Africa and elsewhere.

Toward a Theory of External Assistance for Democratic Consolidation

The historical roots of intellectual and policy support for external promotion of democratization in sub-Saharan Africa and elsewhere suggest possible outlines of a theory of external support for democratic transitions and consolidation grounded in the interests of donor countries and of recipient countries within the context of post–Cold War international relations. The assumptions of U.S. policymakers concerning why and under what circumstances democracy is desirable or not desirable have generally remained inchoate, seeming to imply that democracy is an end in itself wherever it can be introduced. However, the history just outlined suggests a possible implicit rationale for democratization in sub-Saharan Africa. It suggests that the democratization movement in sub-Saharan Africa drew inspiration and strength from both international and domestic African pressures for economic liberalization. External support for African democratization may, therefore, find theoretical and existential justification to the extent that it has emerged as a logical, historical concomitant of donor- and host-country shared political interest in economic liberalization. But whether such a convergence of interest is realistic or not turns on a much wider set of considerations having to do with both the domestic and international impact of democratization and external democratization assistance. First, what are in fact the connections, if any, between domestic democratization and the capacity of both recipient and donor countries to advance their respective interests in terms of domestic and international relations, including policy reform? Second, to what extent and in what ways may foreign assistance actually promote democratic transitions and consolidation?

The task of evolving a credible theory of external assistance for democratization is tied inextricably to a larger task shared by several related schools of contemporary democratic theory—namely, to improve our understanding of the consequences of democratization in less developed regions of the world such as sub-Saharan Africa. First, as suggested at the outset, the global applicability of democratic peace theory rests heavily upon the question of precisely how, if at all, not only established democratic institutions in European countries but embryonic ones in less developed ones contribute to peaceful resolution of conflict domestically as well as internationally. Unanswered questions such as this leave open others—for example, whether democracies *now and in the future* will always refrain from warring with one another. Whether and to what extent democracies exhibit these capacities hinge, in turn, upon thorny problems that democratic peace theory addresses inadequately: How can democracies *domestically* reconcile the interests of their skeptics and opponents with those of its proponents, at least to the minimal level required for democracy to survive and become consolidated? Although the theory holds that democracies do not fight one another, there has been little or no theoretical argument or evidence concerning the capacity of democracies, internationally, to reconcile nondemocracies to their existence—only that when democracies fight nondemocracies they have tended to prevail.

Second, a precondition for success in this inquiry is improved understanding of interrelationships among (1) levels of economic development, (2) formally inaugurated democratic structures and practices, and (3) actual *political organizational capacity* to effect and consolidate both. At least partly because of the considerable extent to which they have been derived from the experiences of generally middle-income countries in southern Europe and in the Americas, pertinent contemporary theories of democratization inadequately address discontinuities among these variables in African and other less developed countries. Political parties, civil society groups, and interest groups (in Africa, at least) have tended characteristically to lack the political organizational capacity to sustain democratic transitions that they have been instrumental in launching and/or to lack the necessary financial resources and political autonomy for this purpose that they would be more likely to possess in countries with higher levels of economic development.[14] These discontinuities may well have been significantly exacerbated by two decades of external pressure upon less developed countries to embrace political and economic liberalization not accompanied by the financial resources and organizational technical assistance necessary to sustain these processes. This contention forms a corollary to Thomas Callaghy's thesis, in Chapter 3 of this volume, concerning the failure of foreign private investors to meet their part of the "implicit bargain" that the World Bank and the International Monetary Fund struck with developing countries: Reform and foreign private investment will follow.

Third, therefore, a theoretical and existential justification for external assistance for democratic transitions and consolidation may prove to be enabling countries to address and mitigate discontinuities that external pressures for reform may have helped to exacerbate.

The theoretical problem of discontinuities among levels of economic development, inauguration of democratic structures and processes, and political organization capacity to promote and sustain them requires further explication. Contemporary theories of democratization have suffered generally from a certain reductionism that appears to be responsible for their seemingly pervasively importation of a crucial hidden, and unexamined, assumption that *levels of political organizational capacity to effect and consolidate democratic transitions vary directly with changing levels of economic development.*

On the one hand, much of the theoretical literature on democratic transitions has appeared tacitly to assume the presence of (1) a polity whose existence and membership are not seriously questioned, (2) increasing levels of political organizational capacity within civil society and political parties to negotiate or impose democratic transitions upon reluctant *ancien régimes,* and (3) political organizational activity roughly commensurate with this capacity. For example, among Huntington's more important contributions has been his insistence on the importance of political institutional capacity in advancing development.[15] In *The Third Wave,* however, in recommending strategies for accommodating *ancien régime* resistance to different patterns of transition to democracy, he tacitly assumes that political parties pressing for democratic transitions *already* enjoy the capacity to negotiate credibly with powerful interests that are expected to yield power.[16] Guillermo O'Donnell and Phillippe Schmitter, in distilling the common themes of transitions, at the time confined mostly to southern Europe and Latin America, sketched a process that stipulated (1) the emergent capacity of civil society to force and sustain transitions and (2) the organization of political parties to contain this power once transitions have occurred in the interests of political stability.[17] But these contentions overlook the level of commitment presumed to exist between both proponents and opponents even to share participation in the same polity (e.g., whether all are prepared to continue and recognize each other's political membership in, say, Uruguay) while pursuing their struggles over whether and how to effect a transition from authoritarianism to democracy.

Each of these assumptions may well have been entirely reasonable in the European and American contexts, the empirical foundation for such assumptions. But each is very much in question in many, if not most, sub-Saharan African countries where levels of socioeconomic development are markedly lower and the fragility of colonially inherited state structures has generally been far more pronounced.

On the other hand, the well-supported proposition that democracy is most likely to be present when a certain level of socioeconomic development has occurred has tacitly imported the assumption that political institutional capacity to sustain democracy will emerge along with increasing economic development. But this literature is of limited pertinence where democratic transitions have been initiated in advance of both the hypothetically required socioeconomic development *and* the necessary political organizational capacity. The empirically well-grounded proposition that democracies are *necessarily* most likely to be found where certain levels of socioeconomic development have been achieved has been questioned, but without reaching the issue of *how* democracy transitions may be brought about and sustained, absent the socioeconomic preconditions.[18]

Moreover, in their important work on *The Political Economy of Democratic Transitions,* Stephan Haggard and Robert Kaufman follow Huntington in emphasizing the importance of institutions, especially parties to processes of economic reform and democratization; but they concede that they are "clearer about the effects of parties on policy outcomes than about the way party systems are established and evolve during the transition process."[19] Yet this is in fact the key issue in many sub-Saharan African transitions: What happens when the actual levels of political organizational capacity may *not* be commensurate with what is required *by the political context in which it takes place*—for example, to (1) sustain or rebuild commitment to the polity itself where there is the fact or risk of state failure (e.g., Somalia), (2) overcome continuing strong *ancien régime* resistance to democratization at the point of transition (especially where elections return an old regime to power, as in Kenya), (3) advance and extend the consolidation of democracy even where resistance is more diffuse and/or moderate (e.g., most African countries), and (4) make democratic structures and practices work effectively to resolve conflict peaceably in both domestic and international theatres as well as to extend and consolidate economic liberalization upon which its long-term survival may well depend.

The record to date clearly indicates a serious, if variable, deficit in the political organizational capacity required to sustain and consolidate democratic transitions in the political contexts of contemporary sub-Saharan Africa. Michael Bratton and Nicolas van de Walle have warned that *ancien régime* Goliaths continue to endanger the livelihood of David-like transitions.[20] The weaknesses of civil society, political parties, and democratically restructured legislatures to consolidate democracy following initial national multiparty elections have been evident to everyone, important indications of success in some quarters notwithstanding. The number of countries that are today failed, failing, or fractured polities, and therefore fall well below the minimal political threshold required even to attempt democratization, has escaped no one's attention.

But are these developments grounds for the Afro-pessimism they have generated? Does the root of the problem lie with the conceptions of democracy being advanced—as Fareed Zakaria has contended, for example?[21] Is the whole project flawed, however it is designed, because it is a post–Cold War reprise of Western neocolonial impositions upon Africa fatally flawed by ineradicable cultural biases? Or, alternatively, have embryonic democratization projects a better chance to overcome residual neopatrimonialism than some suggest? Only time will tell. But in the meantime, another possibility has received less attention than it deserves. Could it be that flaws in the family of contemporary democratic theory schools, as suggested above, have obscured a theoretically and existen-

tially valid focus of external democratization assistance that can constructively address both African domestic and general post–Cold War international circumstances—namely, a sharper focus on strengthening political
organizational capacity commensurate with that required to consolidate
already-launched democratization processes? Should not such a more direct focus on political organizational capacity include attention to what
embryonic democratic institutions themselves can do to stabilize the political context? And is it not possible that external assistance for these purposes, when properly implemented, is an important if not sufficient condition for advancing not only democratization itself but also its claimed
benefits for achieving (1) domestic and international peace and (2) economic development on the basis of liberal economic principles?

In the sections that follow, I explore these issues by considering the theoretical and existential implications of the first few years of U.S. foreign assistance for sub-Saharan African democratization, beginning with the
stated goals of this assistance and continuing with the strategies and practices through which it has been implemented. In the process, I examine the
extent to which the goals and the implementation strategies for external democratization assistance actually centered clearly and effectively on miti-
gating deficiencies in democratic organizational capacity that are apparent
on the ground but tacitly overlooked in much of received theory.

Objectives

The United States elevated African democratization to a central priority
and objective of its foreign policy toward the continent in the 1990s principally in response to (1) frustration with the limited progress achieved
through structural adjustment initiatives in the preceding decade and (2)
opportunities created by the abrupt termination of the Cold War.[22] Other
Western donors followed suit for many of the same reasons. On the one
hand, overseas development assistance to Africa had doubled in the
1980s in support of World Bank– and IMF-led economic liberalization
campaigns, but after a decade it produced *negative* initial results in the
form of shrinking per capita GNP numbers for the continent as a whole,
at a time of rising per capita incomes throughout other world regions.[23] In
these circumstances, Western donors expanded the scope of the campaign
to include political liberalization rather than changing or reversing course
in response to structural adjustment's many critics in and out of Africa
who believed this World Bank–IMF medicine to be counterproductive in
principle and politically dangerous or suicidal in practice. Although political liberalization had achieved fresh prominence in U.S. foreign policy
in the Carter administration's human rights campaign, the democratization objective in the 1990s appears to have been as much a means to the

end of economic liberalization as it was a central objective in its own right. In the expansion of the liberalization agenda, however, there appeared to be little analysis given to a crucial *how* question: How exactly would a liberalized political environment garner or generate the political organizational capacity to have a positive effect on economic liberalization initiatives?

On the other hand, the new foreign policy focus on democratization in Africa was profoundly opportunistic in its response to other seemingly unanticipated outcomes encouraged by structural adjustment initiatives, as well as to the abrupt transformation of international relations brought about by the end of the Cold War. As suggested above, structural adjustment policies encouraged greatly expanded private-sector social, economic, and political initiatives in the form of explosive proliferation of NGOs, previously stimulated by the "new directions" assistance strategies of the 1970s. To similar phenomena, especially in eastern Europe, scholars had previously applied the term *civil society*, freshly resurrected from the annals of classical political philosophy. The end of the Cold War enabled the United States and other donor countries to center more directly on promoting political as well as economic liberalization in less developed countries, notably sub-Saharan Africa.

Former Secretary of State Warren Christopher had observed that "[d]uring the long Cold War period, policies toward Africa were often determined not by how they affected Africa, but by whether they brought advantage to Washington or Moscow."[24] In addition to the intellectual and policy justification for a new emphasis in foreign aid upon political liberalization, there now existed both an expanded international political opportunity to do so and, at least hypothetically, a ready-made receptive constituency within Africa itself. The rapid expansion of democracy in Latin America and southern Europe supplied important encouragement and impetus to the new policy direction. But still unaddressed was the question of *how* an expanded civil society could or would become a more powerful one, capable of effecting and sustaining democratic consolidation.

The evolution of U.S. objectives in promoting democracy occurred during both the Bush and Clinton administrations. At least with respect to the objectives themselves, the change of administrations in 1993 appears to have yielded primarily continuity rather than an abrupt shift of purpose. Statements of objectives by the two administrations reflected not only a broad consensus on the scope of democratization to be fostered but also a sensitivity to both the difficulty of the enterprise and the importance of tailoring programming to individual country circumstances.[25] These statements joined (1) recognition of the centrality of democracy to America's own proclaimed principles and international identity to (2) achievement of parallel progress in sustainable economic development.

But the precise connections between the two processes were not fully explicated or examined.

If the core objectives were first articulated by the Bush administration, the Clinton administration zeroed in on the *general* empirical obstacles to their achievement, if not specifically on the sub-Saharan variants upon them. These objectives included the following:

1. *Free and fair elections*, through strengthened electoral institutions, expanded registration and education of voters, and more professionally managed political parties in order to reduce the phenomena of tainted elections; "nonexistent, ineffectual, or undemocratic political parties"; and the absence of competition for elected positions.
2. *Representative institutions*, through increased professionalism among elected legislators, supported by enhanced staff research, analysis, and drafting capacities in order to overcome ineffectiveness and unaccountability of parliaments.
3. *Strengthened civil society*, through support for professional associations, civic groups, labor unions, business groups, and "other nongovernmental advocacy groups," in order to overcome "the absence or weakness of intermediary organizations, such as labor unions, business associations, media outlets, educational institutions and civic groups."
4. *Executive branch accountability*, through reduction of corruption, strengthened procedures for financial accountability and budget monitoring (including military budgets), and promotion of executive branch watchdogs in the form of ombudsmen, in order to reduce corruption, ineffectiveness, and unaccountability of overly centralized governments.
5. *Law-abiding governance*, through enactment of constitutions (including bills of rights) and reduction of dishonesty and inefficiency in the judicial administration, in order to improve recognition and protection of basic human rights.
6. *Democratic values*, through expanded civic education (including in the schools), strengthened advocacy capacity of NGOs and interest groups, and increased independence of electronic and print media, in order to overcome the effects of pervasive public inexperience with democratic institutions.[26]

With the notable exception of civil-military relations, an area in which long-standing legislation had inhibited USAID's ability to work with military and police administrations, these foci generally established a broad and inclusive scope for democratization assistance. Moreover, they named the institutional shortcomings that needed to be overcome if democracy were to flourish and be sustained. What has been missing in these and other formulations, however, is a clearer focusing upon how these objectives were to be realized in the *political contexts* within which they were newly to be ensconced. Where would the organizational capacity be found or be generated to empower newly instituted democratic processes and structures to survive in the mercurial political circumstances of the continent? How were these new forms to survive, let alone prosper, at the hands of those whose objectives, strategies, and interests were built on profound skepticism regarding democratization, if not outright opposition? And what resources would tribunes of democratic consolidation draw upon or create to advance their cause in competition with myriad other causes and agendas competing for finite human, financial, and organizational resources? The new democratization agendas seemingly neglected to focus upon such problems as these—problems that are immediately practical and at the same time of theoretical importance. Also overlooked was the extent to which advancing democracy may require the formulation of strategies for the *use* of fledgling democratic institutions and processes themselves in helping to overcome these obstacles and in accommodating competing interests and priorities without losing sight of the long-term objective.

Attention to the *political context* in which the capabilities for advancing these objectives must somehow be found or built requires recognition that advancement of democracy in domestic contexts, as with national interests in international contexts, involves the management and uses of power. It requires awareness that democracy's advancement must be gauged by examining its progress in *arenas of contestation* in which the advancement of democracy competes with other interests. And it requires strategies for enabling individuals and groups advocating democracy to compensate for, if not to overcome, the structural weaknesses in their position. Sadly, however, it has too often been the case in sub-Saharan Africa that the advocates of democratization have lacked the political organizational capacity and the financial resources required to sustain and defend fledgling democratic processes and structures *already established*, let alone to extend, broaden, and consolidate their reach. Most important, the outcomes for democracy's interests in arenas of contestation will be affected by the fragility of the political context itself—that is, by the frayed or even failing commitment of contesting groups even to continue to work together within the same polity or to recognize minimal common rules of the game for doing so.

A sharper focus of democratization assistance upon capacity building in the political context in which the democratic causes must joust with competing interests is, thus, a key to the advancement of democracy on the ground, to strengthening weak links in democratic theory, and to establishing a niche for external assistance to democratization. But to what extent has the implementation of democratization assistance in fact centered on the crucial elements of capacity building required?[27]

Implementation

To date, the implementation of U.S. assistance for democratization in sub-Saharan Africa has cast into sharp relief the importance of a keener concentration upon (1) political capacity for increasing its effectiveness in the *political context* in which it is delivered and (2) the *ways and means by which embryonic democratic institutions must themselves survive in and mitigate the tribulations of the overall political context,* as democratic peace theory indirectly assumes they are able to do. As a practical matter, several lightly examined issues have arisen to render more difficult the task of building contextually suited political capacity for implementing democracy more effectively.

Policymaking and the Academy. The first problem concerns the relationships between the academy and policymaking communities. Although it may be extravagant to posit any causal connections, it is difficult not to observe possible parallels between the limitations of contemporary theories of democracy and democratization already outlined and the shortcomings in the way that the Agency for International Development shapes its objectives and strategies for delivering democratization assistance. An issue of considerable philosophical importance, and of significance to the study of the sociology of knowledge as well, underlies this point: What are, need to be, and might be linkages between (1) the arena wherein assistance for democratization is designed and implemented and (2) the academy wherein democracy's "third wave" has ignited greatly expanded interest in the contemporary meaning of democracy? From personal experience as an academic within the USAID policymaking arena, I have observed, on the one hand, a receptivity to and even substantial reliance within the policymaking community on relevant academic insights and methodologies, but also significant obstacles to be overcome for their effective operationalization and use within the bureaucracy; and, on the other hand, limited receptivity within the academy to the idea that it is important and possible for theoretically important insights to emerge from, not just be delivered to, the policymaking/implementation communities. As suggested throughout this chapter, there is much to be gained by overcoming these barriers in the interests of stronger theoretical foundations, more cogent strategic foci, and improved delivery of foreign assistance for democratization in sub-Saharan Africa and elsewhere.

The Focus of Democracy Assistance. Under the Clinton administration the Agency for International Development reorganized itself internally in order to concentrate resources and establish an integrated global focus for its central objectives, which included sustainable economic development, improved health and nutrition, and strengthened environmental protection as well as democracy.[28] Within the new Global Bureau, centers established to address each of the Agency's central objectives have, to a considerable degree, reduced the programmatic scope of geographic bureaus over the work of country-based field missions. However, field missions continue to enjoy abundant discretion in determining how these objectives are to be prioritized and focused upon the circumstances of individual countries. Particularly in Africa, the number of individual country-based missions has been dramatically reduced during the 1990s in response both to intensifying budgetary constraints and to recognition of the need for coordinated regional initiatives (e.g., in the Horn, the Sahel, and southern Africa) that address regional obstacles to realization of the priority objectives.

As a participant in the Clinton administration's initiative to modernize and improve the efficiency of public administration at the federal level (an initiative led by Vice President Gore), USAID required each major unit within its structure (including country-based missions) to formulate more specific strategic objectives supported by sub-objectives or intermediate objectives. Specifically, each unit was obligated to more clearly articulate anticipated program outcomes as well as indicators and measures by which to gauge progress in meeting them. A key problem with this well-intentioned sharpened focusing of democratization assistance, however, appears to have been its emphasis on *monitoring results* as distinct from identifying, harnessing, and/or building the capacities needed to realize the results being sought.

In 1992, twenty-two of the twenty-six remaining country missions in Africa had new or ongoing obligations of funds in support of democratization strategic objectives.[29] In the absence of a detailed analysis of projects designed to implement these strategic objectives, it is impossible to determine with any accuracy the distribution of resources among the several general objectives outlined above. But even without such microanalysis, some important generalizations can be drawn regarding the emphasis of USAID democracy programming.

First, USAID has accomplished a change of emphasis from support for initial multiparty elections, which so galvanized the United States and other donors early in the 1990s, to a broader range of objectives. In effect, then, it has appeared to follow the school of thought that holds that broadening the scope of democratization is at least as critically important to effective democratic consolidation as repetition of national-level free and fair elections—if not more important.[30]

Second, USAID missions have assigned a clear and unmistakable priority to the strengthening of civil society. (Most of the remaining country missions have also assigned a central place to civil society support in their programming on the evident premise of its *continuing* role in extending and consolidating democracy.) Here, too, at least with respect to sub-Saharan Africa, the Agency for International Development appears to have ignored or turned away from an alternative school of thinking about democratic consolidation. That school holds that the business of politics normally belongs to *political* society—to those who by virtue of their elective or appointive positions are professionally engaged in politics. For this school the political role of civil society is *intermittent,* arising to force paradigmatic change upon political society at crisis points in a nation's political life.[31]

Eight out of the ten country missions with which I had occasion to work from 1993 to 1995 had, as of fiscal year (FY) 1995, targeted the strengthening of civil society, although South Africa accounted for by far the lion's share of total resources assigned to this objective within the region.[32] Massive support for civic organizations opposed to apartheid had been a centerpiece of U.S. policy toward South Africa since the mid-1980s. Significantly, however, the continuing resistance and backsliding of some African governments with respect to democratization has not always moved donor countries even to begin to invest more heavily in countervailing civil society capacity in order to counteract and reverse such retrogression to the degree that they did in combating apartheid. There has instead been a tendency simply to decry the weakness of civil society, matched in the literature by skepticism concerning civil society's *potential.* Nevertheless, USAID has balanced clear and important support for the strengthening of civil society with considerable emphasis upon a broader array of other democratization objectives, including strengthening core democratic institutions (particularly legislatures and judiciaries) and improving the implementation of policy and procedural reforms within all branches of national government. Less attention has been devoted to extending democratization to the local level, notwithstanding exceptions in such countries as South Africa, Mozambique, and—after a fashion—Ethiopia.

It is important to understand the extent to which U.S. assistance for democratization has been programmed centrally—particularly since the establishment of the Global Bureau, with its individual centers responsible for spearheading realization of USAID's central objectives. As of FY 1996, the largest obligations for democratization at this level were for democratic trade union development, improved electoral processes, and a broad-gauged and inclusive project directed toward implementing policy change. Democratization assistance to sub-Saharan Africa for the decade as a whole represented just under 6 percent of total nonmilitary development assistance for sub-Saharan Africa (8 percent of obligations incurred during FY 1995 and FY 1996), even if one includes *all* Global Bureau programming, much of which benefited countries in other regions. Of the total existing funding obligations incurred in support of democratization *worldwide*, only 58 percent had been incurred at the country mission level. Particularly noteworthy has been a small but significant increase in democracy programming at the regional level (i.e., the Sahel, southern Africa, and the Horn of Africa) from 3 percent as of FY 1994 to 9 percent in FY 1995 and FY 1996. Ninety percent of the remaining funds programmed in Washington were the responsibility of the Democracy Center within the Global Bureau as opposed to the Africa Bureau.

The importance of Washington-based and regional programming, the inclusiveness of strategic objectives and of some projects, and the high degree of interdependence between elements of democratization in practice are among the reasons it is very difficult to estimate how U.S. democratization resources have actually been apportioned in support of democracy's subcomponents and dimensions. Even with these caveats, it is abundantly clear that one central facet of democracy has been dramatically underemphasized in USAID programming.

Although the core objective of democratization has been a transition from hegemonic single-party (or even nonparty) regimes to *multiparty* democracy, very few resources have been devoted to strengthening political parties in sub-Saharan Africa. Although the literature on contemporary democracy and democratization has tended implicitly to *presume* that opposition parties have the capacity to exert leadership in forcing democratic transitions, negotiating transfers of power with reluctant departing civilian or military dictators, and reestablishing the autonomy of "political society" from "civil society" once the transfer of power has been accomplished, the actual capacities of political parties in sub-Saharan Africa for these purposes have fallen far short of that required for such purposes. The same observation applies to civil society if, instead of postulating an intermittent role for civil society in forcing democratic change upon reluctant governments as the political-society distinction implies, one emphasizes its *continuous* role along with political parties for this purpose.

Yet the Agency for International Development has devoted very few resources to strengthening the operational capacity of weak sub-Saharan African political parties. The National Democratic Institute and the International Republican Institute have undertaken some party training, independent of USAID, under the auspices of their parent National Endowment for Democracy. It appears, however, at least in sub-Saharan Africa, that training has generally been limited in scope and duration to forthcoming elections rather than broad and sustained over a longer term. It also appears that important potential domestic U.S. resources for assisting party development in sub-Saharan Africa—for example, experienced staff of the Democratic and Republican parties as well as present and former elected officials—have not been drawn upon very extensively for this purpose.

What accounts for this omission? One important reason has been a seldom articulated but clearly rooted cultural premise highlighted by USAID's relatively new role in promoting democratization: Career agency employees have appeared to retain a strong sense that its role is and must remain apolitical. The belief has been that USAID constructs development projects for broad national rather than partisan political benefit. Yet the objective of strengthening *multiparty* democracy necessarily involves establishing a more level playing field between established ruling parties and weak fledgling opposition parties. It is difficult to address that objective without appearing, and in fact actually being, partisan on behalf of opposition parties struggling to compete on equal terms.

A more fundamental problem, equally underemphasized by donor agencies even in the context of providing support for impending national elections, has involved working with ruling and opposition parties alike on defining and enforcing laws, regulations, and informal rules of the game for their competition with each other. Ruling parties and opposition parties have, at a minimum, not always become comfortable negotiating with each other on anything, but particularly on such a subject. Yet failure to address these issues has been evident in the shortcomings of elections in new democracies in sub-Saharan Africa and elsewhere. Negotiations and agreements on these matters are essential if multiparty political campaigns as a whole are to be truly free and fair, not just technically correct on election day. Reforming electoral commissions is a necessary but not sufficient requirement for this purpose.

Far clearer than priorities in programmatic resource distributions have been dramatic differences in geographical apportionment of financial resources for democratization between country missions. As of FY 1996, nearly 70 percent of the peoples of sub-Saharan Africa were citizens of countries to which some level of USAID funding for democratization had been applied. However, of the new and continuing funding obligations in that year, 58 percent had been incurred in South Africa, reflecting that mission's long head start in strengthening civil society opposition to apartheid. More generally, 90 percent of new and existing funding obligations for democracy assistance had been incurred by missions serving the countries of eastern (including the Horn), central, and southern Africa, with only the remaining 10 percent being programmed by six missions in West Africa.

Analysis of distribution of USAID democratization resources between countries at different stages of political and economic development reveals few clear patterns. One might expect, and indeed require, that the United States support democratization in those countries that have demonstrated the clearest commitment to that end. Once again, only imprecise means are available for such an estimate. Table 10.1 offers a rough approximation by juxtaposing (1) total obligations to each of twenty-two African countries as of FY 1996, (2) total obligations per capita as of that year, (3) average Freedom House evaluations of country recognition of civil and political liberties between 1991 and 1996, and (4) *changes* in those evaluations during the same period.

There are obvious and important limitations to the quality of these data. However, they at least suggest the hypothesis that there are at best weak connections between the allocation of resources for democratization assistance and country progress toward that end. If the judgments by Freedom House concerning achievement in institutionalizing political and civil liberties are accepted, these data suggest a very poor correlation (.22) between the amount of democracy assistance resources allocated and the democratic record of these twenty-two African countries over the period 1991–1996. An even weaker correlation (−.17) obtains between democracy assistance resources *per capita* and democratic progress in these countries. Similar results obtain vis-à-vis *net change* in democratic practice and resource allocations over the same period and for rank order correlations. The one important correlation (.81) that does obtain—between the level of resource commitments for democratization and country levels of per capita income—disappears when South Africa (with its lion-sized claims on democratization resources) is extracted from the sample. The same fate affects the weaker but still seemingly important correlation (.66) between commitment of democracy resources per capita and per capita income. Rank order correlations produce the same outcomes.

These distributional patterns suggest a continuing insufficient strategic focus in U.S. democracy programming. In such data it is difficult to find answers to core questions: (1) Which countries most deserve U.S. resources building democratization capacity, (2) under what circumstances, and (3) for what purposes? One can make a strong case for competing approaches or even for explicitly allowing them to remain in contention with each other; but still unclear is the extent to which the United States has endeavored to support countries that have made the greatest progress toward democratization, countries that have remained consistently strong performers, and/or countries that are the neediest because they have taken the first crucial but all-important steps away from dictatorship. The same point applies to the matter of supporting democratiza-

TABLE 10.1   USAID Democracy Assistance and African Democratic Progress

	Percent of Total Obligations as of FY 1996		Total Obligations per Capita as of FY 1996		Average Freedom House Evaluations, 1991–1996		Net Change in Freedom House Evaluations, 1991–1996	
	$mil.	Rank	$mil.	Rank	Score	Rank	Score	Rank
Angola	6.5	11	0.61	14	6.15	19	-1.00	19
Benin	0.8	22	0.15	18	2.29	2	+0.50	10
Burundi	11.4	6	1.81	7	6.57	22	-0.50	16
Eritrea	8.4	8	2.37	4	5.20	15	+0.50	10
Ethiopia	14.2	4	0.25	17	5.00	13	+1.00	8
Gambia	2.1	18	1.89	6	4.21	8	-4.50	22
Ghana	10.9	7	0.64	13	4.36	10	+3.00	2
Guinea	7.2	11	1.10	11	5.13	14	0.00	13
Kenya	3.9	14	0.15	18	5.86	17	0.00	13
Liberia	7.6	10	2.77	2	6.15	19	+2.00	4
Malawi	6.5	12	0.66	12	4.07	7	+4.00	1
Mali	3.2	16	0.33	16	2.93	4	+2.00	4
Mozambique	25.6	2	1.58	9	4.29	9	+1.50	7
Namibia	2.7	17	1.77	8	2.43	3	0.00	13
Niger	1.0	20	0.11	21	4.79	11	-0.50	16
Nigeria	2.1	18	0.02	22	5.93	18	-2.00	20
Rwanda	16.4	3	2.56	3	6.21	21	-0.50	16
São Tomé	0.3	21	2.33	5	1.79	1	+1.00	8
South Africa	218.1	1	5.26	1	2.93	4	+3.00	2
Tanzania	3.5	15	0.12	20	5.36	16	+0.50	10
Uganda	8.0	9	0.42	15	4.93	12	+2.00	4
Zambia	13.1	5	1.45	10	3.50	6	-2.00	20

SOURCE: U.S. Agency for International Development Data and Freedomhouse Annual Reports.

tion in countries with stronger and/or more market-based economies versus those that have made the greatest progress or have taken the first critical steps toward becoming market economies.

Insufficient Focus on Political Context. The formulation of a more coherent strategic focus for democratization assistance to sub-Saharan Africa is self-evidently no simple matter, but it is also complicated for theoretical significant reasons that become particularly apparent in the course of working with democratization programs on the ground. First, as discussed above, it is apparent throughout sub-Saharan Africa that strengthening the capacity of embryonic democratic institutions to cope with the difficult political context in which they come into being is a more complicated and critical problem than anticipated in existing theory. In seeking to strengthen democratic institutions, too little energy and too few resources have been devoted to the question of what those fledgling institutions can actually *do* to survive and mitigate the stresses of a political environment in which the continued existence of the polity itself is an issue not far from center stage in many countries. As we have also seen above, this subject represents an important frontier area within contemporary theories of democracy and democratization.

Second, working with host governments on democratization initiatives brings to light the ways in which key elements of democracy appear fundamentally counterintuitive to political leaders who are skeptical of, or outright opposed to, democratization. Part of a more comprehensive capacity-building agenda for democratization would appear to involve greater appreciation of why democracy's merits are not as evident to those who remain unconverted as to true believers. Only in recent years have donors and, also, even the academic community fully acknowledged that shrinking the scope of *government* in the interests of economic liberalization does not diminish the importance of government in supplying the political and policy foundation for a market economy and in shoring up the *state* itself in a context of so much African state failure, fracturing, and fragility. Moreover, all theories of democracy presuppose that citizens are treated as equals for purposes of political participation, even though they are clearly very unequal in terms of economic and political power. Democratic political culture implicitly requires a degree of de facto, tacit acceptance of this ambivalence as a necessary element of democratic practice. My hypothesis is that the nature and necessity of such ambivalence have not been brought home to African skeptics and opponents of democracy to the degree that traditional cultural practices do not enshrine equality of treatment. Certainly U.S.-supported civic education initiatives in that continent appear to give but scant attention to this concept—one that those not born to the democratic manor find very difficult to understand.

Moreover, the concept of freedom of speech and press appears similarly counterintuitive to many of those not culturally schooled in Western democracy. Democratic theory implicitly upholds verbal combat as the appropriate surrogate for what in other contexts might well lead to physical warfare. At the same time, democratic theory implicitly honors the power of words and the marketplace of ideas as an arbiter of political power. It has been my observation that democracy's opponents and skeptics in Africa, as elsewhere, have difficulty with the idea that they must accept the judgment of the marketplace of ideas when they are not obliged to tolerate physical challenges to their power and survival in the form of military coups. This point, elementary to "cradle democrats" but not necessarily so to actual or potential converts, has appeared to be another less than intuitive but essential concept rarely included in civic education programs.

A derivative of this point is that the rationale of institutionalized checks and balances is also less than self-evident to those becoming acculturated to democracy. For those born into democracy, separated power centers increase the chances of vigorous debate of alternatives, of compromises to accommodate conflicting interests, and, ultimately, of wise policy that will strengthen democratic legitimacy and stability. In countries with fragile polities, dispersed centers of power may appear to invite irreconcilable conflict threatening the very existence of the polity itself. Whether, why, and how the virtues of checks and balances can be realized in fragile polities like many of those in sub-Saharan Africa may not be self-evident and, indeed, may represent burning questions in the minds of those whose acceptance of democracy is being sought. For example, Ethiopia's quest simultaneously for a postimperial state and for democratization has been impeded, even endangered, by profound disbelief among many Ethiopians that the new regime's authorship of a confederal constitution will not result in the "Yugoslavianization" of Ethiopia.

Toward Legitimate, Effective External African Democratization Support

It is still too early to assess the impact of the U.S. assistance that has been delivered, because the strategic approach and the theoretical justification for such assistance remain open-ended, controversial subjects. As this chapter has suggested, a historical foundation for assistance to less developed countries seeking to democratize is to be found in the focus of assistance delivered under two contrasting Cold War–era predominant strategies. However, the theoretical basis for such assistance has been underexplored in the current literature on democracy and democratization. The continued inattentiveness of this literature to theoretically significant and empirically daunting aspects of the African condition corresponds to a lack of sufficiently coherent strategic focus in U.S. assistance to sub-Saharan democratization. Specifically, insufficient recognition has been directed to the importance of understanding, cultivating, and employing the *political organizational capacity* of fledgling democratic institutions to survive and mitigate residual opposition to democracy and to overcome the infirmities of singularly fragile African polities. In these important respects the development of effective democratization assistance policies and the formulation of effective theoretical justification for such assistance go hand in hand.

Notes

The author expresses his appreciation to the International Forum for Democratic Studies for generously allowing him the use of its facilities prior to beginning his tenure at the U.S. Institute of Peace.

1. Among the noteworthy and useful contemporary contributions are Thomas Carothers, *Assessing Democracy Assistance: The Case of Romania* (Washington, D.C.: Carnegie Endowment for International Peace, 1996); Thomas Carothers, *In the Name of Democracy: U.S. Policy Toward Latin America in the Reagan Years* (Berkeley, Calif.: University of California Press, 1991); Tony Smith, *America's Mission: The United States and the Worldwide Struggle for Democracy in the Twentieth Century* (Princeton: Princeton University Press, 1994); and Graham Allison, Jr., and Robert P. Beschel, Jr., "Can the United States Promote Democracy?" *Political Science Quarterly* 1, no. 107 (1992), pp. 81–101. Among the very few contributions on assistance for African democratization are Todd J. Moss, "U.S. Policy and Democratization in Africa: The Limits of Liberal Universalism," *Journal of Modern African Studies* 2, no. 33 (1995), pp. 189–211; and Deborah Brautigam, "Governance, Economy, and Foreign Aid," *Studies in Comparative International Development* 3, no. 27 (1992), pp. 3–26.

2. In the flood of recent scholarly attention to this subject, one of the best summaries of the literature remains James Lee Ray, *Democracy and International Conflict: An Evaluation of the Democratic Peace Proposition* (Columbia: University of South Carolina Press, 1995).

3. In fact, the importance of institutionalized value systems was acknowledged (though not emphasized) in both the realist and neorealist literature from the very start. See Hans J. Morgenthau, *Politics Among Nations,* 1st ed. (New York: Knopf, 1948).

4. John Spanier characterized this period as one of "bipolycentrism," in which Cold War alliances shaped a bipolar world but detente enabled the alliance partners to pursue somewhat more independent foreign policies suggestive of a more multipolar world. See John Spanier, *Games Nations Play* (New York: Holt, Rinehart & Winston, 1978).

5. Among the wealth of important literature on this subject, see in particular Coralie Bryant, *Managing Development in the Third World* (Boulder: Westview

Press, 1982); Hollis Chenery et al., *Redistribution with Growth* (New York: Oxford University Press, 1974); David Korten and Rudi Klauss, *People-Centered Development* (West Hartford, Conn.: Kumarian Press, 1984); and Milton Esman and Norman Uphoff, *Local Organizations: Intermediaries in Rural Development* (Ithaca: Cornell University Press, 1984).

6. The first of a continuing series of World Bank reports articulating, evaluating, and defending this strategy was *Accelerated Development in Sub-Saharan Africa: An Agenda for Action* (Washington, D.C.: World Bank, 1981).

7. A pioneering work capturing the political implications of this "revolution" was Goran Hyden, *Beyond Ujamaa in Tanzania: Underdevelopment and an Uncaptured Peasantry* (Berkeley: University of California Press, 1981).

8. An important early article examining this phenomenon is Michael Bratton, "Beyond the State: Civil Society and Associational Life in Africa," *World Politics* 3, no. 41 (1989), pp. 407–430.

9. The evolution of donor thinking on this phenomenon is carefully summarized by Larry Diamond, "Promoting Democracy in Africa: U.S. and International Politics in Transitions," in John W. Harbeson and Donald Rothchild (eds.), *Africa in World Politics*, 2nd ed. (Boulder: Westview Press, 1995), pp. 250–278.

10. The World Bank dramatized its concern with the constructive role of the state in development in its *World Development Report 1997: The State in a Changing World* (New York: Oxford University Press, 1997).

11. Samuel Huntington, *The Third Wave: Democratization in the Late Twentieth Century* (Norman: University of Oklahoma Press, 1991).

12. One of the pioneer works portending an avalanche of subsequent works on this subject was Guillermo O'Donnell and Phillippe Schmitter, *Transitions from Authoritarian Rule: Tentative Conclusions About Uncertain Democracies* (Baltimore: Johns Hopkins University Press, 1986).

13. Representative of this new literature was P. Evans, D. Rueschemeyer, and T. Skocpol (eds.), *Bringing the State Back In* (Cambridge, Eng.: Cambridge University Press, 1985).

14. For a discussion of early patterns of democratic transition in sub-Saharan Africa, see Michael Bratton and Nicolas van de Walle, *Democratic Experiments in Africa: Regime Transitions in Comparative Perspective* (New York: Cambridge University Press, 1997). See also Jennifer Widner (ed.), *Economic Change and Political Liberalization in Sub-Saharan Africa* (Baltimore: Johns Hopkins University Press, 1994).

15. Samuel Huntington, *Political Order in Changing Societies* (New Haven: Yale University Press, 1968).

16. Huntington, *The Third Wave: Democratization in the Late Twentieth Century*.

17. O'Donnell and Schmitter, *Transitions from Authoritarian Rule*.

18. Dankwart Rustow, "Transitions to Democracy: Towards a Dynamic Model," *Comparative Politics* 3, no. 2 (1970), pp. 337–363.

19. Stephan Haggard and Robert Kaufman, *The Political Economy of Democratic Transitions* (Princeton: Princeton University Press, 1995), p. 370.

20. Bratton and van de Walle, *Democratic Experiments in Africa*.

21. Fareed Zakaraia, "The Rise of Illiberal Democracy," *Foreign Affairs* 6 (1997), pp. 22–44.

22. Diamond, "Promoting Democracy in Africa."

23. Ibid.

24. Quoted in ibid., p. 252.

25. *Democracy and Governance* (Washington, D.C.: U.S. Agency for International Development, November 1991); and *Strategies for Sustainable Development* (Washington, D.C.: U.S. Agency for International Development, 1993).

26. See the two documents cited in ibid. for a distillation and merging of these themes.

27. Among the U.S. Agency for International Development's most important projects is one titled "Implementing Policy Change." In Zambia, this project supported a sustained effort to improve the performance of the president's cabinet to reflect the accountability requirements of democracy. The extent and effectiveness of the use of this project for similar purposes elsewhere has not been comprehensively gauged.

28. To these original four central objectives have been added *de facto* human resource development, strengthened scientific capacity, and improved humanitarian assistance as well as cross-sectoral objectives including the promotion of the political, economic, and cultural position of women.

29. The data in this section are derived and adapted from U.S. Agency for International Development, *Congressional Presentation: Statistical Annex, Fiscal Year 1996* (Washington, D.C.: USAID).

30. Defenders of the election-centric approach to consolidation include Huntington, *Political Order in Changing Societies*; Guillermo O'Donnell, "Illusions About Consolidation," *Journal of Democracy* 2, no. 7 (1996), pp. 34–52; and Michael Bratton, "Deciphering Africa's Democratic Transitions," *Political Science Quarterly* 1, no. 12 (1997), pp. 67–93. Representative of a broader conception of the requirements for consolidation is Juan J. Linz and Alfred Stepan, "Toward Consolidated Democracy," *Journal of Democracy* 2, no. 7 (1996), pp. 14–34.

31. One scholar who has been influential in advocating this distinction is Alfred Stepan, *Rethinking Military Politics: Brazil and the Southern Cone* (Princeton: Princeton University Press, 1988).

32. John W. Harbeson, *Democracy and Governance in Eastern and Southern Africa: End of Tour Report* (July 1995). This report was prepared at the conclusion of my service as regional, democracy, and governance adviser for eastern and southern Africa in the Agency for International Development (1993–1995).

PART FOUR

Globalization and a Changing State System

11

Africa and the World Economy: Continued Marginalization or Re-engagement?

NICOLAS VAN DE WALLE

The East Asian economic crisis of 1997 has led to renewed debates within Africa regarding the merits of opening up local economies to the vagaries of global economic forces. The ability of international financial speculators to devastate the economic institutions of the "miracle economies" of East Asia was interpreted by some as a cautionary tale about the dangers of excessive exposure to those forces. In Africa, the crisis provided instant ammunition to the critics of the structural adjustment programs, whose founders were in fact trying to emulate the Asian countries by liberalizing policies regulating international trade and finance.

Deep suspicion about the likely impact of international trade and capital flows on low-income economies constitutes a long tradition in Africa. The view that Africa would not derive substantial benefits from engagement with the world economy, and might actually be weakened by it, was instrumental in the formulation of inward-looking economic policies following independence—most notably import-substitution industrialization (ISI).[1] More recently, the reticence to liberalize the trade regime or pursue reforms to facilitate foreign direct investment can also be explained by this persistent skepticism about the desirability for integration of African economies into the international economy.[2] Indeed, the inability of the structural adjustment programs of the last two decades to bring back economic growth to Africa is argued to be proof that outward-oriented, export-driven development strategies do not work.[3] This argument had been pushed aside in recent years, when it seemed that Africa had finally turned the corner.[4] Today, however, the negative effects of the East Asian crisis on the economies of middle-income countries such as Brazil, Turkey, and South Africa has relegitimated the view that the international economy poses threats to Africa, and that the latter would be better off carefully limiting contact with outside economic agents.

Now is thus a good time to analyze the evolving nature of Africa's relationship to the world economy. Just how integrated is Africa in the world economy? And what impact has structural adjustment had on the level of integration? In this chapter I do not explicitly assess the desirability of specific economic policy options, although I refer to elements of the voluminous literature that does. I instead seek to describe the patterns of engagement and disengagement of the region with the global economy. In particular, I argue that Africa's relationship to the world economy is structured by three sets of related facts. First, African economies have traditionally been extremely reliant on foreign trade. Somewhat paradoxically, Africa has combined high levels of protectionism with high trade dependence. A focus on the export of primary commodities was established during the colonial era and has been maintained by most countries in the region with remarkably little modification. Second, African economies have proved unable to attract and maintain private capital. Foreign direct investment declined to a trickle in the 1980s, whereas equity capital has always been hampered by the weakness of financial intermediation in the region, with the exception of South Africa. Despite arguments to the contrary, the 1990s have not witnessed a significant change in those patterns. Third, African economies have become extraordinarily dependent on foreign aid. Following three decades of continuous growth, African countries receive a level of external public resource flow that is historically unprecedented. These three "stylized facts" regarding Africa's relationship to the world economy are often misunderstood. The first task of this chapter is thus to document them, which I undertake in the next three sections. In each case, the evolution over time and current trends are examined. I then turn to the implications of these three facts for African politics and the renewal of economic growth in the future. I end with some comments on the likely impact on African economies of the East Asian crisis of 1997.

Africa and International Trade

Much of the recent globalization literature implies that the integration of low-income developing countries into international trading networks has increased dramatically in recent years.[5] Indeed, however, the integration of Africa into international trade is long-standing and predates the formal colonization of the region by the Western powers at the end of the nineteenth century.[6] In particular, the slave trade and gold exports and, subsequently, an array of primary commodities constituted a significant volume of trade. As early as the mid-nineteenth century Africa was a leading supplier of palm oil, groundnuts, coffee, and cocoa. Through the political control it gained by the early twentieth century, and thanks to substantial investments in infrastructure, European colonialism would extend the export economy into the African hinterland, allowing access to mineral commodities and oil. By the end of colonialism, Africa accounted for more than 5 percent of total world trade, having benefited from a sustained commodities boom following the Korean War.[7]

For a variety of reasons, Africa's share of world trade has been declining ever since independence and today accounts for less than 2 percent of world trade. Africa's share has declined largely because the continent did not participate in the dramatic growth in global merchandise trade during the last half-century. Thus, African exports grew at a much smaller rate than those of the rest of the world. During the 1960s the differences were minor, but they have been quite striking in the more recent past, as illustrated in Table 11.1. Africa's mediocre trade performance can in turn be explained by the stagnation of its economies, the deterioration in the terms of trade for many of its exports, and its failure to diversify its export base—as well as by policies that often discouraged the export sector.[8]

The colonial era nonetheless fashioned certain patterns in Africa's trading relationship—patterns that have not really changed in the years since then, including the current era of *globalization*. First, the region exported primary commodities to the metropole and in return purchased manufacturing goods. The failure to industrialize since independence has maintained Africa in this international division of labor.[9] As recently as 1993, only a fifth of the average African country's exports were made up by manufacturing, and no country in the region could claim more than a 37 percent share.[10] As a result of the downward price trend for many of these commodities during the last forty years, the reliance on primary commodities has proven costly.

Second, most African countries were reliant on a small number of commodity exports. Here, too, there has been a failure to diversify in the intervening period. In the early 1990s, fewer than a third of all African countries were not dependent on a single primary commodity for at least 50 percent of their total exports. Oil producers such as Nigeria, Congo, and Angola had actually become less diversified in their trade over time, with oil accounting for more than 90 percent of their total exports. Most of the poorest African countries were reliant on a single low-value agricultural commodity: Cashews accounted for 91 percent of Guinea Bissau's

TABLE 11.1   Average Annual Growth Rate (%) of Merchandise Exports, 1980–1995

	1980–1990	*1990–1995*
Sub-Saharan Africa	0.9	0.9
East Asia and Pacific	9.3	17.8
South Asia	6.6	8.6
Latin America and Caribbean	5.2	6.6
High-Income Economies	5.2	5.4
All Low- and Middle-Income Economies	3.0	7.2
World	4.7	6.0

SOURCE: World Bank, *The World Development Report, 1997* (Washington, D.C.: World Bank), p. 243.

exports, coffee for 66 percent of Burundi's exports, cocoa for 92 percent of São Tomé's exports, cotton for 57 percent of Mali's exports, and so on.[11] This reliance on a single commodity has left African economies extremely vulnerable to the volatility in commodity prices. Sudden world price increases for oil or copper have been almost as disruptive to the Nigerian or Zambian economies as the inevitable subsequent decline, which was equally sudden.

Third, each African colony's trade was primarily directed to a single colonial power. The rise of protectionism in the 1930s helped lock African colonies into this pattern, given the imperial preferences that their exports enjoyed in the colonial power's market. Although there has been a diversification of trading partners, notably for oil producers in the region, this colonial legacy remains quite strong. The largest trading partner typically remains the ex-colonial power.[12]

Finally, and perhaps most significantly for the purposes of this chapter, colonialism left a legacy of economies highly dependent on their trade sectors. African governments relied on trade for an extremely high percentage of their fiscal revenues, and the share of the trade sector in GDP was quite high. According to the World Bank, the share of GDP taken up by trade in Africa was 15.8 and 18.9 percent in 1986 and 1996 respectively, compared to 7.9 percent and 17.3 percent for Latin America and 9.1 and 13.1 percent for East Asia.[13]

In sum, independence found most African countries extremely reliant on the exports of a small number of commodities with declining prices to a single trading partner. In the intervening four decades they proved unable to escape this pattern. Indeed, rather than increasing its integration into world markets, Africa has on the whole stood on the sidelines while the rest of the world trading system has expanded. On the one hand, African governments failed to expand or diversify their commodities exports, with some notable exceptions.[14] Specifically, postcolonial governments tended to neglect if not directly undermine their export commodity sectors through a combination of excessive taxation, underinvestment in infrastructure, injudicious nationalization, and disastrous macroeconomic policies that generated overvalued exchange rates and balance-of-payments crises.[15]

On the other hand, governments failed to diversify their economies and, in particular, to promote the development of manufacturing production for the domestic market, which would have reduced their reliance on exports. Most countries tried to create domestic industries through then-fashionable ISI policies. They raised tariffs and used state resources to create industrial parastatals in key "strategic" sectors.[16] Mauritius was a very successful exception to this pattern; it relied only briefly on trade protection to move away from a sugar monoculture economy at independence to a diversified economy driven by an export-led light manufacturing base.[17] Elsewhere, the attempts to implement ISI strategies resulted in an unsustainable mix of uncompetitive industries, rent-seeking corruption, and high budget deficits. Only a handful of countries such as Kenya and Côte d'Ivoire escaped complete disaster.

Africa and Private Capital

A primary cause of the failure of ISI policies proved to be the low level of investment that has characterized most African economies for most of the postcolonial era. Two characteristic components of this situation have been the absence of foreign private capital flows into the region and the large amount of capital flight from it. These two factors are usually treated separately but should be assessed together as they have the same origin: Both local and foreign holders of capital have not found it sufficiently profitable to invest their holdings within most African economies.

There are no systematic data on capital flight from Africa, although most accounts describe it as a significant issue.[18] Hundreds of millions of dollars of annual capital flight from Nigeria have been reported in recent years, whereas Franc Zone countries like Cameroon and Côte d'Ivoire were reputedly suffering from large-scale capital flight in the early 1990s. These two cases highlight the two primary reasons for capital flight: official corruption and an unsustainable macro-economic disequilibrium. Successive Nigerian governments have tolerated large-scale corruption surrounding oil revenues. And in the Franc Zone, the virtual certainty that the exchange rate could not be sustained led investors to seek the shelter of other currencies.

The numbers on private foreign capital are more complete and edifying. In 1996, the total long-term private net resource flow to all developing countries was $247 billion, of which Africa received $4.4 billion, or just under 1.8 percent.[19] These totals included some $3.3 billion in foreign direct investment (FDI), of which more than half went only to Nigeria and Angola for investments in the oil sector. These numbers were rising sharply during the 1990s before the East Asian crisis, in the context of a renewed interest in emerging markets by Western investors. FDI to Africa more than doubled between 1990 and 1997. However, Africa's share of global FDI in 1996 was still half of what it had been in the early 1980s.

The first and almost certainly most important reason for this neglect of Africa by international capital, related to all the other factors undermining investment, has been the low quality of governance in the region. Governance failures have entailed both the content of policy and its implementation. Economists have long argued that the economic policies pursued in the region created various disincentives for investors.[20] Macro-economic uncertainty and overvalued exchange rates resulted from the capricious fiscal and monetary policies pursued by African governments in the 1960s and 1970s. Punitive taxation levels, excessive regulation, and shortsighted controls on the financial sector scared away prospective investors. Foreigners soon turned their attention to economies in other regions of the world that were more hospitable to their investments, whereas African capital soon found ways to escape financial controls and make its way into European banks and their lower-risk dividends.

Since the 1980s, the negative implications of poor economic policy on investment have been well understood by policymakers. Various reform programs have been put in place with the assistance of the international donors to create policy regimes that investors would find more attractive. Even if these programs had been fully implemented, which is far from the case, a broader set of governance failures continues to discourage capital flows into the region.

Thus, surveys of businesspeople consistently reveal that public-sector failures in most countries of the region constitute a major obstacle to private-sector activity.[21] They point to the fact that courts and legal systems often do not function well, given poor documentation as well as uneven and politically mediated applications of the body of commercial law, which is itself complex and contradictory. In addition, the rule of law itself is often unsatisfactory, with growing violence in urban areas and banditry in the countryside of a growing number of countries. Roadblocks in and around the major cities manned by undisciplined and unaccountable police, army personnel, and assorted security units appear to have no function other than to provide income to underpaid officers; but they raise the costs of commerce, sometimes substantially so.[22]

A related scenario has to do with corruption, which is typically more severe in Africa than in other regions of the world, if various cross-regional surveys are to be believed.[23] Corruption not only increases the costs and risks of private investment; it also has a negative fiscal impact by lowering net revenues and perverting the tax effort. The tax burden on "honest" economic agents is increased to the point where they, too, have significant incentives to escape compliance. There is growing evidence, more generally, that corruption reorients government activities away from the provision of public goods and services and toward wasteful investments and rent-seeking. Excessive regulation is sustained because it creates rents, whereas governmental efforts in the delivery of social services in health and education are reduced because they do not.

Corruption provides an incentive for governments to underinvest in administrative capacity, and low capacity, in turn, facilitates corruption. In much of Africa, rent-seeking, patronage, and the private appropriation of public goods should not be conceived of as incidental abuses in weak administrative systems; on the contrary, these practices have often been consciously developed into a system of rule. Building on traditional forms of clientelism, and helping to compensate for low legitimacy and ethnic fragmentation, such practices were in fact quite successful at promoting political stability for weak regimes. Indeed, their political usefulness more than compensated for their economic cost, which is one reason they have proven so resilient.

But even African governments that have gained relatively good reputations for their probity often suffer from a dramatic lack of administrative capacity, which undermines even the most basic government activities. The civil service is underpaid, public statistics are poor or completely unavailable, policies and laws remain unimplemented, and budgets are poorly designed and end up having little impact on expenditure patterns. One result is the poor quality of public services.

These public-sector failures may serve to dissuade investment even more than wrong-headed policies, as they appear to investors to enhance not only risk but also uncertainty. There has been a belated realization in the 1990s of the importance of these issues to economic growth, and the region is now awash in civil service and public-sector reform programs. Yet, governance performance in Africa has been even more difficult to improve than macro-economic policies. One recent survey by the World Bank of its hundred or so efforts to promote civil service reform this decade has admitted with refreshing bluntness that there is little evidence these programs have had much impact at all.[24] Even in instances where the politicians are unambiguously committed to public-sector reform and do not view it as undermining their hold on power, progress will be slow and arduous. For the foreseeable future, low levels of public-sector effectiveness will dissuade investment in most countries in the region.

These governance failures are linked to other factors that undermine the flow of capital to the region. One such factor has been the weakness of financial institutions in the region. The legacy of noncompetitive government-set interest rates, politically rationed access to credit, and gross interference in the internal operation of financial institutions led directly to capital flight and disintermediation as private economic agents lost confidence in financial institutions. An integral component of the crisis of the 1980s was a crisis of the financial sector, which left very few banks operational and little or no capital available for private investment, particularly for medium- and small-sized firms. At the behest of the donors, governments have promoted liberalization of credit as well as financial reforms including deregulation and privatization of the banking sector. In many countries, these reforms will bring about higher rates of savings and investment in time, but they need to be sustained and strengthened so that they appear completely irreversible.

Africa's poor infrastructure constitutes another critical factor deterring foreign investment. The poor quality of telecommunications, public utilities, and the road network raises the cost of doing business, particularly in areas such as manufacturing with a high growth potential. Business surveys invariably suggest that the cost of utilities is higher in African countries than in other low-income countries, and that services are often unpredictable, with costly breakdowns and strikes. Public infrastructure appears to have been one more victim of the reform era. In many countries, the road network is probably in worse shape than it was at independence, as fiscally strapped governments have for too long been allowed to underinvest in maintenance.[25] And in telecommunications, Africa has not kept up with other regions of the world; in fact, its backwardness is increasing.[26]

Finally, the dearth of private capital flows into Africa results from the perceived low quality of the labor force. Literacy rates, particularly in West Africa, continue to lag well behind prevailing levels in comparable low-income countries. After much progress in the 1960s and 1970s, rates have stagnated in many countries. True, there has been dramatic progress in the number of trained professionals across the continent: African countries have gone from a handful of college graduates at independence to literally tens of thousands of them. However, Africa still lags behind every other region of the world in terms of the number of engineers, doctors, and scientists that it produces. Rates on enrollment in tertiary education are estimated to be one-quarter of the level attained in Latin America and one-tenth of the level attained in East and Southeast Asia. Many of the best-trained professionals, moreover, have emigrated to seek employment in wealthier countries. The United Nations Development Program

(UNDP) has estimated that some 50,000 to 60,000 trained professionals left Africa in the second half of the 1980s alone.[27]

The poor health conditions still prevailing in the African region similarly raise labor costs and dissuade investment.[28] Endemic diseases continue to plague large proportions of the population, undermining labor productivity. Progress on the eradication of some of these diseases is possible and has been achieved in the past, but it requires constant vigilance at the regional level. Lapses can be extremely costly, as demonstrated by the growing spread of medicine-resistant strains of malaria and tuberculosis. The frightening tragedy looming on the horizon is the burgeoning AIDS/HIV crisis, which has so far hit southern Africa very hard but spared much of West and central Africa. In countries like Zimbabwe and Botswana, the crisis poses an extraordinary burden on already-overstretched public health systems. Incredibly, estimates from Botswana suggest that AIDS/HIV has reduced the average life expectancy from fifty-four to forty-seven years of age.

Africa and the International Aid System

The third stylized fact about postcolonial Africa's relationship to the rest of the world is its extraordinary reliance on aid. Given the inability of the African countries to access international capital and their declining role in international commerce, it is fair to say that aid has played a hugely important role in linking Africa to the rest of the world.

Africa was not always an unusually large recipient of aid. At independence, total aid flows to the region constituted under 2 percent of GNP—a level comparable to that of developing countries in other regions. As late as 1983–1984, it constituted only 5 percent of GNP. However, in response to each succeeding turn in Africa's downward economic spiral throughout the 1970s and 1980s, the donors increased aid to the region. Aid levels grew by an astounding annual average of more than 5 percent in real terms between 1970 and 1995. (Recent aid flows are described in Table 11.2.) Calls for a "Marshall Plan for Africa" have long been fashionable. Yet, the total flows under the Marshall Plan between 1948 and 1952 probably never exceeded 2.5 percent of Western Europe's GDP.[29] In relative terms, that constitutes roughly one-fifth of current levels of aid to Africa. By 1996, excluding South Africa and Nigeria, the average African country received the equivalent of 12.3 percent of its GDP in annual aid, an amount simply unprecedented in historical terms. In comparison, all other regions of low- and middle-income countries received less than 1 percent that same year.

Africa's current social and economic landscape is profoundly marked by aid: In the typical country, 30–40 donors in addition to 75–125 foreign

TABLE 11.2   Official Overseas Development Assistance to Africa, 1997

	ODA 1996 ($mil.)	ODA 1997 ($mil.)	ODA p.c. ($)	ODA/GNP (%)	Real Annual % Change, 1987–1997 (%)
Angola	544	436	49.0	13.2	
Benin	293	225	52.0	13.5	
Botswana	81	125	54.7	1.7	
Burkina	418	370	39.2	16.5	0.3
Burundi	204	119	31.8	18.2	
Cameroon	413	501	30.2	4.9	6.5
Cape Verde	120	110	307.7	28.6	
CAR	167	92	50.0	17.9	
Chad	305	225	46.1	19.0	
Comoros	40	28	80.0	18.7	
Congo-K	167	168	3.7	3.2	−15.4
Congo-B	430	268	158.7	23.0	3.5
Côte d'Ivoire	968	444	67.5	9.9	3.4
Djibouti	97	87	156.5	−	
Equatorial Guinea	31	24	75.6	13.6	
Eritrea	157	123	42.4	20.6	
Ethiopia	849	637	14.6	14.2	−2.7
Gabon	127	40	112.4	2.6	
Gambia	38	40	33.0	9.7	
Ghana	654	493	37.3	10.5	−1.1
Guinea	296	382	43.8	7.8	
Guinea-Bissau	180	125	165.1	71.4	
Kenya	606	457	22.1	6.7	−4.7
Lesotho	107	93	53.0	8.4	
Liberia	207	95	73.7	−	
Madagascar	364	838	26.6	9.5	6.8
Malawi	501	350	50.0	22.9	−0.6
Mali	505	455	50.5	19.4	−0.4
Mauritania	274	250	117.6	26.4	
Mauritius	20	42	17.7	0.5	
Mozambique	923	963	51.2	43.2	1.0
Namibia	189	166	119.6	5.7	
Niger	259	341	27.7	13.2	−3.2
Nigeria	192	202	1.7	0.4	7.9
Rwanda	674	592	100.1	48.8	6.1
São Tomé	47	33	335.7	117.5	
Senegal	582	427	68.2	12.4	−6.9
Seychelles	19	15	237.5	3.7	
Sierra Leone	196	130	42.3	21.3	
Somalia	91	104	9.3	−	−18.1
South Africa	361	497	9.6	0.3	
Sudan	230	187	8.4	−	−16.9

(continues)

TABLE 11.2   *(continued)*

	ODA 1996 ($mil.)	ODA 1997 ($mil.)	ODA p.c. ($)	ODA/GNP (%)	Real Annual % Change, 1987–1997 (%)
Swaziland	31	27	33.3	2.3	
Tanzania	894	963	29.3	13.7	−1.9
Togo	166	124	39.2	13.2	
Uganda	684	840	34.7	11.3	7.6
Zambia	614	618	66.7	19.3	0.8
Zimbabwe	374	327	33.2	4.5	−1.6
Sub-Saharan Africa total	16,749	15,065	28.1	5.6	−1.1
Sub-Saharan Africa except Republic of South Africa, Nigeria	16,196	14,366	12.3	4.9	

SOURCE: Calculated from Development Assistance Committee (1999).

NGOs fund a thousand or so distinct projects involving 800–1,000 foreign experts. Whereas few public institutions have never received aid, a large proportion of African professionals have benefited from a donor-funded scholarship at some point in their careers. Between a third and a half of total spending on basic health and education is provided by foreign aid. And in most countries of the region, the aid business is typically the second biggest employer in the local economy; surpassed only by government, it is often preferred by young graduates for its greater prestige and much more generous conditions of employment.[30]

Table 11.2 also suggests that the rate of growth of aid to Africa is slowing down after years of rapid continuous growth. This apparent trend has led to alarmist claims about the future of aid. Upon closer inspection, however, the table reveals that overall flows to Africa have declined only by an average of 1.1 percent since 1987. Based on a slightly different set of numbers, Stephen O'Connell and Charles Soludo show that the decline totaled some 24 percent in real terms between 1990 and 1996, but also that it was almost entirely concentrated in Kenya, Somalia, Sudan, and Congo-Kinshasa.[31] Aid to Africa may well suffer declines in the future, given increasing doubts about the effectiveness of such aid, but it remains too early to predict its demise.[32]

Since the early 1980s, the aid system has increasingly been directed at addressing Africa's economic crisis. Although regular aid projects have continued to be implemented, an increasing proportion of total aid flows have been linked to addressing Africa's balance-of-payments and fiscal deficits. The World Bank established the Special Facility for Africa (SFA) in 1984 to mobilize funds more quickly for the region. In 1987, the SFA gave way to the Special Program of Assistance to Africa (SPA), designed to provide quick disbursing loans to highly indebted low-income countries in the region.[33] The IMF soon followed with its own special funds for African adjustment. An array of new lending instruments were devised to channel quick disbursing funds to the region to meet the pressing reform-related needs for finance (e.g., Stand-by Agreements, ESF loans, SAFs, ESAFs, SALS, and SECALS). The World Bank's first structural adjustment loan in Africa was extended to Senegal in 1979. By 1989, more than half of the countries in Africa were in the middle of Bank-funded structural adjustment programs, and in all some thirty-six countries in the region had signed a total of forty-nine adjustment program loans plus an additional forty-one sectoral adjustment program loans with the Bank.[34]

Each of these lending instruments, in turn, put in place or strengthened modalities that expressed in explicit fashion the agreement with recipient governments on the policy reforms to be adopted—namely, the Letter of Intent, the Policy Framework Paper, and the Public Investment Program, to mention only those of the IFIs. A fundamental principle of adjustment aid that emerged concerned *conditionality*. In exchange for continued financial support, African governments agreed to a set of reform measures. Conditionality had always been a feature of aid, but the 1980s witnessed a sharp increase in the "explicitness and detail" of the conditions that donors attached to their aid.[35]

A set of processes came to be established for virtually every country in the region that included regular meetings of the Consultative Group and Paris Club to help them respect their debt servicing obligations. When it became clear that the debt servicing obligations would not be met on a regular basis, various debt forgiveness facilities were also developed. (Examples include the Toronto and Naples terms and the Fifth Dimension.) Between 1980 and 1986, twenty-five countries in the region rescheduled their debts with the Paris Club some 105 times.[36]

Implications for African Politics and the Renewal of Economic Growth

The combination of circumstances I described in the last three sections left the region with a distinct political economy that can also be described. In particular, they made it less likely that adjustment would succeed. True, structural adjustment programs officially sought to alter the patterns noted earlier. Reforms to lower and simplify tariff structures, place reasonable exchange rates in place, and create new incentives for the traded goods sectors were aimed at enhancing trade and reintegrating Africa into the world trading system. Other reforms, to liberalize domestic prices, deregulate financial markets, and privatize the parastatal sector, constituted efforts to make Africa more attractive to investors and generate greater FDI.

But the question remains: What did these programs achieve? The answer is that they achieved some limited progress on policy reform. Quite a large literature has emerged to assess the ability of structural adjustment programs to restore sustainable growth as well as to attain other policy goals such as poverty reduction.[37] However, few observers argue that African economies have undergone fundamental transformation, and the least one can say is that structural adjustment programs have not generally been viewed as a success. This literature tends to be more divided about whether adjustment programs, as conceived, could have been more successful, but it is generally quite united in arguing that few structural adjustment programs were ever fully implemented. Paul Mosley and his colleagues (1991), otherwise strenuous critics of World Bank policies, suggest that fewer than 60 percent of all policy reforms that featured in Bank lending conditionality in Africa were ever implemented. The World Bank's own evaluation unit claimed an implementation rate only modestly higher than that. Once one takes into account subsequent policy reversal, the use of countervailing measures to undo the impact of reforms, and the growing gap between de jure and de facto policy,[38] the effective rate of implementation could actually be considerably lower.

Significant progress had been made on cutting fiscal deficits, which declined from well over 10 percent (excluding grants) at times in the 1970s and 1980s to 9 percent of GDP in 1992 and to 4.5 percent in 1997. Current account deficits have undergone a similar improvement, totaling on average only 4 percent of GDP in 1977. In most countries of the region, liberalization policies brought about significant progress on the elimination of domestic price controls, notably in agriculture. In addition, reform has achieved reductions in nontariff barriers and the liberalization of bank credit and interest rates. Formally drastically overvalued exchange rates have become considerably more realistic. Typically, at the same time, the average size of the state apparatus relative to the economy has not declined appreciably. The pace of privatization has been painfully slow, while very little sustained civil service reform has taken place and fiscal deficits remain substantially too high, even if they have declined somewhat in the 1990s.[39] Nor have structural adjustment programs succeeded in altering Africa's relationship with the rest of the world. Trade liberalization has proven to be particularly intractable, with rates of effective trade protection essentially unchanged in a majority of the region's economies.[40] As a result, Africa is probably the only region of the world where the degree of openness has not increased in the last two decades.[41]

Why have these reform programs not had better success? Many reasons have been offered.[42] But the peculiar combination of international marginalization and significant dependence on foreign aid that I described in previous sections is almost certainly a key factor.

Simply put, ever-increasing donor support sheltered African governments from the consequences of their inability to attract foreign private capital throughout the 1980s and 1990s. Indeed, aid flows probably lessened the likelihood of economic reform, since they helped governments sustain the policy status quo. Despite its harsh rhetoric, donor conditionality on policy reform lending has proven toothless: Donors kept lending to governments whether or not they were implementing reform programs.[43] Had public capital flows into the region abated, the market would have imposed adjustment on governments that were unable to attract private flows.

These arrangements also resulted in a massive increase in international debt.[44] Private Western bankers had not expressed much interest in lending to African countries (with the exception of the oil exporters), so when the debt crisis broke out in Latin America in 1982, debt in Africa tended to be lower relative to the size of the economy, and a much greater proportion of it was public debt.[45] Debt grew rapidly during the 1980s, however, largely because the economic crisis did not improve and African countries continued to receive concessionary public finance despite their inability to service prior obligations. Although the lending has become more concessionary over time, much of the resource flow has been in the form of loans rather than grants. The donors have proven unwilling to accept debt forgiveness, which would otherwise lessen the leverage they felt they needed in order to bring about reform, but they have been willing to provide funding to help African countries service their debt. For instance, Ghana, the star pupil of the IFIs during the 1980s, witnessed its external debt more than double relative to its economy. Overall, sub-Saharan Africa's debt increased by almost a factor of three between 1982 and 1992, even after various debt forgiveness schemes are taken into account.[46]

Another direct consequence of Africa's relationship to the world economy has been the emergence of the *aid dependency syndrome*.[47] By the early 1990s, most African governments had come to be extremely reliant on aid resources. In 1992–1993, aid represented the equivalent of more than 75 percent of African government revenues. In many countries in the region, virtually the entire nonrecurrent component of the budget was now being financed by donors, as was a large part of the recurrent budget.

This high level of aid resources has had an economic impact. There is some evidence that aid creates a "Dutch disease" effect on the exchange rate in the most aid-dependent countries, whereby the currency appreciates and actually hurts the export sector.[48] In some countries, the evidence suggests that governments have substituted donors' resources for their own tax collection efforts, which in turn have progressively declined relative to the size of the economy.[49]

In addition, the institutional impact has been profound.[50] Some African countries have been overrun with donors and their activities. The proliferation of donors and projects has complicated the life of local decisionmakers, who now often need to coordinate the development activities of more than a dozen actors and their different timetables and procedures. Entire ministries have been marginalized from their own areas of responsibility, with sectoral policy increasingly designed in aid missions and donor capitals and implemented by self-standing project units outside of central government; the latter, meanwhile, has lost much of its sense of accountability and responsibility. Having lost their best staff to these units, hampered by the budgetary crisis, and victimized by patronage and corruption, many government structures have withered.

Future Prospects: The Impact of the East Asian Financial Crisis on Africa

After so much bad news coming out of Africa, and for so long, the donor community and African leaders were quick to take credit for the renewal of real per capita growth after 1994. The World Bank estimated that the median country in the region grew by 4.5 percent in 1995–1997, with exports increasing at 7.5 percent. The international financial institutions argued that this renewal of growth demonstrated that the policy reform programs they had long championed were finally reaping benefits.[51] And governments in the region claimed that they were being rewarded by the markets for their discipline and the sacrifices they had made in the previous decade.

These claims all had a kernel of truth. Indeed, as earlier noted, the policy stance of a majority of African governments in the mid-1990s was more conducive to economic growth than at any time in the last two decades, even if reform had been uneven and too slow. Analyses by the World Bank and the IMF[52] suggest, not implausibly, that countries that had gone the furthest on this reform agenda enjoyed the fastest growth rates, whereas nonreformers and countries mired in civil conflict lagged far behind. Indeed, the strong reformers (countries like Mauritius, Ivory Coast, and Mozambique) appeared to predominate among the eleven countries forecasted to continue to grow at 5 percent or higher in 1998. On the other end of the spectrum, of the twelve countries that experienced a fall in real per capita GDP in 1995–1997, four were involved in armed conflicts (Burundi, the Central African Republic, Congo, and the Democratic Republic of Congo).

By the mid-1990s, Africa was also beginning to benefit from the "emerging markets" phenomenon. Long-wary investors were taking a second look at countries like Ghana, Uganda, and Mozambique, whereas the Republic of South Africa (RSA) was being rewarded for its peaceful transition from apartheid with renewed capital inflows. The continent's fifteen mostly nascent and very small stock exchanges were posting significant gains and drawing positive commentary in the financial press.[53]

However, the breadth of this recovery, and its seeming strength, was at least in part an artifact of several essentially temporary, "one-time-only" circumstances that could not have contributed to long-term growth. First, some of the fastest growth was recorded in countries such as Mozambique, Ethiopia, and Uganda, which emerged from civil wars in the late 1980s and early 1990s. Here, too, the spurt of growth was unlikely to be sustained, having resulted from the "one-time-only" benefit of underutilized capacity being put back to work after a long period of instability. Although the return of these countries from a virtual Hobbesian state of nature is something to cheer, we need to remind ourselves that the return of growth in the mid-1990s left most of them poorer than they were at independence.

The optimism of the late 1990s was based on the notion that with the end of these long-standing civil conflicts in the Horn of Africa and southern Africa, the continent might be entering a period of political stability. Overcoming the reputation of being a bad "neighborhood" was viewed as important to attracting private capital back to Africa, and the region's advocates in the policy community probably exaggerated the significance of the end of these civil wars.

Second, the long-delayed devaluation of the CFA franc in January 1994 was a major reason for the good performance in the fifteen CFA countries. Overvaluation had wreaked a devastating impact in countries like Senegal and the Ivory Coast, both of which had suffered through negative growth rates in the years before the January 1994 devaluation. The dramatic improvement in competitiveness helped foster a sharp increase in long-deferred investment, the reactivation of idle productive capacity, and some return of capital flight. The result was an export boom that helped fuel growth. Thus, the average GDP of CFA countries had dropped at an annual rate of −0.1 percent from 1990 to 1994, increasing by about 5.1 percent in 1995–1997.[54]

In sum, Africa benefited from not insignificant progress on the policy and political-reform fronts, but also from some lucky and unusual circumstances in the mid-1990s. This luck appeared to change in 1997–1998. The eruption of new conflicts in the region—with civil war in Congo-Brazzaville in 1997 and in Congo-Kinshasa in 1998, plus the Senegalese intervention in Guinea Bissau, the South African intervention in Lesotho, and the border war between Eritrea and Ethiopia, all in 1998—provided a sobering reminder that African states continue to be extremely vulnerable to internal ethno-regional strife and external border disputes. Given the high profile of Congo-Kinshasa, the renewal of war there will probably reverse a lot of the recent perceptional changes about investment risks throughout Africa. It should be noted that some investments for high-value mineral and oil resources (particularly offshore) are remarkably immune to political instability, as they can easily be enclaved and protected. Thus, when commodity prices are high, certain war-torn countries, such as Sierra Leone and Angola, have actually enjoyed high growth rates. What will most suffer from political instability are productive investments that require law and order, public infrastructure, and effective governments.

But, perhaps more important, the emergence of a massive international financial crisis following a speculative attack on the Thai currency, the Baht, represented a potentially significant exogenous shock to African economies. In the short to medium term, the crisis in Asia is likely to have three somewhat distinct effects on African economies.[55]

First is what might be called a *contagion effect*, whereby speculative panic spreads from country to country through the financial sector, leading to attacks on vulnerable national currencies. This appears to have happened in RSA, where the Rand tumbled some 30 percent between mid-1997 and mid-1998, while total capitalization on the Johannesburg Stock Exchange fell by 30 percent in dollar terms over the same period. As a result, growth estimates were revised sharply downward, to less than 1 percent for 1998.

Elsewhere in the region, however, this impact of the East Asian crisis has been relatively muted, largely because the region has not been sufficiently integrated into international capital markets to be vulnerable to speculative crises. Granted, capital flows from Asia into Africa had been increasing in recent years, but they are now likely to diminish as banks and firms must deal with losses at home. In addition, had the enthusiasm of Western investors for emerging markets continued, middle-income reform successes like Ghana or Ivory Coast would have been poised to start benefiting. Today, the higher risks associated with emerging markets will raise the cost of borrowing for Africa and defer much of these flows. This effect should not be exaggerated, however. It may be true that the crisis in East Asia will make capital much more cautious about emerging markets in the next couple years, but the fact remains that few African countries would have been a significant destination for this capital anyway, at least in the immediate future.

A second, stronger effect of the Asian crisis on Africa is likely to be felt through trade effects. In particular, the resulting slowdown of the world economy has put downward pressures on commodity prices, which are likely to have a much more direct negative impact on the region. Overall, primary commodity prices are down by an estimated 12 percent since the beginning of the East Asian crisis, with sharpest declines for copper, timber, cotton, and oil prices. The decline of oil, especially, is likely to have a significant impact on Africa's oil exporters. By October 1998, oil prices were hovering around $13 a barrel, down 30 percent from the previous two years. Most forecasts do not suggest much improvement in the immediate future, with prices remaining under $15 a barrel through the end of the century, assuming no further deterioration of the world economy due to diffusion effects of the East Asian crisis. Of course, net oil importers in Africa will benefit from these lower prices. Overall, the Bank estimated that price movements would translate into a 7 percent decline in Africa's terms of trade for 1998, after an improvement of 3.3 percent in 1997.

A third effect of the East Asian crisis may be further downward pressure on concessional flows to the region. This outcome is admittedly more speculative, but the provision of well over $100 billion by the West to support bailouts in other regions of the world will almost inevitably put pressure on the flows going to Africa. Peaking at about $19 billion in 1994, official aid flows to Africa have since declined by about a quarter. An increasing share of that total, moreover, is being directed to emergencies rather than to development. The decline in assistance for the latter is likely to continue, particularly as skepticism about aid effectiveness appears to be on the rise in Western public opinion.

The impact of lower aid levels on Africa's economies is not easy to decipher. If the critics of aid are right and concessional support has not only promoted government consumption at the expense of investment but also lessened the incentives to promote economic policy reform, then it could be argued that lower levels of aid may have a salutary effect and force governments to adapt to the global economy. This may well be true, at least in some countries where there is *prima facie* evidence of a level of aid well beyond the government's realistic absorption capacity. On the other hand, if it can be demonstrated that properly administered aid helps governments with the right policy mix to promote growth and alleviate poverty, as argued in several recent studies of aid effectiveness,[56] then an acceleration of the decline in aid will represent a net cost for the region.

Conclusions

The inability of African economies to attract or retain private capital combined with extremely high levels of public assistance to the region has profoundly marked Africa's relationship to the world economy as well as the nature of its domestic political economy. Today may well be a watershed period, as aid flows have started to decrease. The sustainability of the international *regime* I have described in this chapter was largely predicated on ever-increasing aid flows, which allowed African economies to maintain more or less permanent balance-of-payments and fiscal deficits. Declining aid levels in the future will force African governments to finally adjust their economies to the logic of international markets. If the current trends are any indication, however, the decline of aid will be slow and incremental. Will governments then promote policies that are more attractive to private capital? They will have little choice but to do so. Nonetheless, the region's accumulated bad reputation over the last three decades—as well as its long-standing deficiencies in infrastructure, human capital, and governance—will for the foreseeable future deter investors.

Notes

1. Sachs and Warner (1995), pp. 16–17.

2. Bienen (1990) and Rodrik (1998).

3. Several recent contributions include Ake (1996), Stein (1997), Adedeji (1994), and Barratt-Brown (1995).

4. See, for example, the optimistic assessment in Gordon and Wolpe (1998).

5. See, for example, Hoogvelt (1997).

6. Among a large literature, see Fieldhouse (1973), Austen (1987), Cooper (1981), and Munro (1973).

7. Munro (1973).

8. These issues are well covered in Yeats et al. (1996).

9. On industrialization in Africa, see the excellent summary essay by Hawkins (1991). In addition, Riddell (1990) provides useful, if now somewhat dated, case studies.

10. See World Bank (1997c), p. 242.

11. These estimates, from a wide variety of sources, concern the early 1990s and late 1980s. They were collected from Europa Publications (1997).

12. See, for example, Colin et al. (1993).

13. World Bank (1998b), p. 312.

14. The discovery of oil after independence, in such countries as Angola, Gabon, and Cameroon, served to diversify the export base, yet typically led governments to neglect their export agricultural sectors even more.

15. These developments are well discussed in Bates (1981) and Hart (1982).

16. On the role of the parastatal sector in this process, see World Bank (1995).

17. See World Bank (1989).

18. Lensink et al. (1998).

19. World Bank (1999), pp. 206–207. Note that these totals do not include South Africa.

20. The best summary of these deficiencies remains World Bank (1981).

21. These are reported in World Bank (1997c).

22. See *Jeune Afrique* (1997).

23. See, for example, the corruption index reported by Transparency International in its annual reports. Kaufmann (1997) provides a good summary of the issues.

24. Nunberg (1997).

25. Heggie (1994).

26. See, for example, Wilson (1997).

27. On these issues, see Braütigam (1996).

28. World Bank (1994b).

29. O'Connell and Soludo (1998).

30. See van de Walle and Johnston (1997) for a description of these phenomena.

31. O'Connell and Soludo (1998), p. 2.

32. These issues are examined in greater depth in van de Walle (forthcoming).

33. Operations Evaluation Department (1997). See also Ravenhill (1988, 1993), which provide good discussions of the early diplomatic activities around the African crisis, and Kapur (1997).

34. See Jesperson (1993), p. 12.

35. Kapur (1997).

36. Operations Evaluation Department (1997), p. 24.

37. See, among others, World Bank (1988, 1993); Corbo et al. (1992); Mosley et al. (1991); Thomas et al. (1991); and Sahn (1992).

38. Béatrice Hibou (1996) presents a particularly fascinating account of this divergence from trade policy reform.

39. On civil-service reform, see Lienert and Modi (1997) and Nunberg (1997). Commenting on the Bank's own lending for civil service reform, Nunberg candidly admits that she cannot be confident that "our projects have boosted either [the] effectiveness . . . or efficiency [of the civil service]" (p. 5). On the privatization record, see the recent survey by Bennell (1997). And for a good analysis of fiscal adjustment, see Elbadawi (1996).

40. See Rodrik (1998).

41. For cross-regional comparisons, see Sachs and Warner (1995) and World Bank (1996).

42. On the politics of structural adjustment in Africa, see Callaghy and Ravenhill (1994), Lewis (1997), and Bates and Collier (1993).

43. See Collier (1997).

44. Debt issues are covered comprehensively by Thomas Callaghy in Chapter 3 of this book.

45. Lancaster and Williamson (1986).

46. World Bank (1994b).

47. Project 2015 (1996). See also Braütigam (1999).

48. For the case of Kenya, see Younger (1992).

49. Braütigam (1999, pp. 26–28) surveys the available studies.

50. Ibid.

51. See, for example, Fischer et al. (1998) and the World Bank's analyses in World Bank (1996, 1997a).

52. Ibid.

53. Kenny and Moss (1997).

54. On the impact of the devaluation, see Clément et al. (1996).

55. See Harris (1999).

56. World Bank (1998) and van de Walle and Johnston (1997) provide good reviews of the recent literature on this subject.

References

Adedeji, Adebayo. (1994). "An Alternative for Africa," *Journal of Democracy* 5 (October), pp. 119–132.

Ake, Claude. (1996). *Democracy and Development in Africa*. Washington, D.C.: Brookings Institution Press.

Austen, Ralph A. (1987). *African Economic History: Internal Development and External Dependency*. London: James Currey.

Barratt-Brown, Michael. (1995). *Africa's Choices*.

Bates, Robert A., and Paul Collier (1993). "The Politics and Economics of Policy Reform in Zambia." In Robert H. Bates and Anne O. Krueger (eds.), *Political and Economic Interactions in Economic Policy Reform*. Oxford: Basil Blackwell.

Bates, Robert H. (1981). *Markets and States in Tropical Africa: The Political Basis of Agricultural Policies*. Berkeley: University of California Press.

Bennell, Paul. (1997). "Privatization in Sub-Saharan Africa: Progress and Prospects during the 1990s," *World Development* 25, no. 11, pp. 1785–1803.

Bienen, Henry. (1990). "The Politics of Trade Liberalization in Africa," *Economic Development and Cultural Change* 38, no. 4, pp. 713–732.

Bräutigam, Deborah. (1999). "Aid Dependence and Governance." Unpublished manuscript, American University, Washington, D.C., March 5.

_____. (1996). "State Capacity and Effective Governance." In Benno Ndulu and Nicolas van de Walle (eds.), *Agenda for Africa's Economic Renewal*. Washington, D.C.: Overseas Development Council.

Callaghy, Thomas, and John Ravenhill (eds.). (1993). *Hemmed In: Responses to Africa's Economic Decline*. New York: Columbia University Press.

Clément, Jean A. P., Johannes Mueller, Stephane Cosse, and Jean le Dem. (1996). *Aftermath of the CFA Franc Devaluation*, Occasional Paper 138 (May). Washington, D.C.: International Monetary Fund.

Colin, et al. (1993). "D'Un Berlin à un Autre." Paris: Cahiers de L.OECF.

Collier, Paul. (1997). "The Failure of Conditionality." In Catherine Gwin and Joan M. Nelson (eds.), *Perspectives on Aid and Development*, Overseas Development Council Policy Essay Number 22. Baltimore: Johns Hopkins University Press for the ODC.

Cooper, Frederick. (1981). "Africa and the World Economy," *African Studies Review* 24, no. 2/3 (June/September), pp. 1–86.

Corbo, Vittorio, Stanley Fischer, and Steven B. Webb. (1992). *Adjustment Lending Revisited: Policies to Restore Growth*. Washington, D.C.: World Bank.

Elbadawi, Ibrahim. (1996). "Consolidating Macroeconomic Stabilization and Restoring Growth in Africa." In Benno Ndulu and Nicolas van de Walle (eds.), *Agenda for Africa's Economic Renewal*. Washington, D.C.: Overseas Development Council.

Europa Publications. (Various years). *Africa South of the Sahara*. London: Europa Publications.

Fieldhouse, D. K. (1973). *Economic and Empire, 1830–1914*. London: Weidenfeld and Nicholson.

Fischer, Stanley, et al. (1998). *Africa: Is This the Turning Point?* IMF Papers on Policy Analysis and Assessment (May). Washington, D.C.: International Monetary Fund.

Gordon, David, and Howard Wolpe. (1998). "The Other Africa: An End to Afro-Pessimism," *World Policy Journal* 15, no. 1, pp. 49–59.

Harris, Elliott. (1999). "Impact of the Asian Crisis on Sub-Saharan Africa," *Finance and Development* 36, no. 1, pp. 14–17.

Hart, Keith. (1982). *The Political Economy of West African Agriculture.* Cambridge, Eng.: Cambridge University Press.

Hawkins, Tony. (1991). "Industrialization in Africa," in Douglas Rimmer (ed.), *Africa: 30 Years On.* London: James Currey.

Heggie, Ian G. (1994). *Managing and Financing of Roads: An Agenda for Reform,* World Bank Technical Paper no. 275, Africa Technical Department Series. Washington: World Bank.

Hibou, Béatrice. (1996). *L'Afrique est-elle Protectioniste?* Paris: Karthala.

Hoogvelt, Ankie. (1997). *Globalization and the Postcolonial World.* Baltimore: Johns Hopkins University.

Jesperson, Eva. (1993). "External Shocks, Adjustment Policies, and Economic and Social Performance." In Giovanni Andrea Cornia, Rolph van der Hoeven, and Thandika Mkandawire (eds.), *Africa's Recovery in the 1990s: From Stagnation and Adjustment to Human Development.* New York: St. Martin's Press.

Jeune Afrique. (1997). "Le Boom de l'Insecurité." Paris (March 12).

Kapur, Devesh. (1997). "The Weakness of Strength: The Challenge of Sub-Saharan Africa." In Devesh Kapur, John P. Lewis, and Richard Webb (eds.), *The World Bank: Its First Half Century.* Washington, D.C.: Brookings Institution Press.

Kaufmann, Daniel. (1997). "Corruption: The Facts," *Foreign Policy* (Summer), pp. 114–127.

Lensink, Robert, Niels Hermes, and Victor Murinde. (1998). "The Effect of Financial Liberalization on Capital Flight in African Economies," *World Development* 26, no. 7 (July).

Lienert, Ian, and Jitendra Modi. (1997). "A Decade of Civil Service Reform in Sub-Saharan Africa," IMF Working Paper WP/97/179 (December). Washington, D.C.: International Monetary Fund, Fiscal Affairs Department.

Mosley, Paul, et al. (1991). *Aid and Power: The World Bank and Policy-Based Lending in the 1980s.* London: Routledge.

Munro, J. Forbes (1973). *Africa and the International Economy.* London: J. M. Dent & Sons.

Nunberg, Barbara. (1997). "Rethinking Civil Service Reform: An Agenda for Smart Government," Working Paper (June 30). Washington, D.C.: World Bank, Poverty and Social Policy Department.

O'Connell, Stephen A., and Charles C. Soludo. (1998). "Aid Intensity in Africa." Paper presented to the AERC/ODC conference on "Managing the Transition from Aid Dependence in Sub-Saharan Africa," Nairobi, May 21–22.

Operations Evaluation Department. (1997). *The Special Program of Assistance for Africa: An Independent Evaluation.* Washington, D.C.: World Bank.

Ravenhill, John. (1993). "A Second Decade of Adjustment: Greater Complexity, Greater Uncertainty." In Thomas Callaghy and John Ravenhill (eds.), *Hemmed In: Responses to Africa's Economic Decline.* New York: Columbia University Press.

_____. (1988). "Adjustment with Growth: A Fragile Consensus," *Journal of Modern African Studies* 26, no. 2, pp. 179–210.

Riddell, Roger. (1990). *Manufacturing Africa.* London: James Currey.

Rodrik, Dani. (1998). "Why Is Trade Reform So Difficult in Africa?" *Journal of African Economies* 7, Supplement 1, pp. 43–69.

Sachs, Jeffrey, and Andrew Warner. (1995). "Economic Reform and the Process of Global Integration," *Brookings Papers on Economic Activity* 1, pp. 1–118.

Sahn, David E. (1992). "Public Expenditures in Sub-Saharan Africa During a Period of Economic Reform," *World Development* 20, no. 5 (May), pp. 673–693.

Stein, Howard. (1997). "Adjustment and Development in Africa: Towards an Assessment," *African Studies Review* 40, no. 1 (April).

van de Walle, Nicolas. (forthcoming). "Aid's Crisis of Legitimacy: Current Proposals and Future Prospects." *African Affairs.*

van de Walle, Nicolas, and Timothy Johnston. (1997). *Improving Aid to Africa.* Baltimore: Johns Hopkins University Press, for the Overseas Development Council.

Wilson, Ernest J. (1997). "Globalization, Information Technology and Conflict in the Second and Third Worlds: A Critical Review of the Literature." Unpublished manuscript, Rockefeller Brothers Fund.

World Bank. (1999). *Global Economic Prospects and the Developing Countries, 1998/99.* Washington, D.C.: World Bank.

_____. (1998). *Assessing Aid: What Works, What Doesn't and Why.* New York: Oxford University Press for the World Bank.

_____. (1997a). *Global Economic Prospects and the Developing Countries, 1997.* Washington, D.C.: World Bank.

_____. (1997b). *African Development Indicators, 1997.* (On diskette.) Washington, D.C.: World Bank.

_____. (1997c). *The World Development Report, 1997.* Washington, D.C.: World Bank.

_____. (1995). *Bureaucrats in Business: The Economics and Politics of Government Ownership.* Washington, D.C.: Oxford University Press for the World Bank.

_____. (1994a). *Adjustment in Africa: Reforms, Results and the Road Ahead.* Washington, D.C.: World Bank.

_____. (1994b). *Better Health for Africa.* Washington, D.C.: World Bank.

_____. (1989). *Sub-Saharan Africa: From Crisis to Sustainable Growth. A Long-Term Perspective Study.* Washington, D.C.: World Bank.

_____. (1989). *Mauritius: Managing Success.* Washington, D.C.: World Bank.

_____. (1981). *Accelerated Development in Sub-Saharan Africa.* Washington, D.C.: World Bank.

Yeats, Alexander J., Azita Amjadi, Ulrich Reincke, and Francis Ng. (1996). "Did External Barriers Cause the Marginalization of Sub-Saharan Africa in World Trade?" *World Bank Policy Research Working Paper No. 1586* (March). Washington, D.C.: World Bank.

12

Africa's Weak States, Nonstate Actors, and the Privatization of Interstate Relations

WILLIAM RENO

Aid from wealthy states to sub-Saharan Africa is being transformed. A 1995 report from the United States President's Office condemned the post–World War II practice of government-to-government aid to poor countries, arguing that "[a] nation does not develop a vibrant economy through development aid, but by its adoption of an economic system which encourages individual initiative through minimal state intervention." Focusing on U.S. policy, the report observed that "[t]oo often, the U.S. Development Aid Program, acting in conjunction with other donors . . . [has] hindered such transitions by subsidizing statist economic policies."[1] The U.S. Congress cut direct foreign development aid appropriations for 1996 to sub-Saharan Africa by about $130 million, a 20 percent drop from 1992–1995 averages, and there has been substantial pressure in Congress to cut it further.[2] Actual cuts directed at Africa, however, have been offset with new aid for businesses willing to invest in Africa. For example, the Growth and Opportunity Act of 1998 increased funding by $650 million for loan guarantees through the official Overseas Private Investment Corporation (OPIC) and enhanced duty-free access to U.S. markets via the Generalized System of Preferences (GSP).[3] Organization for Economic Cooperation and Development (OECD) member-states have followed a similar course, with modest cuts in Africa aid programs since the mid-1990s, while bolstering support for commercial transactions with Africa.[4]

The shift toward economic aid to Africa through increasingly private channels creates incentives for some rulers to adopt noninterventionist economic policies, as intended. Others, however, incorporate this aid via private channels into their political strategies to weather the collapse of their state institutions. Beneficiaries of the largest amounts of resources include states that currently battle insurgencies as well as states where officials are either unwilling or unable to implement pro-market reforms. Such states should be expected to offer little attraction to overseas donors who insist on policies of economic openness—greater protection of property and contract rights, less regulation of capital movements, and reduced state intervention in internal economies—to attract private investors.

In fact, transnational firms do business in some of Africa's most politically unstable and bureaucratically weak states, including those that visibly abjure a coherent process of policy and institutional reform. In contrast, the firms' responses to supposedly attractive economic policies are highly selective. The interest of some firms in doing business in nonreforming states ensures that these unlikely recipient states will continue to receive aid from the United States through these new channels and occasionally increase their share of aid. Furthermore, these nonreforming recipient states show a marked tendency to relax their efforts to monopolize violence within their globally recognized boundaries. Yet at the same time, rulers of these states increase their capacity to influence developments outside the state's territory. To do this, they manipulate practices and norms associated with global commerce to manage the terms under which foreign firms operate in areas under their de jure control. The link between aid and business in Africa then facilitates rulers' efforts to use firms to fashion a new relationship between themselves and officials in strong states. In other words, the interstate regime of aid, designed to induce conformity in the internal organization of states in a global economy, in fact accomplishes the opposite: a further departure from these global norms.

Here I consider the relationship between rulers of weak states and increasing transnational commerce in the context of a growing "trade, not aid" trend in policies of stronger states, especially the United States. Toward this end, I test the proposition that shifts in foreign aid from African governments to private economic actors reduce state intervention in economic affairs. I examine this model's predictions about ex ante and ex post political constraints on economic reform. As for the ex ante constraints, the evidence drawn from the recent record of aid suggests that those countries exhibiting greater instability and internal disorder continue to receive significant amounts and proportions of the region's share of overseas aid. Even in the context of U.S. state-to-state aid, Angola, ranked near the bottom of indices of economic openness, received $47 million in U.S. assistance in 1997, up from $25 million the year before, and $3 million in 1992, the year of a peace agreement and election that seemed poised to change Angola's statist economy and authoritarian government. As for ex post constraints, the record of recent investment in Africa demonstrates the weakness of connections between economic reform that donor states prescribe and actual increases in transnational commercial transactions that are supposed to respond to "correct" behavior.

I then present a model of aid to African states in which rulers of bureaucratically weak and politically tumultuous states benefit to an unexpected degree. This new aid regime strengthens the political advantages of some economic actors (including rent-seeking officials in institutionally weak states who had sought private wealth through the manipulation of their state offices) and some foreign firms that are especially adept at managing these risky environments. Members of this new partnership develop incentives to preserve the rents (both internally generated and, now, supplied through aid to businesses) and barriers to competition created by internal chaos and bureaucratic weakness. Together, these partners use the very weak state and its globally recognized sovereignty as a commercial resource, and incorporate strong state aid to private business into this strategy. I conclude with some observations about how these unintended outcomes change the international relations between very weak and strong states. In particular, I show how very weak state rulers become unexpectedly adept at garnering resources in the global economy to manage their internal affairs and influence officials in strong states, all without capable formal institutions for economic management or even diplomacy.

Trade, Aid, and Weak States in Theory

Skeptics observe that rent-seeking behavior is ubiquitous in the context of overall scarcity as well as low status and low pay for state officials. Businesses and other interest groups commonly pay for privileged access to these officials, who use their control over state assets and law enforcement for private gain at the expense of a socially optimal allocation of resources. This arrangement, however, makes business in Africa expensive and highly risky, dependent as it is on the personal caprices of officials whose incentives are to maximize their personal short-term gains. These state officials rationally favor an inefficiently large state sector, both to control resources directly and to collect rents from as broad an array of access points to the state as possible.[5] The relationship between private actors and state officials is such that Dennis Mueller famously observes:

"[W]henever there is a rent to be found, a rent seeker will be there trying to get it."[6] This explains seemingly high returns on investment in Africa, variously cited by boosters as between 25 and 34 percent, versus a global average of about 8 percent.[7] This premium, in turn, reflects the difficulty of doing business in bureaucratically weak, internally chaotic states. To boosters of reform, it also suggests that Africa is underexploited, that removing political risk and bad policies will increase Africa's share of foreign investment as bureaucratic and political barriers to investment fall.

Thus when rent-seeking is pervasive, increasing internal resources and foreign aid under state control supposedly hampers growth rather than encouraging it.[8] This proposition appears in official criticisms of direct government-to-government aid in the United States. "Despite decades of foreign assistance," observed an official in President Clinton's office, "most of Africa and parts of Latin America, Asia and the Middle East are economically worse off today than they were 20 years ago."[9] The U.S. Congress echoes the complaint, noting that "[p]overty is largely a condition imposed on people by ill-conceived and repressive economic policies. . . . No amount of foreign aid can make up for the conditions that result from economically unfree economies."[10]

These views resonate in World Bank pronouncements. "[T]oday's large volume of aid poses dangers," noted a 1994 World Bank report on reform in Africa; "it could soften budget constraints and thus finance the postponement of public sector reforms."[11] This concern fits empirical findings in successful cases of reform in East Asia. Richard Doner and Anek Laothamatas, for example, found that spending constraints in Thailand limited unbridled clientelism,[12] a conclusion that clearly argues for limiting direct state-to-state aid in many cases. For Africa, many scholars identify the role that a regular flow of resources from overseas plays in the neopatrimonial ruler's efforts to hold together a coalition of elite loyalists and strategic groups.[13]

This diagnosis of rent-seeking justifies prescriptions for market-oriented reforms, both within recipient countries and in the manner and direction in which aid is distributed. Scholars have also recognized, however, that it is unwise to conclude that apparently successful market reforms automatically end rent-seeking, maintaining the danger that even aid to seemingly committed reformers will end up underwriting corruption and cronyism. Early in the current wave of market reforms in Africa, Thomas Callaghy and Ernest Wilson discovered that "in a continent where the line between the public and the private is often very fine, members of the ruling political or state class have frequently used their influence and state resources, obtained illegally or otherwise, to 'buy' state-owned enterprises."[14] "Reform" in Russia, along with the extensive financial backing of European and U.S. governments, has attracted more recent attention (and condemnation) along these lines. Based on evidence from postcommunist transitions, serious political obstacles to further reform come not from short-term losers but from short-term winners. These groups, which often include current and former state officials, benefit from early distortions of partially reformed economies, then exert political pressure to halt reform at that point.[15] This outcome gives more ammunition to groups and individuals in the United States and elsewhere who claim that even state-to-state aid to committed reformers can go seriously wrong and is an inefficient use of resources.

Despite this pessimism from both rational choice and institutional perspectives, development economists and policymakers have long recognized that the nature of official policies and state institutions does matter to efficiency and economic growth.[16] They observe that governments with poorly functioning government institutions tend to be corrupt; hence most aid to weak states has emphasized what the World Bank calls "capacity building" since the late 1980s.[17] The aim of aid, therefore, is to improve the performance of government institutions—to make corrupt bureaucracies more Weberian in the sense of encouraging meritocracy in appointment and recruitment, stressing career service, and offering reasonable pay and prestige. Yet theoretical and empirical counterarguments justify ending even this kind of direct aid to states as well.[18] Aid to increase bureaucratic efficiency may buy more efficiency among lower-level government officials. It is also possible that aid of this sort will actually reduce the wealth of ordinary citizens. New, efficient institutions can simply encourage more centralized, efficient predation. This is a persuasive reason *not* to give aid to governments, since some rulers have been observed to use more effective state agencies to centralize corruption at higher levels than existed in the past.[19] This line of argument is cited in connection with the U.S. Congress's reluctance to extend further aid to the Yeltsin government in Russia, for example.

The lesson of these findings is not only that reformers should try to control rent-seeking among state officials and make them more competent, but also that reformers should delegate as many economic policy issues as possible to investors and even encourage them to take over critical economic tasks previously reserved for the state. For example, Indonesia's President Suharto contracted out customs services to a Swiss firm, cutting out corrupt Indonesian officials.[20] The aborted post-Suharto Indonesian government proposal to appoint a currency board—effectively replacing the rupiah with the U.S. dollar—represented an even more extreme recognition that no degree of internal institutional reform was likely to root out cronyism and quickly restore investor confidence in Indonesia. So, too, in Africa, where private firms play a prominent role in customs services, tax collection, procurement, and even war fighting.[21] If commercial firms rather than bureaucracies are real agents of reform in weak states, policies of donor states should target these firms as proper channels for aid. A World Bank official carries the argument further: Aid should be directed toward private groups, specifically those that are critical of rent-seeking, including globally competitive firms that demand efficiency and stability in states in return for investment.[22] Thus market forces, not just officials in strong states or creditors, will punish laggard reformers.

Sub-Saharan Africa is a good venue for testing these propositions because its forty-seven countries represent a wide range of state capacity and levels of perceived corruption. Many African countries have also received long-term aid from donor states. Though subordinate to debates about the wisdom of continuing much larger quantities of bilateral and multilateral aid to postcommunist governments, Africa has been at the vanguard of initiatives to privatize the transmission and targets of aid. Relatively marginal to donors in terms of overall aid budgets, Africa has the distinction of being at the forefront of innovation in markets and state politics.

The Evidence

Does trade, or the prospect of future trade, have an impact on U.S. aid to sub-Saharan Africa? And do economic policies of recipient governments influence aid flows, as critics in Congress and the executive branch of U.S. government claim they should? To investigate these potential relationships, I recorded foreign direct investment from all sources and overseas direct aid from the United States for forty sub-Saharan African states from 1992 to 1996.[23] (Provided that policymakers refrain from pursuing noneconomic policy agendas with regard to investors from their own country, growing foreign investment should signal that a country is implementing correct policies and will be increasingly likely to benefit from aid channeled through private actors.) I then investigated the relationship among investment, aid, and three indexes that rate African states alternately on the basis of economic freedom, perceptions of corruption, and political risk.

The first measure, economic freedom, is indexed by the Heritage Foundation and includes such factors as government intervention in economies, openness to trade and investment from abroad, and guarantees of protection of private property.[24] This measure is significant insofar as members of the U.S. Congress refer to it frequently and incorporate its criteria into legislation regulating development aid. The second measure is indexed by Transparency International's Corruption Perceptions Index, based on surveys of businesspeople concerning degrees of corruption in particular countries.[25] Finally, political risk is indexed by the Australian Export Financing Insurance Corporation, which generates ratings of both country political risk and commercial risk.[26]

These data show that even state-to-state U.S. development aid, though declining, is not allocated to countries on the basis of "economic freedom" as defined by the Heritage Foundation. In fact, figures for 1996 show a slight inverse correlation between economic freedom thus defined and allocations. Relatively little of the linear variation in aid allocations is explained by business perceptions of corruption; and almost none, by the Australian government's evaluation of risk.[27]

Why does U.S. aid to sub-Saharan Africa appear to be so impervious to a state's progress toward creating the more open and efficient economies and administrations that critics of rent-seeking support? Are some states so successful in their policies that they no longer require assistance? This does not appear to be the case. Uganda and Ghana, hailed in Washington and among multilateral creditors as models of successful reform, have per capita incomes of $190 and $410, respectively.[28] In fact, these two poor but promising states have seen significant cuts in U.S. aid. Uganda's 1995 allocation of $49 million was reduced to $29 million in 1996. Ghana's aid fell from $54 million to $30 million during the same year. Strategic and humanitarian motivations still appear to play significant roles in aid allocations. Aid to Ethiopia peaked in 1993 and 1994 at around $125 million, as that country demobilized after a war and Eritrea separated from it, both issues in which U.S. officials took an interest. Likewise, the allocations to Rwanda of $194 million in 1994 and $101 million in 1995 appear to have responded to the humanitarian emergency there, as well as to what some observers of U.S. policy regard as U.S. strategic support for the post-genocide Rwandan regime as a counterbalance to regional instability.[29]

The foregoing examples suggest the proposition that the functions of state-to-state aid programs are changing. Direct aid may continue to be an appropriate means of managing low-level strategic interests and responding to humanitarian emergencies. Trade-related assistance, however, finds its way to Africa through other, newer channels. For example, the quasi-official U.S. Eximbank approved $23 million to help finance investment in Ghana's gold mining industry and $316 million in escrow financing to limit risk for investors in Ghana's hydrocarbon industry.[30] If this proposition is correct, it follows that the finding of Peter Schraeder and his colleagues—namely, that trade played a significant role in shaping U.S. aid policy in the 1980s—continues to be true in the 1990s, despite the apparent lack of correlation between state-to-state development assistance and actual or potential trade.[31]

More surprisingly, the behavior of foreign investors appears to be little affected by factors captured in the Heritage Foundation's index of states' adherence to neoliberal economic policies. The behavior of foreign investors in Africa is even slightly negatively correlated to the Australian government's evaluation of risk. Business perceptions of corruption appear to have an impact on investment decisions, though here, too, the correlation between the two factors is quite low.[32]

What explains this ambiguous result? More than foreign aid, foreign investment in Africa varies widely from state to state. In 1996, for example, foreigners invested $912 million in Nigeria and $329 million in Angola, both extremely risky countries by the Australian measure and clearly not serious reformers by the Heritage Foundation measure. Yet Côte d'Ivoire also attracts foreign investment ($223 million in 1996), suggesting that reform policies do promote private capital inflows that may benefit from aid to firms willing to invest in Africa—a contingency that justifies the shift to "trade, not aid" to successful reformers. Ghana, Cape Verde, Swaziland, and Lesotho all rank relatively high on the index of "economic freedom" and low in terms of risk, and each has experienced above-average growth in foreign investment from 1990 to 1997, compared to other African states. Reforms may attract investment. But something else attracts investors in risky cases. Some World Bank researchers suggest that the presence of fixed market advantages, rather than specific government policies, has a greater impact on investment decisions.[33] Perhaps this explains China's odd situation: Ranked almost at the end of the Heritage Foundation list between Chad and Mauritania as "economically unfree," China nevertheless hosted 45 percent of the $90 billion invested in developing countries from abroad in 1995! In fact, a tally of investment by state rankings of risk (see Table 12.1) shows a bipolar distribution of investment. Furthermore, there is a tendency over time for investment to gravitate toward the two poles of low and high risk.

Why is this so? Quite simply, investment goes where the markets are or, in the case of Africa, where opportunities to exploit natural resources and build large infrastructure projects are—calculations that can be influenced by state aid programs that minimize private investors' risks. Investment that relies on small producers or multiple transactions requires a local government administration that is capable of and willing to enforce contracts and provide stable and predictable economic policies. Enclave investment, however, may bring firms that have substantial capabilities to manage their own economic environments. The political implications of this distinction are significant, both in terms of survival strategies of vulnerable regimes and in terms of the significance of high risk for foreign investors. If resources from overseas states increasingly come through commercial channels, officials in states that continue to abjure reform policies, and continue to rank highly on risk indices, may seek new commercial intermediaries to gain access to these resources—pro-

TABLE 12.1   Tally of Investment by State Rankings of Risk

	Risk Moderate (N=7)	Risk High (N=12)	Risk Extreme (N=20)
1980 investment	$52mn	$163mn	$458mn[1]
1996 investment	$146mn	$5mn	$2,017mn

	Risk Moderate (N=7)	Risk High (N=12)	Risk Extreme (N=20)
GNP of group (% of sample)	$17,516mn (11%)	$35,900mn (22,6%)	$105,500mn (66.4%)
Group % total investment (minus Gabon)	6.7% (6.3%)	0.2% (6.1%)	93.0% (87.5%)
Rate of investment (as unit GNP per $)	$119.9	$7,194	$52.6

SOURCES: See website <www.efic.gov.au>.
   World Bank, African Development Indicators, 1997. Washington, DC, World Bank, 1998, p. 82.

vided that they have assets or other advantages to attract foreign investors. To the extent that foreigners care about Africa, and depending on the degree to which this concern is tied to investment and trade, the willingness of foreign investors to do business in weak, unstable states headed by nonreformers gives these officials new, nonstate intermediaries through which to influence officials outside of Africa. Additionally, firms that do invest in spite of high risk can also be expected to play significant roles in the internal strategies of these state rulers—an issue to which I turn next.

The Argument

The shift of financial resources away from state-to-state assistance programs creates new opportunities for the coincidence of short-term interest among firms, rulers of weak states, and officials in non-African states. The long-term impact is quite different, however. This policy, designed to reduce bureaucracy and promote the privatization of economies, plays a major role in helping rulers resolve problems related to their inability to control national territories and impose disciplined hierarchies on associates. "Trade, not aid," which is commonly described as subjecting African rulers to global processes for their own good, ends up as a mechanism through which rulers of weak states can exert influence through private, transnational actors and build political coalitions among these actors and officials in foreign states, while abjuring many of the difficult bureaucratic and administrative tasks commonly associated with internal sovereignty. Rulers of weak states owe much of this newfound capability to the changing nature of assistance from abroad.

Closer examination of overall foreign assistance from the United States to Africa reveals that resources have not diminished very much at all.[34] It is even possible that they have increased, though the increasingly blurred distinction between public and private resources requires redefining the categories in which assistance is measured. This shift in the U.S. assistance program has largely taken place during the Clinton presidency. Upon Clinton's arrival in Washington in January 1992, OPIC insured investments in risky markets, including those in Africa, on a case-by-case basis. The agency extended equity financing to only two investment funds—one concentrating on Asia, the other on Africa—for a total public and private financial commitment of $100 million. By 1998, OPIC had committed about $200 million in equity financing for Africa-oriented investment funds, in addition to underwriting private investments valued at $745 million in Africa. The Clinton administration backed the creation of two private equity funds for investment in Africa: the New Africa Opportunity Fund (NAOF) and the Modern Africa Growth and Investment Company (MAGIC), with combined OPIC resources of $180 million in equity financing. The pending Africa Growth and Opportunity Act will provide another $500 million in equity financing for an Africa infrastructure investment fund.[35] During Clinton's administration, the Eximbank has provided escrow accounts to limit risk for infrastructure and large-project investments valued at $1.3 billion in Africa. Other U.S. agencies have become involved in business investments in Africa, too. The U.S. Department of Transportation, for example, approved $67 million in loan guarantees to Ghana to finance the purchase of two power generators from a U.S. firm.[36]

The Clinton administration recognized that quasi-official investment funds and direct government agency intervention could play a crucial role in foreign policy toward economically marginal areas like Africa that would not otherwise attract large amounts of private investment. Recall that promoting U.S. investment in Africa should, according to standard analysis, reduce rent-seeking behavior among African officials and strengthen preferences for rule-based bureaucratic administration among rulers. Finding less aid with more strings attached, governments in Africa should recognize that greater administrative discipline and economically efficient policies present the best opportunities to tap new resources that respond to market incentives. "A clearly defined policy that trade and investment are the main focus of U.S. engagement with Africa," said the CEO of the U.S.-based Equator Bank, "will make it clear to governments in Africa that an alternative to long-term dependence on foreign assistance will depend on their adherence to internationally accepted practices in areas such as subsidies, protection of intellectual property, illicit payments and dispute settlement."[37] This policy also serves U.S. commercial interests. Referring to the MAGIC fund, which he helped create, Representative Philip Crane noted that "[t]he emerging markets of Africa present enormous potential for U.S. investors. This new fund will greatly improve the climate for U.S. private investment in Africa . . . in keeping with the growing trend toward increasing trade instead of traditional U.S. foreign aid."[38]

The latter aim of policy appears to be met in spite of low "economic freedom" and high risk ratings for many African states—an aim that contradicts the former one. The Australian government service, for example, rates Angola at the top of its risk categories. And the Heritage Foundation rates Angola as among the world's most "economically unfree" states. Despite this status, American entrepreneur Maurice Templesman sought Eximbank financial support for a diamond brokering consortium for his firm, Lazare Kaplan International; Endiama, Angola's diamond marketing parastatal; and Sociedade Generale Miniero, the diamond marketing arm (Uniõ Nacional para a Independencia Total do Angola) of the Union for the Total Independence of Angola (UNITA). Templesman reportedly touted the deal as a way to resolve growing conflicts between UNITA and the Angolan government through providing each with a predictable and visible stake in the diamond wealth of the contested Cuango region.[39] He also reportedly received high-level support for his scheme in Washington. (Prior to Clinton's reelection, he had contributed $145,000 to the U.S. Democratic Party through himself and his companies.) Former National Security Adviser Anthony Lake reportedly instructed an aide to inform OPIC and Eximbank about the proposal. The aide told Angolan President Eduardo Dos Santos that the deal "will take on greater meaning if the U.S. is involved through such mechanisms as Eximbank or OPIC." A State Department official also reported that "Templesman wanted us to tell Ex-Im: This is a foreign policy imperative. We would like you to do it even if it is risky."[40]

In the end, no formal proposal was made. The incident, however, reveals much about the nature of foreign investment in risky countries, in terms of both profit and the political role of foreign investment in the strategies of insecure regimes. First, a firm backed with U.S. government guarantees is likely to carry far more political weight than a firm backed with guarantees from a less powerful country, or one backed with none at all. The U.S. firm's competitive advantage lies in the calculation in the capital of the weak state that crossing a U.S. agency (or a multilateral creditor agency like the Multilateral Investment Guarantee Organization

[MIGO]) will carry greater costs than mistreating a firm that is backed by a less powerful government's agencies. The shift toward "trade, not aid" thus increases the relevance of a transnational firm's home country, especially when that government backs the firm with subsidized finances or risk insurance.[41] Such a firm may receive preferential treatment from officials, including the opportunity to share in rent-seeking opportunities that state officials can selectively provide. Second, the foreign firm's intervention (and the implicit backing of this firm's home state) can boost the weak state ruler's own security. Templesman's proposal could be seen from Luanda's perspective as an opportunity to control territory through the intermediary of a foreign firm. This practice of foreign firm intervention is already common in Angola. For example, the American private security firm Airscan protects a Chevron-Angolan government joint venture in Cabinda's oil fields (which supplies 70 percent of Angola government foreign exchange earnings) and plays a key role in keeping at bay the fighters of the Frente de Liberação do Enclave do Cabinda (FLEC).[42] Similarly, a U.S.-Canadian firm operates and protects a Cuango mining concession with its partner, International Defense and Security.[43] The ruler who is able to attract a foreign firm to an enclave operation not only secures new rent-seeking opportunities for himself and favored associates (long a feature of foreign investment in patronage political systems); he also gains access to more reliable, politically less meddlesome private military forces that can deny these resources to freeriders, yet cannot build indigenous power bases of their own.

From the perspective of officials in non-African states, government subsidization of finances and indemnification of private firms against risk can have a strategic component, provided that it enhances this political relationship between investor and vulnerable regime. To the extent that this relationship is mutually profitable, even if it does not end rent-seeking, U.S. trade officials aggressively seek advantage for "their" firms. Eximbank, for example, provided an $88.5 million loan guarantee for Halliburton Energy Services (of which former U.S. Defense Secretary Richard Cheney is general manager) for a joint venture with the Angolan government oil company, as part of Eximbank's overall $316 million investment in the hydrocarbon sector in Angola. Eximbank also provided Halliburton with a $150 million loan at a low guaranteed interest rate in strife-torn Algeria, and it has taken the lead in securing privileged positions for U.S. firms to develop new gasfields off the coast of Ghana. In addition, U.S. official influence was reported to be crucial for securing favorable treatment for U.S. firms in auctions of new offshore oil blocs in Angola.[44] Ideally, if the investments generate profits or strategic benefits for the "donor" country, officials there reap the additional benefit of having the recipient of "aid" pay for its own benefits—as, for example, when export earnings finance weapons purchases or foreign investment results in increased state control and stability in economically valuable areas.

In some cases, officials in weak states conspire to defraud commercial partners. Toward this end they may depend on their own manipulation of internal regulations and outsiders' willingness to confer sovereign rights on otherwise fraudulent actions. For example, in Guinea, Sierra Leone, and Gambia, investigators for an underwriter discovered that local customs officials were fraudulently recording shortages of goods as they were being unloaded from ships. Armed with customs documents, the nominal receivers of the goods then filed bogus claims, confident that their underwriters would prefer to pay claims rather than launch expensive investigations in dangerous ports in West Africa.[45]

Our main concern here is whether or how this shift in resources from state-to-state channels to private transactions changes the nature of political authority in weak states. Does this policy enforce conformity to a particular standard of internal behavior? Or does the U.S. government assume risk while rulers of weak states and their commercial partners exploit high-risk premiums of investment? From the standpoint of investors, OPIC- or Eximbank-backed investment funds help leverage their investments in high-risk areas. Most OPIC funds use government-guaranteed notes to contribute to two-thirds of the investment, relying on private institutional equity investors for the other third. This means that the fund's earnings, minus low interest rates on government notes, go entirely to the fund's private partners. The willingness of government agencies to underwrite high-risk investments provides private investors with further protection—a relationship that creates the possibility that the provider of subsidized indemnification will also become a new source of rents, both for African regimes and for their private commercial partners.

Here, in fact, we find investment being used as a means to reduce political risk, rather than simply responding to risk as an exogenous market factor. The intervention of foreign state agencies that are willing to offer below-market-rate financing and insurance for firms that do business in high-risk environments effectively commercializes internal security risks for rulers of weak states, too. The cost of reducing these risks is borne by taxpayers in non-African states. Meanwhile, rulers reduce their own political and security threats through profitable partnerships with foreigners. Closer examination of the nature of rent-seeking in regimes facing threats from insurgencies provides a more systematic illustration of the advantages to both local officials and foreign private commercial partners of investment in very risky places.

First, as World Bank and other critics of rent-seeking suspect, a ruler facing significant internal threat will choose an excessive level of state intervention in a national economy to generate rents with which to pay off loyal associates. This behavior, however, does not preclude ruler interest in efficiency. In fact, a ruler may prefer that lower-level officials, or the members of a recalcitrant or threatening group, not share rents. He would then prefer a much smaller government administration, provided that the subordinates or associates within it could be controlled. Herein lies the advantage of foreign investment, particularly that which arrives with partners who have good connections to the security establishments of stronger states or who can occupy and defend enclave territory on their own, denying resources to challengers. Given these advantages, a rent-seeking ruler may continue to lack interest in real bureaucratic reform or the development of indigenous entrepreneurs (from both of which future political challenges may arise), while demonstrating a credible commitment to efficiency as creditors and transnational firms define it.

Furthermore, the commercialization of weak state rulers' risk changes the way that officials in non-African states view and treat the weak state rulers' internal security threats. Angola's military stalemate, for example, clearly debilitates what could be a prosperous economy and threatens to create humanitarian emergencies and refugee migrations that would upset democratic transitions in neighboring southern African states. State-to-state assistance, such as the $132 million spent to support the United Nation's failed UNAVEM II peacekeeping between UNITA and the Angolan government and elections, demonstrates to officials the futility of direct aid in politically risky situations.[46] The $3 billion U.S. expenditure and twenty-six deaths in the 1992–1994 Somalia operation further convinced policymakers of the futility of direct assistance to Africa's worst-off areas.[47] This wariness to intervene or spend large amounts of money in risky places is codified in Clinton's Presidential Decision Directive 25 of 1994, thus reflecting an official reluctance to become embroiled in open-ended financial and political commitments in conflicts outside areas of direct strategic importance to U.S. interests.[48]

At the same time, the academic community lends support to the notion that internal conflicts are resolved when one side wins militarily. Roy Lichlider, for example, finds that 76 percent of the ninety-one conflicts in his sample that he classifies as "civil" between 1945 and 1993 ended only when one side won. Of the negotiated settlements—24 percent—half collapsed, whereupon fighting resumed.[49] In this regard, seeking an end to the Angolan war through the use of firms as intermediaries to broker revenue sharing among combatants, or encouraging firms to supply the recognized government with new sources of revenue and access to private security forces, accords with a preference for military solutions. Paradoxically, the United States appears to have shifted closer to a Soviet pattern of foreign aid that blurred the distinction between commercial and military aid. That is, the spendthrift Soviet "donor" often required recipients of military assistance to trade raw materials useful to Soviet industry to pay for arms purchases from state-run enterprises, or from favored firms attached to Soviet client states.

In the contemporary version, the intermediary is private, though substantial informal links between government officials and firm personnel are common. For example, U.S. State Department officials and the Clinton administration reportedly pressured the Angolan government in 1997 to hire a private U.S. security firm, Military Professional Resources, Inc., staffed by many retired U.S. military officers, to train Angola's army.[50] Directing assistance through these private channels should make U.S. officials more concerned about the fiscal solvency of the Angolan regime, since the regime must have the means to pay for its own assistance. Although ambassadors have long been concerned about a home state's commercial prospects in the country of posting, current practice makes it less surprising that the U.S.-Angola Chamber of Commerce would count current and former U.S. ambassadors to Angola, along with several retired high-level State Department officials, among the members of its board.

Uganda offers another example of the military consequences of a "trade, not aid" foreign aid regime. Even given the difficulties of discovering the extent of (now private) transactions, it is apparent that Uganda is not a large-scale beneficiary of investment subsidies from the U.S. government. OPIC helps finance a pyrethrum extraction operation ($1.9 million) and a satellite data transmission project ($500,000).[51] It is even more apparent, however, that foreign private investment plays an important, and growing, role in the Ugandan regime's efforts to battle four distinct insurgency groups and in the efforts of U.S. State Department officials to help them to do so.

Situated on the southern border of Sudan and the eastern border of Congo, Uganda is of strategic interest to U.S. officials as a rear base for anti-regime Sudan People's Liberation Army (SPLA) rebels. Florida-based Airscan (which is also a member of the U.S.-Angola Chamber of Commerce) also reportedly trains and provides logistical support to Uganda's military in its battle with insurgents.[52] Members of the Ugandan regime have adopted the strategy of incorporating private firms into their own security measures in ways that make rent-seeking compatible with increased economic efficiency. President Yoweri Museveni's half-brother, who oversees anti-insurgency operations, also heads the Ugandan subsidiary of a private South African military service firm. He also has a stake in an arms assembly factory, an air transport company, and a weapons vendor, among others.[53] Uganda's rulers have mastered an eclectic approach, incorporating firms from a variety of backers, including South Africa and China. Nonetheless, U.S. officials have been accused of providing tacit diplomatic support so that some of these supplies end up in the hands of the SPLA.[54] For a state that already attracts complaints from multilateral creditors for spending about 12 percent of its budget on its military, the use of private firms may be one of the few viable ways acceptable to both regime associates and outsiders to expand the regime's military capabilities.[55]

U.S. military policy in Africa promotes this use of private firms to supply assistance. For example, the Joint/Combined Exchange Training (JCET) program, which serves thirty-four African states, incorporates private firms in training operations to minimize the extent of direct U.S. military and political commitments. Likewise, the U.S. Africa Crisis Response Initiative (which helped train Ugandan troops) incorporates private suppliers. Both programs also insulate private elements of assistance from U.S. State Department restrictions regarding military aid to countries with significant human rights abuses.[56] And since assistance can be supplied through private firms, policymakers need not face questions from legislators related to appropriations.

Conclusion

Clearly the connection between reform and investment is variable. In fact, for enclave economies, investors prove able to operate in chaotic environments, in partnership with local rulers to manage local anarchy and to benefit from external order that commercial conventions and foreign governments supply. Though the subject is beyond the scope of this chapter, it is conceivable that some investors who are especially adept at managing local risk may even prefer chaos over internal stability that would attract less adept competitors.[57] Is this relationship a new development, in terms of weak state politics or international relations? It appears to be significant in terms of detaching weak state rule from control over a national territory, save for domination of archipelagos of economically useful areas, often through private proxies. In terms of international relations, the extraterritorial influence of weak state officials flows as much through alliances with global economic actors as from formal diplomatic channels. These strategies also release rulers of weak states from the politically challenging and expensive task of building, or even preserving, significant bureaucratic state institutions in order to rule.

In the preceding pages, we have found that this (externalized) "internal" strategy is tied to policies of economic openness, freedom of capital movements, aggressive promotion of investment from strong states, and a conviction in commercial circles that Africa is underexploited—at least in the sense that risk premiums begin to overwhelm the barriers to investment, just as global commercial practice increases incentives to invest in Africa's weak states. These developments echo previous cycles of the global spread of commerce. Janice Thomson, for example, notes that states did not monopolize the international exercise of violence until well into the nineteenth century. Powerful states used chartered companies and other commercial proxies to build forts, issue money, make war, and acquire territory.[58] Indeed, one could argue that states have contracted out violence to private actors in the more recent past. The Vinnel and Raytheon corporations, for example, have decades-long experience training Saudi troops on behalf of the United States. And air cargo firms as well as various other commercial operators featured in Cold War U.S. aid to Contra rebels in Nicaragua and UNITA in Angola.

Nonetheless, the nature of the recent sharp increase in investment in very weak states in Africa points to a marked shift toward the pattern of shared sovereignty between state and private actors in the conduct of relations between strong and weak states. The statement of the Clinton administration's trade representative, Charlene Barshefsky, that "in an increasingly competitive global economy the United States cannot afford to see a vast region marginalized"[59] recalls colonial-era convictions among strong states that such states have a duty to ensure that Africa's resources do not lie unused for the tasks of civilization. Likewise, the effort is occasionally justified in terms of bringing Africa into conformity with global economic standards. Said an officer of the Seaboard Corporation in reference to the Africa Growth and Opportunity Act, "It is time that Africa be treated as an adult . . . and [be] held responsible for her behavior and growth just as any other adult nation."[60]

From the perspective of the (externalized) "internal" politics of the weak state, ruler efforts to recruit outside commercial partners exhibit similarities to Michael Doyle's notion of "imperialism by invitation," which applied to the nineteenth-century late precolonial era when some of Africa's very weak political authorities battled one another to control trade routes and profit as middlemen in Europe-bound trade.[61] Specifically, these rulers used external commercial transactions to help resolve problems related to their inability to control national territories or mobilize populations.

The contemporary strain, however, is distinguished by a more extensive globalization of the management of economic and political risk. In the wake of failed peacekeeping or peacemaking interventions in the early 1990s, strong states have proven reluctant to exercise significant direct power—even in the former Yugoslavia, which is geographically close to a number of strong states. Likewise, strong states have failed to come to a consensus regarding the use of force in Iraq, a clear case that involves mineral resources of critical strategic importance to industrial economies. Thus the contemporary strong state use of commercial proxies in Africa is likely to offer greater opportunities for rulers of weak states and their commercial partners to act as free riders vis-à-vis the private (as in underwriter conventions, bond rating services, nonstate adjudication of commercial disputes) and state provision of risk management on a global scale. Freeridership in this context faces boundaries that are less firm than those associated with previous cycles of economic globalization. In central Africa, for example, we see even other weak states take advantage of disorder in neighboring states. Leo Mugabe, the nephew of Zimbabwe's President Robert Mugabe, was able to sign a joint venture agreement with Gécamines (Congo's state-owned mining company) and the Zimbabwean state-owned Zimbabwe Defense Industries in a deal financed by Zimbabwean banks close to key political actors in that country.[62] And as I noted earlier in a similar vein, conflict in Congo plays a role in the Ugandan president's use of private companies to help manage Uganda's insurgency problem.

This expanded freeridership, however, is not likely to lead to the increased stability that constitutes the goal of officials in strong states. First, as observed above, investment itself does not necessarily force rulers of weak states to conform to a particular standard of internal sovereignty. Second, and more threatening to regional order, firms and weak state officials who provide mutual benefits tend to bolster local strategies that privilege externalization of conflicts. In Congo, for example, President Laurent Kabila finds few options beyond inviting foreign firms, including those with close attachments to political establishments in neighboring countries, to trade natural resources for weapons or local security. These firms and, in some instances, the states in which they originated become parties to conflict. Especially where neighboring weak state rulers employ this strategy, conflicts threaten to become enmeshed in interlocking commercial alliances and exchanges.

What alternatives exist? Strong states could define a standard of sovereignty, denying sovereignty to rulers who are unable or unwilling to conform to that standard. This measure, however, would require a significant political shift away from post–World War II global conventions recognizing the right to self-determination of former colonies in the form of unqualified state sovereignty. It would also require a significant commitment of resources from officials in strong states, entailing massive state-to-state aid to weak state administrations to build capable and effective public bureaucratic institutions. This action in turn, however, would violate current economic and fiscal orthodoxy in nearly all stronger states. Thus the developments described above are likely to persist, insofar as regional disorder does not pose a serious threat to the strategic interests of strong states and the fiction of sovereign equality can be maintained in the face of the costs of economic and political freeridership in the context of this order.

Notes

1. U.S. Congress, Senate, Committee on Foreign Relations, Subcommittee on International Economic Policy, Trade, Oceans and Environment, Prepared Statement, July 24, 1993, pp. 12–13.

2. U.S. Congress, House of Representatives, "Foreign Operations, Export Financing, and Related Programs Appropriations Bill," September 15, 1998, p. 6. The report notes, however, that government aid to Africa matches the previous year's level, though more of it is to be distributed through nongovernment channels.

3. U.S. International Trade Commission, *U.S.-Africa Trade Flows and Effects of the Uruguay Round Agreement and U.S. Trade and Development Policy* (Washington, D.C.: USITC, 1997).

4. Organization for Economic Cooperation and Development, *Geographical Distribution of Financial Flows to Developing Countries* (Washington, D.C.: OECD, 1998), p. 22.

5. This relationship is spelled out in Joel Migdal, *Strong Societies and Weak States* (Princeton: Princeton University Press, 1988). Migdal makes the important point that rent-seeking in the context of regime insecurity, where efficient bureaucracies harbor political rivals, generates bureaucracies that are designed to produce rents and are incompatible with reform that permits an independent articulation of agency interest. For interpretations of rent-seeking in Africa more generally, see Robert Bates, *Markets and States in Tropical Africa* (Berkeley: University of California Press, 1981); and Richard Sandbrook, *The Politics of Africa's Economic Recovery* (New York: Cambridge University Press, 1993).

6. Dennis Mueller, *Public Choice II* (New York: Cambridge University Press, 1989), p. 241.

7. An official at the Overseas Private Investment Corporation claimed that investments in Africa generated a 28 percent return in 1997, versus 8.5 percent worldwide. See "OPIC in Africa" (June 1998), available at www.opic.gov/SUB-DOCS/public. The vice-chair of the African Development Fund asserted that investments in Africa returned an average of 33 percent in 1996. See Carol Castiel, "Trade: America's New Approach," *West Africa* (May 19, 1997), p. 718.

8. This point is made more generally in Terry Lynn Karl, *The Paradox of Plenty* (Berkeley: University of California Press, 1997).

9. U.S. Congress, Senate, Committee on Foreign Relations, "Foreign Aid Reduction Act of 1995: Together with Additional and Minority Views," Y1.1/5, pp. 104–195.

10. U.S. Congress, House of Representatives, "International Responsibility and Self-Sufficiency Act of 1998," H.R. 3256, February 24, 1998, Sec. 2(2).

11. World Bank, *Adjustment in Africa* (New York: Oxford University Press, 1994), p. 14.

12. Richard Doner and Anek Laothamatas, "The Political Economy of Structural Adjustment in Thailand," in Stephen Haggard and Steven Webb (eds.), *Voting for Reform: Political Liberalization, Democracy and Economic Adjustment* (New York: Oxford University Press, 1994); M. G. Rao, "Accommodating Public Expenditure Policies: The Case of Fast-Growing Asian Economies," *World Development* 26, no. 4 (April 1998), pp. 673–694. The recent economic crisis in East Asia has pro-

duced plenty of counterevidence that reduced state expenditure is compatible with continued clientelism.

13. See, for example, Peter Lewis, "Economic Statism, Private Capital, and the Dilemmas of Accumulation in Nigeria, *World Development* 22, no. 3 (March 1994), pp. 437–451; Christopher Clapham, *Africa and the International System* (New York: Cambridge University Press, 1996).

14. Thomas Callaghy and Ernest Wilson, "Africa: Policy, Reality or Ritual?" Raymond Vernon (ed.), *The Promise of Privatization* (Washington, D.C.: Council on Foreign Relations, 1988), pp. 224–225.

15. Joel Hellman, "Winners Take All: The Politics of Partial Reform in Postcommunist Transitions," *World Politics* 50, no. 2 (January 1998), pp. 203–234; Danny Kaufman and Alex Kaliberda, "Integrating the Unofficial Economy into the Dynamics of Post-Socialist Economics," in Bartlomiej Kaminski (ed.), *Economic Transition in the Newly Independent States* (New York: M. E. Sharpe, 1996), pp. 81–120.

16. Mancur Olson, "Big Bills Left on the Sidewalk: Why Some Nations Are Rich and Others Poor," *Journal of Economic Perspectives* 10, no. 2 (Spring 1996), pp. 3–24.

17. See, for example, World Bank, *Adjustment in Africa*, p. 15.

18. This skepticism with specific regard to Africa finds a voice in the World Bank. See Jacqueline Coolidge and Susan Rose-Ackerman, "High-Level Rent-Seeking and Corruption in African Regimes" (Washington, D.C.: World Bank Private Sector Development Department and Foreign Investment Advisory Service, June 1997).

19. This is a common complaint regarding reform in postcommunist states where "oligarchs" have centralized control over resources to shape new political networks. The argument underlying the argument is contrary to the conclusions of the influential Andrei Shleifer and Robert Vishney, "Corruption," *Quarterly Journal of Economics* 108, no. 3 (August 1993), pp. 599–617. These authors were leading advisers to Anatoli Chubais, then chairman of the Russian Privatization Ministry.

20. Manuela Saragosa, "Importers Adjust to Return of Indonesia Customs Office," *Financial Times*, April 11, 1997, p. 8.

21. See, for example, Herbert Howe, "Private Security Forces and African Stability: The Case of Executive Outcomes," *Journal of Modern African Studies* 36, no. 2 (June 1998), pp. 307–331.

22. Mamadou Dia, *Africa's Management in the 1990s and Beyond: Reconciling Indigenous and Transplanted Institutions* (Washington, D.C.: World Bank, 1996).

23. I omitted Liberia and Somalia from my analysis because most relief allocations to these states were not, properly speaking, state-to-state transfers—especially in the case of Somalia, where formally recognized state structures ceased to exist in December 1990. The aid measures are from Organization for Economic Cooperation and Development, *Geographical Distribution* (Washington, D.C.: OECD), and the foreign investment data are from World Bank, *African Development Indicators* (Washington, D.C.: World Bank, 1997), p. 82.

24. Heritage Foundation, "1997 Index of Economic Freedom—Country Rankings," available at www.heritage.org/index/rankings.html.

25. Transparency International, "1998 Corruption Perceptions Index," available at www.transparency.de/documents/cpi/index.html.

26. Export Finance Insurance Corporation, "Country Risk Assessment," available at www.efic.gov.au/grading.html. This index has the virtue of free web access, in contrast to the expensive indices of private vendors.

27. Variations in aid and perceptions of corruption show the strongest correlation, with a Pearson's coefficient of .332—indicating that about 10 percent of the linear variation in aid correlates to corruption.

28. World Bank, *World Development Report 1998* (New York: Oxford University Press, 1998), table 1.

29. Kathi Austin, *Stoking the Fires: Military Assistance and Arms Trafficking in Burundi* (New York: Human Rights Watch Arms Project, December 1997).

30. U.S. International Trade Commission, *A Comprehensive Trade and Development Policy for Countries of Africa* (Washington, D.C.: USITA, 1998).

31. Peter Schraeder, Steven Hook, and Bruce Taylor, "Clarifying the Foreign Aid Puzzle: A Comparison of American, Japanese, French, and Swedish Aid Flows," *World Politics* 50, no. 2 (January 1998), pp. 294–323.

32. Comparison of perceptions of corruption and investment produces a Pearson's coefficient of .399, indicating that about 16 percent of linear variation in investment correlates to perceptions of corruption.

33. Harinder Singh and Kwang Jun, "Some New Evidence on Determinants of Foreign Direct Investment in Developing Countries" (Washington, D.C.: World Bank, 1996).

34. In fact, it has become increasingly difficult to measure trade assistance, as OPIC and other agencies now invoke commercial confidentiality arguments against releasing specific data. For criticism of this practice on the part of OPIC, see U.S. Congress, House of Representatives, Appropriations Committee, Subcommittee on Foreign Operations, Export Financing and Related Programs, "FY '99 Appropriations, Human Rights Issues," April 1, 1998.

35. Africa Growth and Opportunity Act, H.R. 1432, S.778.

36. James Bennet, "Throngs Greet Call by Clinton for New Africa," *New York Times*, March 24, 1998, p. 1.

37. Testimony of John P. Kearney, CEO, HSBC Equator Bank on Behalf of the U.S.–South Africa Business Council Before the United States Congress, House Subcommittee on Trade, April 29, 1997.

38. Quoted in U.S. Congress, House of Representatives, "Hearings of the Trade Subcommittee of the House Ways and Means Committee, Expanding Trade with Sub-Saharan Africa," April 29, 1997.

39. "Diamond Dealer Turns Peacemaker," *Mail and Guardian* (Johannesburg), August 15, 1997.

40. Quoted in Susan Schmidt, "DNC Donor with an Eye on Diamonds," *Washington Post*, August 2, 1997, p. 1.

41. This point is also made in Robert Wade, "Globalization and Its Limits: Reports of the Death of the National Economy Are Greatly Exaggerated," in Suzanne Berger and Ronald Dore (eds.), *National Diversity and Global Capitalism* (Ithaca: Cornell University Press, 1996).

42. Al J. Venter, "U.S. Forces Guard Angolan Oilfields," *Mail and Guardian*, October 10, 1997; Al J. Venter, "Winds of War Set to Blow Across Angola," *Jane's Intelligence Review* 10, no. 10 (October 1998), pp. 37–39.

43. "The Crackdown Begins," *Africa Energy and Mining*, January 28, 1998.

44. Patrick Smith, "Cursed for Their Mineral Wealth: Business in War Zones," *Financial Mail* (Johannesburg), August 14, 1998, p. 30.

45. John Mason, "Cargo Cheats Receive Shot Across the Bows," *Financial Times*, March 31, 1998, p. 19.

46. The dollar figure is cited in Margaret Joan Anstee, *Orphan of the Cold War: The Inside Story of the Collapse of the Angolan Peace Process, 1992–3* (New York: St. Martin's Press, 1996), p. 14.

47. Harry Johnston and Ted Dagne, "Congress and the Somalia Crisis," in Walter Clarke and Jeffrey Herbst (eds.), *Learning from Somalia* (Boulder: Westview Press, 1996), pp. 197, 202.

48. U.S. Department of State, Bureau of International Organization Affairs, "Clinton Administration Policy on Reforming Multilateral Peace Operations" (PDD 25), Publication No. 10161, February 22, 1996.

49. Roy Lichlider, "The Consequences of Negotiated Settlements in Civil Wars, 1945–1993," *American Political Science Review* 89, no. 3 (September 1993), pp. 681–690.

50. Kevin O'Brien, "Freelance Forces: Exploiters of Old or New-Age Peacekeepers?" *Jane's Intelligence Review* 10, no. 8 (August 1998), p. 43.

51. "U.S. Bilateral Aid," *Indian Ocean Newsletter*, May 10, 1997.

52. Yves Goulet, "Washington's Freelance Advisors," *Jane's Intelligence Review* 10, no. 7 (July 1998), pp. 38–41; "Advisors for UPDF," *Indian Ocean Newsletter*, January 31, 1998.

53. On the business interests of Salim Saleh (Caleb Akwandanaho), see Yunusu Abbey and Grace Matsiko, "Saracen to Sell Guns to Civilians," *New Vision* (Kampala), July 19, 1997; "South Africa Arms Uganda," *New African* (May 1997), p. 32; and "Mercenaries and Security," *Indian Ocean Newsletter*, July 5, 1997.

54. Kathi Austin, *Stoking the Fires: Military Assistance and Arms Trafficking in Burundi* (New York: Human Rights Watch Arms Project, December 1997).

55. In this regard, the Ugandan regime mixes commercial entrepreneurialism with military operations in homegrown firms, too. For example, the private firm Renaissance 2000 reportedly recruits and trains anti-insurgency units. As coup-weary rulers must recognize, it is best that it is not the military that defends the regime.

56. This insulation of policy generates criticism in Congress. See Foreign Operations Bill.

57. An intriguing inquiry into this prospect can be found in Jedrzej George Frynas, "Political Instability and Business: Focus on Shell in Nigeria," *Third World Quarterly* 19, no. 3 (September 1998), pp. 457–478.

58. Janice Thomson, *Mercenaries, Pirates, and Sovereigns: State-Building and Extraterritorial Violence in Early Modern Europe* (Princeton: Princeton University Press, 1994).

59. Castiel, "Trade: America's New Approach."

60. Quoted in ibid.

61. Michael Doyle, *Empires* (Ithaca: Cornell University Press, 1986).

62. "Mining Project in Congo," *Indian Ocean Newsletter* 12 (September 1998).

13

Western and African Peacekeepers: Motives and Opportunities

JEFFREY HERBST

In the debate over peacekeeping, one of the most important, but least examined, assumptions is that there is an unambiguous commonality of interests between Western and African peacekeepers. In fact, the major U.S. African peacekeeping effort, the African Crisis Response Initiative (ACRI), is explicitly based on the premise that the United States should provide training to African troops who will do the actual peacekeeping. Similarly, France, the Nordic countries, and the United Kingdom, among others, are all attempting to increase the African capacity to intervene in states that have failed, may soon experience catastrophic institutional collapse, or are a threat to their regions. In this chapter I argue that it is not at all obvious that Western countries and potential African intervenors have the same motivations or desire similar outcomes. Indeed, given the particular nature of state failure in Africa, which helps determine who the likely intervenors are to be, the assumption of a commonality of interests may be especially problematic.

Are We All Peacekeepers Now?

There was a brief moment, as the Cold War ended and the cheers from Desert Storm still rebounded across Washington, when the United States saw itself as leading at least some peacekeeping efforts in Africa and in other parts of the developing world. The United States had been support-ive of the explosion of UN peacekeeping activity, which began once the superpower deadlock in the Security Council had ended, and George Bush did put American soldiers first in line when the United Nations in-tervened in Somalia in December 1992. The euphoria, however, was short-lived. Although many contributing factors were implicated (cost, the cumbersome nature of UN exercises, the uncertain outcome of many operations), there is no doubt that the peacekeeping world changed fun-damentally, on October 3, 1993, when eighteen American soldiers were killed in Somalia. The subsequent public revulsion caused the United States to develop a new, much more skeptical stance toward international intervention. As Presidential Decision Directive (PDD) 25, released in May 1994, noted: "It is not U.S. policy to seek to expand either the num-ber of U.N. peace operations or U.S. involvement in such operations," and the document went on to promise "to continue to apply even stricter standards" when recommending the involvement of U.S. personnel in in-ternational operations."[1] The cost of the Somalia operation and the dis-tasteful images of peacekeepers at war with local armies (who were adept at keeping women and children in the frontlines) also soured many other Western nations on peacekeeping.

The result of the West's new passivity was quickly evident in Rwanda, where the genocide of the Tutsi by the Hutu began on April 6, 1994. On April 21, 1994, the Security Council, having been chastened by Somalia, actually voted to decrease significantly the small UN force already in Rwanda despite the fact that the scale of the ethnic carnage was quickly becoming evident. The international community simply did nothing as perhaps 800,000 of the 1.1 million Tutsi in Rwanda were killed in a three-month period. The U.S. delegation, led by then-Ambassador Madeleine Albright, actively worked to slow UN intervention, demanding addi-tional safeguards and worrying about the cost of a new operation. It took the permanent powers of the Security Council some time even to admit that genocide was occurring in Rwanda, presumably for fear that they might be obliged to act under the Genocide Convention.

Within Africa, there had, of course, always been a desire to have Africans lead interventions. Despite the achievement of independence by most African countries in the early 1960s, foreign military intervention by the ex-colonial powers and others highlighted the fragility of the newly won political power and served to strengthen the historic memory of colonial domination. As General R. P. Mboma, chief of Tanzania's Peo-ple's Defense Force, noted, "At the time of the Organization of African Unity's inception in 1963, the heads of African states were convinced that Africans had an 'inalienable right' to control their own destiny."[2] Thus, *West Africa*, the major news weekly on the continent, called as early as

1964 for an "African Fire Brigade" that could serve as an interpositional force in international conflicts (e.g., between Ethiopia and Somalia, Rwanda and Burundi, and Morocco and Algeria) and that would also address domestic upheavals in individual countries. *West Africa's* motivation was the debacle in Tanganyika where British troops had to intervene to quell a revolt by the East African country's restive army, a profound embarrassment given then-President Julius Nyerere's clarion calls for an end to all foreign influence and his criticism of Western powers during the Cold War.[3] However, it was the catastrophe in the Congo—where outside intervention by the United Nations, Belgium (the former colonizer), and other powers, apparently motivated by Cold War concerns, ended in the death of Congolese President Patrice Lumumba—that solidified the African view that foreign intervention, even under humanitarian guise, would always be problematic.

The African reading of the failures in Somalia and Rwanda only reinforced the belief that reliance on the international community would continue to be highly problematic. For many African countries, the fundamental challenge posed by Somalia was clear: Would the United States, the last remaining superpower, allow Mohamed Fareh Aideed and his few hundred fighters to chase it out of Mogadishu? When the question was answered in the affirmative, the implausibility of Western peacekeeping even in the new world order became self-evident. As William Nhara, coordinator of conflict prevention and research in the OAU's Division of Conflict Management, noted, "Regional organisations should realise that there is a need to take on the primary responsibility for their own problems, especially those relating to issues of peace, security and stability. This is necessary as Africa's external partners are increasingly less enthusiastic about sharing its problems."[4]

Western powers, especially the United States after Somalia, were also anxious to encourage the notion that conflict management could be subcontracted out to regional organizations. After several missteps, in early 1997, the United States unveiled the ACRI. The United States proposed to provide training to several African countries in order to develop a capacity for peacekeeping that might, at some future date, be mobilized. By mid-1997, Washington was able to obtain commitments from seven African countries (Ethiopia, Ghana, Malawi, Mali, Senegal, Tunisia, and Uganda) to allow eight battalions (Ethiopia agreed to provide two) to be trained. Under the training program, about sixty trainers from U.S. Army Special Forces units headquartered at Fort Bragg are sent to each African country for sixty days to provide basic soldiering skills and special training relevant to peacekeeping (e.g., an emphasis on refugees, and some advice on how to deal with humanitarian organizations).[5] About $1 million worth of communications equipment is provided to each battalion. A total of $15 million was budgeted by the United States for the ACRI in fiscal 1997 and $20 million in fiscal 1998.[6]

American officials have gone to considerable lengths to state that they are not leading the African peacekeeping initiatives, especially after earlier diplomatic miscues when the United States seemed to suggest that it wanted to help create and help lead a force for intervention (the ill-fated African Crisis Response Force). As U.S. Ambassador in charge of the ACRI Marshall McCallie notes, "Essentially, what we are doing and others are doing would be training units that would be able to respond to a crisis." Indeed, the American description of the ACRI seems to go out of its way to ask for leadership by others. Again, McCallie's briefing is informative:

> What we are suggesting is not a force. What we are suggesting is a—almost a clearinghouse. It would be an association without membership. It would be an informal gathering of states that are interested in peacekeeping in Africa. And they would address what type of training would be useful, what type of joint exercises would be useful.[7]

Similarly, a former senior American official described the ACRI as "a coalition of the willing."

The desire to leave peacekeeping to the Africans became even more heartfelt after the collapse of the UN peacekeeping effort in Angola in 1998. This operation, like the one in Somalia, cost well over a billion dollars, led to the deaths of dozens of peacekeepers, and left the country in ruins. The Somalia and Angola operations probably guarantee that Africa will not witness another significant UN operation for many years. The dream of a new world order for Africa, where the international community would help secure peace, lasted roughly seven years.

Thus, for a variety of historical, tactical, and relatively recent reasons, "African solutions to African problems" have been embraced across the world as the operational code for future peacekeeping operations in Africa. No one believes that African countries alone can conduct formal peacekeeping operations, and there has been very serious work done on how African and Western forces might cooperate during internationally mandated operations and on what kind of training is necessary to provide. However, it is clear that the emerging vision of peacekeeping foresees African soldiers as the backbone of any intervention force. Further, especially as disgust with UN operations increases, there is a significant desire to "subcontract" the decisionmaking process to African countries, either the OAU or subregional groupings such as the Southern African Development Community (SADC). One of the stated contingencies ACRI-trained troops might respond to is an intervention authorized by a regional grouping of African states.

The Africanization of peacekeeping is an important development in the international relations of the continent. Much of the African discussion of diplomacy in the decades after independence until 1990 centered on the virtues of foreign intervention. In the context of the Cold War, when the superpowers and the great powers (especially France and the United Kingdom) had at least some strategic interests in Africa, such a focus made sense. Also, only the superpowers and the great powers had the ability to project force inasmuch as most African armies in the 1960s were exceptionally weak. Thus, most of the major intervenors in the Congo crisis in the mid-1960s were non-African: Belgium, the United States, the USSR, and the United Nations.

However, the end of the Cold War has meant the end of superpower and great-power strategic interests in Africa. It is impossible, for instance, to imagine the United States intervening in the Democratic Republic of the Congo (DROC) to help defeat the secession of Katanga province as the United States and its allies did twice in the 1970s when President Mobutu faced separatist threats. At the same time, some African armies have matured and are, in a halting manner, able to project force over distance, especially if they are not challenged by a well-organized army. Thus, all of the intervenors in Zaire during the endgame of the Mobutu era in 1997 were African: The Ugandans, Rwandans, Angolans, and Zambians all played significant roles, and minor roles were played by several other African countries including Ethiopia. Thus, the fact that peacekeeping is increasingly being seen as an African responsibility is part of a larger process that is leading to the development of much more profound and important international relations within Africa. It is not much of an exaggeration to say that the history of international relations in Africa is just beginning.

Prospects for Benign Intervention

A core assumption of the peacekeeping literature is that intervenors enter a country with the best of intentions. This assumption, seemingly problematic given the oft-repeated refrain in international relations that countries act according to their interests, came about because of the manner in which peacekeeping evolved after World War II. The classic type of peacekeeping that the "blue helmets" of the United Nations are associated with is the creation of an interpositional force between armies that have agreed to a cease-fire. These peacekeeping forces were mandated under Chapter Six of the UN Charter, which required that the peacekeepers be neutral and prohibited them from using force unless they were attacked. The peacekeeping forces were usually composed of forces from countries that not only had no interest in the conflict but had no obvious interests in the area. Thus, for example, a Ghanaian contingent has long had a significant presence in the UN peacekeeping force in the Golan Heights. The countries that supplied the peacekeepers were motivated by exceptionally high UN per diems, which made peacekeeping a profitable activity; by the prospect of their armies being equipped and trained by the United Nations; and by a commitment to internationalism, albeit at a very low price.

After the Cold War, when it seemed briefly that the remaining superpower would be intimately involved in peacekeeping operations, the assumption of the neutral intervenor could be retained. For instance, few could suggest an ulterior motivation for the U.S. intervention in Somalia: The United States had no traditional interests (strategic or economic) in Somalia, and it seemed obvious that George Bush had been motivated largely by humanitarian concerns.

That international power politics in Africa is now beginning poses an important challenge for peacekeeping. International relations in Africa during the first three decades after most countries gained independence in the early 1960s were very genteel: Very few countries attacked one another and, even when they did, they had no territorial ambitions. For instance, Tanzania invaded Uganda in 1979 to overthrow Idi Amin, not to annex Uganda. Even South Africa's destabilization efforts against its neighbors in the 1980s were primarily attempts to influence the policies of the majority-ruled countries, not to change the borders of the region. Lesotho or Swaziland would not exist today if South Africa had any real territorial ambitions. Within that environment, an assumption that intervention by African countries might be benign was at least plausible. However, now that at least some African countries appear to be acting in a more traditional manner—whereby they project power to further their own parochial interests—an assumption that intervention can be benign is obviously much more problematic.

Indeed, Africa for the first time is witnessing the rise of what might be called revolutionary states. Countries such as Uganda, Eritrea, and Rwanda now have leaders who came to power through unconventional means, largely by waging war within their nations after establishing their own armies. In addition, both the Eritreans and the Rwandans have contempt for many of their fellow African states, the OAU, and the international order. The Eritreans are still bitter because their struggle for decolonization from Ethiopia was simply ignored by the outside world for many years. The Tutsi government in Rwanda believes that it must act independently after the world watched but did not act as the old Hutu government carried out a genocide of the Tutsi population in 1994. It is thus hardly surprising that the Rwandan government, despite its small size, has tried to forcibly change the international order in central Africa and that Eritrea has been fighting against all of its neighbors, including a major land war against Ethiopia in 1999. As Henry Kissinger wrote in a different context, "Whenever there exists a power which considers the international order or the manner of legitimizing it oppressive, relations between it and the other powers will be revolutionary."[8] Thus, the search for peacekeepers comes at precisely the moment when at least some in Africa are beginning to question the fundamental premises of the diplomatic practices that have guided the continent since independence. Although the rise of the new men in Rwanda, Uganda, and Eritrea was initially celebrated because they were believed to possess a stronger commitment to democracy, the way they came to power may pose novel threats to the regional order.

Are There Benign Hegemons in Africa?

Indeed, when intervention is left to the neighbors, as it increasingly is in Africa, the assumption of the benign and neutral intervenor must be examined carefully. Obviously, the most plausible scenario for benign peacekeeping would be for a very large country to lead an intervention in a much smaller country that was, at best, largely extraneous to its own concerns. The international relations literature has long recognized that for a collective good to be produced, one country may have to take on costs disproportionate to the benefits it expects to reap. In particular, it has been noted that many of the post–World War II institutions that have come to guide the international economy were created by the United States as a superpower that was willing to absorb costs that were higher than the benefits it would be able to garner in the short term.[9] A benign hegemon might absorb similar costs to promote peace within a neighbor's realm, even if the immediate benefits were not proportionate.

The question of a benign regional hegemon that might lead a peacekeeping effort is especially pertinent in Africa, given the distribution of country size across the continent. Africa is composed of a large number of countries that are small and only a very few that are large (see Table 13.1).

Indeed, although the average population of African countries is 12.4 million, the median is only 6.5 million—a clear indication of an unequal population distribution. There are only four countries (all over 30 million in size) that could conceivably play the role of regional hegemon: Nigeria (111 million), Ethiopia (56 million), Democratic Republic of the Congo (43.8 million), and South Africa (41.5 million). Three of these countries (Ethiopia, Nigeria, and South Africa) also have three of the four largest armies in Africa.[10]

The model intervention by a benign hegemon is probably the effort led in 1994 by President Nelson Mandela, assisted by other southern African

TABLE 13.1   Distribution of Country Size in Africa

Population	Number of Countries
Less than 2 million	13
2–5 million	8
6–10 million	12
11–19 million	7
20–29 million	3
30 million or more	4

SOURCE: World Bank, *African Development Indicators on Diskette, 1997* (Washington, D.C., 1997).

leaders, to prevent a royal coup by Lesotho's King Letsie III. South Africa so dominates Lesotho that it could not be said to be largely motivated by its own interests. Further, the moral stature of Nelson Mandela and the fact that the intervention was designed to prevent a coup preempted any discussion that South Africa was nothing other than a benign intervenor seeking to ensure the status quo.

However, there are few places in Africa where a similar scenario could be played out. Indeed, the disastrous 1998 intervention by South Africa into Lesotho was probably the best possible demonstration that good intentions by themselves are not enough. It is also obvious that no other leader has Mandela's stature, so the motives of countries when they intervene must at least be examined. Further, what is startling about the current regional situation in Africa is that, outside of southern Africa, where South Africa is the natural leader and is relatively stable by the standards of the neighborhood, all of the other big countries are in serious trouble, even by the standards of their regions, and cannot plausibly play the role of disinterested regional hegemon. Nigeria, by dint of its large population, dominates West Africa; however, its continual domestic political and economic problems long ago ended any discussion that it might be a neutral regional policeman. Nigeria has intervened in parts of the region, but, as discussed below, many of the domestic pathologies it suffers from essentially travel with its troops to foreign countries. In central and East Africa, the Democratic Republic of the Congo is the natural hegemon, but it has been dysfunctional as a country for so long that the capital, Kinshasa, cannot project power over its own territory, much less into other countries, in a professional and unbiased manner. And Ethiopia, though the dominant country in the Horn of Africa, is only very slowly recovering from the decades-long civil war that eventually led to the independence of Eritrea in 1993. Given its profound poverty and ethnic divisions, Ethiopia also cannot play the disinterested big brother.

Indeed, it is striking that Africa's largest countries, with the exception of South Africa, are more likely to be discussed as destinations for peace-keepers than as benign hegemons leading disinterested interventions. DROC has been the destination for a variety of intervenors for several years now, and both Nigeria and Ethiopia, given the centrifugal pressures they are experiencing, are routinely discussed as possible failed states. The problems of many countries in Africa—populations that are atomistically dispersed across a rural hinterland, low and declining tax bases, security forces that are poorly equipped and ill-trained, and the uncertain strength of national identity—become especially pernicious in large countries where capitals find that their writ of authority dissipates over the vast distances that their countries encompass. Indeed, far from size being correlated with power, as has traditionally been the case in the international relations literature, it appears that significant size, within the African context, is a relatively good predictor of poor state performance. It is telling that of the African countries participating in the ACRI, only Ethiopia is among the largest and the only one that would normally be thought of as a natural intervenor.

Buying Disinterested Intervenors

The other prospect for benign intervention would be if African countries were subsidized by the international community to intervene in areas where they would not normally have interests. If they did not have immediate interests and they were on the international payroll, assuming benign intervention might be tenable. However, it seems unlikely that the international community will be willing to pay the price to buy neutrality. For instance, the ACRI comes with no guaranteed funding except for the limited training it provides. It is hoped that funding to get the ACRI-trained troops to their targets and to sustain them will be provided by the international community on an ad hoc basis.

However, the failure of the international community to provide disinterested parties with funding has been a major problem for peacekeeping in Africa. Thus, Tanzania's participation in the intervention in Liberia—a good example of an intervention where there were no obvious national interests at stake—was persistently hampered by an inability to secure outside funding from the United States or the United Nations.[11] The non-Nigerian forces that originally constituted part of the ECOMOG force in Liberia (Ghana, Sierra Leone, Gambia, and Guinea) eventually left, in part because they were not willing to pay the costs of an extended intervention even in a country that was a neighbor. African countries, which became accustomed to having all expenses paid when participating in the old-style Chapter Six interventions sponsored by the United Nations, now clearly recognize that finance is a formidable barrier to intervening in conflicts where their immediate interests are not at stake. Nor are the impediments to disinterested intervention limited to African countries. When former UN Secretary-General Boutros Boutros-Ghali called upon sixty non-African states to form a standby force for Burundi, only one (Bangladesh) volunteered.[12]

Disinterested intervention is also hampered by logistics. The ability to move forces is crucial to peacekeeping. The official U.S. doctrine for peacekeepers notes simply, "Transportation by air, land, and sea is the 'linchpin' of your operation."[13] Logistics is obviously especially important if the countries to intervene are chosen because they are not in the neighborhood and therefore presumably do not have an immediate agenda involving the domestic politics of the destination country. However, there is no chance of any African country or set of countries having such a capability to intervene in another region for the foreseeable future. Even South Africa has only an extremely limited capability to project power, given that most of its forces during the apartheid period were developed to prevent border incursions. Without a strong and robust logistical capability, the ACRI or any other proposal will not be able to get around the central paradox of peacekeeping in Africa: Those that are willing to intervene without an ulterior motive beyond humanitarian concerns do not have the capacity to project the necessary force.

As a result, benign peacekeeping is exceptionally difficult for most African nations. For instance, the 1998 intervention by Senegal into Guinea Bissau—to prevent chaos in that country after a profound split developed within that country's military—turned out exceptionally poorly. Indeed, despite the fact that the Senegalese military has received significant assistance from both the United States and France, its forces, by themselves, were not able to dislodge rebel military units from their quickly built fortifications. This was an especially disappointing performance because the minimal goal of the ACRI and French training was probably for the Senegalese to at least have the capacity to intervene in Bissau.

Thus, disinterested intervention in Africa, ironically, usually happens under the sponsorship of Western nations. Zimbabwe and Botswana both had units in Somalia, perhaps as clear an example of disinterested intervention as is possible, during Restore Hope. Indeed, the United States and the United Nations had made it a high priority to attract African nations that would lend more legitimacy to the intervention. Similarly, the African units that have participated in peacekeeping operations in Angola and Mozambique did so under UN sponsorship and were therefore on the UN payroll. Although several African countries clearly stated that they wanted to form an intervention force during the genocide in Rwanda, their volunteerism came to naught when the United Nations and the major powers indicated that they would not be interested in sponsoring an intervention.

Intervention with a Motive

Instead of benign intervention, what is clear from the very recent history of international relations in Africa is that many of the most dramatic and effective instances of intervention have been carried out by parties with a profound motive in a particular type of intervention. The Rwandan/Ugandan intervention in former Zaire in 1997, which led to Laurent Kabila coming to power, was done specifically to eliminate the security threat posed to Kampala and, especially, to Kigali, by Hutu groups based in eastern Zaire. The effectiveness of this operation (the refugee camps were emptied, millions of Hutu were returned to Rwanda, and the armed Hutu groups lost some of their best sanctuaries and their lifeline to international assistance) stands in stark contrast to the endless dithering by non-Western powers over intervention first in Rwanda in 1994 and then in Zaire in 1996 as the refugee crisis became dramatic. That Rwanda, small by almost any measure, was able to help establish, support, and, to some extent, direct a successful (on its own terms) intervention into its much bigger neighbor clearly demonstrates how peculiar the relationship between size and power has become in Africa and just how great the possibilities of intervention are for a country with strong motives.

Angola also demonstrated in 1997 that it was possible to dramatically change the course of a country when it sent a significant armed force to Congo-Brazzaville to overthrow the democratically elected government of Pascal Lissouba and replace him with former dictator Denis Sassou Nguesso. The Angolans had found Nguesso to be a more attractive leader as they sought to end their own civil war by cutting off outside support for the Union for the Total Independence of Angola (UNITA).

Nigeria's interventions, first in Liberia (1990) and later in Sierra Leone (1997), present a more complicated case. The initial movement into Liberia was motivated in part by humanitarian concerns, especially worries over the fate of Nigerians residing in Liberia. The Liberian intervention also attracted several African partners, and the Nigerian forces in both Liberia and Sierra Leone were legitimated post hoc by the international community. However, the Nigerian interventions could hardly be considered disinterested. In addition to humanitarian concerns, then-Nigerian President Ibrahim Babangida sent forces to Monrovia to help his ally and friend Samuel Doe stay in power. The Nigerian forces proved able to hold Monrovia but could not defeat the forces of Charles Taylor in the Liberian interior. Indeed, the pathologies of Nigeria's patron-client system soon transferred to Liberia as some local commands in ECOMOG

began to make significant money through mineral and logging concessions.[14] Despite many years of fighting, the Nigerian forces did not prevent the war from spilling over into Sierra Leone and, in the end, had to
ratify the election of Taylor, even though they had fought for many years
to keep him from coming to power.

In Sierra Leone, the 1997 coup against President Ahmed Tejan Kabbah
was eventually reversed (the putative motivation for the Nigerian intervention), although the country suffered from several rounds of brutal
conflict. As of this writing (mid-1999), the situation has not stabilized. Intervention in either Liberia or Sierra Leone would have been a complicated and difficult task for any country. However, the fact that Nigeria
had significant interests in both cases, and, at least in Liberia, developed a
panoply of patronage opportunities, probably combined to make a successful intervention unlikely to impossible.

Finally, intervention by African countries in their neighbors for nonhu-
manitarian reasons may increase as a response to other interventions, especially in the context of the rise of revolutionary states. Thus, when
Uganda and Rwanda helped support a second uprising in eastern Zaire
in 1998—this time, to overthrow their former puppet Laurent Kabila—
Angola, Namibia, and Zimbabwe sent troops to protect Kinshasa and to
defeat the invaders. The motivations underlying intervention by Luanda,
Windhoek, and Harare, when all three were suffering from drastic economic conditions at home, are not clear; but their rhetoric suggested that
they were extremely unhappy about Rwandan and Ugandan adventurism. It may be the case that Kabila had managed to extend his own web of
commerce and patronage to these other countries. Whatever their motivation, and this particularly complicated episode may not be untangled for
years, it is clear that no one could confuse Angola, Namibia, and Zimbabwe with disinterested peacekeepers modeled on the old Chapter Six
operations.

Policy Implications

In the international relations literature, there is a clear divide between
peacekeeping and intervention. Such a dichotomy was possible because,
in the classic instances of peacekeeping, forces sent to ratify the ends of
conflict were clearly endorsed and supported by the international community. Intervention, on the other hand, was something that states did to
further their own parochial interests. However, in Africa, there will probably be a much hazier boundary between intervention and peacekeeping.
The international community no longer wants to ratify and support as
many peacekeeping operations, especially in Africa, because the United
States and the major European powers no longer want to pay the bill. At

the same time, at least some African countries will argue that, from their national perspectives, there is no difference between peacekeeping on the cheap and intervention. Rwanda and Uganda had clear peacekeeping concerns (given the over-the-border incursions by Hutu groups) when they sponsored the intervention in eastern Zaire, and Luanda also had, at least by its own lights, a need to cut off possible support from UNITA flowing from Congo-Brazzaville. Similarly, Angola, Namibia, and Zimbabwe have all argued that their 1998 intervention in DROC was done to further the cause of international peace in the face of external aggression, an argument that also eventually convinced Nelson Mandela (who had initially opposed further internationalization of the conflict).

However, if peacekeeping and intervention are synonymous in Africa, it should be understood that most armed interventions will be designed to further the interests of the intervenors. It is unlikely that the interventions will be designed with a high priority assigned to respecting human rights, and the forces involved may not be trained according to the emerging norms for peacekeepers. Most important, the intervention may be designed not to promote peace in an unbiased manner but, rather, to help those parties in the host country that are friendly with the intervenor. African militaries that intervene may also find that they develop new commercial interests in the host country, as happened with Nigeria in Liberia, that further divert them from the cause of peacekeeping and peacemaking in an unbiased manner.

In short, there are many policy implications that should be understood, given the new realities of international relations in Africa and the fact that benign intervention in peacekeeping cannot simply be assumed. First, Western countries must understand that they are playing with fire when they prepare African armies for peacekeeping, especially as that training always involves a significant combat element. After the trainers go home, the United States and other Western nations lose whatever control they may have had over the units trained and the material provided. African countries may therefore be more tempted to intervene in the affairs of neighbors even if they lack the resources to be the benign intervenor farther afield. It may be only a matter of time, to take the worst-case scenario, before ACRI equipment provided to Ugandan troops is found in the hands of pro-Ugandan rebels operating in eastern DROC. Even for the ACRI countries, chosen explicitly because they were least likely to embarrass the United States, there is also the possibility that ACRI equipment could be used in internal operations against domestic opponents. This is especially likely in Senegal and Uganda, where there is significant armed internal opposition to Dakar and Kampala. African governments will use their armies to counter whatever security threats they perceive and will simply not leave equipment or units on the shelf because they received training from Western countries. Indeed, these may be the units and equipment that are called upon to go into the field first.

Second, Western countries are going to have to confront the problem that the countries they have identified as possible peacemakers are not those with the most capable armies who are most likely to intervene. It is particularly striking that the ACRI does not target Kenya, Zimbabwe, South Africa, Angola, and Nigeria. Those countries have armies far more likely to be able to intervene in something other than a UN-sponsored operation (precisely the type of operation that will happen less and less in Africa) than Malawi or Tunisia. They also have, by African standards, at least some ability to project power. The reason those armies have not been targeted for training is that their governments have serious bilateral problems with the United States, including controversies over the democratization process and human rights abuses. However, if the United States and other Western countries are going to have some role in intervention as increasingly implemented by African countries, it is obviously important to deal with those countries most likely to intervene. The international community has indicated that it is not going to provide the resources for benign intervention, so it must recognize that only those with interests are going to intervene. Of course, the United States and other Western countries may have so many problems with the government of Zimbabwe or Angola (to take only two examples) that they will not aid the countries most likely to intervene. It should be absolutely clear to Western countries, however, that they are going to become increasingly extraneous to the process of peacekeeping and intervention as it is played out on the African continent. There appears to be no likelihood that this dilemma will ease in the years to come; indeed, it will probably only get worse.

Third, the United States and other Western countries must recognize that breaches of sovereignty cannot be selectively endorsed. The United States and the major European countries all but officially welcomed the obvious Rwandan/Ugandan intervention to overthrow Mobutu in 1997. This violation of the territorial boundaries of Zaire was applauded because Mobutu's neighbors were doing what the West desired but was not willing to do itself: get rid of the dictator who had so impoverished Zaire. However, the United States and other Western countries therefore had no ability to complain when the Rwandans and Ugandans sponsored the invasion of DROC in 1998 to overthrow Kabila. Indeed, even the Western protest against the Angolan invasion of Congo-Brazzaville in late 1997 was muted because the United States and European countries were in a weak position, having welcomed the Rwandan/Ugandan invasion of Zaire only a few weeks before. Either countries are sovereign or they are not.

This issue will become even more complicated in light of the stated desire by the United Nations to subcontract interventions to regional organizations. However, in cases where the dirty work (fighting) is subcontracted, it must be recognized that international norms are also being subordinated. Indeed, Rwanda, Uganda, and other countries aiding the two incursions into Zaire/DROC could state with credibility that they were a far more cohesive and capable regional grouping than many of the official debating societies that litter the African continent. The African intervenors may have received encouragement from the repeated statements at the United Nations and in the West that regional groupings should solve Africa's problems.

Conclusion

The ambition for African solutions to African problems is an admirable one. It signals the end of the West's patronizing attitude toward Africa and is another indication that the dream of true political independence for the countries south of the Sahara is increasingly becoming a reality. However, African solutions to African problems also mean that the West will be increasingly less able to determine how intervention and peacekeeping are implemented. Currently, the United States and European countries appear to want the best of both worlds: letting the Africans do the fighting but hoping that they will pay attention to Western sensibilities. In the brutal world of international relations, which parts of Africa are finally beginning to resemble, such hope is far-fetched. The United States and the European countries are going to have to deal with African intervenors on African terms or realize that they are irrelevant.

Notes

1. See "Key Elements of the Clinton Administration's Policy on Reforming Multilateral Peace Operations," reprinted in Paul Taylor, Sam Daws, and Ute Adamczick-Gerteis (eds.), *Documents on the Reform of the United Nations* (Aldershot, Eng.: Dartmouth/Hants, 1997), pp. 125, 127.

2. R. P. Mboma, "The Role of Regional Bodies in Preventive Diplomacy and Peacekeeping," in Jakkie Cilliers and Greg Mills (ed.), *Peacekeeping in Africa II*, vol. 2 (Johannesburg: South African Institute of International Affairs, 1996), p. 109.

3. "African Fire Brigade," *West Africa*, February 15, 1964, p. 169.

4. William Nhara, "The OAU and the Potential Role of Regional and Sub-Regional Organisations," in Cilliers and Mills (eds.), *Peacekeeping in Africa II*, vol. 2, p. 100.

5. Training is done by U.S. Special Forces because they are the lead units on all foreign U.S. military training.

6. Ambassador Marshall McCallie and Colonel David E. McCracken, "On the Record Briefing" (July 28, 1997), which can be found at www.state.gov/www/regions/africa/acri_briefing_970728.html. See also Steven Metz, "Testimony," House Subcommittee on Africa, October 1, 1997.

7. McCallie and McCracken, "On the Record Briefing."

8. Henry A. Kissinger, *A World Restored: Metternich, Castlereagh and the Problems of Peace, 1812–1822* (Boston: Houghton Mifflin, 1957), p. 2.

9. These issues are discussed by Robert O. Keohane in *After Hegemony: Co-Operation and Discord in the World Political Economy* (Princeton: Princeton University Press, 1984).

10. The Nigerian army, at 89,000 soldiers, is the same size as the Sudanese army. See Arms Control and Disarmament Agency, *World Military Expenditures and Arms Transfers, 1996* (Washington, D.C.: ACDA, 1996), pp. 58–98.

11. Mboma, "The Role of Regional Bodies in Preventive Diplomacy and Peacekeeping," p. 116.

12. Herbert Howe, "Lessons of Liberia: ECOMOG and Regional Peacekeeping," *International Security* 21 (Winter 1996/1997), p. 145.

13. Joint Warfighting Center, Joint Task Force, *Commander's Handbook for Peace Operations* (Fort Monroe, Va., 1997), p. VI-5.

14. See, for instance, William Reno, *Warlord Politics and African States* (Boulder: Lynne Rienner Publishers, 1998), p. 105.

14

The Crisis in the Great Lakes

RENÉ LEMARCHAND

No other crisis encapsulates more tellingly the perverse effects of the post–Cold War era than the brutal civil war sweeping across the Great Lakes region of Africa (here referring to Rwanda, Burundi, Uganda, and eastern Congo). Nowhere else in the continent are the destabilizing side-effects of global disengagement from East-West issues more evident, the "criminalization"[1] of the state more calamitous for the civil society, and endemic violence more savagely visited on innocent civilians. Nowhere else are the prospects for democracy more distant, and the challenge faced by the international community more daunting.

Besides raising fundamental questions about the rights—and physical survival—of distinct ethnic communities, and their ability to live in peace with each other after suffering untold casualties, the immediate problem is to stop the destruction and bloodshed, and work out the conditions of a negotiated settlement. These issues are made all the more intractable, however, by the sheer number of political actors involved, the diversity of interests at stake, and the fluidity of domestic and international alliances.

At the time of this writing (February 1999) no fewer than eight states are militarily involved, officially or unofficially, in the Congo: Rwanda, Uganda, and Burundi on the side of the rebellion, and Angola, Zimbabwe, Namibia, the Sudan, and Chad on the side of the Kabila government. To this must be added a number of opposition groups from neighboring states: Angola's Union for the Total Independence of Angola (UNITA), Uganda's Alliance of Democratic Forces (ADF), some elements from the all-Hutu, militant wing of Burundi's Conseil National pour la

Défense de la Démocratie (CNDD), and the remnants of the Hutu militias from Rwanda, the so-called *interahamwe*.

Differences in the scale of these states' involvement reflect their respective capabilities as well as the diversity of their motivations. Security concerns are crucial to an understanding of Rwanda's military occupation of large areas of North and South Kivu. Although Rwanda's security problems are shared by Uganda, both derive substantial economic benefits from their free access to the mineral wealth of eastern Congo, much of which is being used to cover the costs of their military involvement. Although strategic considerations are paramount in explaining President Eduardo Dos Santos's decision to back Kabila, his most reliable ally against the external threats posed by UNITA's bases in the Congo, these have little to do with Zimbabwe's involvement. Prospects of economic and financial gains, however illusory, have weighed far more heavily in President Mugabe's choice of allies. Behind UNITA's decision to support the rebellion lie both strategic and economic interests: Only through the export of Angola's diamonds—a large portion of which is now being marketed in Kigali, Kisangani, and Kampala—can UNITA find the foreign exchange needed for the purchase and servicing of its huge military arsenal, as well as for the salaries of foreign mercenaries.

The diversity of interests at stake is one reason for the extreme fragility of the rival coalitions; another is the absence of effective leadership, military and civilian, coupled with the plurality of geopolitical fields in which insurgents and incumbents are facing each other. Though claiming indigenous roots, the "rebellion" is very largely an externally sponsored insurgency, in which Rwanda and Uganda are the key players. It unfolds in geographically distinct arenas and under the leadership of different politico-military factions. Its principal theaters include North and South Kivu, Maniema, North Shaba, and the large swath of territory extending north and west of Kisangani. In these "liberated areas," representing approximately one-third of the Congo, three national armies, each under a separate operational command, are in charge of maintaining "peace and order"—the Rwandan and Ugandan armies, and the dissident FAC forces. To this must be added hundreds of Rwanda-trained ethnic Tutsi from eastern Congo, the so-called Banyamulenge, as well as a sprinkling of Tutsi elements from the Burundi army.

The same impression of fluidity and fragmentation emerges from the local counterinsurgencies generated by the rebellion in North and South Kivu. The most significant in terms of numbers and geographical spread is the Mai-Mai movement, a guerrilla group that attracts the sympathies of a large cross-section of elements indigenous to North and South Kivu, and is frequently operating in alliance with the *interahamwe* militias. The presence of CNDD fighters from Burundi has also been reported in South Kivu, along with loyalist FAC units previously stationed in the Kivu (essentially made up of Katangan elements). The only glue holding this disparate group of counterinsurgents together is their common hatred of "foreign" occupying forces and their Banyamulenge allies.

Against Conventional Wisdom

To make sense of this otherwise confusing situation, we must embrace a number of counterintuitive notions. The first commonplace assumption that needs to be challenged is that the Rwanda genocide was the only genocide recorded in the region's history; another is that the horrors of the Rwanda holocaust are largely reducible to a long-standing atavistic conflict between Hutu and Tutsi; a third is that the Rwanda killings (like other crises elsewhere in the region) are self-contained, inscribed, as it were, in the specificity of their ethnic map and historic past, and thus to be understood in isolation from each other.

On each count the evidence suggests a very different state of affairs. The sheer magnitude of the Rwanda killings has all but eclipsed from public attention at least two other genocides: the 1972 genocide in Burundi, resulting in the massacre of at least 100,000 Hutu (some would say twice as many), and the genocide perpetrated against Hutu refugees in eastern Congo, resulting in the extermination of tens of thousands at the hands of the Rwandan army.[2]

Although the immediate circumstances of such atrocities differ, they can hardly be attributed to long-standing differences between Hutu and Tutsi. Exclusion, rather than a clash of culture or civilization, is the key to an understanding of the crisis in the Great Lakes: The exclusion of Hutu elements from a meaningful share of power in Burundi, the exclusion of Tutsi residents in Rwanda (and the "near abroad") from participation in the social and political life of the country, and the withdrawal of citizenship rights from the Banyarwanda populations of eastern Congo are critical elements behind the hardening of Hutu-Tutsi relations in Rwanda and Burundi and the simmering conflict between Banyarwanda and non-Banyarwanda in eastern Congo.[3]

The regional underpinnings of the crisis are inseparable from the massive refugee flows generated by ethnic strife. Broadly speaking, the typical scenario is one in which exclusion leads to insurrection, insurrection to repression, and repression to the exodus of tens of thousands of refugees across boundaries, which in turn become the vehicles of further violence in their countries of asylum. The effect of refugee diasporas on the polarization of the host societies is again inseparable from the presence in all three countries of indigenous communities (Hutu and Tutsi) with which they could readily identify. To this point we shall return in a moment.

We begin with a general overview of the regional factors underlying the current crisis, followed by a brief sketch of its historical antecedents. Next, we turn to a discussion of the two critical turning points in the chain of events leading to the civil war: the 1996 Rwanda-sponsored Congo insurrection, under the nominal leadership of Laurent Kabila, resulting in the overthrow of the Mobutu regime, and the 1998 rebellion, following Kabila's fateful decision to cut his ties with his Tutsi "sponsors." Finally, we look at the wider dimensions of the crisis, taking into account the balance of forces between the Kabila coalition and the rebellion as well as the divisions and discords within each camp.

The Regional Context

Behind the uniformities—ecological, cultural, and linguistic—that give the Great Lakes region its distinctive character lies the stark reality of its violent history (see Table 14.1). Genocide is deeply etched in the collective memory of its people. But the roots of genocide are inscribed in the wider social context. Underlying the volatility of political forces at work in the region are three irreducible realities that have set the scene for subsequent confrontations.

The first is the lack of coincidence between ethnic and geographical maps. Hutu and Tutsi are found not only in Rwanda and Burundi but also in North and South Kivu, southern Uganda, and western Tanzania. David Newbury estimates that there are roughly 10 million people speaking Kinyarwanda, and 15 million if Kirundi are included in the total.[4] In North Kivu alone, about half the total population of some 3.5 million were identified as Kinyarwanda-speaking in 1993, and of these about 80 percent were Hutu and 20 percent Tutsi. Although many came during and after the colonial era, their presence reaches back to precolonial times—in fact, long before the birth of centralized state systems in Rwanda and Burundi. The heaviest concentration of what used to be called the Banyarwanda (i.e., the people from Rwanda) before 1994 are found in the Rutshuru and Masisi territories of North Kivu. Thousands of Hutu from Burundi have settled in the Ruzizi valley in South Kivu, alongside the border with Burundi. And some fifteen or twenty thousand Tutsi from Rwanda live in the high plateau area south of Uvira, in and around Mulenge (hence the term *Banyamulenge* to describe the Tutsi pastoralists inhabiting the area).[5]

The significance of this regional configuration is best captured by Samuel Huntington's characterization of the "kin country syndrome," a situation in which ethnic fault lines tend to replicate each other across na-

TABLE 14.1 Chronology of Hutu-Tutsi Violence and Refugee Flows in the Great Lakes Region, 1959–1999

Year	Rwanda	Burundi	North and South Kivu	Refugee Flows
1959–1962	Hutu revolution: Exodus of some 300,000 Tutsi			200,000 Tutsi refugees flee to Burundi; 78,000 to Uganda, 36,000 to Tanzania, and 22,000 to North and South Kivu
1963		Abortive raid into Rwanda by Tutsi refugees from Burundi, causing massacre of thousands of Tutsi residents in Rwanda		
1964–1965			Hundreds of Tutsi refugees join Muleliste rebellion	
1972		Genocide of 100,000–200,000 Hutu by Tutsi army		60,000–80,000 Hutu flee to Tanzania and Rwanda
1973	Anti-Tutsi pogroms; hundreds killed in southern Rwanda			
1988		Hutu uprisings in northern Burundi; 10,000–20,000 Hutu killed by Tutsi army		30,000 Hutu flee to Rwanda
1990	FPR invasion of Rwanda			
1991	Massacre of hundreds of Bagogwe/Tutsi by Hutu			
1993			Anti-Banyarwanda uprising resulting in massacre of 10,000 Hutu and Tutsi	
1993		First Hutu president assassinated, causing an estimated 30,000 Tutsi killed by Hutu; as many Hutu are killed by the army		300,000 Hutu flee to Rwanda

1994	Genocide of Tutsi and moderate Hutu, resulting in death of 1 million people, mainly Tutsi		1 million Hutu flee to North and South Kivu; another 1 million, to Tanzania, Burundi, and Uganda
1996/July		Thousands of Tutsi residents of North Kivu killed by Hutu militias (*interahamwe*)	
1996/October	An estimated 400,000 refugees return to Rwanda	Rwandan army (RPA) attacks refugee camps in North and South Kivu	At least 600,000 Hutu refugees flee into the interior of the Congo, while some 400,000 return to Rwanda
1997		Ethnic cleansing of refugees by Rwandan army; some sources estimate 200,000 were killed, others claim no more than 30,000	
1998/August	Outbreak of Rwanda-instigated anti-Kabila rebellion	Massacre of thousands of ethnic Tutsi in Kinshasa and Kisangani; hundreds of pro-Kabila troops massacred in Goma	Thousands of refugees from North and South Kivu flee to Tanzania

NOTE: Although the figures in this table are based on the best evidence available, their reliability is open to question. They convey little more than an order of magnitude. One of the most controversial issues concerns the number of Hutu refugees who came back to Rwanda after the destruction of their camps in North and South Kivu (Congo) in November 1996, and, among those who stayed behind, how many were killed by the Rwandan army. Interviews with NGO workers present in Rwanda at the time indicate that approximately 400,000 to a half-million at the most returned to Rwanda, rather than 700,000 as claimed by the Kigali authorities (and the U.S. Embassy). No exact count of the returnees was taken. Human Rights Watch, Médecins sans Frontières, and UNHCR suggest that as many as 200,000 Hutu refugees and *genocidaires* could have been killed by the Rwandan army in the course of search-and-destroy operations in eastern Congo. For a different, though somewhat tendentious, interpretation, see Howard Adelman, *Early Warning and Humanitarian Intervention: Zaire, March–December 1996*; report commissioned by International Alert's Forum on Early Warning and Early Response (March 1999).

tional boundaries, thus creating a deadly potential for ethnic conflict to expand and escalate. "As the conflict becomes more intense," Huntington writes, "each side attempts to rally support from countries and groups sharing its civilization. Support in one form or another, official or unofficial, overt or covert, material, human, diplomatic, financial, symbolic or military, is always forthcoming from one or more kin countries or groups."[6] In the mobilization of ethnic fault lines across boundaries lies one of the keys to an understanding of the dynamics of violence in the Great Lakes.

Demographic data reveal another fundamental reality—the sheer density of population and resulting pressures on land throughout the region. Rwanda is at the top of the list of all African states in terms of population density, with Burundi and North Kivu close behind. A country of an estimated 1 million people at the turn of the century, Rwanda claimed 7.6 million on the eve of the genocide, with an average of 336 inhabitants per square kilometer (according to 1979 statistics) and, in some areas, almost twice this number.[7] Burundi reveals a similar pattern, with an average of 220 per square kilometer. The figures for North Kivu indicate much the same densities in the high-lying areas of the Congo–Nile Crest. It is not a matter of coincidence if the most densely populated areas—Masisi and Rutshuru—are also the sites of the most intractable land disputes. Speaking of Masisi, one observer notes that "competition for access to, and control over, increasingly scarce land resources originates in these demographic facts; and so do ethnic politics."[8] Historically, the frequency and severity of famine conditions bear testimony to the persistence of land scarcity as a key source of hunger and poverty: In Rwanda alone, no fewer than eleven famines were recorded from 1895 to 1945,[9] the latest occurring in 1990, four years before the genocide.

There is more, however, to chronic starvation than the mutually reinforcing constraints of demographic forces and climatic disturbances. Colonial policies also played a role. The profoundly negative impact of colonial policies is nowhere more evident than in North Kivu: By 1935 the Comité National du Kivu (CNK), a chartered company set up in 1928, proclaimed some 200,000 hectares to be "vacant land" and proceeded to turn them into protected parklands and plantations. Meanwhile, yielding to the pressures of the colonat, the CNK played a key role in "facilitating" the influx of tens of thousands of immigrants from Rwanda, ostensibly to provide European planters with a cheap labor force.[10] What was seen at the time as a solution to Rwanda's overpopulation became part of the problem in Kivu. And what one administrator described as "an act of humanity and a duty that will allow the development (mise en valeur) of certain uninhabited regions of the Kivu"[11] would soon open a Pandora's box of grave economic and social problems, not the least of which stemmed from the large-scale appropriation of cultivable land by migrant families.

The presence of sizable refugee populations in all four countries of the region is the third major contextual element in the background of the current crisis. In eastern Congo the adverse effects of colonial policies on indigenous land rights were greatly magnified after independence (1960) by chronic outflows of refugees from Rwanda. The first, consisting primarily of Tutsi elements, occurred in the early 1960s, during the "social revolution" (1959–1962) that led to the overthrow of the Rwanda monarchy and the capture of power by politicians claiming to represent the will of the Hutu majority. The last and by far the most consequential was the 1994 exodus of an estimated 1 million Hutu to Goma and Bukavu fleeing the advance of Paul Kagame's Rwanda Patriotic Front (RPF) in the wake of the genocide. As much as the social, economic, and environmental dislocations caused by the scale and frequency of refugee movements, what needs to be stressed is the profoundly divisive impact of their presence on the host communities.

Reduced to its simplest expression, the dynamics of violence in the Great Lakes involves the transformation of refugee-generating violence into violence-generating refugee flows.[12] The pattern repeats itself again and again in one state after another, culminating with the invasion of Rwanda by Paul Kagame's Tutsi "refugee warriors" on October 1, 1990. Long before that, Tutsi refugees from Rwanda became a major vehicle of ethnic conflict in Burundi (and to a lesser but significant extent in Uganda and eastern Congo); the same phenomenon came about, in reverse fashion, when tens of thousands of Hutu refugees poured into Rwanda after the 1972 genocide of Hutu in Burundi; and again in eastern Congo in 1994, following the massive influx of Hutu refugees into North and South Kivu. The refugee problem is thus inextricably bound up with the dynamics of ethnic conflict throughout the region.

A detailed account of the circumstances that have led to massive refugee flows from one state to another and back again is beyond the scope of this discussion. The best we can do here is to consider a brief historical overview of the major events that have accompanied the region's bloodstained descent into hell.

Historical Threads

Rwanda is where it all began. Although the Rwanda revolution carried few premonitions of the regional tragedy to come, it emerged in retrospect as the defining moment when an anti-Tutsi, anti-monarchical upheaval sowed the seeds of wider confrontations. Between 1962, when Rwanda became an independent republic under Hutu rule, and the 1994 genocide, the entire region became the site of a chronic Hutu-Tutsi struggle, accompanied by massive bloodshed.

Every single event of importance recorded during those thirty-two years is in one way or another traceable to the Rwanda revolution[13]—the fall of two monarchies (Rwanda in 1962, Burundi in 1966); the assassination of two leading Hutu personalities in Burundi (Prime Minister Pierre Ngendadumwe in 1965, and President Melchior Ndadaye in 1993); the military takeovers (the 1973 coup in Rwanda and the 1965, 1976, 1987, and 1996 coups in Burundi); the 1972 Hutu insurrection in Burundi, leading to the genocide of Hutu in the same year; the rural uprising in North Kivu in 1993; the 1990 invasion of Rwanda by the RPF, and the 1994 genocide of Tutsi and Hutu; and the transformation of North and South Kivu into a privileged sanctuary for cross-border raids into Rwanda and Burundi.

The most obvious of such threads is that which links the exodus of some 78,000 Tutsi refugees to Uganda between 1960 and 1963 and the 1990 invasion of Rwanda by the offspring of the very same refugee diaspora, under the banner of the RPF. Although there is no direct, unbroken chain of causality between the two, any more than between the 1990 invasion and the 1994 genocide, in each case the causal connection, however distant, is nonetheless undeniable.

Far less evident is the impact of the Rwanda revolution on the 1972 Burundi genocide, and of this genocide on the capture of power by President Juvenal Habyalimana in Rwanda. The key to both events lies in the critical role played by refugee movements as vectors of contagion.

Although Burundi's ethnic map bears obvious similarities to that of Rwanda, relations between Hutu and Tutsi were not nearly as conflict-ridden as in Rwanda.[14] The principal lines of cleavage at the time of independence (1962) were not between Hutu and Tutsi but between rival princely factions identified with distinctive dynastic lineages (Bezi versus Batare). The hardening of ethnic lines was the direct outcome of the presence in the country of tens of thousands of Tutsi refugees from Rwanda. Although few of their kinsmen in Burundi could remain insensitive to their plight, many were the Hutu who looked to republican Rwanda as the model polity for Burundi—particularly so after being robbed of their electoral victory in the 1965 elections. By then the die was cast. Following an abortive Hutu-sponsored coup in 1965, a number of leading Hutu personalities were arrested and shot, and the army was purged of most of its Hutu officers and troops. The crunch came in 1972, following a Hutu-instigated uprising in the south, causing untold casualties among the Tutsi population. The ensuing repression took the form of a genocide of just about every educated Hutu, including schoolchildren and university students. Between 100,000 and 200,000 perished at the hand of the all-Tutsi army, while tens of thousands fled to Rwanda and Tanzania.[15]

In Rwanda the backlash was felt almost instantly. The epicenters of anti-Tutsi violence were the secondary schools (notably Shyogwe and Nyanza) and the National University of Rwanda, where hundreds of Tutsi were massacred under the proddings of *comités de vérification d'identité* and *comités de salut public* headed by local politicians.[16] Things rapidly got out of hand. As President Gregoire Kayibanda, a southerner, pleaded for moderation in an effort to stop the killings, his move was quickly countered by a group of army officers and politicians from the north. With the proclamation of the Second Republic by Major General Juvenal Habyalimana on July 5, 1973, power passed into the hands of northerners. From then on Rwanda was ruled by civilian and military elites whose outlook and dispositions were conspicuously hostile to any meaningful sharing of power with representatives of the Tutsi minority.

Long before Habyalimana's capture of power, the impact of the Rwanda revolution in eastern Congo was dramatically brought to light during the "Mulelist" insurgency in 1964–1965, when hundreds of Tutsi refugees joined hands with the rebels.[17] Their alliance with the Mulelistes—whose leading light in South Kivu was Laurent Kabila—was purely instrumental. Their immediate objective was to use the Kivu as a base for recapturing power in Rwanda, not unlike the Hutu militias some thirty years later. Although the raids launched into Rwanda by Tutsi commandos—the so-called *inyenzi*, or "cockroaches"[18]—ultimately failed, the costs in terms of revenge killings of Tutsi civilians inside Rwanda were little short of horrendous, prompting some observers to describe them as genocide. Again, the parallel with the massacre of civilians triggered by cross-border raids by *interahamwe* in the months following the RPF invasion is striking. So, too, is the parallel between the many tiffs and misunderstandings that developed between the *inyenzi* and their Mulelist comrades, on the one hand, and the similarly conflictual relationships between Laurent Kabila's ADFL and its Rwandan patrons, on the other. Ironically, the leading role assumed by Kabila during the 1964 insurgency must have weighed heavily in Kagame's decision to use him as the spearhead of the anti-Mobutist crusade in 1996, and yet his reliability as an ally proved just as questionable in 1996 as it had been in 1964, for reasons excellently described by Che Guevara in his posthumous account of his involvement in eastern Congo rebellion.[19]

The effects of the Rwanda revolution on Kivu society were felt long after the collapse of Mulelistes. The influx of tens of thousands of Tutsi refugees profoundly altered the social fabric of the province, while planting the seeds of the highly contentious nationality question. Unlike the earlier generations of Banyarwanda who settled in the Kivu under CNK auspices, the refugees who fled the flames of the revolution were no ordinary migrants. Most were highly educated and relatively wealthy, and quickly developed ties of solidarity with ethnic Tutsi in the Congo as well as among other refugee diasporas in the region. They made the most of their resources to place some of their kinsmen in strategic positions in the Congo's national and provincial power structures, and in time emerged as an influential business community in Kinshasa as well as in Goma (North Kivu) and Bukavu (South Kivu). Their principal spokesman in Kinshasa was Bisengimana Rwewa, a Tutsi refugee who served as Mobutu's chief of staff until 1977. Like many of his kinsmen Bisengimana became one of the largest landowners in the Kivu. Through all kinds of shady deals with customary authorities of Nande and Hunde origins, hundreds of thousands of acres were sold to Tutsi refugees and converted into ranches and plantations, resulting in the eviction of hundreds of peasant families from their traditional landholdings.

In this situation of growing land shortages and social tension lie the roots of the violent eruption that swept across Masisi in 1993, causing an estimated 10,000 deaths and the displacement of some 250,000 people.[20] Significantly, much of this violence was directed against all Banyarwanda, irrespective of their ethnic identities. Even though many Hutu and Tutsi claimed precolonial roots in the region, both groups were viewed by the non-Banyarwanda as foreign interlopers, working hand in hand with corrupt tax collectors and chiefly authorities, and globally responsible for exploiting the indigenous inhabitants of the province.

As the foregoing suggests, there was more at stake here than a growing scarcity of land resources. The land problem and the nationality question were two sides of the same coin. Although the land issue was clearly paramount in the minds of the rural masses, for the urban politicians who claimed indigenous roots in the Kivu the real threat came from the insistence of the Banyarwanda to be recognized as bona fide citizens of the Congo. Citizenship rights meant the right to participate in the political life of the province—and to buy land.

For all the hostility surrounding their claims, until 1981 the Banyarwanda could legitimately point to a 1972 law, pushed through parliament at the request of Bisengimana, that recognized the citizenship rights of all Banyarwanda and Barundi residing in the Congo as of January 1, 1950. In 1981, with Bisengimana no longer in a position to make a difference, the 1972 law was repealed and replaced by far more restrictive legislation. According to the nationality law of June 29, 1981, citizenship rights could be granted only to "those persons who could show that one of their ancestors was a member of a tribe, or part of a tribe, established in the Congo prior to October 18, 1908," when the Congo formally ceased to be a "Free State" and became a Belgian colony.[21] Behind the palpable ineptitude of this stipulation lies a clear intention to collectively deprive all Banyarwanda of their citizenship rights.

Pushing back the date of residence for citizenship to 1908 meant that not only the Tutsi "fifty niners" (i.e., the refugees from the 1959 revolution in Rwanda) but also the descendants of the tens of thousands of Hutu migrants brought into the Kivu to work on European plantations were now to be treated as foreigners. Nothing could have done more to bring Hutu and Tutsi together in their shared frustrations and insecurities in the face of this utterly absurd and profoundly unjust situation.

The seismic shocks of the Rwanda genocide from April to June 1994 and the subsequent flight of over 1 million Hutu refugees across the border quickly dissolved their fragile partnership as a disenfranchised Banyarwanda community. Almost overnight, identities crystallized around Hutu and Tutsi labels. Caught in the cross fire of Hutu-Tutsi hatreds, local militias of Nande warriors—the Mai-Mai—initially turned against ethnic Hutu in Masisi, only to switch sides when Tutsi communities offered an easier target. The refugee camps, meanwhile, were transformed into recruiting grounds for the training of *interahamwe* militias. The presence of humanitarian NGOs did little either to prevent the recruitment of these militias or to stop the flow of arms into the camps.

In the spring and summer of 1996, the Rwanda cancer rapidly metastasized through North and South Kivu. The predominantly Hutu region of Masisi (North Kivu) is where the killings began, when, in May of that year, an estimated 800 Tutsi who had taken refuge in the Mokoto trappist monastery were slaughtered by gangs of *interahamwe* and local Hutu. The Mokoto tragedy was only a prelude to even more appalling massacres of Tutsi. The killers, meanwhile, received the full backing of local authorities, including the governor of South Kivu, Kyembo wa Lumona, whose violent anti-Tutsi diatribes did not go unheeded ("What do you do when you run into a snake on the road? You kill him!"). That Kagame would not sit idle in the face of this alarming situation was made clear during his trip to Washington in August: If the international community was not prepared to act to prevent further bloodshed and threats to Rwanda's security, he would.

As armed raids into Rwanda became more frequent and the impotence of the international community more painfully evident, the new rulers of Rwanda did what no one else had the will or capacity to accomplish. In October 1996 units of the Rwanda Patriotic Army (RPA), assisted by Banyamulenge elements, launched a series of deadly raids against each of the dozen or so refugee camps strung along the borders with Rwanda and Burundi, killing thousands and sending an estimated 400,000 running for their lives while approximately the same number chose to return to their homeland.[22] In bringing Armageddon to the shores of Lake Kivu, Vice-President Paul Kagame nurtured an insurgency that would eventually turn against him and unleash forces that he never suspected would reach such intensity.

The 1996 Watershed:
The Rise (and Demise?) of Laurent Kabila

The nemesis visited upon the refugee camps touched off tectonic shifts that would radically alter the political landscape of the region. By far the most significant stemmed from the dialectic that so closely linked insurrection to retribution: With the emergence of Laurent Kabila as the head of the Alliance of Democratic Forces for the Liberation of the Congo (ADFL), the stakes were raised far beyond the immediate objective of making the Kivu safe for Rwanda. The aim was to wrestle the Mobutist monster to the ground and make the whole of the Congo safe for Rwanda.

While public attention was largely focused on the resurfacing of Kabila under the protective wing of his Rwandan patron, and on the collapse of the Mobutist state seven months later, at least three other sideshows were going on, involving search-and-destroy operations against armed opponents from Uganda, Burundi, and Rwanda.

The Ugandan thrust was directed at the presence in northeastern Congo of armed elements of the Alliance of Democratic Forces (ADF), whose hit-and-run raids into Uganda had become a major source of insecurity in the Kasese area. The ADF bases were thoroughly cleansed in the course of joint military operations between the Ugandan army and Kabila's men.[23]

The Burundi operation was targeted against Leonard Nyangoma's CNDD militias and their armed affiliates, the Forces pour la Défense de la Démocratie (FDD), many of whom were operating from the refugee camps between Bukavu and Uvira in South Kivu. In a matter of days the camps were reduced to ashes by RPF-trained Banyamulenge and ADFL troops, sending approximately 50,000 Hutu back to Burundi, where many were summarily executed by the Burundi army. The attackers then marched north toward Goma, to join hands with FPR units before moving against the Rwanda refugee camps.

The Rwanda "sideshow" is better described as a human tragedy of appalling proportions.[24] Close to a million refugees lived in these camps. That some served as rear bases for *interahamwe* militias and ex–Forces Armées Rwandaises (FAR) troops is undeniable. Equally obvious is the fact that not all refugees were *interahamwe*, nor were all involved in the killings in Rwanda. In the strategic thinking of the Rwandan authorities, however, the distinction seemed irrelevant. It took the attackers only twenty-four hours to destroy the largest camp (Mugunga), providing shelter for some 200,000. A week or so later, the job was completed. While hundreds of thousands trekked back to Rwanda, the destruction of the camps triggered a huge exodus of refugee populations across thousands of miles into the interior of the country, only partially diminished by the wanton killings of thousands of them by Rwandan troops. Predictably, the horrors that have accompanied the "neutralization" of the refugee camps deepened the abyss between Hutu and Tutsi, making the search for a modus vivendi all the more problematic.

Just as a solution of sorts—though by no means final—had been found to the refugee problem, the Tutsi of eastern Congo developed their own solution to their identity problem. The Tutsi frame of reference simply evaporated from their vocabulary, giving way to an altogether different ethnic configuration. Thus a new tribe came into being, the Banyamulenge.

The use of *Banyamulenge* as an omnibus term to designate all Tutsi elements residing in the Congo is more than just an interesting case of ethnogenesis; it signals the emergence of the ethnic Tutsi—numbering possibly half a million—as a politico-military force that had to be reckoned with, and makes plain their determination to claim "authentic" roots as Congolese citizens. Nonetheless, the label could hardly conceal the ambiguity of their status.[25] Although the term serves as an identity marker designed to settle once and for all the nationality question, there can be little doubt about their divided loyalties. Many (especially among the younger generations) look to Rwanda for guidance and protection. Just as they provided the RPF with crucial military support when the time came to "deal" with the refugees, in return they expect Rwanda to remain their strongest ally in their struggle to make good their claims to citizenship, even if it means a head-on confrontation with Kinshasa. This mutuality of interests is what Kabila failed to understand.

Orchestrated by Kagame, assisted by troops from Rwanda, Uganda, and Angola, applauded by almost every state in the continent, the ADFL campaign against Mobutu was harnessed to a common will—to overthrow Mobutu's dictatorship and prepare the ground for democracy. Mobilizing support against Mobutu was relatively easy; how to cement disparate political forces after Mobutu's overthrow proved immensely more difficult. The swiftness of Kabila's military campaign outpaced his capacity to put in place a viable administration. Furthermore, as opposition and civil society forces rushed into the vacuum left by Mobutu's demise, Kabila detected new threats on the horizon. Rather than give in to the demands of opposition parties, he turned against them. His "state of grace" proved short-lived.

There are few examples of the popular legitimacy of a self-styled revolutionary leader soaring and collapsing in such a brief interval. Kabila's ineptitude in handling the demands of the civil society and the domestic opposition for democratic reforms must be seen as one of the main reasons behind his plummeting popularity in the months following his rise to power. Another stemmed from his overwhelming dependence on Banyamulenge and Rwandan elements.

That Kabila would not stand as the long-awaited apostle of democracy was made clear in his inaugural speech as president of the Congo's Third Republic on May 29, 1997: The National Conference—which for many Congolese embodies the basic principles from which a transition to democracy must proceed—was ruled out as the basis for a new constitutional order. It belonged to a Mobutist past that had to be jettisoned lock, stock, and barrel into the dustbin of history. So, too, were the political parties, particularly Etienne Tshisekedi's Union for Democracy and Social Progress (UDSP). Although Tshisekedi stood as the fiercest opponent of the Mobutist dictatorship, his treatment at the hands of Kabila was even worse than the one he endured under Mobutu. The civil society fared no better. Appropriately described by Peter Rosenblum as being in essence "a liberal, pluralist movement linked through churches, non-governmental organizations, and donors to the United States and Western Europe," it could not be seen by Kabila otherwise than with utter suspicion.[26] If any doubts remained about Kabila's dispositions, these were quickly dispelled by the arrest and incarceration of dozens of civil society leaders and journalists in the months following his inauguration.

Nor could this "Mobutisme sans Mobutu" syndrome leave the international community indifferent, least of all the United States. Secretary of State Madeleine Albright's visit to Kinshasa in December 1997 turned out to be a near-disaster as Kabila took advantage of a press conference to reiterate his intention to come down hard on the opposition, ending his tirade with a mocking smile and a cynical "Vive la démocratie!"[27] The $10 million assistance package earmarked by the United States was then dismissed as amounting to little more than "pocket change." Two months later it was the turn of President Clinton's special envoy, Jesse Jackson, to gain a firsthand appreciation of Kabila's ways. After meeting with Tshisekedi, Jackson was sternly taken to task for violating diplomatic protocol, and Tshisekedi rusticated to his home province (Kasai Oriental).

Although other donors remained wary of providing financial assistance, the United Nations, meanwhile, became involved in a long and inconclusive struggle with Kabila's government over the fate of the tens of thousands of refugees allegedly killed by ADFL and Rwandan troops in the course of their exodus. In early 1997 the public outcry over the refugee question resulted in the appointment of a UN investigatory commission headed by Special Rapporteur Roberto Garreton. Though authorized by Kabila to carry their mandate, the UN investigators had no sooner set foot in Kinshasa than they ran into endless problems. After Kabila insisted that Garreton be replaced, another team was sent to Kinshasa, but with no greater success. Following one complication after another—including arrests, harassment, and local protests clearly engineered to block the work of the forensic experts—in March 1998, a year after it had been appointed, the commission left Kinshasa, empty-handed.[28]

Kabila's stonewalling could not have made clearer his utter dependence on Kigali. What evidence there is about the circumstances surrounding the massacre of refugees suggests that the RPA was far more heavily involved than the ADFL: In blocking the work of the UN commission, Kabila was evidently taking his marching orders from Kigali.

If further proof were needed of Kabila's subservience to Rwanda, one could point to the growing influence of certain key Banyamulenge personalities in his entourage, most notably Bizima Karaha, minister of foreign affairs; Deogratias Bugera, minister for presidential affairs and former secretary-general of the ADFL; and Moise Nyarugabo, his personal secretary. Nor could one fail to notice the commanding presence in Kinshasa of Tutsi-looking, Swahili- or Kinyarwanda-speaking elements. This was even more true of Goma and Bukavu, where scores of Rwandan and Banyamulenge troops could be seen patrolling the streets, clutching their AK-47s. As anti-Tutsi sentiment became more widespread, Kabila increasingly came to be seen as a stooge of Kagame. As 1997 drew to a close the choice he faced was a difficult one: either to hang on to his Rwandan protectors, at the cost of suffering a further loss of legitimacy, or to free himself of their embrace and face the consequences. By mid-1998 Kabila had made his choice—and the consequences proved fatal to his regime.

The 1998 Rebellion: A Replay of 1996?

Signs of an impending crisis between Kinshasa, on the one hand, and Kigali and Kampala, on the other, could be detected as early as May 17, 1998, when Kagame and Museveni declined Kabila's invitation to attend a regional summit on the occasion of the first anniversary of the Third Republic. The sacking a few weeks later of Army Chief of Staff James Kabare, a Rwandan Tutsi with years of service in Kagame's RPA, did little to ease the tension. The crunch came on July 27 with Kabila's announcement that all foreign troops would be expelled from the Congo. The next day, six planeloads of Tutsi and Banyamulenge troops flew out of Kinshasa. Sensing the danger, Bizima Karaha, Deogratias Bugera, and Moise Nyarugabo hastily packed their bags and left the country. By yielding to the mounting anti-Tutsi sentiment, the Congo's new king turned the king-makers into his bitterest enemies.

The sense of outrage felt by Kagame struck a responsive chord among several Congolese opposition figures whose distaste for Kabila exceeded their grievances against the Rwandans. The crisis offered them a unique opportunity to use Rwanda's support to turn the tables on Kinshasa. Like Kabila in 1996, they knew that the road to Kinshasa passes through Kigali; and like Kabila they quickly realized the need for a homegrown, authentically Congolese vehicle to lend credibility to their plans. Thus came into existence, on August 16, the Congolese Rally for Democracy (CRD).

By then a full-scale rebellion was under way in eastern Congo. On August 6, Goma, Bukavu, and Uvira were in rebel hands. After killing scores of Katangan troops suspected of loyalty to Kabila in Goma, the rebels had little difficulty in persuading other units to join their movement. The prize catch was General Jean-Pierre Ondekane's Tenth Battalion, the FAC's biggest and best-trained military unit. At this juncture, with an unerring instinct for the jugular, Kagame airlifted some six hundred Banyamulenge and Rwandan soldiers from Goma to Kitona, a major military airbase about 200 kilometers west of Kinshasa, where they linked up with the local FAC garrison. The key towns of Moanda and Matadi were seized almost immediately. By August 17 the huge hydroelectric dam at Inga, the main source of electric power for Kinshasa, was under rebel control. With the flick of a switch Kinshasa was plunged into darkness and its water supply cut off. Then, precisely when Kinshasa seemed about to cave in, Angola saved the day. On August 22, an estimated 3,500–4,000 Angolan troops surged from the Cabinda enclave and with tanks and heavy artillery attacked Kagame's men from the rear. With the backing of Luanda's 66th Mechanized Regiment the Angolans quickly recaptured Moanda, Kitona, Matadi, and Inga, thus decisively redrawing the battle lines. Fleeing the Angolan attacks from the west, on August 26 the rebels made a last-ditch effort to seize Kinshasa, only to concede defeat.

Despite its setback in the west, the rebellion quickly picked up momentum in the east. After the capture of Kisangani on August 23, rebel troops struck out north and west, and with the strong backing of the Ugandan army took one town after another: Bunia, Buta, Bumba, Isoro, and Aketi. With the fall of Kindu, the strategic capital of the Maniema, on October 12, the rebellion scored a major victory. Besides giving the rebels and their allies free access to the mineral resources of the region, the path was now cleared for a further advance south toward Kasongo, Kabalo, Kabinda, and the diamond-rich Kasai province.

On the surface, the 1998 rebellion had all the earmarks of a replay of the 1996 anti-Mobutist insurrection. In both instances, the initiative came from Kigali, with the enthusiastic support of Kampala; the points of ignition, logically enough, were Goma and Bukavu, with the Banyamulenge acting as the spearhead of the movement; and the two sets of insurgents had little in common besides their shared aversion to the Kinshasa regime.

But the differences were no less significant. Except for the Kivu region, where violence has remained fairly constant, the 1996 anti-Mobutist insurrection did not result in major bloodshed among Congolese. The same cannot be said of the 1998 rebellion, in which the cost in human lives was without precedent. Both sides were responsible for unspeakable atrocities against civilian populations—as shown by the massacre of hundreds Tutsi residents of Kinshasa and Lubumbashi (in the name of what some government-controlled media referred to as the Hamitic threat to the Bantu people) and by the innumerable revenge killings perpetrated by Banyamulenge and Rwandan troops against the communities of North and South Kivu. Two of the worst massacres occurred in Kasika (South Kivu) in August 1998, when more than a thousand people were killed at the hands of Rwandan troops, and in Makobola (South Kivu) in January 1999, when an estimated five hundred people lost their lives in similar circumstances.[29] This is how a representative of one local NGO described the slaughter in Masika:

> On August 23 and 24, after suffering serious losses around the Lutambi escarpment, Kinyarwanda-speaking elements unleashed the full force of their anger against the peaceful civilian and ecclesiastical communities. They killed and raped. They destroyed and burned houses, seized the crops and cattle from Kasika to Kilungutwe, over a distance of ten kilometers. The number of dead is 1,094.[30]

Other examples could be cited from almost every other "liberated area." The scars left by such atrocities will not easily be forgotten, or forgiven.

Partly as a consequence of internal disagreements over the behavior of Rwandan troops, intense rivalries have surfaced among presumptive leaders and factions, between them and their external sponsors, and between the sponsors themselves (Rwanda and Uganda).

In May 1999 the CRD split into two warring factions, the Rwanda-backed CRD-Goma, headed by Emile Ilunga, a Luba of Katangan origins, and the Uganda-backed CRD-Kisangani, headed by Ernest Wamba dia Wamba, an exile academic of Bakongo origins. Although personal rivalries played a role, the critical factor behind the crisis lies in the long simmering tensions behind the so-called "reformateurs", committed to enlarging the representativeness of the CRD's directing organs, and the old-guard Mobutists. The former include, besides Wamba dia Wamba, Jacques Depelchin, a crypto-Marxist academic of Belgian-Fulero origins, and Arthur Zahidi Ngoma, former president of the opposition party Forces of the Future (FOF); among the ex-Mobutists are found such well-known turncoats as Lunda Bululu, a former law professor who served as cabinet director and prime minister under Mobutu, and Alexis Mwamba Tambwe, who served as managing director of the Customs Office under Mobutu. By then, however, a third anti-Kabila movement had emerged in the Equateur region, the Congo Liberation Movement (CLM), led by Jean-Pierre Mbemba, son of a well-known businessman and former supporter of Mobutu. Enjoying the full backing of Uganda, the CLM appears to have very close relations with the CRD-Kisangani (as shown by Wamba dia Wamba's decision to rename his movement CRD-Liberation Movement).

Follwing an armed confrontation between the two CRD factions over the control of Kisangani, in August 1999, Rwandan and Ugandan troops jumped into the fray, and for four days fought each other tooth and nail on behalf of their respective clients, leaving some 200 soldiers and civilians dead. Although the Rwandan authorities later claimed that this unfortunate turn of events had "in no way affected the cordial relations enjoyed by the two countries," the battle for the control of Kisangani is more than just a case of external patrons being reluctantly drawn into a factional struggle. It reflects a deadly competition between rebel factions and their foreign allies over access to the Congo's mineral wealth. A multiplicity of informal networks, ranging from the commercial to the criminal, flourish in the interstices of the rebellion. Ugandan and Rwandan army men are deeply involved in the war economy. While some peddle influence and protection for material rewards, others (especially Rwandans) engage in looting and theft on a grand scale, making off with vehicles, machine tools, radios, and TV sets. For most Congolese, the war is a colossal catastrophy; for others it is a golden opportunity.

Factional divisions are just as pervasive among the pro-Kabila forces fighting the rebellion on its eastern flank. Although the hard-core FAR/Interahamwe are Kabila's major ally against Rwanda, many have switched sides, offering their services to highest bidder. The Hutu militias from Burundi are equally fragmented. Perhaps the only exception are the Mai-Mai, consisting at first of a losse assemblage of Nande and Hunde warriors from North Kivu, and now claiming considerable support from a broad social spectrum in the urban and rural sectors of the region. The Mai-Mai are making maximum political capital of the bitterly anti-Rwandan feelings of the indigenous populations of North and South Kivu, a sentiment, one might add, which is also shared by a number of Banyamulenge who refuse to be seen as the instrument of Rwandan imperialism.

By far the most significant contrast, however, between 1996 and 1998 is found in the scope of external interventions, their effect on the balance of forces between insurgents and incumbents, and their repercussions outside the Congo. To this dimension we shall turn in a moment. Suffice to note here that, in the short run at least, the consequences of the rebellion were precisely the opposite of what it hoped to achieve. For one thing,

Kabila's image as a "nationalist-leader-victim-of-external-aggression" has been magnified out of all proportion, casting his dictatorial, thuggish style into temporary oblivion. At no other time in his political career did he enjoy greater popularity at home and abroad. Although Kagame deserves full credit for this sudden surge of nationalist sentiment, he also must be seen as partially responsible for its ugliest manifestations—the killing of hundreds of Tutsi in an orgy of xenophobic hatred. Again, until the outbreak of the rebellion Kabila had very few friends in the continent; but after becoming the victim of "external aggression" he ended up with more support from more states than any past or present African leader confronting a domestic insurrection.

International Dimensions

External intervention in the Great Lakes region did not begin in 1998. No other part of the continent has been so thoroughly exposed to the penetration of so many international actors on so many occasions, and with so few positive results. International NGOs, UN agencies, Western powers, informal transnational networks—all have had a piece of the action at one point or another. And all bear some degree of responsibility for either doing too little too late, or too much at the wrong time on behalf of the wrong party.

In the latter category the French deserve pride of place. As has been repeatedly emphasized, France's political and military backing of Habyalimana's government, before, during, and after the genocide, has contributed in no small way to the enhancement of the capabilities of a long-discredited regime and the creation of expectations of continued support for its policies.[31] The performance of the UN Assistance Mission to Rwanda (Minuar), on the other hand, has been criticized for the opposite reasons. Regardless of what accounted for its paralysis during the genocide, there is little question that its failure to act was one of the many factors that encouraged the butchery. It is equally clear that the Clinton administration is open to much the same criticisms for refusing to explicitly acknowledge the genocide while it was going on, and doing nothing to prevent it.[32] Nor are international NGOs free of blame. However commendable on moral grounds, humanitarian assistance is never neutral. This point was driven home immediately after the genocide, when over a million Hutu refugees walked across the border into eastern Zaire: Nothing was done to disarm the *interahamwe* and ex-FAR in the camps, or to prevent them from monopolizing food supplies in order to strengthen their hold on the refugee population.[33] By action and by omission, some would argue, humanitarian NGOs became complicit in the cross-border raids launched against Rwanda by Hutu extremists. It is all too easy, however, to pick on NGOs and ignore the role of other actors. Suffice it to note that it was Mobutu, not the NGOs, who played a major role in facilitating the flow of arms to Hutu extremists in the camps. Today, as in the more recent past, the sheer number of external actors, each with different goals and priorities, makes its resolution all the more complicated.

The current crisis marks a decisive expansion of African involvement and a corresponding decline in the role of Western powers. Not counting Kabila's FAC and the various armed factions fighting on the side of the rebellion, seven armies have jumped into the fray. The Angolan Armed Forces (AAF) were the first to move in to provide the providential backing that prevented the rebels from capturing Kinshasa after the raid on Kitona, but Zimbabwe, Namibia, Chad, and the Sudan promptly sent in reinforcements, with Zimbabwe contributing the largest contingent (8,000 to 10,000 troops).

Whether this foreign armada can turn the tide is very doubtful, however, considering the sheer size of the country, the unfamiliarity of the troops with the terrain, their inability to communicate with local populations, and the lack of effective coordination among various units. Their reluctance to engage the rebels on their turf means that the initiative must come from the FAC. But Kabila's ragtag army, consisting largely of teen-age soldiers (the kadogos) and Katangan "Tigers,"[34] is no match for the 6,000 Rwandan and Ugandan troops equipped with armored cars, BM-21 multiple rocket launchers, and anti-aircraft missiles.

The rebellion, moreover, has drawn significant benefits from cross-border alliances based on ethnic ties. In the Equateur region, for example, Jean-Pierre Bemba was able to capitalize on his Ngbaka origins to attract the support of a substantial number of former mutineers from the Central African Republic (CAR), mostly of Yakoma origins (a group closely re-lated to the Ngbaka). In the Orientale province, elements of the Southern People's Liberation Army, Sudan's principal armed opposition move-ment, fought alongside the rebels in Buta and Isiro. And in South Kivu, a number of Tutsi troops from the Burundi army are reported to have joined the RPA-Banyamulenge coalition in fighting Mai-Mai militias.

Tactical cross-border alliances work both ways, however. Just as Hutu extremists from North Kivu have found potential allies among their kins-men from Rwanda and Burundi, the Nande of Butembo (North Kivu) were able to enlist the support of Bakonjo elements from the Ruwenzori-based National Army of Liberation of Uganda (NALU), with whom they share strong ethnic ties. Mobilized ethnicity thus transforms international boundaries into a sieve, allowing free passage of armed groups from one national arena to another.

The counterpart of the "soldier without borders" phenomenon is the smuggler, for whom borders are a necessary condition of his trade. Which in turn points to another form of external penetration: the extension of contraband networks—ranging from drugs to diamonds, and from gold to guns—from Europe and South Africa to the Great Lakes and beyond. Much of this illicit trade follows a two-way traffic in which gold and diamonds are smuggled out of the Congo to Uganda, Rwanda, and Burundi, with the proceeds used to smuggle weapons back into the country. Rwanda, not exactly known for its diamond production, now has five diamond marketing agencies (*comptoirs*). A large portion of the trade is in the hands of Ugandan army officers, who also act as middlemen for the export of diamonds from the UNITA-controlled mines in Angola. Burundi's gold exports have increased significantly, and so have Uganda's. Museveni's half-brother, General Salim Saleh, has a major stake in the weekly shipment of gold from the Office des Mines d'Or de Kilo-Moto (Okimo) and the Societé Minière et Industrielle du Kivu (Sominki). According to one eyewitness account, "In Kilo-Moto the Ugandans have kicked out all Congolese; every Tuesday and Friday a Ugandan jet lands in Durba and takes the loot to Kampala."[35] Among the several armed groups fighting the rebellion, the *interahamwe* appear to derive important benefits from the narcotics trade. According to a report of the UN commission investigating illegal arms flows, "Rwandan ex-FAR, *interahamwe* and other armed groups (based in Mombasa and Dar es Salaam) are directly involved in the drugs trade . . . and there is credible information that ex-FAR officers continue to conduct recruitment and fund-raising operations in Kenya to purchase arms intended for use against the Rwandan government."[36]

Secret shipments of arms to the region come from many sources, some in South Africa, others from as far as Bulgaria, described by one observer as "the arms bazaar for rebels and terrorist organizations of every political, ethnic and religious persuasion . . . including the Hutu militia who were responsible for mass killings in Rwanda."[37] In a recent piece of investigative journalism Al Venter notes that "weapons are coming into the region from just about everywhere. For instance there were 47 contracts from dozens of countries to supply arms or equipment, expertise and/or training, etc. to the Burundi government or to armed Hutu rebels attached to organizations such as the CNDD, Palipehutu, Frolinat or FDD."[38] South African manufacturers are at the top of the list of arms suppliers to Rwanda, with Armscor, Kunene Brothers Holdings, and Alpha-5 claiming the lion's share of the trade. French and Belgian arms brokers are also involved. A Belgian citizen with the implausible name of Geza Mezozo is reported to have sold 8,000 American M-16 rifles to Kabila, as well as an undisclosed quantity of weapons to "numerous countries, including Burundi, Congo-Brazzaville, Tanzania, Uganda and Nigeria."[39] Whereas the Bulgarian state marketing agency, Kintex, along with the country's largest arms manufacturer, Arsenal, have reported to have sold weapons to Hutu militias, much of Kabila's military hardware comes from Zimbabwe Defense Industries (ZDI). It is a sad commentary on the logic of privatization that the whole of the Great Lakes has become a free-trade area for arms merchants, drug traffickers, gold and diamond smugglers, and plain thugs, transforming the region into a prime example of the "criminalization of the state" syndrome.[40]

The Backlash

In such circumstances it is easy to see why the search for a negotiated solution becomes something of a catch-22 situation. The sheer fragmentation of forces creates its own dynamic, so that, even if a peace accord were to break the deadlock, there is no certainty that it will be heeded by the warring factions on the ground. As the fighting continues, armed groups of various stripes develop a vested interest in keeping the pot boiling. The Liberian scenario casts an ominous shadow on the prospects for peace in the region.

Nonetheless, it is equally clear that the involvement of African states in the conflict has exacted an exorbitant price in their respective domestic arenas, and that the time will come when the burden of intervention exceeds the expected benefits. Their eventual withdrawal from the scene, along with the growing pressures of the international community and the Congolese civil society, will leave Kabila with no other option than to open peace negotiations.

A brief inventory of the domestic difficulties faced by the participants in the conflict would include the following:

1. In Angola the all-out offensive unleashed by UNITA against the AAF has resulted in the recapture of most of the territory lost since 1994, making it imperative for President Dos Santos to recall thousands of troops previously fighting in the Congo. Once seen as the most promising breakthrough in the thirty-year civil war, the 1994 Lusaka protocol has been shot to bits, and with the UN observers now out of the country, the fighting has resumed on an unprecedented scale.

2. In Zimbabwe the political and economic costs of military involvement (estimated at 1 million U.S. dollars a day) have come home to roost, causing violent antiwar protests in the capital city. The powerful Zimbabwean Confederation of Trade Unions (ZCTU) has been among the most vocal critics of President Mugabe's adventurism. Many of its criticisms have been echoed by human rights organizations, including the Catholic Commission for Justice and Peace. Adding to the frustrations felt by Zimbabweans over the costs of the war is their realization that certain key members of the

government and the military stand to reap huge profits from commercial contracts with the Kabila government. Mugabe's popularity is at its lowest ebb since independence.

3. In Congo-Brazzaville, just as the UNITA offensive got under way in Angola, the pro-UNITA Ninja and Zulu militias, respectively identified with former President Pascal Lissouba and the maverick politician Bernard Kolelas, turned against President Denis Sassou Nguesso's Cobra militias, sowing chaos in many parts of the capital city, killing scores of people, and causing a major exodus of city dwellers to rural areas.

4. With Zimbabwe and South Africa at odds on how to handle the conflict, the Southern African Development Community (SADC) has become the major diplomatic casualty of the Congo crisis. Not only is President Mandela openly critical of Mugabe's involvement on Kabila's side, but their disagreement on basic foreign policy issues has further exacerbated personal rivalries between them, making cooperation in other areas, such as trade, tariffs, and banking arrangements, all the more difficult.

What ultimate impact these ominous developments will have on the domestic politics of Kabila's allies is a matter of speculation. Beyond question is the fact that they have already seriously weakened his military capabilities. Furthermore, the war has exacted a horrendous price in both the rebel-held areas and those still under Kinshasa's control. There is growing popular disaffection in the face of the disastrous consequences of Kabila's economic and fiscal policies, most notably his decision to forbid the use of foreign currencies in commercial transactions. In the "liberated areas," chronic insecurity and economic hardships have translated into a quasi-universal hatred of "foreign occupants" and their domestic allies.

Six months after the outbreak of the rebellion the crisis would seem "ripe for resolution," yet the record of a half-dozen abortive peace conferences is hardly cause for optimism. So far, procedural issues—concerning whether to include or leave out delegates from the rebellion and their Rwanda and Ugandan allies—have been the main stumbling block, as Kabila has consistently refused to talk to "the enemies of the nation."

Kabila's obduracy notwithstanding, efforts to work out a peace plan acceptable to all parties have gone apace. Some of the more promising proposals have come from the Congo's civil society, with the Conseil National des Organisations Non-Gouvernementales (CNONG) playing a major role. At the heart of these proposals are four major talking points: (1) agreement on conditions of a cease-fire; (2) withdrawal of all foreign armed forces from the Congo; (3) intervention of a multilateral peace-

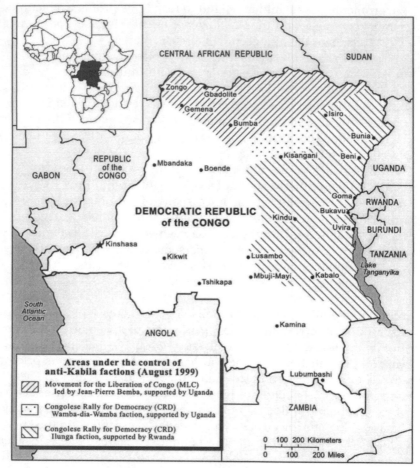

MAP 14.1   Approximate areas under the sway of anti-Kabila factions,
August 1999

keeping force; and (4) a return to the resolutions and institutional reforms of the Sovereign National Conference (1991) as the only basis for
the reconstruction of the state. This agenda was the subject of extensive
discussions during two major conferences organized by Congolese
NGOs in collaboration with Western and Congolese academics in
Antwerp and Montreal in January 1999. Its core proposals were also discussed at the conference organized by Synergies-Africa at Morat
(Switzerland) on November 23–24, 1998, and at the OAU-sponsored conference in Ouagadougou on December 17–18, 1998. But the parties to the
conflict have yet to take them into account as a basis for a negotiated solution.

After weeks of bitter wrangling over which of the two CRD factions should claim to represent the rebellions, agreement on a cease-fire was finally reached in Lusaka (Zambia) on July 10, 1999. The belligerents have agreed to an immediate cessation of hostilities, and to a time table for the withdrawal of foreign troops and the disarmament of militias. Key provisions include the setting up of a Joint Military Commission (JMC) consisting of two representatives from each of the belligerent parties, the deployment of a UN peace-keeping force under chapter 7 of the UN Charter, and the organization of a Congolese National Dialogue intended to pave the way for a new constitution. The JMC's principle responsibilities are to investigate cease-fire violations, develop mechanisms to disarm the militias and monitor the withdrawal of foreign troops.

Although there is no denying the significance of this long-awaited diplomatic breakthrough, the obstacles to the peace process launched by the Lusaka accords are painfully evident. Quite aside from the continuing frictions between the rival CRD factions, the prospects for the disarmament of the militias are highly problematic. Given the nature of the terrain, their wide dispersion throughout eastern Congo, and continuing access to gun-runners it is highly unrealistic to expect the ex-FAR, *interahamwe*, ADF, and Mai-Mai to disarm within 120 days after the signature of the accords. For the Mai-Mai and other guerrilla movements, their exclusion from the Lusaka peace process means that they have no other choice but to keep fighting. Nor is it clear that the UN chapter 7 force will be put in place any time soon, and then have the military, logistical, and financial capabilities to get the job done. If so, the continued presence of armed militias in eastern Congo will be seen by Rwanda as an excellent pretext for maintaining its troops on the ground.

Just as violations of the case-fire are to be expected, it would be little short of miraculous if the "national dialogue" were to take place on schedule, or indeed if something resembling a consensus were to emerge among Congolese parties on how to restore peace and chart a new path towards democracy. Nonetheless, given the alternative, the international community has no other option but to believe in miracles, and make every effort to make them happen. Despite their shortcomings, the Lusaka accords deserve the strongest support on the part of all concerned, for this is Africa's best chance to bring its "first world war" to an end.

Notes

For his searching comments on an earlier version of this chapter, I wish to record my indebtedness to Ambassador Richard W. Bogosian, Special Assistant to the State Department on the Greater Horn of Africa Initiative (GHAI). He is fully exonerated of whatever errors of facts and interpretation I may have committed. The fluidity of the situation in the Great Lakes makes it impossible for any account of the state of the play to remain valid for very long; it will be readily apparent to the reader that this chapter has remained virtually untouched since its completion in February 1999.

1. For a discussion of this concept, see Jean-François Bayart, Stephen Ellis, and Beatrice Hibou, *The Criminalization of the State in Africa* (Oxford: James Currey/Bloomington: Indiana University Press, 1998), pp. 79ff.

2. See R. Lemarchand, "Genocide in the Great Lakes: Which Genocide? Whose Genocide?" *African Studies Review* 41, no. 1 (April 1998), pp. 3–16.

3. For a fuller discussion of exclusion as a source of conflict, see R. Lemarchand, "Patterns of State Collapse and Reconstruction in Central Africa: Reflections on the Crisis in the Great Lakes Region," *Afrika Spectrum* 32, no. 2 (1997), pp. 173–193.

4. David Newbury, "The Invention of Rwanda: The Alchemy of Ethnicity," unpublished manuscript, p. 14. Newbury identifies four groups of "Rwandan speakers" outside the boundaries of present-day Rwanda: (a) the so-called Bachiga (or Bakiga) of southern Uganda, (b) the Banyabwisha located north and south of Lake Rweru (Edward) in the zone of Rutshuru (Congo), (c) the Kinyarwanda speakers who live north and west of Lake Kivu, alongside the border with Rwanda, and (d) the communities that came into being as a result of "the frequent movement across Lake Kivu by people on both sides of the lake," many of whom "retained their Rwandan culture and used this to set themselves apart from earlier inhabitants in the area" (pp. 16–17).

5. The presence of this group in the Mulenge area of South Kivu is traceable to precolonial intra-Tutsi struggles in Rwanda. In this context the term refers to the historic Banyamulenge; it has received a far more inclusive connotation since 1996, referring to all Tutsi elements living in eastern Congo, regardless of the date of their arrival. See Jean-Claude Willame, *Banyarwanda et Banyamulenge* (Paris: L'Harmattan, 1997).

6. Samuel Huntington, *The Clash of Civilization and the Remaking of World Order* (New York: Simon and Schuster, 1995), p. 272.

7. These figures are taken from David Newbury's excellent analysis of the impact of ecology on the Rwanda genocide, "Ecology and the Politics of Genocide: Rwanda 1994," *Cultural Survival Quarterly* 22, no. 4 (Winter 1999), pp. 32–35. See also Christian Thibon, "Croissance et perceptions démographiques: Une politique démographique intégrée; quelques interrogations préalables," *Revue Tiers Monde* 28, no. 106 (April-June 1986), pp. 297–308.

8. Bucyalimwe Mararo, "Land, Power and Ethnic Conflict in Masisi (Congo-Kinshasa), 1940–1994," *International Journal of African Historical Studies* (forthcoming).

9. James Fairhead, "Food Security in North and South Kivu," report to Oxfam (mimeo, 1989), passim.

10. See Catherine Newbury, *The Cohesion of Oppression: Clientship and Ethnicity in Rwanda (1860–1960)* (New York: Columbia University Press, 1988), pp. 159–179.

11. R. Spitaels, "Transplantation de Banyarwanda dans le Nord du Kivu," *Problèmes d'Afrique Centrale* 2 (1953), p. 100.

12. This is the central theme in Myron Weiner's outstanding comparative analysis of refugee movements worldwide: "Bad Neighbors, Bad Neighborhoods: An Enquiry into the Source of Refugee Flows," *International Security* 21, no. 1 (1996), pp. 5–42. In a different vein, see Liisa H. Malkki, "Refugees and Exile: From 'Refugee Studies' to the National Order of Things," *Annual Review of Anthro-*

pology 24 (1995), pp. 495–523; and, by the same author, *Purity and Exile: Violence, Memory and National Cosmogony Among Hutu Refugees in Tanzania* (Chicago: University of Chicago Press, 1995).

13. For a background discussion, see R. Lemarchand, *Rwanda and Burundi* (London: Pall Mall Press, 1970); and Newbury, *The Cohesion of Oppression*.

14. See R. Lemarchand, *Burundi: Ethnic Conflict and Genocide* (Cambridge, Eng.: Cambridge University Press/New York: Woodrow Wilson Center Press, 1995).

15. For a fuller discussion of the 1972 genocide, see ibid., ch. 5.

16. Ironically, one of the most rabidly anti-Tutsi among these local Hutu politicians is none other than Pasteur Bizimungu, currently Rwanda's president. The information in this paragraph is drawn from a lengthy interview in Nairobi in December 1997 with the late Seth Sedashonga, who served as minister of interior under Kagame, until forced to resign in 1995. There is every reason to believe that his assassination in Nairobi, in May 1998, was planned by Kagame's security services.

17. See R. Lemarchand, *Rwanda and Burundi*, pp. 211ff, and, on the role of the leading Tutsi "guerillero," Joseph Mudandi, p. 388; see also the fascinating details drawn from Che Guevara's diary in William Galvez, *Le Rêve Africain du Che* (Bruxelles: Editions EPO, 1998), pp. 146ff.

18. For an interesting comparison of the *inyenzi* with their recent reincarnation as Kagame's warriors, the *inkontanyi*, named after one of Rwanda's precolonial armies, see Filip Reyntjens, "Les mouvements armés des réfugiés rwandais: Rupture ou continuité?" *Mélanges Pierre Salmon, Civilisations* 15, no. 2 (1992), pp. 170–182.

19. "I always thought," wrote Che, "that he did not have enough military experience; he was an agitator, who had the stuff of a leader yet lacked seriousness, aplomb, knowledge, in short this innate talent that one senses in Fidel the minute you met him" (quoted in Galvez, *Le Rêve Africain du Che*, pp. 97–98); elsewhere Che calls him a "womanizer and a party goer." Further references to Kabila during the 1964 rebellion can be found in Benoit Verhaegen (ed.), *Rébellions au Congo*, Vol. I (Bruxelles: CRISP, 1966). What promises to be the definitive biography of Kabila is currently being written by Erik Kennes at the Institut de Politique et de Gestion du Développement (RUCA), which is affiliated with the University of Antwerp.

20. See F. Reyntjens and S. Marysse (eds.), *Conflits au Kivu: Antécédents et Enjeux* (Antwerp: Centre for the Study of the Great Lakes Region of Africa, 1996).

21. For a summary of the legislation affecting nationality rights of the Banyarwanda, see Reyntjens and Marysse, *Conflits au Kivu*, pp. 20ff; see also R. Lemarchand, "Ethnic Violence, Public Policies and Social Capital in North Kivu: Putnam Revisited," paper presented at the workshop on "Creation and Breakdown of Social Capital in Sub-Saharan Africa," University of Antwerp, December 4–5, 1998.

22. The official figure cited by the Rwandan government, and uncritically endorsed by the U.S. Embassy in Kigali, is 700,000 returnees. No one has kept count of the returning refugees, however; the consensus of several NGO workers on the ground is that not more than 400,000 or 500,000 refugees walked back to Rwanda.

23. See Gérard Prunier, "The Great Lakes Crisis," *Current History* 96, no. 610 (May 1997), pp. 193–199.

24. See ibid.; and Erik Kennes, "La Guerre au Congo," in *Afrique des Grands Lacs, Annuaire 1997–1998* (Antwerp: Centre d'Etude de la Région de Grands Lacs/Paris: L'Harmattan, 1999), pp. 231–272.

25. There is something of the "outpost people" mentality about the Banyamulenge, a mentality that Neal Ascherson describes as involving "two delusive mental syndromes"—one being a "skewed and paranoid awareness of the external world" (in this case, of the wider Congo society) and the other "dominance." Ascherson goes on to say that "[t]he outposter must constantly remind himself of who he is by displaying his power over the others." See Neil Ascherson, *Black Sea* (New York: Hill and Wang, 1995), p. 101. (Of course, it would be highly misleading to treat all Banyamulenge as fitting into the same mold.) Today there is a growing tendency among certain Banyamulenge leaders to keep their distance vis-à-vis their Rwandan allies, fearing that they will eventually bear the brunt of the strong anti-Rwandan sentiment of the local Congolese populations.

26. Peter Rosenblum, "Kabila's Congo," *Current History* (1997, no. 619), p. 195.

27. Ibid., p. 199.

28. See UN Security Council, *Report of the Secretary-General's Investigative Team Charged with Investigating Serious Violations of Human Rights and International Humanitarian Law in the Democratic Republic of the Congo*, S/1998/581, June 29, 1998.

29. On the Makobola massacre, see Karl Vick, "Brutal Clash in Congo Left Behind Few Clues," *International Herald Tribune*, January 14, 1999, p. 2.

30. Quoted in Héritiers de la Justice, *Situation des Droits de l'Homme en RDC, Cas du Sud Kivu* (Bukavu, October 16, 1998), p. 6.

31. This fact is openly acknowledged in the report of the commission of investigation appointed by the French National assembly. See *Mission d'Information sur le Rwanda: Enquête sur la Tragédie Rwandaise (1990–1994)*, Tome I, vols. 1 and 2, as well as the individual testimonies in Tome III (Paris: Assemble Nationale, 1998).

32. See Holly Burkhalter, "A Preventable Horror?" *Africa Report* (November-December 1994), pp. 17–21.

33. For a critical commentary on the role of NGOs in Africa, see Alex de Waal, "Democratizing Aid in Africa," *International Affairs* 73, no. 4 (October 1997), pp. 623–637.

34. The "Tigers" is the name given to the descendants of the Katangan gendarmes trained by Moise Tshombe during the Katanga secession in 1960; most fled to Angola after the collapse of the secession. Some 2,000 Tigers fought with the ADFL during the 1996 rebellion and were subsequently incorporated into the FAC.

35. Quoted in *Réseau Congolais d'Information* (RECINFO), Bruxelles, February 1999.

36. "Great Lakes Rebel Activities Financed by Drugs Trade," *IRIN Reports*, November 19, 1998. See also IRIN@ochoa.unon.org.

37. Quoted in Raymond Bonner, "Bulgaria Becomes a Weapons Bazaar," *New York Times*, August 3, 1998, p. 3.

38. Al Venter, "Arms Pour into Africa," *New African* (January 1999), p. 11.

39. Ibid.

40. See Bayart, Ellis, and Hibou, *The Criminalization of the State in Africa*; and Patrick Chabal and Jean-Pascal Dalloz, *Africa Works: Disorder as Political Instrument* (Oxford: James Currey/Bloomington: Indiana University Press, 1999), pp. 79ff.

15

Reconciling Sovereignty with Responsibility: A Basis for International Humanitarian Action

FRANCIS M. DENG

The end of the Cold War was greeted with relief throughout the world. It was assumed that the era of global tension and insecurity was over and that humanity had ushered in a new world order that would guarantee peace, security, and respect for the universal principles of human rights and democratic freedoms. The reverse has of course been the case. With the disappearance of the bipolar alliance system and control mechanisms of the Cold War, a process of violent disintegration became the plight of many states, especially under formerly oppressive regimes. And indeed, as the situations in the former Yugoslavia, the former Soviet Union, and chronic crises and new explosions on the African continent testify, since the end of the Cold War, conflicts around the world have resulted in unprecedented humanitarian tragedies and, in some cases, have led to partial and even total collapse of states.

This development has brought pressures for global humanitarian action, sometimes involving forced intervention, as well as an urgent quest for peacemaking and peacekeeping around the world. The response of the international community to this mounting toll of post–Cold War tragedies, emanating mostly from internal conflicts, has inevitably begun to erode traditional concepts of sovereignty in order to ensure international access to the affected masses within state borders. This access, in turn, has generated a reaction from vulnerable states, designed to reassert the traditional principles of sovereignty and territorial integrity. The resulting tug-of-war is acquiring a cross-cultural dimension that is confronting the international community with severe dilemmas, for both positions represent legitimate concerns.

Much has been said and written about the processes of economic, political, and cultural globalization that the post–Cold War world is supposedly undergoing. There is, however, a process of fragmentation and localization that is concurrently under way, but which has not received commensurate attention. In Africa and indeed in many parts of the world, the state is undergoing a formidable national identity crisis in which sovereignty is being contested. This crisis is rooted primarily in the problems of racial, ethnic, cultural, and religious diversities, rendered conflictual by gross disparities in the shaping and sharing of power, national resources, and opportunities for social, cultural, and economic development.

Indeed, the fate of the state in the post–Cold War international system is essentially dualistic in nature. During the Cold War, there was a tendency to relate all the problems around the world to the ideological confrontation of the superpowers. But in the post–Cold War era, problems are now being better understood in their proper national and regional context, where internal conflicts, violations of human rights, denial of democracy, and mismanagement of the economy are the pressing problem areas. In confronting these problems, the state is being pulled in opposite directions by the demands of various local groups and the pressures of globalization of the market economy and universalizing political and cultural trends. The assignment of responsibility for addressing these challenges must also recognize the fundamental shift that has taken place in the post–Cold War era. Dependency is being replaced by national responsibility and accountability. This new scenario implies recasting sovereignty as a concept of responsibility for the security and general welfare of the citizens, with accountability at the regional and international levels.

The guiding principle for reconciling these positions is to assume that under normal circumstances, governments are concerned about the welfare of their people, will provide them with adequate protection and assistance, and, if unable to do so, will invite or welcome foreign assistance and international cooperation to supplement their own efforts. The conflict arises only in those exceptional instances when the state has collapsed or the government is unwilling to invite or permit international involvement, though the level of human suffering dictates otherwise. This is often the case in civil conflicts characterized by racial, ethnic, or religious crises of national identity in which the conflicting parties perceive the affected population as part of "the enemy." It is essentially the need to fill the vacuum of moral responsibility created by such cleavages that makes international intervention such a moral imperative.

The paradox of the compelling circumstances that necessitate such intervention is that the crisis has gone beyond prevention and has become an emergency situation in which masses of people have fallen victim to the humanitarian tragedy. Since it is more costly now to provide the needed humanitarian relief than it would have been at an earlier stage, the obvious policy implication is that the international community must develop normative and operational principles for a doctrine of preventive intervention. Such an approach would require addressing the root causes of conflict, formulating normative guidelines, establishing the mechanisms for an appropriate institutional response, and developing strategies for timely intervention.

The Magnitude of the Crisis

The events in the former Yugoslavia, the latest dramatization of which is the horrific situation in Kosovo, and in several hot spots in the former Soviet Union, demonstrate that the crisis is truly global. As former UN Secretary-General Boutros Boutros-Ghali observed in his *Agenda for Peace:* "Poverty, disease, famine, oppression and despair abound, joining to produce 17 million refugees, 20 million displaced persons and massive migrations of peoples within and beyond national borders. These are both sources and consequences of conflict that require the ceaseless attention and the highest priority in the efforts of the United Nations."[1]

Although the global dimension of the crisis needs to be stressed, it is fair to say that some regions are more affected than others. Africa is perhaps the most devastated by internal conflicts and their catastrophic consequences. Of an estimated 20 to 25 million internally displaced persons worldwide, over 10 million are African, as are 6 million of the 17 million refugees throughout the world. It was in Africa—specifically, Rwanda—that the world witnessed a genocide comparable to the horrors of Nazi Germany. In the Sudanese conflict, nearly 2 million people are estimated to have died since the resumption of the civil war in 1983; about a quarter perished as a result of war-induced famine and related humanitarian tragedies. In Liberia and Sierra Leone, untold atrocities have been perpetrated by all sides to the conflicts. And of course the collapse of Somalia stands out as an example of the threat looming over a number of fragile and vulnerable states on the continent.

African leaders, diplomats, scholars, and intellectuals have recognized the plight of their countries and their people and are demonstrating a responsiveness commensurate to the challenge, recently culminating in a series of interrelated initiatives. Among them are the Africa Leadership Forum's Conference on Security, Stability, Development and Cooperation in Africa (CSSDCA), embodied in the Kampala Document before the OAU since 1991; the International Peace Academy (IPA) Consultations on Africa's Internal Conflicts, first launched at Arusha in March 1992; and the OAU Mechanism for Conflict Prevention, Management and Resolution, proposed by Secretary-General Boutros-Ghali in 1992 and adopted by the Summit in Cairo in June 1993. In introducing his proposals to the Council of Ministers in Dakar, Senegal, in 1992, the secretary-general said:

> Conflicts have cast a dark shadow over the prospects for a united, secure and prosperous Africa which we seek to create. . . . Conflicts have caused immense suffering to our people and, in the worst case, death. Men, women and children have been uprooted, dispossessed, deprived of their means of livelihood and thrown into exile as refugees as a result of conflicts. This dehumanization of a large segment of our population is unacceptable and cannot be allowed to continue. Conflicts have engendered hate and division among our people and undermined the prospects of the long-term stability and unity of our countries and Africa as a whole. Since much energy, time and resources have been devoted to meeting the exigencies of conflicts, our countries have been unable to harness the energies of our people and target them to development.[2]

In the consultation organized by the OAU and the IPA in Addis Ababa (May 18–21, 1993), the president of the International Peace Academy, Olara Otunnu, spotlighted the magnitude of the crisis when he said: "There is a 'curse' stalking the African continent. Entire societies are being decimated by internecine wars. Indeed, some states have simply collapsed in the wake of these conflicts, and more countries could potentially be exposed to the same fate. What can be done to stem this tide of self-destruction? This is one of the most important and urgent challenges facing Africa."[3]

The regional focus is important, not only for appreciating the context of conflict but also for devising an appropriate response at that level before pursuing further measures at the international level. To respond at either level, however, Africa must address the issue of sovereignty.

The Issue of Sovereignty

Protecting and assisting the masses of the people affected by internecine internal conflicts entail reconciling the possibility of international intervention with traditional concepts of national sovereignty. With the post–Cold War reapportionment of responsibility for addressing these problems, primary responsibility is now placed on the states concerned, with a graduated sharing of responsibility and accountability at the subregional and regional levels and, residually, throughout the international community, both multilaterally and bilaterally. In this emerging policy framework, national sovereignty acquires a new meaning. Instead of being perceived as a means of insulating the state against external scrutiny or involvement, it is increasingly being postulated as a normative concept of responsibility. National sovereignty thus now requires a system of governance that is based on democratic popular citizen participation, constructive management of diversities, respect for fundamental rights, and equitable distribution of national wealth and opportunities for development. For a government or a state to claim sovereignty, it must establish legitimacy by meeting minimal standards of good governance or responsibility for the security and general welfare of its citizens and all those under its jurisdiction. Fulfillment of these standards, in turn, requires the formulation of a normative framework stipulating standards for the responsibilities of sovereignty and a system of accountability at the various interactive levels, from national to subregional and regional to international. The consensus now is that the problems are primarily internal and that, however external their sources or continued linkages, the responsibility for solutions, especially in the post–Cold War era, falls first on the Africans themselves. The time has long since come to stop blaming colonialism for Africa's persistent problems.

The irony, however, is that the principal modern agent of Africa's political and economic development and the interlocutor in the international arena is the state, itself a creature of foreign intervention. Although Africans have, for the most part, accepted the state with its colonially defined borders, African states lack the indigenous roots for internal legitimacy. Even worse, citizen participation is for the most part minimal; indeed, the state is often not representative or responsive to the demands and expectations of its domestic constituencies. It is important in this context to distinguish between recognizing the unity and territorial integrity of the state and questioning its policy framework, which might be attributable to a regime or might be structural in nature. A structural problem would require a fundamental restructuring of the state to meet both the internal standards of good governance and the international requirements of responsible sovereignty.

Failure on the one level usually implies failure on the other. When a state fails to meet the standards prescribed for membership in the international community, thereby exposing itself to external scrutiny and possible sanctions, it is likely to assert sovereignty and cultural relativism in an attempt to barricade itself against alleged foreign interference. Sovereignty has evolved enough not only to prescribe democratic representation but also to justify outside intervention. As one scholar of international law has observed:

In the process, the two notions have merged. Increasingly, governments recognize that their legitimacy depends on meeting a normative expectation of
the community of states. This recognition has led to the emergence of a community expectation: that those who seek the validation of their empowerment patently govern with the consent of the governed. Democracy, thus, is
on the way to becoming a global entitlement, one that increasingly will be
promoted and protected by collective international processes.[4]

Another has argued that

[t]here is a clear trend away from the idea of unconditional sovereignty and
toward a concept of responsible sovereignty. Governmental legitimacy that
validates the exercise of sovereignty involves adherence to minimum humanitarian norms and a capacity to act effectively to protect citizens from
acute threats to their security and well-being that derive from adverse conditions within a country.[5]

During the extensive consultations conducted in connection with the UN
study on internally displaced persons, representatives of several governments commented that national sovereignty carries with it responsibilities
that, if not met, put a government at risk of forfeiting its legitimacy. One
spokesperson for a major power even said, "To put it bluntly," if governments do not live up to those responsibilities (among which he specified
the protection of minority rights), "the international community should intervene by force."[6] Similar views have been expressed by representatives of
African countries who were voicing a global humanitarian concern.

Such pronouncements have almost become truisms that are rapidly
making narrow concepts of legality obsolete. When the international
community does decide to act—as it did when Iraq invaded Kuwait,
when Somalia descended into chaos and starvation, and (albeit less decisively) when the former Yugoslavia disintegrated, especially in Kosovo—
controversy over issues of legality will become futile or of limited value
as a brake to guard against precipitous change.

One observer summarized the new sense of urgency regarding the
need for an international response, the ambivalence of the pressures for
the needed change, and the pull of traditional legal doctrines as follows:

In the post–Cold War world . . . a new standard of intolerance for human
misery and human atrocities has taken hold. Something quite significant has
occurred to raise the consciousness of nations to the plight of peoples within
sovereign borders. There is a new commitment—expressed in both moral
and legal terms—to alleviate the suffering of oppressed or devastated people. To argue today that norms of sovereignty, non-use of force, and the sanctity of internal affairs are paramount to the collective human rights of people, whose lives and well-being are at risk, is to avoid the hard questions of
international law and to ignore the march of history.[7]

The conclusions of a 1992 international conference on human rights protection for internally displaced persons—attended by human rights specialists, experts from humanitarian organizations, international lawyers, UN and regional organization officials, and government representatives—underscored the extent of the changes in perspectives on the confrontation between the universal standards of human rights and the parochialism of traditional ideas of sovereignty. The report on the conference states that the "steady erosion" of the concept of absolute sovereignty is making it easier for international organizations, governments, and nongovernmental organizations to intervene when governments refuse to meet the needs of their populations and when substantial numbers of people are at risk. The concept of sovereignty, it continues, is becoming understood more in terms of conferring responsibilities on governments to assist and protect persons residing in their territories—so much so that if governments fail to meet the obligations, they risk undermining their legitimacy.[8] The scrutiny of world public opinion as represented by the media makes it difficult for governments to ignore these obligations or defend their failure to act.

The report further notes that "participants considered it essential for the international community to continue to 'chip away' and 'pierce' narrow definitions of sovereignty so that sovereignty would not be a barrier to humanitarian intervention."[9] But to intervene is not an easy choice. In 1991 former UN Secretary-General Javier Perez de Cuellar highlighted this dilemma when he said: "We are clearly witnessing what is probably an irresistible shift in public attitudes towards the belief that the defense of the oppressed in the name of morality should prevail over frontiers and legal documents." But he also asked, "Does [intervention] not call into question one of the cardinal principles of international law, one diametrically opposed to it, namely, the obligation of non-interference in the internal affairs of states?"[10] In his 1991 annual report, he wrote of the new balance that must be struck between sovereignty and the protection of human rights:

> It is now increasingly felt that the principle of non-interference with the essential domestic jurisdiction of States cannot be regarded as a protective barrier behind which human rights could be massively or systematically violated with impunity. . . . The case for not impinging on the sovereignty, territorial integrity and political independence of States is by itself indubitably strong. But it would only be weakened if it were to carry the implication that sovereignty, even in this day and age, includes the right of mass slaughter or of launching systematic campaigns of decimation or forced exodus of civilian populations in the name of controlling civil strife or insurrection. With the heightened international interest in universalizing a regime of human rights, there is a marked and most welcome shift in public attitudes.

To try to resist it would be politically as unwise as it is morally indefensible. It should be perceived as not so much a new departure as a more focused awareness of one of the requirements of peace.[11]

Preferring to avoid confronting the issue of sovereignty, de Cuellar called for a "higher degree of cooperation and a combination of common sense and compassion," arguing that "we need not impale ourselves on the horns of a dilemma between respect for sovereignty and the protection of human rights. . . . What is involved is not the right of intervention but the collective obligation of States to bring relief and redress in human rights emergencies."[12]

In *An Agenda for Peace*, de Cuellar's successor, Boutros Boutros-Ghali, wrote that respect for sovereignty and integrity is "crucial to any common international progress"; but he went on to say that "the time of absolute and exclusive sovereignty . . . has passed," that "its theory was never matched by reality," and that it is necessary for leaders of states "to find a balance between the needs of good internal governance and the requirements of an ever more interdependent world."[13] As one commentator noted, "The clear meaning was that governments could best avoid intervention by meeting their obligations not only to other states, but also to their own citizens. If they failed, they might invite intervention."[14]

But although negative interpretations of sovereignty prevail as "a prerogative to resist claims and encroachments coming from outside national boundaries—the right to say no," the question can be, and has been, posed as to whether erasing the doctrine of sovereignty from the minds of political leaders would reduce those forms of human suffering associated with extreme governmental failure. "Would such an erasure strengthen sentiments of human solidarity on which an ethos of corrective responsibility and individual accountability depends?"[15] The withdrawal of the international community from Somalia once the humanitarian intervention proved costly in American lives, the astonishing disengagement from Rwanda in the face of genocide in 1994, and the indifference to the atrocities and gross human rights violations in Liberia, Sierra Leone, and Sudan, to mention just a few examples—as contrasted to the dramatic, high-tech intervention on behalf of the Kurds in Iraq and the Albanians in Kosovo—prompt a resounding "no" answer to the question. Selectivity in the manner and scale of response is the fundamental reality.

Although sovereignty as such is no longer a barrier to intervention on human rights and humanitarian grounds, the determining factor is the political will of other states based on national interest, combined with a compelling level of humanitarian concern. However, assertions of sovereignty can also be invoked by powers lacking the will to become involved. Since intervention is often costly in terms of lives and materiel, it is convenient to avoid it unless imperative national interest dictates otherwise. Sovereignty then elicits benign conformity to the principle of noninterference or provides a convenient excuse for inaction. If the constraints of sovereignty against justifiable intervention are to be circumvented, and, more important, if governments and other controlling authorities such as insurgent movements are to be inspired or at least motivated to discharge their obligations, it is necessary to prescribe "normative sovereignty," or "sovereignty as responsibility."[16]

The ambivalence about intervention by the international community arises not only from reluctance to become involved but also from motives for external intervention, which are by no means always altruistic. Self-interest therefore dictates an appropriate and timely action in terms of self-protection. This was the point made by the secretary-general of the Organization of African Unity, Salim Ahmed Salim, in his bold proposals for an OAU mechanism for conflict prevention and resolution. "If the OAU, first through the Secretary-General and then the Bureau of the Summit, is to play the lead role in any African conflict," he said, "it should be enabled to intervene swiftly, otherwise it cannot be ensured that whoever (apart from African regional organizations) acts will do so in accordance with African interests."[17] Criticizing the tendency to respond only to worst-case scenarios, Salim also emphasized the need for preemptive intervention: "The basis for 'intervention' may be clearer when there is a total breakdown of law and order . . . and where, with the attendant human suffering, a spill-over effect is experienced within the neighbouring countries. . . . However, pre-emptive involvement should also be permitted even in situations where tensions evolve to such a pitch that it becomes apparent that a conflict is in the making."[18]

The secretary-general went so far as to suggest that the OAU should take the lead in transcending the traditional view of sovereignty, building on the African values of kinship, solidarity, and the notion that "every African is his brother's keeper."[19] Considering that "our borders are at best artificial," Salim argued, "we in Africa need to use our own cultural and social relationships to interpret the principle of non-interference in such a way that we are enabled to apply it to our advantage in conflict prevention and resolution."[20]

In traditional Africa, third-party intervention for mediation and conciliation is always expected, regardless of the will of the parties directly involved in a conflict. Even in domestic disputes, relatives and elders intercede without being invited. Indeed, "saving face," which is critical to conflict resolution in Africa, requires that such intervention be unsolicited. But of course African concepts and practices under the modern conditions of the nation-state must still balance consideration for state sovereignty against the compelling humanitarian need to protect and assist the dispossessed.

The normative frameworks proposed by the OAU secretary-general and the UN secretary-general's *Agenda for Peace* are predicated on respect for the sovereignty and integrity of the state as crucial to the existing international system. However, the logic of the transcendent importance of human rights as a legitimate area of concern for the international community—especially where order has broken down or where the state is incapable or unwilling to act responsibly to protect the masses of citizens—would tend to make international inaction quite indefensible. Even in less extreme cases of acute internal conflicts, the perspectives of the pivotal actors on such issues as the national or public interest are bound to be sharply divided both internally and in terms of their relationship to the outside world. After all, internal conflicts often entail a contest of the national arena of power and, hence, sovereignty. Every political intervention from outside has its internal recipients, hosts, and beneficiaries. Under those circumstances, there can hardly be said to be indivisible national sovereignty behind which the nation stands united.

Furthermore, it is not always easy to determine the degree to which a government of a country devastated by civil war is truly in control when, as often happens, sizable portions of the territory are controlled by rebel or opposing forces. Frequently, though a government may remain in effective control of the capital and the main garrisons, much of the countryside in the war zone will have practically collapsed. How would a partial but significant collapse such as this be factored into the determination of the degree to which civil order in the country has broken down? A government cannot present a clear face to the outside world when it keeps others from stepping in to offer protection and assistance in the name of sovereignty after allowing hundreds of thousands (and maybe millions) to starve to death when food can be made available to them; to be exposed to deadly elements when they could be provided with shelter; to be indiscriminately tortured, brutalized, and murdered by opposing forces, contesting the very sovereignty that is supposed to ensure their security; or to otherwise allow them to suffer in a vacuum of moral leadership and responsibility. Under such circumstances, the international community is called upon to step in and fill the vacuum created by such neglect. If the lack of protection and assistance is the result of the country's incapacity, the government would, in all likelihood, invite or welcome such international intervention. But where the neglect is a willful part of a policy emanating from internal conflict, preventive and corrective interventions become necessary.

It is most significant that the Security Council, in its continued examination of the secretary-general's *Agenda for Peace*, welcomed the observations contained in the report concerning the question of humanitarian assistance and its relationship to peacemaking, peacekeeping, and peacebuilding.[21] In particular, the council established that, under certain circumstances, "there may be a close relationship between acute needs for humanitarian assistance and threats to international peace and security";[22] indeed, it "[noted] with concern the incidents of humanitarian crises, including mass displacements of population becoming or aggravating threats to international peace and security."[23] The council further expressed the belief "that humanitarian assistance should help establish the basis for enhanced stability through rehabilitation and development" and "noted the importance of adequate planning in the provision of humanitarian assistance in order to improve prospects for rapid improvement of the humanitarian situation."[24]

Absolute sovereignty is clearly no longer defensible; it never was. The critical question now is under what circumstances the international community is justified in overriding sovereignty to protect the dispossessed population within state borders. The common assumption in international law is that such action is justified when there is a threat to international peace. The position now supported by the Security Council is that massive violations of human rights and displacement within a country's borders may constitute such a threat.[25] Others contend that a direct threat to international peace as the basis for intervention under Chapter Seven of the UN Charter has become more a legal fiction than the principle justifying international action, nearly always under conditions of extreme humanitarian tragedies.

To avoid costly emergency relief operations, the international community must develop a response to conflict situations before they deteriorate into humanitarian tragedies. Such a response calls for placing an emphasis on peacemaking through preventive diplomacy, which in turn would require an understanding of the sources of conflicts and a willingness to address them at their roots.

Addressing the Causes of Conflict

In most countries torn apart by war, the sources and causes of conflict are generally recognized as inherent in the traumatic experience of state-formation and nation-building, complicated by colonial intervention and repressive postcolonial policies. The starting point, as far as Africa is concerned, is the colonial nation-state, which brought together diverse groups that were paradoxically kept separate and unintegrated. Regional ethnic groups were broken up and affiliated with others within the artificial borders of the new state, and colonial masters imposed a superstructure of law and order to maintain relative peace and tranquillity.

The independence movement was a collective struggle for self-determination that reinforced the notion of unity within the artificial framework of the newly established nation-state. Initially, independence came as a collective gain that did not delineate who was to get what from the legacy of the centralized power and wealth. But because colonial institutions had divested the local communities and ethnic groups of much of their indigenous autonomy and sustainable livelihood, replacing them with a degree of centralized authority and dependency on the welfare state system, the struggle for control became unavoidable once control of these institutions passed on to the nationals at independence. The outcome was often conflict—over power, wealth, and development—that led to gross violations of human rights, denial of civil liberties, disruption of economic and social life, and the consequential frustration of efforts for development.

As the Cold War raged, however, these conflicts were seen not as domestic struggles for power and resources but as extensions of the superpower ideological confrontation. Rather than help resolve them peacefully, the superpowers often worsened the conflict by providing military and economic assistance to their own allies.

Although the end of the Cold War has removed this aggravating external factor, it has also removed the moderating role of the superpowers, both as third parties and as mutually neutralizing allies. The results have been unmitigated brutalities and devastations. It can credibly be argued that the gist of these internal conflicts is that the ethnic pieces that were put together by the colonial glue, reinforced by the old world order, are now pulling apart and that ethnic groups are reasserting their autonomy or independence. Old identities, undermined and rendered dormant by the structures and values of the nation-state system, are reemerging and redefining the standards of participation, distribution, and legitimacy. In fact, it may be even more accurate to say that the process has been going on in a variety of ways and within the context of the constraints imposed by the nation-state system.

The larger the gap in the participation and distribution patterns based on racial, ethnic, or religious identity, the more likely the breakdown of civil order and the conversion of political confrontation into violent conflict. When the conflict turns violent, the issues at stake become transformed into a fundamental contest for state power. The objectives may vary in degree from a demand for autonomy to a major restructuring of the national framework, either to be captured by the demand-making group or to be more equitably reshaped. When the conflict escalates into a contest for the "soul" of the nation, it turns into an intractable zero-sum confrontation. The critical issue then is whether the underlying sense of injustice, real or perceived, can be remedied in a timely manner, avoiding the zero-sum level of violence. As the report of the Arusha Consultation put it, "The general conviction was that, despite their apparent diverse causes, complex nature and manifold forms, internal conflicts in Africa were basically the result of denial of basic democratic rights and freedoms, broadly conceived; and that they tended to be triggered-off by acts of injustice, real or imagined, precisely in situations where recourse to democratic redress seemed hopeless."[26]

The report summarized the challenge of conflicts as symbolizing a quest for justice:

> The most comprehensive set of "preventive measures" in this regard was thought to be the development and maintenance of a democratic state in which, among other things, civil society was vibrant, there was effective justice and the rule of law, there was equitable access to political power and economic resources by all citizens and groups, the various regions of the country were treated fairly and equitably in all matters of public concern, and there was sufficient economic growth and development to ensure reasonably decent livelihood or at least realistic hope for social progress.[27]

Viewing the crisis from the global perspective, it is also pertinent to recall the words of UN Secretary-General Boutros-Ghali, who observed in *An Agenda for Peace:* "One requirement for solutions to these problems lies in commitment to human rights with a special sensitivity to those of minorities, whether ethnic, religious, social or linguistic."[28] On the need to strike a balance between the unity of larger entities and respect for the sovereignty, autonomy, and diversity of various identities, the secretary-general further noted:

> The healthy globalization of contemporary life requires in the first instance solid identities and fundamental freedoms. The sovereignty, territorial integrity and independence of states within the established international system, and the principle of self-determination for peoples, both of great value and importance, must not be permitted to work against each other in the period ahead. Respect for democratic principles at all levels of social existence is crucial: in communities, within states and within the community of states. Our constant duty should be to maintain the integrity of each while finding a balanced design for all.[29]

Where discrimination or disparity is based on race, ethnicity, region, or religion, it is easy to see how it can be combated by appropriate constitutional provisions and laws protecting basic human rights and fundamental freedoms. But where discrimination or disparity arises from conflicting perspectives on national identity, especially one based on religion, the cleavages become more difficult to bridge. In some instances, religion, ethnicity, and culture become so intertwined that they are not easy to disentangle. Such is the case in the Sudan, where Islam has gained momentum and is aspiring to offer regionwide and, indeed, global ideological leadership. Islam in the Sudan has been closely associated with Arabism, which also gives the movement a composite ethnic, cultural, and religious identity, even though the Islamists themselves espouse the nonracial ideals of the faith. The composite identity of Islam and Arabism poses the threat of subordination to non-Muslims, who also perceive themselves as non-Arabs. It is consequently resisted, especially in the South.

What makes the role of religion particularly formidable is that there are legitimate arguments on both sides of the religiously based conflict. On the one hand, the Islamists, representing the Arabized Muslim majority, want to fashion the nation on the basis of their faith, which they believe does not allow the separation of religion for the state. The non-Muslims, on the other hand, reject this, seeing it as a means of inevitably relegating them to a lower status as citizens; they insist on secularism as a more mutual basis for a pluralistic process of nation-building. The dilemma is whether an Islamic framework should be used to encompass a religiously mixed society, imposing a minority status on the non-Muslims, or whether secularism should be the national framework, thereby imposing on the Muslim majority the wishes of the non-Muslim minority. The crisis in national identity that this dualism poses is that there is not yet a consensus on a framework that unquestionably establishes the unity of the nation; during most of the colonial period, the country was governed as two separate parts in one, and since independence, it has intermittently been at war with itself over the composite factors of religion, ethnicity, race, and culture.

The report of the Arusha Consultation states: "Two sociological factors were considered pivotal in the internal conflict equations in Africa. One was religious fundamentalism, the other, ethnicity. Both needed to be carefully monitored."[30] Monitoring them is, indeed, both critical and urgent since they are at the core of the challenge of nation-building in countries that are religiously, ethnically, and culturally mixed, especially where these forms of identity correlate with and deepen internal divisions.

If responsibility for Africa's problems is now being assigned to the Africans as represented by their states, the logic should extend down to embrace citizen participation—a process that might be termed the challenge of localization. This process would broaden the basis of participation to include not only the wide array of organizations within the now popular notion of civil society but also, and primarily, Africa's indigenous, territorially defined, local communities, with their organizational structures, value systems, institutional arrangements, and ways of using their human and material resources.

Given its centrality and pervasiveness, ethnicity is a reality no country can completely afford to ignore. Thus, African governments have ambivalently tried to dismiss it, marginalize it, manipulate it, corrupt it, or combat it in a variety of ways. But no strategic formula for its constructive use has been developed[31]—this despite the fact that an overwhelming majority of Africans, however urbanized or modernized, belong to known "tribal" or ethnic origins and remain in one way or another connected to their groups. Indeed, as one African scholar noted, "urban populations straddle the two geographical spaces—urban and rural—with the result [that] the politics of one easily spills into the politics of the other."[32] The other side of this spectrum is flexibility or adaptability that allows considerable room for molding identity to suit changing conditions or serve alternating objectives, some destructive.

Ethnic identities in themselves are not conflictual, just as individuals are not inherently in conflict merely because of their different identities and characteristics. Rather, it is unmanaged or mismanaged competition for power, wealth, or status broadly defined that provides the basis for conflict. Today, virtually every African conflict has some ethno-regional dimension to it.[33] Even those conflicts that may appear to be free of ethnic concerns involve factions and alliances built around ethnic loyalties. Analysts tend to hold one of two views regarding the role of ethnicity in these conflicts. Some see ethnicity as a source of conflict; others see it as a tool used by political entrepreneurs to promote their ambitions.[34] In reality, it is both. Ethnicity, especially when combined with territorial identity, is a reality that exists independently of political maneuvers. To argue that ethnic groups are unwitting tools of political manipulation is to underestimate a fundamental social reality and to assume that members of the group lack value judgment on the issues involved. On the other hand, given the emotional fervor and the group dynamics of the identity issues it evokes, ethnicity is clearly a resource for political manipulation and entrepreneurship, which African states are loath to manage constructively. Ethiopia, after Eritrea's breakaway, can claim credit for being the only African country that is trying to confront the problem head-on by recognizing territorially based ethnic groups, granting them not only a large measure of autonomy but also the constitutional right of self-determination, even to the extent of secession.[35] Ethiopia's leaders assert emphatically that they are committed to the right of self-determination, wherever it leads. But it can also be argued that giving the people the right to determine their destiny leads them to believe that their interests will be safeguarded, which should give them a reason to opt for unity.

Self-determination does not necessarily mean secession. After all, one of the options of self-determination is to remain within the state. But perhaps even more significant is the reconceptualization of self-determination as a principle that allows people to choose their own administrative status and machinery within the country.[36] It has been noted that internal self-administration "might be more effectively used in a way that would help avoid suffering of the kind that so regrettably became commonplace when communities feel that their only option is to 'fight for independence.'"[37]

In that sense, self-determination becomes closely associated with democracy and protection of minorities and not conterminous with independence. As Sir Arthur Watts, one of the principal proponents of internal self-determination, has observed, independence is a complicated process that can be traumatic. For many communities, it is not necessarily the best option. Often, no advantage is gained by insisting on independence, excluding other kinds of arrangements, especially if they would grant a community all it wants without the additional burdens of a wholly independent existence.[38]

Ultimately, the only sustainable unity is that based on mutual understanding and agreement. Unfortunately, however, the normative framework for national unity in modern Africa is not the result of consensus. Except for a very few cases, as in postapartheid South Africa, Africans won their independence without negotiating an internal social contract that would forge and sustain national consensus. Of course, the leaders of various factions, ethnic or political, negotiated a framework that gave them the legitimacy to speak for the country in their demand for independence. Political elites certainly negotiated a common ground for independence in Zimbabwe, Namibia, and, with less satisfactory results, Angola. And independent leaders debated over federalism in Nigeria and ethnic representation in Kenya, Uganda, and the Ivory Coast (Côte d'Ivoire). Indeed, in virtually every African country, independence was preceded by intense dialogue and negotiation between various groups, parallel to negotiations with the colonial powers. But these were tactical agreements to rid the country of its colonial yoke and, in any case, were elitist negotiations that did not involve the grass roots, as the South African negotiations did through a broad-based network of political organizations and elements of civil society.

Typically, the constitutions that African countries adopted at independence were drafted for them by the colonial masters and, contrary to the authoritarian modes of government adopted by the colonial powers, were laden with idealistic principles of liberal democracy to which Africa had not previously been introduced and in which it had no experience. The regimes built on these constitutions were in essence grafted foreign conceptualizations that had no indigenous roots and therefore lacked legitimacy. In most cases, they were soon overthrown with no remorse or regrets from the public. But these upheavals involved only a rotation of like-minded elites or, worse, military dictators, intent on occupying the seat of power vacated by the colonial masters. They soon became their colonial masters' images. In the overwhelming majority of countries, the quest for unity underscored the intensity of disunity, sometimes resulting in violent conflicts, many of which have intensified in the post–Cold War era—as evidenced by Burundi, Congo, Liberia, Sierra Leone, Somalia, Rwanda, and Zaire, now the Democratic Republic of Congo. African states must respond to the demands of justice, equity, and dignity by the component elements or risk disintegration and collapse. As Michael Chege noted in a different context, "It is time to bring this highly varie-gated menu to African statesmen and citizens and to convince them that self-determination of groups need not always lead to the feared disinte-gration of the present states into a myriad of small ethnic units."[39]

There are four policy options for managing pluralistic identities. One is to create a national framework with which all can identify without any distinction based on race, ethnicity, tribe, or religion. This is clearly the most desirable option. The second option is to create a pluralistic frame-work to accommodate diversity in nations that are racially, ethnically, cul-turally, or religiously divided. Under this option, probably a federal arrangement, groups would accommodate each other's differences with a uniting commitment to the common purpose of national identification and nondiscrimination. For more seriously divided countries, the third option may be some form of power sharing, combined with decentraliza-tion that may expand federalism into confederalism. Finally, where even this degree of accommodation is not workable, and where territorial con-figurations permit, partition ought to be accepted.

Operational Strategies of Intervention

Although addressing the issue of sovereignty and the root causes of con-flict are critical prerequisites to intervention, formulating credible opera-tion principles is the most pivotal factor in the equation. These principles relate to institutional mechanisms and strategies for action, both preven-tive and corrective.

Ideally, from an institutional or organizational perspective, problems should be addressed and solved within the immediate framework, with wider involvement necessitated only by the failure of the internal efforts. Hence conflict prevention, management, or resolution progressively moves from the domestic domain to the regional and, ultimately, to the global levels of concern and action.

As already noted, those conflicts in which the state is an effective ar-biter do not present particular difficulties since they are manageable within the national framework. The problem arises when the state itself is a party to the conflict. Under those conditions, external involvement be-comes necessary. In the African context, it is generally agreed that the next-best level of involvement should be the OAU, but there are constraints on the role of the OAU. One such constraint has to do with limited resources, both material and human. But perhaps even more debilitating is the question of political will, since, in the intimate context of the region, governments feel they are subject to conflicts arising from the problematic conditions of state-formation and nation-building and are therefore prone to resist any form of external scrutiny. And since the judge of today may well be the accused of tomorrow, there is a temptation to avoid confronting such problems. The result is evasiveness and benign neglect. Beyond the OAU, the United Nations is the next logical organization, for it represents the international community in its global context. But the UN suffers from the same constraints affecting the OAU, though to a lesser degree. It, too, must deal with the problem of resources and the reciprocal protectiveness of vulnerable governments.

As recent events have demonstrated, the role of the major Western powers acting unilaterally, multilaterally, or within the framework of the United Nations—though often susceptible to accusations of strategic motivation—has become increasingly pivotal. The problem in this regard is more one of their unwillingness to become involved or their lack of adequate preparedness for such involvement. Perhaps the most important aspect of the involvement of Western industrial democracies in foreign conflicts is the fact that these nations are often moved to act by the gravity of the humanitarian tragedies involved. Thus, their involvement is both an asset in terms of arresting the tragedy and a limitation in terms of preventing the tragedy at an earlier stage. Even with respect to humanitarian intervention, lack of preparedness for an appropriate and timely response is generally acknowledged as a major limitation.[40]

Nevertheless, some argue that there is a strong presumption that the interests of these countries are powerfully engaged and that they will eventually be driven to uphold and promote such interests through humanitarian intervention in crisis situations. Industrial democracies, they further argue, cannot operate without defending standards of human rights and political procedures that are being egregiously violated. Indeed, they themselves cannot prosper in an irreversibly international economy if large, contiguous populations descend into endemic violence and economic depression. Given these compelling reasons and the lack of preparedness for any well-planned response, the United States and Western European countries are particularly prone to crisis-induced reactions that are relatively easy to execute and, indeed, more symbolic than effective in addressing the substantive issues involved.

There will always be elements in a country who welcome intervention, especially among the disadvantaged groups to whom it promises tangible benefits. But since intervention is, of course, a major intrusion from the outside, resistance on the grounds of national sovereignty or pride is also a predictable certainty. For that reason, the justification for intervention must be reliably persuasive, if not beyond reproach: "The difference between an intervention that succeeds and one that is destroyed by immune reaction would depend on the degree of spontaneous acceptance or rejection by the local population."[41]

To avoid or minimize this "immune reaction," such an intervention would have to be broadly international in character. The principles used and the objectives toward which the intervention is targeted must transcend political and cultural boundaries or traditions and concomitant nationalist sentiments. In other words, it must enjoy an effective degree of global legitimacy. "The rationale that could conceivably carry such a burden presumably involves human rights so fundamental that they are not derived from any particular political or economic ideology."[42]

The strategy for preventive or corrective involvement in conflict should constitute gathering and analyzing information and otherwise monitoring situations with a view toward establishing an early warning system through which the international community could be alerted to act. The quest for a system of response to conflict and attendant humanitarian tragedies was outlined by the UN secretary-general when, referring to the surging demands on the Security Council as a central instrument for the prevention and resolution of conflicts, he wrote that the aims of the United Nations must be

> To seek to identify at the earliest possible stage situations that could produce conflict, and to try through diplomacy to remove the sources of danger before violence results;
>
> Where conflict erupts, to engage in peacemaking aimed at resolving the issues that have led to conflict;
>
> Through peace-keeping, to work to preserve peace, however fragile, where fighting has been halted and to assist in implementing agreements achieved by the peacemakers;
>
> To stand ready to assist in peace-building in its differing contexts: rebuilding the institutions and infrastructures of nations torn by civil war and strife; and building bonds of peaceful mutual benefit among nations formerly at war;
>
> And in the largest sense, to address the deepest causes of conflict: economic despair, social injustice and political oppression. It is possible to discern an increasingly common moral perception that spans the world's nations and peoples, and which is finding expression in international laws, many owing their genesis to the work of this Organization.[43]

These principles are covered in the comprehensive framework of the proposed Conference on Security, Stability, Development and Cooperation in Africa, developed by the Africa Leadership Forum under the leadership of General Olusegun Obasanjo—at that time, former head of state of Nigeria. A conference held in Kampala in 1991—involving more than five hundred participants from different walks of life across the continent, including former and incumbent heads of state—adopted the Kampala Document, which spelled out the principles of the CSSDCA. It was subsequently submitted to the OAU for adoption by the heads of state, where a few (but vocal) members, fearful of the radical reform agenda it represented, blocked it. The CSSDCA has since remained on the OAU's shelves, supposedly under further study in preparation for reconsideration by the heads of state. Meanwhile, General Obasanjo, after being imprisoned by the dictator General Sani Abacha, convicted on a fabricated charge of treason, was released by General Abdelsalam Abubakar, who assumed the leadership of the country following Abacha's sudden death. Abubakar coaxed the country back to electoral democracy, and General Obasanjo, viewed overwhelmingly as the leader who could successfully manage the transition back to sustainable democracy, was persuaded to run in the presidential elections, which he won by a large margin. With Obasanjo back at the helm of Nigeria's leadership, it is expected that the CSSDCA will be reactivated and that his influence and the more favorable international and regional environment will facilitate the chances of success in having the framework adopted by the heads of state.

The action envisaged to address conflict situations and their humanitarian consequences is a three-phase strategy that would involve monitoring developments to draw early attention to impending crises, interceding in time to avert the crisis through diplomatic initiatives, and mobilizing international action when necessary.[44] The first step would be to detect and identify the problem through various mechanisms for information collection, evaluation, and reporting. If a sufficient basis for concern were established, the appropriate mechanism would be invoked to take preventive diplomatic measures and avert the crisis. Initially, such initiatives might be taken within the framework of regional arrangements—for example, the Conference on Security and Cooperation in Europe, the Organization of American States, or the Organization of African Unity. In the United Nations, such preventive initiatives would naturally fall on the secretary-general, acting personally or through special representatives. If diplomatic initiatives did not succeed, and depending on the level of human suffering involved, the secretary-general might decide to mobilize international response, ranging from further diplomatic measures to forced humanitarian intervention not only to provide emergency relief but also to facilitate the search for an enduring solution to the causes of the conflict. A strategy aimed at this broader objective would require a close understanding of the causal link between the conditions and developments leading to the outbreak of the crisis.

Conclusion

Africa's turbulent transformation, initiated by colonial scramble for the continent in the nineteenth century, contained by external domination for much of the first half of the twentieth century, reactivated by the independence movement at the second half of the century, and subdued by the Cold War bipolar control mechanism, is now gaining a renewed momentum of self-liberation from within. The context in which this is taking place is poised delicately between globalization and isolation, bordering on the marginalization of Africa. Paradoxically, ideological withdrawal by the major powers is being counterbalanced by pressures for humanitarian intervention. This situation calls for a more cost-effective sharing of responsibility, with the Africans admittedly assuming the primary role and their international partners lending a distant, but affirmative, helping hand.

The policy framework that apportions responsibilities in accordance with the emerging scale places the first tier of responsibility on the state. At the next level up the international ladder, regional actors are increasingly being challenged and motivated by the realization that their own national security is closely connected with the security of their neighbors. This realization has propelled a range of initiatives in which neighbors offer their good offices for third-party mediation in internal conflicts but, if their counsel is not heeded, intervene unilaterally or collectively to achieve their objectives.

A number of African leaders have embraced programs of political and economic reforms that would enhance regional security and stability. Some of their peers remain doggedly committed to authoritarian methods of governance. The international community, weary of shouldering responsibility for Africa's problems, is striving to win the leaders' intent on reform, give them the support they need to carry out their programs, and thereby provide them with the incentive to do so in earnest. These measures imply the stipulation of national sovereignty as responsibility with regional and international accountability.

An important dimension of such accountability is the reform of state structures, institutions, and processes to be more equitable in their management of diversities. This reform will require pushing the process of reversing Africa's international dependency to enhance the autonomy of internal actors, ethnic groups, and members of civil society in order to mobilize and engage them in self-reliant processes of governance and sustainable development. The state has been the intermediary and often the bottleneck in the chain of Africa's dependent relationship with the outside world. The required reform must broaden the scope of decision-making through extensive and genuine decentralization. It must make a more constructive use of indigenous structures, values, and institutions for self-governance and self-sustaining development from within. Governments genuinely committed to reform should have no difficulty in supporting this approach, whereas those that insist on centralization of authority wittingly or unwittingly expose their authoritarian disposition and risk regional and international scrutiny or admonition and, possibly, condemnation and reprisals.

The time is certainly opportune for reconciling sovereignty with the responsibilities of good governance. In balancing national sovereignty and the need for international action to provide protection and assistance to victims of internal conflicts and humanitarian tragedies, certain principles are becoming increasingly obvious as policy guidelines.

First, sovereignty carries with it responsibilities for the well-being of the population. It is from this precept that the legitimacy of a government derives, whatever the political system or prevailing ideology. The relationship between the controlling authority and the populace should ideally ensure the highest standards of human dignity but at a minimum it should guarantee food, shelter, physical security, basic health services, and other essentials.

Second, in the many countries where armed conflicts and communal violence have caused massive internal displacement, the countries are so divided on fundamental issues that legitimacy—and, indeed, sovereignty—are sharply contested. This is why there is always a strong faction inviting or at least welcoming external intervention. Under those circumstances, the validity of sovereignty must be judged, using reasonable standards to assess how much of the population is represented, marginalized, or excluded.

Third, living up to the responsibilities of sovereignty implies that there is a transcendent authority capable of holding the supposed sovereign accountable. Some form of an international system has always existed to ensure that states conform to accepted norms or face the consequences, whether in the form of unilateral, multilateral, or collective action. Equality among sovereign entities has always been a convenient fiction; it has never been backed by realities because some powers have always been more dominant than others and therefore have been explicitly or implicitly charged with responsibility for enforcing the agreed-upon norms of behavior.

Fourth, such a role imposes on the dominant authority or power certain leadership responsibilities that transcend parochialism or exclusive national interests and serve the broader interests of the community or the human family.

When these principles are translated into practical action in countries torn apart by internal conflicts, a number of implications emerge. For example, sovereignty cannot be an amoral function of authority and control; respect for fundamental human rights and humanitarian principles must be among its most basic values. Similarly, the enjoyment of human rights must encompass equitable and effective participation in the political, economic, social, and cultural life of the country, at least as a widely accepted national aspiration. This system of sharing must guarantee that all individuals and groups belong to the nation on an equal footing with the rest of the people, however identified; they must also be sufficiently represented and not discriminated against on the basis of the prevailing views of identity.

To ensure that these normative goals are met or at least genuinely pursued, the international community as represented by the United Nations is the ideal authority. The imperatives of the existing power structures and processes may, however, require that authority be exercised by other powers capable of acting on behalf of the international community. Multilateral action may therefore be justified under certain circumstances. Any type of less collective action should be closely circumscribed to avoid its exploitation for less lofty objectives of a more exclusively national character—objectives that may erode the transcendent moral authority of global leadership for the good of all humankind.

As a polarity emerges between those African governments committed to participatory democracy, respect for human rights, and responsible international partnership and those bent on repression and resistance to reform, the international community should adopt a dual strategy that effectively supports reform with positive incentives and discourages resistance with punitive sanctions. Living up to the responsibilities of sovereignty implies a transcendent authority capable of holding the supposed sovereign accountable. Although the international community has made some progress in responding to humanitarian tragedies, much more needs to be done to ensure that governments adhere to the responsibilities of sovereignty by ensuring the security, fundamental rights, civil liberties, and general welfare of their citizens and all those under their domestic jurisdiction.

Although the world is far from a universal government, the foundations, the pillars, and perhaps even the structures of global governance are taking shape with the emergence of a post–Cold War international order in which the internally dispossessed are bound to benefit. Unmasking sovereignty to reveal the gross violations of human rights is no longer an aspiration; it is a process that has already started. Governments and other human rights violators are being increasingly scrutinized for such violations. What is now required is to make them fully accountable and to provide international protection and assistance for the victims of human rights violations and unremedied humanitarian tragedies within their domestic jurisdiction. In other words, what is called for is not something entirely new but, rather, an intensification and improvement of what has already been unfolding.

Notes

1. Boutros Boutros-Ghali, *An Agenda for Peace: Preventive Diplomacy, Peacemaking and Peacekeeping* (New York: United Nations, 1992), p. 7.

2. Boutros-Ghali, in a statement of his proposals to the Council of Ministers in Dakar, Senegal, in 1992. The main documents in these three areas of African initiative are as follows: "The Kampala Document Toward a Conference on Security, Stability, Development and Cooperation in Africa" (Kampala, Uganda: Africa Leadership Forum and Secretariat of the Organization of African Unity and the United Nations Economic Commission for Africa, 1991); Dent Ocaya-Lakidi, *Africa's Internal Conflicts: The Search for a Response*, Report of an Arusha, Tanzania, High-Level Consultation, March 23–25, 1992, prepared for the International Peace Academy; OAU, Council of Ministers, Fifty-sixth Ordinary Session, *Report of the Secretary-General on Conflicts in Africa: Proposals for an OAU Mechanism for Conflict Prevention and Resolution* CM/1710 (L.VI) (Addis Ababa: Organization of African Unity, June 22–27, 1992); OAU, Council of Ministers, Fifty-seventh Ordinary Session, *Interim Report of the Secretary-General on the Mechanism for Conflict Prevention, Management and Resolution* CM/1747 (L.VI) (Addis Ababa: Organization of African Unity, February 15–19, 1993); and OAU, Council of Ministers, Fifty-seventh Ordinary Session, *Report of the Secretary-General* CM/Plen/Rpt (L.VII) (Addis Ababa: Organization of African Unity, February 15–19, 1993). Also pertinent to the issues involved is UN Secretary-General Boutros Boutros-Ghali's report, *An Agenda for Peace*, originally published as document A/47/277 S/24111, June 17, 1992.

3. Cited in Ocaya-Lakidi, *Africa's Internal Conflicts*, p. 3.

4. Thomas M. Franck, "The Emerging Right to Democratic Governance," *American Journal of International Law* 86 (January 1992), p. 46.

5. Richard Falk, "Sovereignty and Human Dignity: The Search for Reconciliation," in Francis M. Deng and Terrence Lyons (eds.), *African Reckoning: A Quest for Good Governance* (Washington, D.C.: Brookings Institution, 1998), p. 13.

6. Francis M. Deng, *Protecting the Dispossessed: A Challenge for the International Community* (Washington, D.C.: Brookings Institution, 1993), p. 14.

7. David J. Scheffer, "Toward a Modern Doctrine of Humanitarian Intervention," *University of Toledo Law Review* 23 (Winter 1992), p. 2.

8. Refugee Policy Group, *Human Rights Protection for Internally Displaced Persons: An International Conference* (Washington, D.C., June 1991), p. 7.

9. Ibid.

10. UN press release SG/SM/4560, April 24, 1991; cited in Gene M. Lyons and Michael Mastanduno, *Beyond Westphalia: International Intervention, State Sovereignty and the Future of International Society* (Hanover, N.H.: Dartmouth College, 1992), p. 2. Portions of this statement are also cited in Scheffer, "Toward a Modern Doctrine of Humanitarian Intervention," p. 262.

11. Javier Perez de Cuellar, *Report of the Secretary-General on the Work of the Organization* (New York: United Nations, 1991).

12. Ibid., p. 13.

13. Boutros-Ghali, *An Agenda for Peace*, p. 5.

14. Scheffer, "Toward a Modern Doctrine of Humanitarian Intervention," pp. 262–263.

15. Falk, "Sovereignty and Human Dignity," p. 12.

16. Francis M. Deng, Sadikiel Kimaro, Terrence Lyons, Donald Rothchild, and I. William Zartman (eds.), *Sovereignty as Responsibility: Conflict Management in Africa* (Washington, D.C.: Brookings Institution, 1996).

17. OAU, Council of Ministers, *Report of the Secretary-General on Conflicts in Africa.*

18. Ibid.

19. Ibid.

20. Ibid.

21. Note by the president of the Security Council, S/25344, February 26, 1993.

22. Ibid., p. 1.

23. Ibid., p. 2.

24. Ibid.

25. Ibid.

26. Cited in Ocaya-Lakidi, *Africa's Internal Conflicts*, pp. 9–10.

27. Cited in ibid., pp. 18–19.

28. Boutros-Ghali, *An Agenda for Peace*, p. 9.

29. Ibid., pp. 9–10.

30. Cited in Ocaya-Lakidi, *Africa's Internal Conflicts*, p. 78.

31. Donald Rothchild, *Managing Ethnic Conflict in Africa* (Washington, D.C.: Brookings Institution, 1997), pp. 20–21.

32. Mkandawire, "Shifting Commitments and National Cohesion in African Countries," p. 15.

33. Roberta Cohen and Francis Deng (eds.), *The Forsaken People: Case Studies of the Internally Displaced* (Washington, D.C.: Brookings Institution, 1998).

34. According to one source, ethnicity is important in African politics because it serves as an "organizing principle of sound action," which makes it "basically a political . . . phenomenon." See Naomi Chazan et al., *Politics and Society in Contemporary Africa* (Boulder: Lynne Rienner Publishers, 1988), pp. 110, 120. And as UN Secretary-General Kofi Annan observed in a paper presented to an international conference on "The Therapeutics of Conflict," when he was still undersecretary-general for Peacekeeping Operations: "Many [of the civil wars] have also been perceived as showing strong symptoms of ethnic conflict. Ethnic conflict as a symptom is, at best, extremely difficult to assess. . . . Ethnic differences are not in and of themselves either symptoms or causes of conflict; in societies where they are accepted and respected, people of vastly different backgrounds live peacefully and productively together. Ethnic differences become charged—conflictual— when they are used for political ends, when ethnic groups are intentionally placed in opposition to each other." See Kofi Annan, "The Peacekeeping Prescription," in Kevin M. Cahill, M.D. (ed.), *Preventive Diplomacy* (New York: Basic Books, 1996), p. 176.

35. The Constitution of the Federal Democratic Republic of Ethiopia (Addis Ababa, December 8, 1994) provides in Article 39, Number 1, that "[e]very nation, nationality and people in Ethiopia has an unconditional right to self-determination, including the right to secession." It also states in Article 39, Number 3, that "[e]very nation, nationality and people in Ethiopia has the right to a full measure of self-government which includes the right to establish institutions of government in the territory that it inhabits and to equitable representation in regional and national governments."

36. This is the essence of the proposal that the state of Liechtenstein presented to the General Assembly of the United Nations in 1991—a proposal that aimed at establishing a new international legal framework in which self-determination, defined primarily as self-administration, might be pursued within the existing state framework. See Wolfgang Danspeckgruber and Sir Arthur Watts (eds.), *Self-Determination and Self-Administration: A Sourcebook* (Boulder: Lynne Rienner Publishers, 1997).

37. Ibid., p. 1.

38. Sir Arthur Watts, "The Liechtenstein Draft Convention on Self-Determination Through Self-Administration," in ibid., p. 23.

39. Cited in a review of Francis M. Deng, "Africa and the New World Disorder," *The Brookings Review* (Spring 1993), p. 3. For a more comprehensive discussion of ethnic diversity in the context of democratization, see Chege's article, "Remembering Africa," in *Foreign Affairs* 71, no. 1 (1992), pp. 146–163.

40. John Steinbruner, "Civil Violence as an International Security Problem," memorandum dated November 23, 1992, addressed to the Brookings Institution Foreign Policy Studies Program staff. See also Chester A. Crocker, "The Global Law and Order Deficit: Is the West Ready to Police the World's Bad Neighbors?" *Washington Post*, December 20, 1992, p. C1.

41. Steinbruner, "Civil Violence as an International Security Problem."

42. Ibid.

43. Boutros-Ghali, *An Agenda for Peace*, pp. 7–8.

44. For a more elaborate discussion of these phases as applied to the crisis of the internally displaced, see the UN study in document E/CH.4/1993/35 and the revised version of that study in Francis M. Deng, *Protecting the Dispossessed: A Challenge for the International Community* (Washington, D.C.: Brookings Institution, 1993). This study was considered by the Commission on Human Rights at its forty-ninth session, during which its findings and recommendations were endorsed and the mandate of the special representative of the secretary-general was extended for two years to continue to work on the various aspects of the problem presented in the study.

Index